"In a highly accessible style yet with deep and wide scholarship, John Pilch, an international authority on the biblical social world, leads us, like a trustworthy tour guide, through the highways and byways of the ancient world. Thanks to his work, the Bible becomes alive to us again as God's Word in human words. I most strongly recommend this handbook to both scholars and general readers."

— PETER C. PHAN
Georgetown University

"An award-winning predecessor volume by John Pilch (*The Cultural Dictionary of the Bible*) proved enormously useful for my undergraduate biblical-studies classroom. This new compilation of articles once again demonstrates Pilch's rich knowledge of biblical culture and provides readers with many satisfying insights. *A Cultural Handbook to the Bible* will well serve students, clergy, and university-level teachers."

— DOUGLAS E. OAKMAN
Pacific Lutheran University

"Once more Pilch has given us what we have come to expect from him — thorough knowledge from Middle Eastern and Mediterranean cultures giving new and unexpected insights into the texts of the Bible. Short essays on a wide range of topics provide answers to the curious Bible reader, and bibliographies give students tools to pursue their own explorations into the fascinating world of the Bible. This is a book to enjoy and learn from!"

— HALVOR MOXNES
University of Oslo

A Cultural Handbook to the Bible

John J. Pilch

WILLIAM B. EERDMANS PUBLISHING COMPANY
GRAND RAPIDS, MICHIGAN / CAMBRIDGE, U.K.

Published 2012 by

Wm. B. Eerdmans Publishing Co.

2140 Oak Industrial Drive N.E., Grand Rapids, Michigan 49505 /
P.O. Box 163, Cambridge CB3 9PU U.K.

Printed in the United States of America

18 17 16 15 14 13 12   7 6 5 4 3 2 1

Library of Congress Cataloging-in-Publication Data

Pilch, John J.
    A cultural handbook to the Bible / John J. Pilch.
        p.   cm.
    Includes bibliographical references and indexes.
    ISBN 978-0-8028-6720-9 (pbk.: alk. paper)
    1. Bible — Handbooks, manuals, etc.   I. Title.

    BS417.P54   2012
    220.9'5 — dc23

                    2012007734

www.eerdmans.com

For my colleagues and friends in:

The Context Group: A Project on the Bible in Its Socio-Cultural
Context;

The Social Sciences and New Testament Interpretation Task Force
at the Catholic Biblical Association of America; and

The Social Scientific Criticism of the New Testament Section at the
Society of Biblical Literature

who have inspired, encouraged, and nurtured my research and
publications over more than four decades

with heartfelt appreciation and gratitude

Contents

Contents

Preface

From 1993 to 2006, I wrote a bimonthly article in *The Bible Today* (Collegeville, MN: The Liturgical Press) under the heading "A Window into the Biblical World." The aim of these articles was to show how insights from Middle Eastern culture drawn from the social sciences (Cultural Anthropology, Middle Eastern Anthropology, Medical Anthropology, and others) helped to situate the Bible in its proper cultural context. For example, the "salt" statements of Jesus recorded in the Gospels (Matt 5:13; Mark 9:49-50; Luke 12:49; 14:34-35) have nothing to do with seasoning or preserving foods. Rather, they reflect the use of salt in the Middle East to facilitate the burning of the common fuel — camel and donkey dung — in the ovens. The articles that appeared from 1993 to 1997 were published in *The Cultural Dictionary of the Bible* (Liturgical Press, 1999). In 2000 this book won an award from the Catholic Press Association and was subsequently translated into Italian (*Il Sapore della Parola,* Áncora, 2001) and Polish (*Słownik Kultury Biblijnej,* Edycja św. Pawła, 2004).

In this sequel to that book, I have collected the articles published in that journal from 1998 to 2006 and arranged them thematically under eight headings. Some articles could probably fit under more than one heading, so the arrangement is somewhat arbitrary. However, this is not a book one would read from beginning to end. It is not a book to be read at one sitting. Most readers will quite likely consult the Table of Contents and select a topic that catches attention at the moment.

A special feature of this book and its predecessor is that each article applies insights from the social sciences to the interpretation of biblical passages, topics, and themes. The references listed under "Further Reading" are primarily the social-science resources consulted and secondarily biblical resources that have applied these social-science insights to select segments or books of the Bible. For example, the Further Resources for the part on the Family lists the anthropological resources I consulted in writing each of those chapters (e.g., Broude, Francoeur, and Shapiro) and biblical resources which have applied such insights in interpreting their topics (e.g., Campbell, Malina, and Malina and Rohrbaugh). With this book, readers should be able to become acquainted with social-scientific sources and methods, and also be able to see how biblical scholars utilizing these resources are able to produce fresh, Middle Eastern, culturally plausible interpretations of that Middle Eastern document known as the Bible.

The challenge that remains, then, is how to translate those Middle Eastern understandings to other non–Middle Eastern cultures, situations, and problems. For example, if marriage, adultery, and rape in the Bible do not mean what they mean in Western and other cultures, what can a Bible reader draw from this information? How can a Bible reader bridge the gap between that culture and her or his own? Again, in the Further Readings on Family, I list two very useful resources, books by Augsburger, and Stewart and Bennett. These two books can serve as basic sources for anyone who wants to address the challenge that the Bible hurls at teachers, preachers, and readers. Perhaps this present book and its predecessor can assist.

For an Index of References to the Roman Lectionary, see my web site: http://mysite.verizon.net/vzewdxtw/drjohnjpilchwebpage/id67.html.

Feast of St. Francis of Assisi
October 4, 2011

JOHN J. PILCH
The Odyssey Programs
Johns Hopkins University

Part One

THE COSMOS

In our lifetime, human beings have put various satellites into orbit, become travelers to the moon, and sent exploratory probes deep into outer space. Our knowledge of the universe has expanded dramatically. Yet when contemporary Christians speak about heaven (the sky) and earth and hell, they neglect to notice that these concepts as currently understood carry centuries of outdated intellectual baggage. A close examination of these and related concepts as they appear in the Bible will give readers a fresh appreciation of how our ancestors in the faith understood their cosmos, and what they had in mind when they used these terms.

1. Hell

In the worldview of traditional "holy men" and "holy women" (often called shamans by anthropologists) the Tree of Life is a key way of understanding the cosmos. (This concept appears to have nothing in common with the mythological biblical Tree of Life in Gen. 2:4b–3:24, which is a source of life.) In traditional shamanic reflection, the universe is like a gigantic, cosmic tree. The analogy is vegetative rather than animal. The change of seasons and the change of skyscapes and landscapes are rather like the cycle of a tree than like the behavior of animals. From the flat-earth perspective of these traditional holy men and women, the universe is like a unique tree, the Tree of Life, that stands at the very center of the universe. Its roots contain the lower world, which is the habitat of power animals and the abode of dead souls and/or helper spirits. Its trunk contains the middle world, the spiritual counterpart or "parallel" to the world in which human beings live. This middle world contains the spirit or essence of all things. It is the "real" world behind the visible world. It is sometimes called "alternate reality," though that more properly describes the upper world. The branches of the Tree of Life contain everything that exists inside and outside our galaxy. Shamans, or holy men and/or women in each culture, take spirit journeys in trance in order to visit these three worlds (Pilch 2011: 48-60). Ezekiel (e.g., Ezek. 3:14-15) and John (e.g., Rev. 4:1-2) are two holy men in the biblical tradition who visited one or another of these worlds (Malina and Pilch 2000).

Anthropologists are quick to point out that the lower world is not hell. They claim that hell is a designation that first occurred in the agricultural religions such as Christianity (Goodman and Nauwald 2003: 68). While this claim is basically correct, it must be nuanced. This is all the more necessary if that notion of hell includes a presumed fire. While the idea of hell is most common [especially] in the popular understanding of Christianity, there is no Hebrew or Greek word in the Bible that can be appropriately translated "hell" in English. Moreover, much of the theological freight that "hell" carries in the modern popular understanding emerged in the period of time following the biblical period.

Hell

The English word "hell" derives from the Middle English word *helle* (related to the Old German *Hölle* and Old English *hel*, which is associated with the underworld goddess, *Hel*). It is the base of the verb *helan*, which means "to hide," "cover," or "conceal." Hell is the word most commonly used to translate the Hebrew word *Sheol*, the Latin and English word *gehenna* (from the Hebrew *Ge-Hinnom*), and the Greek word *hades* in the Bible. Insofar as the English word reflects the meanings "hide," "cover," or "conceal," it is appropriate since in the Bible this place ("hell") was located somewhere beneath the earth (e.g., Job 14:13 [Sheol]; Isa. 14:9 [Sheol]; Matt. 11:23 [Hades]). The element of fire or flame that appears in *gehenna* (Matt. 5:22; 18:9) or *hades* (Luke 16:23-24) is a subsequent development. However, this development was neither systematic nor clearly demarcated. In general, the Hebrew and Greek terms identify the abode of the dead, and in this regard the terms coincide with the shamanic understanding of the lower world.

Sheol

This Hebrew word is the most common name for the abode of the dead (65 times in the Hebrew Bible). It is sometimes translated as the "netherworld," but it was not primarily a place of punishment. Though its etymology is debated, the word probably derives from the Hebrew verb "to ask" (*šāʾal,* the same root as for the name of Saul). This etymology is culturally plausible because the ancients sought advice from the dead. When faced with an attack from the Philistines (1 Sam. 28), King Saul first sought advice from God, who, however, did not respond through the customary channels: dreams, the Urim, or prophets (1 Sam. 28:6). Then Saul consulted a medium who brought up the deceased Samuel.

Anthropologists confirm what the biblical record reports: People who seek to learn the will of God, whose abode is in alternate reality (specifically the upper world of the shamanic Tree of Life), will induce or hope to experience an alternate state of consciousness or awareness (e.g., dreams, visions, and the like). God routinely communicates with human beings in alternate states of awareness (1 Sam. 3:1ff.). They may also seek the assistance of a prophet (holy man, or "shaman"), who by definition has easy access to the realm of God and can mediate favors and information from that realm.

After the death of Samuel, a prophet who had this kind of access to the realm of God, Saul, banished all mediums and fortune-tellers from the country (1 Sam. 28:3). In the absence of a holy man/prophet, people might be tempted to seek out these alternate — but forbidden (see Deut. 18:9-11) — sources of recourse to alternate reality in which answers to questions and solutions to problems are often discovered by those who visit there. When Saul failed to obtain answers to his questions from the usual approved sources mentioned above, he turned to one of the alternative sources banned by Deuteronomy and banished by him(!): a medium at Endor (1 Sam. 28:7).

Saul requests of the medium: "Divine for me by a spirit, and bring up for me whoever I shall name to you" (1 Sam. 28:8; Scurlock 2009). The Hebrew phrase translated "medium" would be literally translated "a woman who is mistress of ghosts," in other words, a person who has access to and is capable of interacting with the spirit world. Spirits include those who abide in the lower world in the Tree of Life. Some scholars doubt that this is the ancient conception, yet anthropologists would argue in favor of its plausibility. They would identify this "ghost" as a "familiar" spirit or a helper spirit even in antiquity. At the very least, the medium that Saul consulted was successfully able to contact the lower world where the dead and familiar helper spirits abide. Samuel rises from this lower world and communicates to Saul God's will that Saul and Israel should fall into the hands of the Philistines.

As already noted, the netherworld is not primarily a place of punishment; it is simply the abode of the dead. The place is dark (Job 17:13); silence pervades (Ps. 31:17). Those who dwelt in this place were called "shades" (*rĕpā'îm;* Isa. 14:9). In Greek thought, the word "shades" describes ghosts or spirits, but in Israel the word describes beings who are but a "shadow" of their former selves. In other words, they no longer have the fullness of being experienced in life on earth. Most are even unable to remember God (Ps. 6:5), an unimaginable and unbearable experience for an Israelite. Though the characteristics of existence in Sheol are peculiar to Israel, the basic concept as the dwelling place of the dead remains similar to the shamanic concept as already noted.

In the period of Second Temple Judaism (520 B.C.E. to 70 C.E.), however, the understanding of Sheol underwent some development. Though initially it was considered the final and permanent place for the dead (Isa. 38:10) in a "shadowy" or hollow existence, in this period Sheol was conceived of as an intermediate place to be followed at some point by reward or punishment. Moreover, the Hellenistic concept of the immortality of the soul began to influence Israelite thinking about existence after death (Wis. 8:19-20; 9:15; 15:8). Some now began to believe that the souls of the righteous went immediately to God at death and would receive new bodies at the resurrection, while the wicked remained in Sheol (Dan. 12:2; Josephus, *Jewish War* 3.374-75).

In the Greek Bible, Sheol is usually translated as "Hades," but it doesn't relate to the Hades of Greek mythology. In the New Testament period (and a little earlier) Sheol/Hades came to be understood as a place of punishment for sin (Matt. 11:23; Luke 16:19-31).

A synonym for Sheol, namely, "the pit" (Hebrew *bôr;* e.g., Ps. 28:1), also appears sixty-five times in the Old Testament. Often it is in parallelism with Sheol: "O LORD, you brought me up from the netherworld *(šĕ'ôl);* you preserved me from among those going down into the pit *(bôr)*" (Ps. 30:4). The image of humans who were created from dust (Gen. 2:7) returning to dust (Gen. 3:19) at death created the image of the abode of the dead as a dusty, dirty place (Job 7:21).

Gehenna

This Greek name derives from the Aramaic *Ge-Hinnam*, which in turn relates to the Hebrew *Ge-Hinnom*, the Valley of Hinnom, or, perhaps more accurately. the Valley of the Son of Hinnom. At one time, the family of Ben Hinnom owned most of the land. It is located south and southwest of Jerusalem. Ancient Canaanites were said to have practiced rituals of child sacrifice here, and some Israelites (e.g., Ahaz [2 Chron. 28:3; 2 Kings 16:3]) continued that kind of sacrifice to Canaanite gods. Jeremiah (626-587 B.C.E.) denounced the practices, and King Josiah's reform sought to end them (640-609 B.C.E.). According to some archaeologists, in later times (certainly in the New Testament period) the place was likely a crematorium for unclean animals and criminals as well as a dump where temple refuse was burned. (The burial ground Hakeldama [Acts 1:19] associated with the death of Judas [Matt. 27:3-10; Acts 1:16-19] is located in the eastern part of the Valley of Hinnom.) Though no archaeological evidence for this kind of garbage dump has been found for the first century, the association of "fire" with Gehenna in Matthew (5:22; 18:9) suggests that this was indeed the case.

It was especially in the writings of later Second Temple Judaism (620 B.C.E.–70 C.E.) that the punishments of the wicked included smoldering fire. "Then I [Enoch] looked and turned to another face of the earth and saw there a valley, deep and burning with fire. And they were bringing kings and potentates and were throwing them into this deep valley" (*1 Enoch* 54:1-2). Later rabbinic tradition in the Babylonian Talmud said that an entrance to the underworld was located in the Valley of Hinnom (*'Erubin* 19a). In the New Testament, Gehenna was considered to have been prepared for Satan and his retinue (Matt. 25:41). In addition, here the soul reunited with its reconstituted body at the resurrection will be destroyed by eternal fire (Matt. 10:28; Mark 9:42-48).

Doctrine

Many of these biblical ideas were combined and amplified in doctrinal debates and statements in postbiblical times. The Athanasian Creed (end of fifth century C.E.) described hell as a place of eternal punishment for sin. The Fourth Lateran Council (1214) said that sinners who go to hell will be punished "with different punishments." The Second Vatican Council did not mention hell at all. The *Catechism of the Catholic Church* (1994) treats hell at some length, but in general concludes: "The chief punishment of hell is eternal separation from God, in which alone man can possess the life and happiness for which he was created and for which he longs." This is similar to the statement by the Church of England, which a few years earlier declared that there was no physical fire in hell. Thus readers of the biblical evidence through the centuries in general appear to have distinguished carefully between the actual punishment sinners experience in some place and the culturally conditioned descriptions of the nature of that punishment reported in some parts of the Bible.

Conclusion

The word "shaman" describes a holy person (holy man/holy woman) peculiar to Siberia, where they were first identified and studied. All cultures recognize holy persons (men and women) but name and describe them differently. By the same token, while the belief systems of cultures are in some ways similar, they are also different in specific features. The Tree of Life conception peculiar to Siberian shamans is not the same as the Tree of Life in biblical literature and the culture that produced it. Nevertheless, the conception of places such as a lower, middle, and upper world associated with the Siberian tree also exist in Israelite culture. In general, the understanding of the lower world as the abode of the dead with helper spirits and power animals is similar in Siberian shamanism and in the biblical world (except perhaps for power animals, though see Job 12:7). The Israelite interpretation of the lower world as Sheol, Gehenna, or Hades, however, differentiates it from the Siberian shamanic concept. Further, these three biblical concepts evolved in meaning and function over millennia to the present. The contemporary Catholic understanding of hell as "eternal separation from God" for those dead who merited this punishment is clearly not the Siberian shamanic understanding of the lower world. Similarities and differences always help sharpen our understanding of familiar realities.

2. Heaven

Jesus taught his disciples to pray in this way: "Our Father who art in heaven . . ." (Matt. 6:9). The phrase "Father in heaven" was Jesus' customary way of referring to God (Matt. 5:16, 45; 6:1, 9; 7:11, 21; 10:32, 33; 12:50;

16:17; 18:10, 14, 19). The Greek word translated "heaven" literally means "sky." To understand what the biblical authors have in mind, perhaps it might be a good idea to drop the word "heaven" from Bible translations entirely. The biblical reference is always and only to the sky. The Greek plural form in this phrase (Matt. 6:9: *en tois ouranois*) was probably influenced by the Hebrew *šāmayim* (or Aramaic *šĕmayin*), which the Greek translates. However, the Greek word occurs most often in the singular. According to the *Oxford English Dictionary,* the word "heaven" first appeared in eleventh-century translations of the Bible (Gen. 1:1), but its ulterior etymology is unknown. Scholars note that heaven is understood differently in the Bible and in theology. In the Bible, heaven refers either to the physical sky above the earth or to the realm of God. In theology, heaven usually refers to the eternal destiny and destination of believers, the ultimate goal of human existence.

Heaven: The Physical Sky

The first creation story in Genesis reports how God created the world on the foundation of a watery abyss. God made a dome (or "firmament") to separate these waters into a mass above the dome (Ps. 148:4) and a mass beneath the dome (Gen. 1:6-7). God named this dome "the sky" (*šāmayim,* Gen. 1:8). It is as firm and solid as the earth (Job 37:18), yet the psalmist says that God stretched out the heavens "like a tent" (Ps. 104:2; see also Isa. 40:22). This sky is supported by pillars (Job 26:11).

A countless number of stars (Gen. 15:5) were affixed in the sky (Gen. 1:14-18), but the sun and moon coursed across it. There were also windows in the sky (Isa. 24:18) through which God could shower the earth with gifts or punishments: rain (Gen. 7:11; Luke 4:25; Acts 14:17), manna (Exod. 16:14; Ps. 78:24), even the wind or spirit (Num. 11:31; Job 26:13; Ps. 135:7; Jer. 10:13; Matt. 3:16; Acts 2:2; 1 Pet. 1:12).

The sky serves as a vehicle for audio-visual communication from God. "He works signs and wonders in the sky and on earth" (Dan. 6:27). The rainbow is one such sign (Gen. 9:12-17). Thunder, the "voice of God," is another such sign (Exod. 20:22; Jer. 25:30). Meteorological phenomena announce God's intentions to those who know how to interpret them (Luke 21:11, 25).

Perhaps the most important and often overlooked feature of the sky is the opening that allows one to travel from the earth to the other side of the sky, where God abides. According to the ancient Israelite tradition, God

created an open sky for Adam "so that he might look upon the angels singing the triumphal song. And the light, which is never darkened, was per-
petually in paradise" (2 *Enoch* 31:2-3). Of course, after the disobedience of
the first creatures that opening to the other side of the sky was closed. In
fact, Israelite tradition in general believed that this hole or opening was
permanently closed. Yet God could open it as desired. Isaiah begs God to
do just that: "O that thou wouldst rend the heavens [plural: *šāmayim*] and
come down" (Hebrew Isa. 63:19; RSV Isa. 64:1).

Where is this opening located? Many ancient peoples believed that the
opening was located directly above the earthly residence of their god. For
ancient Israel, the opening was directly above God's temple in Jerusalem.
This explains why Jesus could not ascend to God in Galilee after his resurrection, since the opening was not located there.

The tradition mentions people who had access to the realm of God and
traveled there. These were mainly holy people like Enoch (see Gen. 5:21-23
and the books of Enoch dating from the third century B.C.E. to the third
century C.E.) but especially prophets like Elijah (2 Kings 2:11), Daniel
(Dan. 7–12), Ezekiel (Ezek. 1:1), and John (Rev. 4:1-2). The sky opened at Jesus' baptism (Mark 1:10//). Just before he died, Stephen looked through the
opening over Jerusalem and saw Jesus standing before God (Acts 7:56).
Though he was in Joppa at the time, Peter had a vision of food descending
through the same opening in the sky (Acts 10:11). These journeys to the sky
and visions of the realm of God occurred in what contemporary cognitive
neuroscience has identified as an alternate state of consciousness, or a level
of human awareness that is different from ordinary "waking" consciousness. This is how God has physically equipped human beings to communicate with the deity and the realm of God (1 Sam. 3:1).

Heaven: The Realm of God

The postexilic and intertestamental literature manifests growing curiosity
about heaven as the abode of God and God's attendant beings. The
prophet Micaiah reports this experience: "I saw the LORD sitting on his
throne, and all the host of heaven [Hebrew *šāmayim*, thus literally the sky]
standing beside him on his right hand and on his left" (1 Kings 22:19). The
throne is the symbol of royal authority in a monarchic society. It symbolizes the monarch's ability to effectively control the behavior of the kingdom's subjects and to extract loyalty from these subjects. In ancient sky
lore, a throne constellation was very well known. The famous Farnese

sphere depicting the chief constellations of the second century B.C.E. places the throne of Caesar near the North Pole over Leo and Cancer (Malina 1995: 90-93). Another familiar throne in the sky is that of Cassiopeia. The constellation Virgo-Isis is the throne in Hellenistic Egyptian sky lore. In the Israelite tradition, Isaiah wrote: "Thus says the Lord: The sky is my throne" (Isa. 66:1 LXX). And Matthew's Jesus echoes this belief: "But I say to you, Do not swear at all, either by heaven [the sky], for it is the throne of God, or by the earth, for it is his footstool . . ." (Matt. 5:34-35; see also Matt. 23:22).

Notice also that God does not live alone. Micaiah saw the "host of heaven." Originally this phrase referred to the stars (Gen. 2:1; Deut. 4:19), but eventually it extended to beings in the realm of God (1 Kings 22:19; Luke 2:13). In the book of Revelation (4:4), John saw twenty-four elders seated on thrones around God's throne. These are celestial beings, other inhabitants of the realm of God (Malina 1995: 93-97). In astrological lore, they are called decans, truly significant astronomic beings of antiquity, astral deities. In Revelation, they form a core group around God's throne similar to the scene witnessed by Micaiah. Here these beings regularly worship God and sing celestial songs of praise to God (Rev. 4:10; 5:11, 14; 7:11; 11:16; 19:4). They know God's cosmic plan and share it with prophets (Rev. 5:5; 7:13). They are also in the entourage of the cosmic Lamb (Rev. 5:6) and pay personal homage as well as the homage of other beings to the Lamb (Rev. 5:8). There is no doubt that these decanal thrones belong to the "thrones or dominions or principalities or authorities" over which Jesus Messiah has preeminence in Colossians 1:16.

Still other celestial beings live in the realm of God. Raphael is one of seven holy angels (or sky servants) who stand in the presence of God (Tob. 12:15). According to Daniel, "a thousand thousand served him, and ten thousand times ten thousand stood before him . . ." (Dan. 7:10). Even Satan lived in heaven as an associate (Job 1:6; 2:1) before he was cast out (Luke 10:18; Rev. 12:7ff.).

Multiple Heavens

References to "heaven and the heaven of heavens" or "the highest heaven" (Deut. 10:14; 1 Kings 8:27; Neh. 9:6; 3 Macc. 2:15; etc.) led some to speculate about the actual number of heavens. The phrase "heaven and the heaven of heavens" prompted the conclusion that there were at least two and maybe three heavens. God lived in the highest one. This may be the third

9

heaven to which Paul made a sky journey (2 Cor. 12:2). Greek Baruch (11) knows of five heavens. The *Testament of Levi* 2ff. speaks of seven heavens, which became a common belief after the second half of the second century c.e. The number seven may be due to Babylonian influence. In that tradition the seven heavens are layered atop each other, and one must travel through all of them to reach the realm of Anu. Finally, *Slavonic Enoch* (22) recognizes ten heavens (Pilch 2011: 73-88).

In addition, Paul considers heaven synonymous with Paradise (2 Cor. 12:3), a Greek word used in the Septuagint for the garden of Eden (Gen. 2:8-10). Jesus' use of this word in his promise to the criminal: "Truly, I say to you, today you will be with me in Paradise" (Luke 23:43) reflects the association of Eden with the abode of the righteous dead already evident in *1–2 Enoch* and *4 Esdras*. In the New Testament, heaven is clearly the destiny and destination of righteous believers (2 Cor. 5:1; Eph. 2:6; Phil. 3:20; Rev. 11:12). Yet heaven in these instances is less a place than a presence or, more accurately, being with God for all eternity. Heaven, especially in Matthew, is a metonym for God. Anything that comes from heaven comes from God (Dan. 4:23; John 3:27). Anything that is "in heaven" is "with God." Thus when Jesus says to Peter: "I will give you the keys of the kingdom of heaven, and whatever you bind on earth shall be bound in heaven, and whatever you loose on earth shall be loosed in heaven" (Matt. 16:18; see also 18:18), the phrase "the kingdom of heaven" is Matthew's version of the phrase in the other Synoptics, "the kingdom of God." Whatever Peter decided will be affirmed by God.

Conclusion

It is very useful to keep in mind the differences between the Bible and theology in their use of the word "heaven." Readers of the Bible can't go wrong by substituting "sky" all the time, whether referring to the physical sky or to the divine realm, the abode of God and the spirits. When contemporary theologians speak of heaven, they usually are referring to a human state or condition of bliss and happiness which is rooted in the vision and enjoyment of God, technically called the "beatific vision." The fact that Jesus is there with his body (as is his mother Mary) and human beings are also present corporeally does not allow the denial of heaven as a place. That, however, is not the primary understanding. As hell in the Bible is the abode of the dead, so heaven is the abode of God and of righteous believers.

3. Earth

This reflection upon earth in the Bible completes the consideration of the three segments of the mythological Tree of Life, a shamanic concept for understanding the cosmos. Having examined the roots (the lower world where the dead abide) and the branches (the upper world or sky where God and the righteous dead abide), we now focus on the trunk, which contains the middle world, the spiritual counterpart or "parallel" to the world in which human beings live. This middle world contains the spirit or essence of all things. It is the "real" world behind the visible world. However, human beings in general believe that the world they inhabit, the earth, is the "real" world. Can these conflicting concepts be reconciled? How are we to understand the trunk of the Tree of Life?

The Tree of Life

Anthropologists have gathered extensive information about the mythological Tree of Life or Tree of the World (the *axis mundi*) from cultures around the world (Goodman 1990: 200-204; Gore 2009: 107-9). In the Norse tradition, it is an ash tree, Yggdrasil. Its roots and branches hold the cosmos together. For the Greeks, it was a fig or oak tree. Many traditions believe it to be the yew tree. In Siberia it is birch, and according to the Siberian Yakut, the tree grows at the navel or vulva of the Earth Mother (see Ps. 139:15). Here the moon does not wane nor the sun set. Summer is everlasting. The cuckoo calls forever.

A Hungarian myth reports that only holy men and women ("shamans") can reach this tree. "But only that person can find this tree, only he can discover where it is, who is born with teeth, and who for nine years has taken only milk for nourishment. That kind of person is a *táltos* [Hungarian shaman, or holy person]. This marvelously tall tree grows in a special place so that only such a man of knowledge can get to it. Other people merely hear of it, but can never see it" (Diószegi 1958: 270-71). Since only specially sensitive persons can reach this tree, they alone can see and work in that world which is parallel to the one in which human beings live. Is there evidence for this in the Bible? Let us examine the understandings of the earth in the Bible and explore how they relate to the trunk of the Tree of Life or Tree of the World.

The Earth

Two Hebrew words in the Bible are translated "earth": *'ădāmâ* and *'ereṣ* (Greek *gē*). The word *'ădāmâ* can mean soil (Gen. 2:5), land or country (Gen. 47:19), or the whole earth (Gen. 12:3). In general, however, it refers to the fertile regions in which human beings can lead a sedentary life tilling the soil or pasturing their flocks. The *'ădāmâ* is only part of the whole earth *('ereṣ)* that also includes the wilderness where no human beings dwell (Job 38:26; Isa. 6:11; Jer. 2:6). The word *'ereṣ* is an antithesis to the physical sky (most often translated in the Bible by the misleading word "heaven"). The phrase "heaven [sky] and earth" that appears forty times in the Revised Standard Version of the Bible reflects a belief in a bipartite division of the universe (e.g., Gen. 14:19; Matt. 11:25, etc.). There are also indications of belief in a tripartite division of the universe: "You shall not make for yourself a graven image, or any likeness of anything that is in heaven above, or that is in the earth beneath, or that is in the water under the earth" (Exod. 20:4; Ps. 146:6; Acts 4:24). Yet another tripartite view includes sky, earth, and netherworld: "and no one in heaven or on earth or under the earth was able to open the scroll or to look into it" (Rev. 5:3; see also Phil. 2:10). The Bible clearly indicates that the Israelites did not have a consistent view of the cosmos, nor did they attempt like the Babylonian sages to construct one. Thus the contradiction of placing Sheol, a cosmic ocean, or an abyss under the earth (see Jonah 2:2-6).

What remains consistent about the earth, however, is that it is perceived as a flat disk (Isa. 40:22; Job 26:10) set quite firmly upon solid foundations (Ps. 18:15; Prov. 8:29) or on pillars (1 Sam. 2:8; Job 9:6). An older view of the earth considered it to be like a square piece of cloth suspended by its four corners (Job 38:12-13; Isa. 11:12; Rev. 7:1). Janzen sums it up thus: Earth is "the habitation of human beings, viewed physically as land, soil, or ground, geographically as a region, politically as a state, territory, or country, cosmically as the opposite of heaven, and symbolically as the entirety of material existence."

The "Real" World

Janzen's description requires some refinement. States and countries did not exist in antiquity, and earth is properly the opposite of sky rather than heaven. But his claim that the earth symbolically represents "the entirety of material existence" is correct. Anthropologists call this consensual reality. This is the world in which human beings live and which they agree is "real." Alternate reality is parallel to consensual reality. This is what the trunk of the Tree of Life designed by holy men and women represents.

One clue to the "real" world behind the visible world (consensual reality) is the concept of the navel or center of the earth (Heb. *ṭabbûr*, highest part or center). This concept, so common in the ancient world, is mentioned only once in the Bible. In the Gog and Magog oracles, Ezekiel announces that the foe from the north (Ezek. 38:15) will attack those "who dwell at the center [or navel] of the earth" (Ezek. 38:12). These are God's people in Jerusalem, for earlier God announced: "This is Jerusalem; I have set her in the center of the nations, with countries round about her" (Ezek. 5:5).

In antiquity, each culture built the earthly residence (temple) of its deity under the deity's residence in the sky (alternate reality). There was a hole in the sky over this place on earth through which people could have access to the divine realm (the branches of the Tree of Life). Jesus ascended to the Father from the Mount of Olives after his resurrection, because the hole in the sky was in the environs of Jerusalem (over the temple) and not in Galilee.

Earlier in the Israelite tradition it seems that Bethel was considered the navel. This is where Jacob saw angels of God ascending and descending on a ladder that reached to the sky. "This is none other than the house of God, and this is the gate of heaven [or hole in the sky]," exclaimed Jacob at the end of his sleep (an alternate state of consciousness, Gen. 28:17).

Presumably the deity could visit the earth through the same hole. In another early Israelite tradition (see Gen. 11:5), the navel of the earth was Babylon (about 50 miles south of Baghdad), the center of Hammurabi's empire. Those who built a tower to the sky here knew where the hole was because God came to visit Babylon, descending through that hole in the sky. Earlier in Babylonian tradition, Nippur (about 100 miles south of Baghdad) was the navel of the earth. It was in this vicinity that Ezekiel experienced God in alternate states of consciousness and communicated God's will as he learned it in visions to fellow exiles. Thus, holy men and women like the patriarch Jacob and the prophet Ezekiel can find the Tree of Life and gain insight from the middle world on that Tree, the "real" world, to apply to life on earth where human beings live.

On Earth as in Heaven

Some ancient cultures thought that life on earth shared in and should imitate life in the sky. This is not exactly the intent of Jesus' prayer: "Thy will be done, on earth as it is in heaven" (Matt. 6:10). The point is that God is Lord or Master of the entire cosmos (Josh. 3:13; Ps. 97:5; Mic. 4:13; Zech. 4:14). "Heaven [the sky] is my throne, and the earth is my footstool" (Isa. 66:1). Life on earth is best lived in accord with God's will. The challenge for the inhabitants of the earth is to learn that will and then fulfill it. Learning God's will is possible in the middle world of the Tree of Life, the parallel to the world human beings inhabit.

In the story of the healing of the paralytic (Matt. 9:1-8), Jesus at first announces that God has forgiven his sins. That is the force of the passive voice "are forgiven." God in the divine realm is the agent. In the ensuing discussion with his opponents, Jesus says, "But that you may know that the Son of man has authority on earth to forgive sins . . ." (Matt. 9:6). The power (or authority) to forgive sins is available in alternate reality, can be acquired there, and can be brought to consensual reality. As a holy man (Mark 1:24), Jesus had access to alternate reality and could broker favors from there to consensual reality quite in line with holy men and women in all cultures.

Further, Jesus the holy man empowers Peter (Matt. 16:19) and the disciples (18:18) with authority to make decisions on earth that will be upheld in the divine realm. This is something new and extraordinary in the biblical record. Though it is not explicitly stated, it is quite likely implied that these leaders will make an effort to learn the real nature of reality by visits to the middle world and also to the divine realm to learn God's will and designs for fulfilling life on earth.

Conclusion

Useful as the shamanic Tree of Life model has been for appreciating the Bible's perspective on the cosmos, the Israelite tradition also expected a new earth and new sky (see Isa. 65:17-20; 66:22; Rev. 21:1, 4). In contrast to contemporary belief in evolution, the ancients believed in devolution (Malina and Pilch 2006: 352-53). Pessimistic as this may sound, the biblical tradition contained a divine promise of a renovated world and a transformed cosmos. There will be no sea (= chaos) in this new world or cosmos. It will have a new Jerusalem, but no temple. God will be the Temple. There will be no sun or moon since God and the Lamb will illumine the city. John explicitly states that he learned this information in altered states of consciousness (Rev. 1:10). He took sky journeys to the Throne (Rev. 4:2) and elsewhere (Rev. 17:3; 21:10). Perhaps he also gained some insight from visits to the middle world of the Tree of Life, the "real" earth.

4. Imaginary Mountains in Matthew

The evangelist Matthew deliberately highlighted mountains in his account of the career of Jesus. Though sometimes he names the mountain (e.g., Mount of Olives, Matt. 24:3), most often he doesn't (e.g., a mountain in Galilee, Matt. 28:16). In general, scholars agree that Matthew's mountain references intend to associate Jesus with Moses, the exodus, or other elements in the Israelite tradition. These familiar literary and theological interpretations have been modified and enriched by culturally sensitive interpretations. Professors K. C. Hanson (1995: 147-70) and Philip F. Esler (1995: 171-77) conducted a ritual analysis of the events that took place on the unnamed mountains in Matthew. A ritual is a social procedure by which persons are transformed from one social situation to another. Hanson and Esler concluded that in these narratives, Matthew proposed rituals which his community of believers and perhaps subsequent communities might imitate and thereby seek to achieve transformation. A review of these narratives with additional cultural background would seem to confirm their conclusion

Mountains in Palestine

There are two major mountain chains in ancient Palestine. West of the Jordan River lie the western highlands (or the central mountains) running north and south in three distinct ranges. The Israelites first settled in this range: Galilee, Manasseh, Ephraim, and Judah. Roads in this range have tended to follow the ridges. East of the Jordan lie the eastern highlands (or the Transjordanian mountains), which extend from Mount Hermon in the North to Edom in the South. The mountains vary in size but some are more than 3,500 feet high.

The Role of Mountains

The Bible reflects the many ways in which human beings use mountains.
Some live there (Gen. 36:8) or take refuge there as needed (Matt. 24:16).
Shepherds pasture animals on mountains (Luke 8:32). People assemble
there for ritual purposes (Josh. 8:30-33), and some are buried there
(1 Kings 23:16). Deities are associated with mountains (e.g., Baal [Baal-
zephon] with Mount Zaphon or Mount Casius in Phoenicia [see Ps. 48:2];
Yahweh with Horeb [see Exod. 3:1; 4:27; 18:5; etc.] or Sion [Pss. 2:6; 48:3;
99:9; Isa. 11:9; etc.]).

Moreover, mountains are an important symbol in the political religions
of the eastern Mediterranean as sites of political-religious temples. Consider the temples in Babylon, Delphi, Gerizim, and Zion. Indeed, in the
Hebrew language the same word *(hêkāl)* means both temple and palace.
Similarly, mountains distant from inhabited areas are considered places of
divine abode (e.g., Olympus, Zaphon, Sinai). Finally, these notions also attach to humanly constructed "mountains" with political-religion symbolism: ziggurats and pyramids.

Consulting biblical passages where "mountains" are mentioned reveals
that the word is used ambiguously. Sometimes it describes a range (Gen.
31:21), at other times a single mount (Exod. 3:1) or a part of a mountain
range (Josh. 21:21). The common element is reference to an elevation of
some kind, though not always very high.

Meaning of Mountains

The ambiguous use of the term "mountain" and frequent references (as in
Matthew) to unnamed mountains beg for a working definition. Richard
Buxton, a classics scholar, defines mountain (Greek *oros*) as "a height outside inhabited and cultivated space" (Buxton 1992: 2). A mountain cannot
be defined simply in terms of physical height. The important element is its
contrast with a cultivated area. In a specifically Egyptian context, mountain *(oros)* may signify the desert in contrast with the fertile and cultivable
Nile valley.

Elaborating this definition still further, Buxton discusses imaginary
mountains. These are the frequent unnamed mountains found in stories
about deities, heroes, and relations between deities and mortals. In this
context, the imaginary mountain seems to have three characteristics. It is
"outside and wild." Being outside, mountains are for outsiders. Shepherds,

bandits, and other deviants are associated with mountains. The imaginary mountain is also "before," that is, it is humanity's first place of habitation. Ezekiel (28:13-14) seems to reflect such a creation story that located Eden on "the holy mountain of God," which can be plausibly linked with Genesis 2:10-14, where four rivers would flow out of Paradise located on a mountain.

Thirdly, and most relevant to this discussion, the imaginary mountain is a "place for reversals." Things normally separated are brought together. Social relationships and normal social behavior may be reversed on the imaginary mountain. Likewise metamorphoses take place on mountains. Metamorphoses are processes that collapse distinctions between things.

Matthew's Imaginary Mountains

Hanson has identified five mountain scenes in Matthew and analyzed them as reflecting a ritual process in which Jesus and/or the other participants are transformed or changed. Matthew presents them to his community as rituals to be imitated. The mountains in these scenes fit the definition of imaginary mountains. Moreover, three of these scenes are experiences in alternate states of consciousness (ASC). The persons in the report are on an imaginary mountain in alternate reality. Their experience tallies well with the customary cultural expectations of ASCs. Adding the ASC dimension to these three scenes strengthens Hanson's proposal that in each instance, disciples are directed to imitate what is presented (mimesis).

The Mountain of Initiation-Ordeal (Matt. 4:1-12)

This episode reports how the devil tests Jesus' spiritual strength, loyalty, and obedience. It clearly echoes themes from Deuteronomy (8:2-5). Jesus passes the test. Critics point out that the mountain is only one of three places — the last one — where Jesus is tested. In actuality, the test takes place in the wilderness (Matt. 4:1). In a literal sense, this is true. And yet Jesus enters alternate reality since he travels from the presumed plain to the pinnacle of the temple, and finally to a high mountain. Without hesitation, the author describes the scenes of alternate reality displacing the original wilderness location, expecting the audience to understand.

What about the disciples? Matthew dramatically depicts Peter's failure of his test as a disciple (Matt. 26:69-75). The story is not about the impressive lies Peter tells. Lying is an accepted strategy in this culture for preserving honor and avoiding trouble. The story rather highlights Peter's failure to remain loyal to Jesus, particularly after two very loud and quite public boasts that he would be loyal, even unto his death if necessary (Matt. 26:33, 35). Hanson cautions that the danger inherent in any ritual is that it will either be done wrong or that it will not be successfully completed. Small wonder that Jesus would teach followers to pray "lead us not into temptation [the test]" (Matt. 6:13).

The Mountain of Instruction (Matt. 4:25–8:1)

Like Sinai, this imaginary mountain is a place where revelation comes from God to the community by means of a mediator. Jesus (a broker) puts people (clients) in touch with God, the author of the commandments (Patron). This is the normal Mediterranean process of patronage. Here the unnamed mountain of instruction also manifests another characteristic of imaginary mountains: they can express a range of symbolisms (they are multivalent). This mountain symbolizes revelation and instruction but also creation. A new community is created here. Hence like other imaginary mountains, this one too is an umbilicus, or a point of creation. In this passage Matthew once again echoes Old Testament themes, notably from Exodus 19 through 24. On this mountain, Jesus is portrayed as a master who initiates others as disciples and transforms their status.

Mountain of Healing (Matt. 15:29-31)

Here the lame, maimed, blind, mute, and others are transformed from brokenness to wholeness. Jesus heals these people. Healing restores meaning to people's lives. In this instance, those who were excluded from worshiping in the temple are returned to the holy community of God by being transformed through the healing process. The scene reports a re-creation, or a new creation.

The power Jesus wielded over every kind of brokenness he shares with the Twelve. They are to continue the healing, integration, and inclusivity Jesus has initiated. The imagery of Ezekiel 34, where the mountain is a dangerous place where sheep get lost, sick, or injured, is replaced with the hill of Yahweh's blessing. This scene may have provided Matthew with a model for this ritual of transformation.

The Mountain of Epiphany (Matt. 17:1-8)

This passage is a very obvious report of an alternate state of consciousness experience Jesus had conjointly with three privileged disciples: Peter, James, and John (Pilch 2011: 124-45). In the event itself, Jesus and the three, independently yet simultaneously, gain insight into Jesus' true identity (God's Son) and are advised to heed him (more so than Moses and Elijah). The status of Jesus and of the disciples is heightened even as Jesus' exalted status is revealed.

Hanson believes that this narrative prepares for the appearance of the resurrected Jesus at the commissioning (in the final report). From the perspective of ASC experiences, such a replicable experience (a ritual) does indeed familiarize a person with alternate reality and those who abide there already and permanently: God, the risen Jesus, those already transformed, as Paul describes in 1 Corinthians 15:51.

If Isaiah reports an ASC experience in the temple (Isa. 6), surely others had one too. The psalmist captures the basic Israelite belief: "They will go from strength to strength and see the God of gods on Zion" (Ps. 84:8 NAB). Matthew's report about Jesus' transfiguration appears to echo the experience of Moses (Exod. 24:15-18; 34:29-35). The history of Christian liturgy suggests that this was the kind of experience early believers expected in worship (Pilch 2004: 170-80). As Esler observes, this scene very clearly has a mimetic aspect. "The words from heaven: 'This is my Son, the Beloved, he enjoys my favor: Listen to him' (17:5 NJB) are matched by the first part of Jesus' final instruction to the disciples to obey everything which he had commanded them (28:20)" (Esler 1995: 173-74).

The Mountain of Commissioning (Matt. 28:16-20)

Here on another imaginary mountain, the transformed (risen) Jesus in turn transforms his inner circle from an inwardly oriented, tightly knit, fictive kin-group to an outwardly directed group of teachers and disciple makers. Earlier (Matt. 10), the Twelve were commissioned to preach, heal, raise the dead, and cast out demons, but only among the lost sheep of the house of Israel. They were not to go among the Samaritans, or the Gentiles. Here (Matt. 28:16-20) their ethnic focus is extended to fellow ethnics living in minority enclaves outside Galilee and Judea. They also receive new tasks: to teach and baptize these.

This is the third ASC experience among Matthew's five imaginary

mountain reports. Having learned more about Jesus' identity in the transfiguration, they now recognize the risen Jesus himself in his farewell appearance to them. His very last words assure his continued presence in
their midst. He is ever accessible.

Matthew begins this final report by indicating that while some worshiped him, others doubted (28:17). In a culture where ASC experiences are
considered routine and normal, the doubt could not have concerned the
experience itself. The gospel reports that they already had such experiences
with Jesus (e.g., walking on the Sea, 14:22-32). The doubt plausibly concerned the fact that Jesus was raised, was alive. This is, after all, the only appearance to the disciples that Matthew reports. But since the Greek word
translated "doubted" can also be translated "hesitated," perhaps that is
preferable. Some drew the immediate and obvious conclusion, while others (momentarily?) hesitated.

According to Hanson, the equivocal response on the part of some might
reflect Matthew's word of caution that perhaps not all, even among the
leaders, were prepared to or capable of accepting this experience. One of
the dangerous aspects of ritual is that a participant may be unsuccessful in
completing it. Perhaps the evangelist is alerting the reader or listener to
that danger. Some might still be pleading: "We want to see Jesus!" (John
12:21). As those Hellenists sought out Andrew, whom they deemed the appropriate broker, believers who hesitate might similarly be in search of the
appropriate mediator.

Conclusion

The five imaginary mountain scenes created by Matthew are quite in accord with his predilection for fives and his intention to associate Jesus with
Moses. It is significant that three of these scenes are experiences in alternate reality. If these five mountain scenes present rituals that work transformations, the three alternate states of consciousness experiences serve
the ritual process very well. Listeners to or readers of Matthew's presentation of Jesus as a model worthy of imitation can enter that process with
greater confidence by means of the pan-human experience of ASCs. "I am
with you always, to the close of the age" (28:20).

5. A New Sky and a New Earth

When the sky opened for Ezekiel, he saw visions of God and heard a voice giving him instruction and direction (Ezek. 1–7). When the sky opened at Jesus' baptism, the Spirit came upon him and a voice declared him to be a beloved and pleasing Son (Mark 1:10-11). After his resurrection, Jesus was lifted up into the sky and disappeared from the sight of his apostles (Acts 1:11). John the Revealer traveled through an "open door" in the sky and arrived at the throne of God, where he saw and heard many things (Rev. 4:1-11). Where does the sky open? What is this opening? Why do these and other prophets see and learn new things in the sky? What did ancient people know about the sky?

The "Heavens"

A concordance search of the Revised Standard Version of the Bible discloses that the word "sky" appears twelve times, but the word "heaven/heavens" occurs 750 times. (In the NRSV "sky" appears 27 times, notably in Gen. 1 where it never occurs in the RSV; and "heaven" occurs 698 times). Both English words translate the same Hebrew and Greek words! As the Italian proverb puts it, "Every translator is a traitor" *(traduttore, traditore).* The English word "heaven" carries so many centuries of theological freight that a reader does well to avoid it and use "sky" unless completely implausible in context. "Sky" will give us a better understanding of the experiences of Ezekiel, Jesus, and John the Revealer.

The ancients did not have electricity to distract them with movies, TV, and computer games. Scholars realize that they paid an incredible amount of attention to the earth with its plants and animals and to the sky with its animate beings: stars and constellations. They knew and catalogued all these things quite extensively.

Hole in the Sky

The priestly conception of the world reflected in Genesis 1 is familiar to most readers of the Bible. The earth is a flat saucer resting on pillars covered by a dome on the other side of which are waters. There is water and an underworld beneath the saucer, too. This fifth-century-b.c.e. Israelite perspective differed considerably from the fourth-century-b.c.e. Hellenistic view of the universe. For these Mediterranean neighbors, the earth was a still and stable sphere located at the center of the universe and surrounded by the sun, moon, and five planets (also spherical in shape), which traversed around the earth in separate orbits. Greek and Roman philosophers as well as the Fathers of the Church held this opinion. Modern Western readers need to continually remind themselves of the impact Alexander's conquest of the world had on everyone as it spread the Greek language and the storehouse of Greek knowledge. It was Washington Irving's 1828 novelistic biography *The Life and Voyages of Christopher Columbus,* a work of fiction, that spread the lie that until Columbus's time everyone believed that the world was flat.

The ancients agreed that this universe was a closed system enclosed by a vault or firmament. The high god or gods lived on the other side, and there was an opening that allowed access to the other side. That opening, of course, was located over the place where the deity's temple on earth was located. In the Israelite tradition, this was Jerusalem. Jesus had to ascend to heaven from Jerusalem, since the hole was there and not in Galilee. John the Seer on Patmos and Ezekiel the prophet in Mesopotamia could travel through that opening by means of experiences in alternate states of consciousness, an everyday pan-human experience among more than 90 percent of the planet's population according to anthropological studies (Bourguignon 1974).

View from the Other Side

As American schoolchildren are familiar with globes of the earth, the ancients from the sixth century B.C.E. forward were familiar with globes of the universe viewed from the "outside." There is a very famous Islamicate globe in the Smithsonian Institution, but the Farnese sphere from the second century B.C.E. is perhaps better known. These globes are a collection of bands along which each planet, sun, and moon travels, with the earth at the center. They also present the constellations along its band, the zodiac. Pictures of these globes help a Bible reader understand what Ezekiel and John the Seer are reporting. Both prophets traveled through the hole in the sky to gain a view of this universe from God's perspective.

The view is from the throne of God (Ezek. 1:26; Rev. 4:2). Modern readers are apt to imagine this as a seat, but the ancients knew and saw it as a constellation. The Farnese sphere shows a throne near the North Pole over the constellations Leo and Cancer. The Romans identified a constellation as the throne of Caesar. There was also a throne for Cassiopeia. In the Vatican Museum, there is a second-century-c.e. sculpture from the Villa Albani showing Jupiter, the head of the Roman Pantheon, seated on a literal throne in the center of the zodiac supported by Atlas.

The Israelite tradition knew that God's throne was in the sky. "The LORD is in his holy temple, the LORD's throne is in heaven [the sky]" (Ps. 11:4; see also 103:19; 123:1, etc.). Matthew's Jesus knows this too: "he who swears by heaven [the sky], swears by the throne of God and by him who sits upon it" (23:22; cf. 5:34). Ezekiel (1:26; 10:1) describes the constellation rather well: "Above the firmament over their heads there was the likeness of a throne, in appearance like sapphire." The color of a sapphire is mainly yellow, but often blue, and at times orange. One might begin to imagine colors of the rainbow (red, orange, yellow, green, blue, and violet, and sometimes indigo between blue and violet). Ezekiel's description concurs (1:28): "Like the appearance of the bow that is in the cloud on the day of rain, so was the appearance of the brightness round about [the throne]."

Four Equatorial Constellations

Just as the earth has an equator, so too the sky has an equator projected from the earth. The sky also has a central point at the north, where the pole and the polar star are located. The yellow color of the sapphire is also the color of the polar star. This is not a fixed spot, but rather the central point of control, the center of the vault of the sky and the four equidistant constellations along the equator. The four living creatures that Ezekiel (1:10) saw in his alternate state of consciousness suggest the four constellations at four opposite points of the equatorial zodiac. These are: Scorpio-man (human face), Leo (face of lion), Taurus (face of ox), and Pegasus (a flying creature, face of eagle). John the Revealer saw the same constellations (Rev. 4:6-7): "the first living creature like a lion, the second living creature like an ox, the third living creature with the face of a man, and the fourth living creature like a flying eagle."

The point of the content of Ezekiel's and John's visions is not that the constellations determine fate. Rather, since the sky, its planets, and its constellations were created by God at the beginning of creation, an inspired seer who can read the sky correctly by being privy to God's view of the cosmos can understand and interpret current events as reflecting God's will from all eternity. The difference may be difficult to grasp. Essentially it is God's will rather than the animate constellations that direct life and history. God's will is set at creation when the constellations came into being.

Sky Wars and Satan

Luke's Jesus claims that he saw "Satan fall like lightning from heaven [the sky]. Behold, I have given you authority to tread upon serpents and scorpions, and over all the power of the enemy; and nothing shall hurt you" (Luke 10:18-19). Hippolytus (*Refutation of All Heresies* 4.47) cites Aratus to note that there is in the sky "an enormous and prodigious monster, (the) Serpent; and that this is what the devil says in the book of Job to the Deity, when (Satan) uses these words: "I have traversed earth under heaven, and have gone around (it) [Job 1:7]." Hippolytus says that the Dragon/Serpent is located near the North Pole, from which vantage point he can see everything.

John the Revealer appears to reflect this perspective when he writes: "Now war arose in heaven [the sky], Michael and his angels fighting against the dragon; . . . they were defeated and there was no longer any place for them in heaven [the sky]. And the great dragon was thrown down, that ancient serpent, who is called the Devil and Satan, the deceiver of the whole world . . ." (Rev. 12:7-9). Thus, it is highly plausible that Jesus and John both recount a vision each had in an alternate state of consciousness. Reading the sky according to the traditional lore as it has been interpreted by the Israelite tradition, they see an event — a sky war — that took place before humans were created. Jesus may also be referring to constellations when he mentions serpents and scorpions.

According to Israelite tradition, Michael defeated the serpent (starry dragon) and exiled it from the sky to earth, where it later met the first human beings. In the Israelite tradition, Job 1 reflects the period when Satan was still in the sky. The "J" tradition (Gen. 3) reports him to be on the earth before the creation of the first human beings, so that the star war took place earlier. The star-war story appears to have been shaped by another ancient star-war story about darkness (Scorpio) causing the sun/light (Orion) to flee. Orion (sun) shamed Artemis (moon), so Scorpio (darkness) came to the rescue and wounded and then slew Orion. Thus the saying that at the rising of Scorpio (darkness) in the East, Orion flees at the western sky (Malina 1995: 166-71).

Traces of this appear in Isaiah. "The stars of the sky and Orion and the whole array of the sky will not give light" (Isa. 13:10 LXX). "In that day, the LORD with his hard and great and strong sword will punish Leviathan the fleeing serpent, Leviathan the twisting serpent, and he will slay the dragon that is in the sea" (Isa. 27:1; the Septuagint version talks about the crooked or dishonest dragon-serpent). Notice that the ancients were not concerned about consistency nor ashamed of inconsistency. Sky knowledge was cumulative. Each culture added and adapted data, and applied its insights to matters or events in need of understanding and interpretation. Above all, the challenge was to discover and understand God's will. The sky offered a ready reference for that task.

Conclusion

When the Assyrians gained world dominance in the eighth and seventh centuries B.C.E. and conquered Israel, the Northern Kingdom, pagan worship of the stars became attractive, tempting, and popular. Amos warns that exile will be God's punishment for the house of Israel when it adopts Kaiwan (probably Saturn) as "your star-god" (Amos 5:26). During the reign of Hoshea, Israel forsook all the commandments of the Lord, "and worshiped all the host of heaven" (= stars; 2 Kings 17:6). Subsequently, King Josiah attempted to put an end to this idolatry: "he deposed the idolatrous priests . . . those also who burned incense to Baal, to the sun, and the moon, and the constellations, and all the host of the heavens" (2 Kings 23:5). The effort was in vain.

Modern readers of the Bible have long misunderstood these appropriate condemnations to mean that Israelites should have nothing at all to do with the sky and its animate beings (stars, planets, constellations, etc.). A careful and critical reading of the Bible shows that people like Ezekiel, Jesus, and John the Revealer were recognized by their peers as astral prophets. This kind of prophet knows the sky very well and interacts with star-related, celestial personages to learn the will of God. The written narratives in the Bible record the circumstances in which they learned this (in trances or other alternate states of consciousness), the interactions themselves (the content of the visions, what is seen and/or heard), and the consequences (the impact or the meanings of the phenomena in the sky). One could learn much about God from reading the sky. Ironically, this enlightening reading can only be done in the dark.

FURTHER READING: THE COSMOS

Bourguignon, Erika. 1974. *Culture and the Varieties of Consciousness.* An Addison-Wesley Module in Anthropology, no. 47. Reading: Addison-Wesley.
Buxton, Richard. 1992. "Imaginary Greek Mountains." *Journal of Hellenistic Studies* 112: 1-15.

Diószegi, Vilmos. 1958. *A sámánhit emlékei a magyar népi müveltségben.* [The Tokens of Shamanic Belief in the Hungarian Popular Cultivation.] Budapest: Akadémiai Kiadó. 1998 reprint.

Esler, Philip F. 1995. "Mountaineering in Matthew: A Response to K. C. Hanson." Pp. 171-77 in *Transformations, Passages, and Processes: Ritual Approaches to Biblical Texts.* Edited by Mark McVann. Atlanta: The Society of Biblical Literature.

Goodman, Felicitas D. 1990. *Where the Spirits Ride the Wind: Trance Journeys and Other Ecstatic Experiences.* Bloomington and Indianapolis: Indiana University Press.

Goodman, Felicitas D., and Nana Nauwald. 2003. *Ecstatic Trance: A Workbook.* Havelte: Binkey Kok.

Gore, Belinda. 2009. *The Ecstatic Experience: Healing Postures for Spirit Journeys.* Rochester: Bear.

Hanson, K. C. 1995. "Transformed on the Mountain: Ritual Analysis and the Gospel of Matthew." Pp. 147-70 in *Transformations, Passages, and Processes: Ritual Approaches to Biblical Texts.* Edited by Mark McVann. Atlanta: The Society of Biblical Literature.

Janzen, Waldemar. 1992. "Earth." *Anchor Bible Dictionary* 2: 242-48.

Malina, Bruce J. 1995. *On the Genre and Message of Revelation: Star Visions and Sky Journeys.* Peabody: Hendrickson.

Malina, Bruce J., and John J. Pilch. 2000. *Social Science Commentary on the Book of Revelation.* Minneapolis: Fortress.

———. 2006. *Social Science Commentary on the Letters of Paul.* Minneapolis: Fortress.

Pilch, John J. 2004. *Visions and Healing in the Acts of the Apostles: How the Early Believers Experienced God.* Collegeville, MN: The Liturgical Press.

———. 2011. *Flights of the Soul: Visions, Heavenly Journeys, and Peak Experiences in the Biblical World.* Grand Rapids and Cambridge: Eerdmans.

———. 2011. "Holy Men and Their Sky Journeys." Pp. 48-60 in *Flights of the Soul: Visions, Heavenly Journeys, and Peak Experiences in the Biblical World.* Grand Rapids and Cambridge: Eerdmans.

———. 2011. "Music in Second (Slavonic) Enoch." Pp. 73-88 in *Flights of the Soul: Visions, Heavenly Journeys, and Peak Experiences in the Biblical World.* Grand Rapids and Cambridge: Eerdmans.

———. 2011. "The Transfiguration of Jesus: An Experience of Alternate Reality." Pp. 124-45 in *Flights of the Soul: Visions, Heavenly Journeys, and Peak Experiences in the Biblical World.* Grand Rapids and Cambridge: Eerdmans.

Scurlock, Joann. 2009. "Necromancy." *New Interpreters' Dictionary of the Bible* 4: 248.

Part Two

EARTH

.

In the previous part, we reflected upon the earth as part of the cosmos as biblical culture understood it. In this part we reflect upon aspects of the earth in which our ancestors in faith lived: caves, swamps, desert, snakes, and the like. While these may seem like self-evident concepts, our reflections will show how the biblical authors attached a wide array of symbolic as well as literal meanings to these simple realities.

1. Desert and Wilderness

When I first came from the East Coast to attend college in the Midwest, my classmates from Chicago used to speak about playing baseball in the "prairies." I didn't recall Carl Sandburg describing this aspect of Chicago in his famous poem. My only acquaintance with the prairie was from Hollywood films about cowboys or country-Western songs such as: "Oh bury me not on the lone prairie." As a native of Brooklyn, New York, I struggled to imagine large, empty, windblown, sandy tracts of land scattered within the metropolis of Chicago where my friends went to play baseball.

Confused and exhausted by the mental challenge of imagining this scenario, I finally asked them to describe a prairie. When they said that it was an empty space between houses in a neighborhood, large enough in which to play baseball, I immediately recognized the reality to be a "lot." In my hometown, Brooklyn, kids used to play stickball in the lot. A tenant without access to a backyard would take the dog for a walk to the lot. In the neighboring Italian neighborhood, the lot was also the place where people dumped the grapes from which the must had been pressed to make wine. In this context, a lot was not a particularly desirable place to play anything, least of all baseball. Still, kids accommodated to "sandlot" baseball.

Readers of the Bible in Western civilization face a similar challenge. When Jesus' disciples ask him how they can find bread to feed 4,000 in the desert (Matt. 15:33//Mark 8:5), a Western reader typically imagines a large tract of sand, a hot sun burning the grains, a place without water. Where is such a desert in Palestine? How did that large a number of people get there? Why did they go, apparently without provisions of any sort?

Deserts

The desert just described is called an absolute desert, that is, a region where rain almost never falls. In the Middle East, such a desert is found only in the Sahara (which is the Arabic word for desert, thus making the phrase "Sahara desert" a tautology), the peninsula of Arabia, and Iran. The deserts in Syria, Transjordan, the Sinai, and Palestine are tame deserts. Rain tends to fall every winter (the "wet" season), especially in March and April. The storms are sudden and heavy, frequently causing threatening flash floods. The foolish person who built a house on sand (Matt. 5:26) is probably someone who built on crusted-over alluvial soil in a wadi. When the rains fell, the winds blew, and the floods came, all was washed away. Not only was the foundation faulty, but the rains were exceptionally forceful.

Deserts in Antiquity

Social geographers point out that deserts in antiquity are not so designated primarily on the basis of climate or geology. In general, the term "desert" designates a space with minimal human occupation. In particular, it is a place devoid of cities, or, in technical terms, a place minimally structured by the presence of coherent political communities. This is how Paul divides the world: city, wilderness, and sea (2 Cor. 11:26). He boasts of being a "citizen of no mean city" (Tarsus, Acts 21:39). After all, outside the city nothing of social worth exists.

In the second century B.C.E., Gaius Gracchus referred to Tuscany as a desert in spite of the fact that this region contained large estates developed by hordes of slaves. This observation highlights yet another feature of a desert. It is a place inhabited by barbarians, who are by nature little inclined to live in cities. In such an ethnocentric perspective, barbarians are considered intermediate beings between the human and animal kingdoms. They are fated to be slaves, but slavery allows them to improve their lives in some way.

Terms for Desert

Four Hebrew words are commonly used to express the idea of desert. Midbar ("desolate land," "wilderness") is most common. The book of Numbers in the Hebrew Bible is known as *bĕmidbar* (in the wilderness), the fifth word of the first verse. In Job 38:26, the Lord (speaking of himself) asks who has brought "rain on a land where no man is, on the desert in which there is no man." *ʿărābâ* describes the dry plain of the Rift valley, especially south of the Dead Sea. "Make straight in the desert a highway for our God" (Isa. 40:3). It also describes plains (as of Moab; Num. 22:1). *Yĕšîmôn* ("wasteland") ordinarily refers to the slopes of Judah that overlook the Dead Sea. In the exodus, the Israelites wandered, among other areas, in a region northeast of the Dead Sea "from Bamoth to the valley lying in the region of Moab by the top of Pisgah which looks down upon the desert" (Num. 21:20). But the word also denotes savage, waterless places devoid of human habitation, suitable only for beasts. "He found him in a desert land, and in the howling waste of the wilderness" (Deut. 32:10).

Ḥărābâ designates "dry land, dry, uninhabitable area." ". . . and the LORD drove the sea back by a strong east wind all night, and made the sea dry land . . ." (Exod. 14:21). It also describes ruins, as Ezekiel (5:14) uses this word to describe a desolate Jerusalem. The first three Hebrew words can also be translated as "wilderness." Indeed, in many passages, two of the first three words are paired, thus indicating that they are used synonymously, interchangeably.

Deserts and Their Surroundings

Because of the contrasting relationship of inhabited areas (cities and villages) with uninhabited areas (deserts and wildernesses), the uninhabited areas are known by the names of the towns they adjoin. Thus when David became aware that Saul was plotting evil against him, he retreated to the strongholds in the wilderness, in the hill country of the wilderness of Ziph, a rocky area south of Hebron (see 1 Sam. 23:14). From there David moved to the wilderness of Maon, and then to the wilderness of En-gedi (1 Sam.

24:1). Indeed, uncivilized people like bandits, criminals, and renegades were forced to seek escape in the desert or wilderness.

Desert Inhabitants

In addition to outcasts, other fit inhabitants of the desert would include wild animals, spirits, and barbarians. In biblical times, the "wild" animals of the desert included the owl (Ps. 102:6), the ostrich (Lam. 4:3), the vulture (or pelican, Hebrew is uncertain; Ps. 102:6), the wild ass (Jer. 2:24), the fox (Ezek. 13:4), and the jackal (or dragon, Mal. 1:3). Mark's comment (1:14) that Jesus was driven by the spirit out into the wilderness where he was with the wild animals paints a scene that is commonplace and readily familiar.

It is plausible that Luke and Matthew omit mentioning the wild animals because they want to highlight Jesus' encounter with a spirit, the devil. As they and their audiences knew, spirits typically inhabit deserted, waterless places (Matt. 12:43-45//Luke 11:24-26). Deserted places are fit only for wild animals and spirits, not for human beings (see also Isa. 34:14).

Barbarians form an interesting case. The ancient Mediterranean world divided all humanity into two groups: Greek-speaking (i.e., civilized) and non-Greek-speaking (i.e., non-civilized or barbarians). It is in this sense that the inhabitants of Malta are called barbarians in Acts 28:2, 4 (RSV "natives"). In the Corinthian community, those who speak an unknown language are similarly called barbarians (1 Cor. 14:11). From this perspective, Paul classified his fellow ethnics who did not speak Greek as barbarians (Rom. 1:14). Of course, none of these are living in the desert or wilderness, yet it is but a small step from here to the consideration that barbarian tribes, like the Parthians, do not live in true, civilized regions, but rather in the desert or wilderness. This is true no matter what actual geography may indicate.

The Baptist in the Desert

John the Baptist emerges in the desert preaching a message of repentance (Mark 1:4) and exhorting to baptism of repentance for the forgiveness of sins. The fact that he is located near the Jordan yet is considered to be in the desert indicates that deserts were not considered to be waterless stretches of sand. On the contrary, the desert in which John lives and preaches is a desolate area, uninhabited by human (civilized) beings but where water could be and actually was available. John's nourishment (locusts and wild honey) is also uncivilized food, that is, food which city people would not ordinarily eat.

Feeding Crowds in the Desert

The gospel stories popularly known as feeding the crowds with "loaves and fishes" (5,000 — Mark 6:30-34//Matt. 14:13-21//Luke 9:10-17//John 6:1-13; 4,000 — Mark 8:1-10//Matt. 15:32-39) report that the crowd was located in an "isolated" place (5,000) or a "desert" place (4,000). The same Greek word (*eremos,* translated "lonely," "isolated," "desert," etc.) occurs in all accounts except John's. The traditional site is Heptapegon (Arabic *Tabgha*), approximately two miles east of Bethsaida, quite possibly the "home village" of Peter, Andrew, Philip, James, and John. In the year 30 c.e., Herod Philip elevated Bethsaida to the status of a Greek polis and named it Julias in honor of Emperor Tiberius's mother, Livia-Julia.

Even without being able to determine the precise location of this event, the consideration of purchasing food indicates that the crowd is not anywhere close to kinsfolk who could provide for them as needed. The number itself is very likely hyperbole, since this would be larger than the population of very few urban settlements in Palestine of this time.

Many interpreters identify a plausible connection between this gospel story and the Exodus report of God feeding the Israelites in the wilderness. Can our reflection on desert/wilderness add anything else? Perhaps.

Because it was outside of civilized, that is, human habitation, the desert is normally perceived to be chaos and not an appropriate place for a meal. It was impossible to observe the proper procedures in this context for preparing the food or the requirements of ritual purity, according to Leviticus. Yet Jesus manages not only to provide food sufficient for this multitude, but food that is quite desirable and readily available in this locale. Fish would be difficult to come by anywhere else but in the environs of the Sea of Galilee. Bread, of course, is the staple in that diet. The stories therefore present Jesus as providing acceptable nourishment and blessing it, that is, acknowledging God's beneficence in providing the food. Jesus is clearly master over desert and wilderness. As he deals harmoniously with wild animals (Mark 1:14) in the desert, so he provides nourishment that is acceptable to the people and pleasing to their God in a place that customarily is entirely out of bounds, uncivilized, filled with risk, danger, and threat to life.

31

Conclusion

Reading always involves imagination. Authors count on it, for they creatively manipulate the reader's imagination in order to direct them to fresh insight. Desert and wilderness in the ancient world carried stock meanings. Basically these were places unfit for human (civilized) existence. That Jesus could enter these regions and emerge successfully from an encounter with wild animals and hostile spirits is truly remarkable. Moreover, that he could provide for his audience with nourishment for the mind, for the meaning of life, and for the body in a place not normally associated with meeting these needs, speaks of an incredible relationship with God, who replicates at Jesus' behest what God did for his people in the exodus. Once again the evangelists demonstrate how capably they can reshape familiar traditions to offer new insight.

2. Caves

In 1947, a Bedouin boy from the Ta'amireh tribe searching for a stray sheep tossed a rock into a cave near Wadi Qumran. Instead of the bleat of an animal struck or frightened by the stone, or the sound of stone striking against stone, the boy heard the crash of something breaking. Eventually, he found the pottery in which were contained the first of many exciting discoveries in the area, notably the manuscripts now known in general as the Dead Sea Scrolls. In 1952 as scholars recognized the importance of the discoveries, explorers made soundings in some two hundred caves on a line five miles north and south of Qumran, searching for other discoveries.

Why are there so many caves in this region? Are there many other caves throughout the land? What purpose(s) did they serve? Did people assign them any special significance?

Caves in Syro-Palestine

The geology of Syro-Palestine is characterized chiefly by chalk, limestone, and sandstone. The soft quality of these materials accounts for the many natural caves and other openings in the rock such as tombs, carved out by human efforts. Caves are found in Galilee, Mount Carmel, Samaria, Judea, the Shephelah, and the Negev. Moreover, many of these caves are quite large. The geographer Strabo (1st cent. B.C.E.) describes a cave near Damascus that could hold 4,000 men! The Deuteronomic Historian recounts the time when David had to flee for his life from Saul to the city of Adullam in the region south or west-southwest of Bethlehem. He hid there in a cave, and some four hundred men joined him (1 Sam. 22:1-2). The root of the Hebrew word for Adullam means "turn aside," "a retreat, or refuge," signaling some of the uses to which caves were put.

Caves as Domestic Dwellings

The prehistoric caves near Mount Carmel give some glimpses into human habitations from about the year 150,000 B.C.E. when the Tabu cave was first inhabited. At that time this cave was at the seashore, but the sea level dropped to its present level around 80,000 B.C.E. When this cave became uninhabitable, the people moved to the el-Wad cave nearby. Though it was occupied chiefly between 40,000 and 20,000 B.C.E., the most interesting information we have derives from a still later time (12,000 to 10,000 B.C.E.) called the Natufian period. In Syro-Palestine, this culture left traces of basket weaving, the use of bows and traps for hunting animals, and an assortment of fishing nets. Moreover, they developed a distinctive naturalistic art featuring animal and human figures which may have been connected with fertility rites. Because they buried their dead within their settlements, often under the floor of the living quarters, scholars have learned much from the remains.

The Bible itself gives indications that people lived in or used caves at other periods, too. Lot lived in a cave with his daughters after the destruction of Sodom and Gomorrah (Gen. 19:30). Though it is frequently interpreted as a symbol for the maiden's home, the reference in the Song of Solomon to the Lover seeking his Beloved ("dove") in the clefts of the rock, or the covert of the cliff, could literally point to a human (as well as a bird's) cave dwelling (Song 2:14).

Other Uses for Caves

When they were no longer used primarily as places to live, some people used caves for storage. Grains and other durable goods were frequently placed in containers and stored or hidden in caves. Animals were sheltered in caves, especially when living quarters were built at the mouth of the cave. Bandits and political agitators or targets of political vengeance took refuge in caves. Josephus reports how Herod literally smoked the

Galilean rebels out of the caves to murder them above the plain of Arbela (*Jewish War* 16.4). Finally, caves were used as burial places. Abraham purchased the Cave of Machpelah to serve as a family tomb in which to bury Sarah (Gen. 23:17-20). Other patriarchs were buried here, too (Gen. 49:28-33). Lazarus was buried in a cave (a vertical shaft tomb) with a stone laid across it (John 11:38).

A Triad of Caves

In the fourth century c.e., Eusebius, the famous Bishop of Caesarea in ancient Palestine around 260-339, identified three special caves associated with key events in the life of Jesus. These were the cave in which Jesus made his first epiphany (Bethlehem), the cave in which he struggled with and conquered death (his tomb in Jerusalem), and the cave associated with his ascension on the Mount of Olives. This triad of caves became very important for subsequent pilgrims to Palestine. A modern reader is naturally skeptical to hear of a "cave" associated with the ascension. Are the other suggestions more plausible?

To answer this question, one must remember that the Bible, like many ancient documents, is an example of high context literature. This kind of literature leaves much to the imagination because the author assumes the hearers or listeners know the scenes described so well that they can supply the correct details. With regard to Eusebius's triad of caves, the New Testament does not mention a cave associated with the birth of Jesus or with the ascension. The Synoptics describe the tomb in which Jesus was buried as newly hewn out of the soft rock, and it could plausibly be understood as a cave. Where then did Eusebius, a generally reliable and trustworthy source, obtain this information about the caves?

The Cave at Bethlehem

A tradition that Jesus was born in a cave in or near Bethlehem goes back to Justin, a native of Palestine. "But when the Child was born in Bethlehem, since Joseph could not find a lodging in that village, he took up his quarters in a certain cave near the village; and while they were there Mary brought forth the Christ and placed Him in a manger . . ." (Justin, *Dialogue with Trypho* 78.12-13; ca. 155-161 c.e.). Origen (*Contra Celsum* 1.51, ca. 247 c.e.) is the first to identify a specific cave in Bethlehem as the actual place of Jesus' birth. In the fourth century, Jerome lamented that from the time of

Hadrian (135) to Constantine (ca. 300) the cave in which Jesus was born was overshadowed by a grove sacred to Tammuz (Adonis) the lover of Venus.

The Dominican archaeologist, Fr. Jerome Murphy-O'Connor, accepts this tradition of Jesus being born in a cave as plausible and credible (Murphy-O'Connor 2008: 230). So too do the Franciscan archaeologists, Fr. Bellarmino Bagatti and Emanuelle Testa (Bagatti 1971: 111). Murphy-O'Connor suggests retranslating "she laid him in a manger because there was no room for them in the inn" (Luke 2:7) as "she laid him in a manger because they had no space in the room." Joseph took his wife to the cave area at the back of the house-cave (rather than the less plausible "inn"), where she might give birth safely removed from the risks of a house crowded with adults. The manger in which Mary placed the newborn Jesus would be a normal item of "furniture" since the cave area of the house-cave served as the shelter for animals.

The Cave-Tomb

According to the New Testament, Jesus died and was buried in Jerusalem, in a rock-tomb carved by human effort. Eusebius calls it a cave, but some contemporary scholars observe that such a tomb is not a cave, strictly speaking. It would seem that this fine distinction was not significant in antiquity. Still, the tomb which visitors to Jerusalem view today is certainly not a cave, nor is it located in a cave. The tomb has been carved away from its original location and was situated here when Constantine built the basilica to enclose it. Moreover, this present-day tomb retains very little of the tomb originally identified as Jesus' because Caliph Hakim's soldiers hacked it down in 1099. Still other scholars believe that the real tomb of Jesus was further south of this location and will probably never be found. Nevertheless, Murphy-O'Connor accepts as valid and credible the earliest traditions that the Holy Sepulcher basilica does indeed identify the actual location of the tomb (Murphy-O'Connor 2008: 49).

Intriguing as this scholarly debate may be, modern readers might consider other perspectives not usually included in these discussions. The fact that Jesus was buried in Jerusalem in the tomb of a stranger instead of being "gathered to his people" in Galilee (see Gen. 25:8; 35:29; 49:29, 33) to "sleep with his fathers" (see 1 Kings 2:10; 11:43; 14:31; 15:8) posed a serious problem for his family. Such a burial deprived Jesus of his proper place in family ancestry. The family cave-tomb was a key element in this part of ancient life. Not to be buried in it was a serious tragedy.

On the other hand, the gospel information that some of those who sought or visited Jesus' final resting place experienced him alive in altered states of consciousness experiences such as visions strongly suggests that they knew the location of the actual cave-tomb. Such experiences were and continue to be common in the Middle East. Moreover, visions of the risen Jesus quite alive helped his followers to realize that despite apparent severance from appropriate family ties, the earthly life of Jesus was pleasing to God, who gave evidence of this judgment by raising Jesus from the dead. In immediately subsequent decades or centuries, pilgrims who shared these cultural convictions could firmly hope for similar experiences if they visited the right holy place.

The Ascension Cave

Some scholars suggest that in associating the location of the Jesus' ascension with a cave just below the summit of the Mount of Olives, Eusebius betrays some "political" motivations that prompted him to manipulate traditions to highlight a triad of caves linking Jerusalem, the Mount of Olives, and Bethlehem. Tradition identified a cave below the summit as the place where Jesus shared special instruction with his disciples. Further, archaeologists point out that it is solidly probable that after the Last Supper, Jesus prayed not in the "garden" but rather in a cave near Gethsemane where he was arrested. Archaeological evidence indicates that the cave of Gethsemane was used for agricultural storage during the Roman period. It would have been a good place to pray and to sleep during the cold, dew-filled spring nights at Passover time. Though Jesus ascended to the Father quite likely from the summit of the Mount of Olives, it would seem that Eusebius's manipulation of tradition was possible because of special significance that had already adhered to some caves on the Mount of Olives.

Mystical Caves

Franciscan archaeologists Bagatti and Testa noted references to "mystical" caves in Cyril of Jerusalem and Origen among other early Church Fathers (Bagatti 1971: 111). They included this insight in their larger hypothesis about the nature and development of early Christianity in Palestine. Though recent studies have challenged this hypothesis and the special significance of these caves, the challenge appears to overlook a basic datum from culture and archaeology (Taylor 1993). Once a place is considered holy by anyone, it tends to remain holy forever. The same location may well be used and reused as a sacred place by different groups.

The Bagatti and Testa reflections on the significance of caves in the early decades and centuries after Jesus died highlight another key purpose of caves in the ancient world. They were places at which a person could make contact with God or with the world beyond this one and its inhabitants. God communicated with Elijah in a cave (1 Kings 19:9, 13) in an experience that took place in an alternate state of consciousness. At a difficult time in his life, Jesus prayed to the Father in a cave at Gethsemane (Luke 22:41), and the canonical but hotly debated verses in Luke (22:43-44) describe his alternate reality experience of a consoling angel. Anyone who shared these cultural convictions about caves could expect to enjoy similar experiences by visiting the same sacred spot.

Conclusion

Eusebius's triad of caves reminds the modern Bible reader that many pieces of important information that illuminate the biblical texts are found outside the Bible. Archaeology contributes insights. So, too, do other disciplines like cultural anthropology. Eusebius appears to have reported oral traditions which he judged to be reliable and trustworthy to hand on, even as he reinterpreted certain elements of that oral tradition. Still, Eusebius resisted the pilgrims' admiration for the actual places where Jesus' feet might have touch the ground, as it were. His focus was rather the extent to which a place could make Jesus and the gospel universally known. Perhaps Eusebius's caution about pilgrim beliefs caused him to overlook the significance of caves in his and many world cultures as places where humans could encounter the divine.

3. Swamps

When the new king arose over Egypt who did not know Joseph, he sought to reduce the Hebrew population and keep it in check lest in time of war it join the enemy (Exod. 1–2). First the king sentenced them to "hard labor," but when that turned out to be ineffective, he turned to infanticide. He commanded that the midwives allow female infants to live but to kill the males. One clever Hebrew woman saved her son, but after three months, when it became difficult to hide him, she made a basket of papyrus, daubed it with bitumen and pitch, placed the boy in it, and hid it among the reeds *(sûp)* at the river's edge. The Pharaoh's daughter found him, adopted him, and called him Moses (Hebrew *Mōšeh*) because she had drawn *(māšâ)* him out of the water.

The story of Moses' origins is paralleled in the legends of other ancient heroes. Sargon I, king of Agade, founder of the first empire in history (Akkadian, ca. 2300 B.C.E.), was similarly saved from danger in infancy by being placed in a basket of reeds sealed with pitch and set on the river to float to safety. Romulus, the legendary founder and first king of Rome, and his twin brother, Remus, were also left in a marsh next to the Tiber River. The still water of the marsh preserved the children from the strong current, thus allowing them to live by saving them from certain death.

All cultures transform and shape the space they live in. They give it meaning. Swamps, marshes, deserts, woods, mountains — all these places are at the edges of humanized space, which consists of cities and farmland. The choice to settle and remain in one place is an alternative to nomadic or hunter-gatherer existence, wandering from place to place.

Swamps and Marshes

An area of wet land permanently or periodically covered with water and characterized by growths of reeds, shrubs, and the like is variously known as a swamp, marsh, bog, fen, or morass. In the Hebrew tradition as in others, life emerged from such a wet, primordial chaotic landscape (Gen. 1). Chaos here is essentially thick night and limitless waters. Prior to creation there is no dry land, no life of any kind, and certainly no human society, civilization, or culture.

As the entire story line makes clear (Gen. 1–11), God created humans, they failed the deity, and God sent a flood and re-created humankind, restoring for it the landscape destroyed by the waters. Water in this story line is both death-dealing and life-giving. This feature endows the swamp and marsh with ambiguity. It is a border area, yet it has no border. The swamp or marsh lies between dry land and water. It is at the edge.

St. Ambrose (ca. 340-397) seems aware of the ambiguity: "After that old moisture remaining from the flood had grown warm from the rays of the sun, the slime of the wet marshes swelled with the heat, and fertile seeds of life, nourished in that life-giving soil, as in a mother's womb, grew and in time took on some special form" (*Hexaemeron* 1.8.28).

Swamps and Life

Bible readers are familiar with the story of Moses leading the Israelites across the Sea of Reeds *(yam sûp)* to safety while the chariots of the pursuing Egyptians sank into the swamp as the driving wind subsided and the waters returned (Exod. 14:19-30). In view of the death-dealing and life-giving qualities of the swamp, the implicit significance of this event would be so evident to the ancient readers that there would be no need to spell it out. This is yet one more illustration of the Bible as a high context document. Such literature trustingly leaves much to the listener's or reader's imagination, since that significance is widely attested not only in Hebrew sacred literature but also in the literature of other contemporary cultures.

In his description of the restoration of Judah, Ezekiel (47:1-12) describes a life-giving river that flows from the sanctuary and brings life (trees on the banks, fish in the water) to the desolate wilderness of Judah and turns the Dead Sea into a body of fresh water. However, swamps and marshes will not become fresh (v. 11). Commentators interpret this as indicative of divine benevolence providing salt for humankind. In a culture which did not know the advantages and disadvantages of salt as a seasoning, this is a questionable interpretation. Moreover, in a country where water is scarce it is implausible that people would deliberately stimulate thirst that could not be quenched. On the other hand, remembering that salt is a key ingredient of ancient fuel (camel and donkey dung) and has the ability to sustain fires, the salt may well be intended for use in the burnt-offering sacrifices in the restored temple, which is what Ezekiel 40–48 describes. Salt was one ingredient in concocting the incense for use in the temple (Exod. 30:35).

Marshes of the Jordan

Two Maccabee brothers, Jonathan and Simon, avenged the murder of their brother John by ambushing the murderers, the sons of Jambri, whose center of operations was at Medaba (spelling varies: Medeba, Medaba) near the northeast tip of the Dead Sea. Then they retreated to the marshes of the Jordan, knowing that Bacchides would retaliate (1 Macc. 9:42). These marshes are the heavily wooded area at the southernmost end of the Jordan River close to the entrance to the Dead Sea. It is a large, swampy area.

This small piece of information relates to another characteristic of marshes and swamps noted by social geographers. Just as swamp or marsh life was thought to include dangerous animals (ferocious wild boars, snakes, and the like), it was also thought to be the proper residence of inferior humanity, like brigands or guerilla warriors. The marsh or swamp is, after all, a no-man's-land.

The Romans knew that certain barbarian people were swamp humanities: the Scythians, the Sarmatians (not to be confused with Samaritans), the Gauls, the Britons, and the Germans. These were known to live comfortably and move relatively unharmed in places like swamps and marshes that were impenetrable yet threatening. These barbarian peoples knew how to take advantage of the deceits of chaotic and wild spaces. Such people were natural enemies of the ordered Roman landscape produced by civilized people.

Where Jesus Was Baptized

John's gospel suggests that Jesus may have been baptized in "Bethany *beyond* the Jordan" (1:28). No evidence has yet been found for the existence of such a spot on the *east* side of the Jordan. The earliest map of Palestine (ca. 560 C.E.), a mosaic on the floor of an Orthodox church in Madaba, about fifteen miles east of the river, identifies a place roughly in line with Jericho, named Bethabara (see Judg. 7:24), on the *west* side of the river, as the spot where Jesus was baptized. Origen (around 185-253 C.E.), too, identified Bethabara on the west side of the river as the Bethany mentioned by John.

According to tradition, Bethabara might be one of the fords of the (Judean) wilderness (see 2 Sam. 15:28; 17:16), perhaps Mahadat el Hajalh, or Halajah ford. Of course, a ford is not a swamp or a marsh. Still it is another association with the life-sustaining or life-threatening aspects of water in human experience. The ford provides safe passage across the river.

John's was a baptism of repentance for the forgiveness of sin, that is, for renewed life. Like fellow ethnics, Jesus comes to this border area, on the edge between the land and the river, and accepts John's offer. He seeks and obtains renewal of life: "This is my Son, my beloved, with whom I am well pleased." Wherever the actual location may be, the significance of baptism in a "safe" spot on the river is not lost on the participants and audience.

Swamps and the Past

Jesus' offer to give the Samaritan woman living water (John 4:10) is a reference to running water, which connotes life. Stagnant water is unmoving, somewhat abnormal, putrid, dead, and therefore associated with death. The link is not so much with death itself as with the past. While the swamps and marshes are associated with safeguarding life in the case of some ancient heroes, they are primarily places of decay and putrefaction. As a chaotic jumble of water, earth, and vegetation that dies and rots there, the swamps and marshes remind people of the ancestors, who also decay in the earth. The dead have taken leave of society and culture and returned to Chaos, as it were. Recall that primordial Chaos in the Israelite tradition is essentially thick night and limitless waters. The chaos of the swamps and marshes always poses a threat. When the waters returned to that marsh of reeds, clogged the chariot wheels, and caused their enemy to perish, "Israel saw the Egyptians dead upon the shore" (Exod. 14:30). Whether they were left there or buried properly, the decaying process of these fallen Egyptian warriors was already begun. Its occurrence in a border area highlighted the impression on those who witnessed it.

Swamps and the Divine

In Greek culture, Dionysus and Artemis were associated with marshes and swamps. Seneca notes how the darkness of the waters and the immeasurable depth of some swamps consecrated them. In Roman Gaul, rivers, springs, lakes, and marshes were considered haunts of deities and similar beings.

Biblical scholars point out that Israelite tradition about Creation differs from those of its neighbors. Other Creation stories report a battle between deities that somehow contributes to the origin of the Cosmos. In Genesis, the mighty wind of God hovers over the thick night and limitless waters. God is definitely in control of Chaos.

Conclusion

An experienced guide of the Florida everglades was impressing the tourists in his boat with his ability to locate alligators in the water where others could see nothing. After a while, one tourist asked him about the butterflies that seemed to be hovering near the alligators. "What butterflies?" he asked. He had never noticed them before.

A concordance search for the words "swamp," "marsh," and the like turns up precious few references in the Bible. Yet such border areas most certainly were familiar to people whose land was bounded on one side by the Mediterranean Sea and on the other by the Sea of Galilee, the Jordan River, and the Dead Sea. Not only did historical events such as the flight through the Sea of Reeds and the crossing of the Jordan bring these border areas to mind, but the ritual practice of baptism in both the Judaic and Messianist traditions did the same. It is precisely the widespread familiarity of such associations among the ancients that prompted them to consider it unnecessary to mention or explain such realities. What these people left their non-Mediterranean descendants is a high context document, the Bible. Only by entering and appreciating that cultural world can a modern reader begin to sharpen perception and learn to read between the lines to discover what our ancestors in the faith took for granted.

4. Snakes

In the Middle Ages, a distinct type of natural history book known as a bestiary developed and became quite popular. A bestiary collected and reported descriptions and moralistic and religious interpretations of actual and mythical animals. To explore how one might compile a comparable bestiary for the animals that are mentioned in the Bible, let us focus briefly on the snake or serpent.

Animals

The Hebrew Bible uses the word "life" to describe any living creature, including animals. The serpent that tempts God's first creatures is described as a "living creature of the field" (Gen. 3:1; see also Gen. 2:19, 20). The English word "beast," which often appears in the preceding references, more commonly translates the Hebrew word *běhēmâ,* an animal of the ox group, but the word eventually extended to designate any quadruped (see Gen. 1:24). The Hebrew and Greek words for serpent in the Bible are generic words (*nāḥāš* and *ophis* respectively). Perhaps the sacred author of the Genesis story deliberately selected a generic word so that it might be capable of both actual and symbolic interpretations.

Actual Snakes

There were several species of poisonous and nonpoisonous snakes in ancient Palestine. The Hebrew Bible mentions *petên* (Deut. 32:33), *tannîn*

(Exod. 7:9, 12), *śārāp* (Num. 21:4-9), and *šĕpîpōn* (Gen. 49:17), among others, which are usually translated as "asp," "adder" or "viper." Ethnozoologists caution that it is impossible to classify the snakes mentioned in Hebrew according to modern, English-language nomenclature. All we can say is that the ancients knew poisonous and nonpoisonous snakes and knew how to differentiate them. They saw snakes in the desert lying in the hot sand or gliding over rocks (Prov. 30:19). They knew that the bite of some snakes could be deadly (Num. 21:6-9). Poisonous snakes also hid between the stones of the walls of a house (Amos 5:19; Eccles. 10:8).

Charming Snakes

The ancients also knew how to charm snakes, that is, how to render them harmless (Ps. 58:33-36; Eccles. 10:11; Isa. 3:3; Jer. 8:17; Sir. 12:13; Jas. 3:7). The practice is still popular in the Middle East and Far East. The snake is sensitive to sound through its tongue, and the most venomous snakes appear to be the most sensitive. Many contemporary charmers defang the snake for "insurance." The charmer plays a monotonous tone on a shrill pipe which eventually causes the snake to rise out of its basket (or from a crack in wall) and begin to move in rhythm to the music. More daring charmers can grab a snake in a way that renders it powerless, and eventually the exhausted snake can be taken captive.

Symbolism and the Snake

Everyone is familiar with the talking serpent in Genesis who deceived the first creatures and caused them to disobey God (Gen. 3). About a thousand years later, the author of Revelation interprets this animal to be "the great dragon, . . . that ancient serpent, who is called the Devil and Satan, the deceiver of the whole world, . . . [who] was thrown down to the earth, and his angels were thrown down with him" (Rev. 12:9). Subsequent Christian tradition selectively combined the information from the two passages, applied the insights to Mary the mother of Jesus, and created the statue of Mary with a snake under her feet.

With these divergent interpretations, we can begin to explore the symbolic meaning of the snake. The Hebrew word for serpent, *nāḥāš*, is a homonym of the root which means "to practice divination, to divine, to observe signs" *(nḥš)*. In Genesis 15, like Genesis 3 a Yahwist narrative, Joseph indicates that he learned the Egyptian magical practice of divination by observing the effects of objects thrown into a cup of water (*nḥš* appears in vv. 5, 15). If, true to character, the Yahwist is punning or deliberately evoking the homonym in Genesis 3:1, this helps understand the designation of the serpent as the most cunning, shrewd, or crafty of all the animals. This word also has a positive meaning — shrewd, sensible, or prudent — as in Proverbs 12:23 (perhaps also Matt. 10:16). Since everything that God created is very good (Gen. 1:31), the reader might imagine that the serpent is good too, for up until this point in the Yahwist's story (beginning at Gen. 2:4b), there is no indication that any of God's creatures is hostile to God or other creatures. Indeed, since the serpent knows the mysterious properties of this tree (Gen. 3:5) which God created and described to the man (Gen. 2:15-17) even before God created the serpent (Gen. 2:19), this is a most extraordinary serpent, perhaps even capable of ferreting out the secrets of God.

That positive impression doesn't last long, however, because in Genesis 3:4-5 the crafty serpent accuses God of lying ("you will not die"; compare Gen. 2:17) and jealousy ("you will be like God"). The serpent now is clearly an enemy of God. He tells the couple that if they eat of the tree of the knowledge of good and evil, they will be like God, knowing good and evil. They will know and be able to predict the outcome of events. Very shortly, the woman recognizes the snake's true character in this experience: a deceiver (Gen. 3:13).

The snake's punishment returns the story to "actuality" as the ancients understood it. It will crawl on its belly (if it was considered previously to have been a quadruped of some sort, such as a dragon or lizard, it now has lost its legs), and it will eat dirt (the ancients thought they perceived this in the snake's behavior; see Isa. 65:25; Mic. 7:17). Its offspring, whether poisonous or not, will be hated and hunted by humans since they know the actual danger of real snakes. This is a plausible reading of these elements of the Yahwist's story, which combines an actual and symbolic interpretation of the snake.

Snakes and Magic

Magic in antiquity belonged to the realm of power. Peasant populations were largely powerless and subject to uncontrollable power from many quarters. Magic claimed to possess power independently of any superior being, hence it was appealing because it could be beneficial and might entail less indebtedness to the benefactor than one might owe to God. Magic was widespread in Israel (Lev. 19:31; 20:6; 2 Kings 21:6; 23:24) and practiced also by women (Exod. 22:18; Lev. 20:27; Ezek. 13:17-23). In these contexts, magic amounts to a revolt against God. The Lord reminded Isaiah: "And when they say to you, 'Consult the mediums and the wizards who chirp and mutter,' should not a people consult their God? Should they consult the dead on behalf of the living?" (Isa. 8:19).

The Egyptian magicians who served the Pharaoh were able to make a snake as stiff as a rod and then return it to its normal flexibility (Exod. 7:9-12). We already understand how snake charmers are able to render snakes harmless by grabbing them in a certain way. The deed is impressive none-theless. But the sacred author intends to demonstrate that God is more powerful. Not only can Aaron replicate the Egyptian magician's magic feat, but Aaron's snake/rod swallowed up their snakes/rods. Once again, there is an interplay, overlap, and perhaps even contradiction between the snake/rod in actuality and in symbolism.

Snakes and Life

The ancients believed that because the snake shed its skin, it continued to live on forever. Hence the snake became a symbol of eternal life. In the Gilgamesh Epic, the hero exerts strenuous efforts to obtain the plant named "Man becomes young in old age," but a serpent steals it, eats it, and sheds its slough (11.261-89; *Ancient Near Eastern Texts Illustrating the Old Testament* 96b). This understanding of the snake as a life-giving animal is reflected in the Bible, too. During the exodus, many people died of snake bites in the desert. In response to Moses' prayer for help, God instructed him to make a bronze model of a fiery serpent and set it on a pole. Anyone bitten by a snake who would look at it would live (Num. 21:6-9). The life-giving symbol remained in the Israelite repertoire and was worshiped as such until destroyed by Hezekiah (2 Kings 18:4) because of its ready association with Baal. While some Israelites perhaps understood the serpent in its exodus context as symbolizing Yahweh as the source of life (see Hos. 6:2), no doubt others transferred this to Baal. John's Jesus appears to have adopted the positive view of the bronze serpent and applied it to himself (John 3:14-15). Of interest to our reflection is that, once again, the actual source of potential death (snake) can also serve as a symbol of eternal life, a combination of contradictions.

The Talking Snake

Some scholars have noted that talking animals are familiar already from Aesop's fables (ca. 6th cent. B.C.E.). True enough, but are talking animals a clever fictional strategy or might this relate to a real-life experience? If they relate to a real-life experience, what kind of experience might that be? More importantly, how would an ancient reader (or listener) understand a talking snake? Or could the talking snake be another example of the blurring of boundaries between actual and symbolic animals?

In the Genesis story, the author uses the pluperfect tense when saying the snake had been the shrewdest of the animals, indicating that it no longer is. He had the ability to speak, but no longer does. Originally it was a friend and helper to humans, but in this story the snake changed its role. In real life, each culture identifies a category of persons we call "shamans" (our etic interpretation), but these cultures call such a person a "holy man/woman" (their emic understanding), that is, someone who has ready access to the deity and to alternate reality. This access takes place in ecstatic trance during which the holy man/woman learns solutions to problems or discovers new direction in life. In many cultures, this person also obtains an animal guide who reveals its wisdom and bestows its distinctive power on the visionary.

In ecstatic trance, holy men/women, or shamans, are able to heal the sick, change the weather, foretell the future, control the movement of animals, and converse with spirits and spirit-animals. In the Genesis story, the Lord God put the first man into a trance in order to create Eve from one of his ribs (Gen. 2:21). The first human creatures were obviously capable of entering an alternate state of consciousness. The tenth-century-B.C.E. Yahwist author of the story very likely had the same capability. In this state, communication with animals is possible and customary. Yet again, the author has made actual and symbolic understanding overlap in his story.

Conclusion

The South African anthropologist David Lewis-Williams observes that each culture has its own symbolic bestiary. The meanings people attach to animals differ from culture to culture and even within a culture. Thus, the snake may simultaneously symbolize evil and regeneration, and it may simultaneously be the cause of death and symbol of eternal life. In addition, the animals that are most prominent in a culture's thought have not one but a range of meanings or associations. In any context, one of these associations is emphasized while the other associations are muted but still present and contributing to a powerful penumbra of significance. The symbolic understanding of an animal draws all these associations together. Such central animal symbols are powerful and highly emotive precisely because they have a range of associations, some of which may even be contradictory, as we have noted in this brief survey of the snake in biblical literature.

Yet all these associations of snakes were certainly related. They formed a coherent pattern of meanings that derived, ultimately, from an understanding of the cosmos and the places of and relationship between animals and people in different parts of the cosmos. Thus, they differ by contexts and emphases rather than by radically different and separate "meanings," which is why interpreting the word "snake" on the basis of philology alone is inadequate.

5. Dragons

All the references to a dragon in the New Testament appear only in the book of Revelation (12; 13; 16; 20). The author, however, has associated a variety of concepts with the dragon by which he designates an ancient archenemy of God. For instance, he wrote: "And the great dragon [red in color, v. 3] was thrown down, that ancient serpent, who is called the Devil and Satan, the deceiver of the whole world — he was thrown down to earth, and his angels were thrown down with him" (Rev. 12:9). Reflecting upon dragon and concepts associated with it will help a reader to understand the image John the Seer presents as well as the source of his imagery.

Dragon Essentially a Snake

The Greek word translated "dragon," *drakōn,* is often a synonym for the Greek word for snake *(ophis),* reflecting the common understanding in antiquity that the dragon was essentially a snake or serpent. Anthropologists are quite familiar with this mythological being, that is, a colossal serpent or dragon, which appears in the folklore of many different societies all over the world. Felicitas Goodman (1994: 2-3) reflects on a few. There is the giant snake twisted around the Indo-European Tree of the World. In Central Asia, there is a tradition about a dragon in the sky, which, when it shakes, rains animals and brings fertility to the earth. Then, there are China's winged, crested dragons with enormous claws that fight each other in the clouds. Hungarian dragons have multiple heads (three, five, or even seven) and abduct the daughter of the king. Huge serpents looking like rattlesnakes are featured on many pyramids of Central America. The American Southwest, Mayan, and Aztec cultures even know of a feathered serpent! Such wide distribution and varying characteristics attest to the venerable antiquity of this legendary being.

"To an anthropologist," Goodman writes, "it looks like the Australian aborigines, with their culture going back 40,000 years, had the original revelation: the earth is the mighty serpent, and on it live the spirits of the ancestors in the shape of 'lozenges,' in their elongated form actually suggesting feathers. . . . In its passage over the earth, the original myth underwent many transformations, but the Indian tradition is actually the closest to the unimaginably ancient source, if not in substance, at least in the tenaciously held memory of form" (Goodman 1994: 2-3).

In the Middle East, generally speaking, the dragon, like the snake it resembled, was considered an evil and harmful creature. The dragon John describes in Revelation is precisely such a creature. It stands "before the woman about to give birth, to devour her child when she gave birth" (Rev. 12:4 and throughout this chapter). Yet Greece and Rome recognized a dragon that had beneficent powers. It dwelled in the inner parts of the earth and possessed keen vision. In the Far East, the dragon is considered a benevolent creature. Among the Chinese, it symbolizes heaven, activity, the male element (yang) of yin-yang. As we noted in our reflection on snakes, the meanings people attach to animals differ from culture to culture and even within a culture.

Dragon in the Old Testament

The Hebrew word *tannîn* (plural, *tannînîm*) designates serpent, dragon, and sea monster, reflecting the basic Mediterranean understanding that a dragon, though a mythical creature, is essentially a snake. Thus, the person who trusts in God will "tread on the lion and the adder; . . . the young lion and the serpent [*tannîn;* NAB reports dragon] you will trample under foot" (Ps. 91:13 RSV; see Jesus' promise in Luke 10:19). By the power of God, Aaron's rod turned into a snake (*tannîn,* clearly not a dragon), but the Pharaoh's assistants were able to replicate the feat (Exod. 7:8-13). John's association of the serpent of Genesis 3 with the dragon he describes in Revelation is therefore not unusual. Interpreting the dragon, however, requires additional information.

In general, the dragon in the Old Testament is a malevolent creature, posing a threat to human beings. Jeremiah compares Nebuchadnezzar, king of Babylon, to a dragon who has swallowed Jerusalem, filled its belly with her delights, and then spit her out (51:34). Ezekiel similarly compares the Pharaoh to a sea dragon (29:3; 32:2) whom God will catch with a net (12:13) and will expose on land as prey for beasts and birds to devour (29:1-16). This is how God treats sea monsters (or sea dragons) in general (Ps. 74:13-14).

Yet not all sea monsters are malevolent. After all, God created them (Gen. 1:21; sometimes translated "whales"), and everything God created was good (Gen. 1:31). Malevolent sea monsters, however, are associated with Leviathan (Isa. 27:1) and Rahab (Job 26:12; Ps. 89:11; Isa. 51:9), both considered personifications of primeval chaos (Gen. 1:2). Still, God has dominion over the sea/chaos and all rebellious creatures, who were either killed or subdued at creation (Ps. 74:13-14). Indeed, the psalmist exhorts them: "Praise the LORD from the earth, you sea monsters and all deeps!" (Ps. 148:7).

The Dragon in Revelation

John has explicitly identified the dragon with the serpent in Genesis 3 and has additionally identified these as the devil and Satan (12:9). Devil (*diabolos* in Greek) means "accuser" and Satan (from the Hebrew *śāṭān*) is actually a Persian loanword referring to an undercover agent who tests loyalties for a king. The classic example in the Bible is Satan in Job 1–2. A modern example is King Abdullah, the young son of King Hussein who succeeded his father as king of Jordan. Shortly thereafter it was reported in the press that he traveled the country in disguise seeking opinions from ordinary citizens about the "new" king and the government. He was testing not only the loyalty of the citizens but the behavior of government employees. Recall that the serpent in Genesis 3 similarly tested the loyalties of the first creatures to God the Creator. Those who test loyalties do so by deception, by pretending to be someone else, or by making leading (or misleading) statements to catch an unsuspecting citizen off guard. Epictetus (*Discourses* 4.13.1.5), a first-century Stoic philosopher, describes the tactics of Roman soldiers traveling incognito precisely in this way in order to test loyalty to Caesar. The one who failed the test was hauled off to prison!

49

Identity of the Dragon

Scholars in general tend to associate John's dragon in Revelation with the sea monster(s) mentioned in the Old Testament. In part they base this on Revelation 12:15: "The serpent, however, spewed a torrent of water out of his mouth after the woman to sweep her away with the current," and perhaps 12:18: "it took its position on the sand of the sea," that is, the seashore. Yet if the dragon is identical with the serpent of Genesis 3, that serpent is not a sea monster but is rather already on earth when the first creatures are created. Moreover, in that story line it seems that the serpent once had legs since henceforth it will crawl.

When Jesus claims: "I have observed Satan fall like lightning from the sky. Behold, I have given you the power to 'tread upon serpents' . . ." (Luke 10:18), he is referring to an ancient piece of Israelite lore which Jesus may well have remembered or seen in a trance experience. Trance experiences are culture specific; the interpretation derives from the lore of the culture. John reports quite accurately the Israelite tradition concerning a mighty battle between Michael and his angels and the dragon and its angels (Rev. 12:7-9). In the end, the dragon and its angels were thrown down to earth by Michael. Since the serpent/dragon is already on earth to test the first creatures, it was created previously, along with the stars of the sky, hence at the very earliest stages of cosmic creation, a time before human beings and the appurtenances of the earth were created, as reported in Genesis 1.

John's Sources

Where did John sharpen this insight? Like other astral prophets in the Israelite tradition (e.g., Daniel) and outside of it (e.g., Berossus), John finds traces of the time before human time in the sky and its constellations. Four times in Revelation, the author explicitly states that he learned the content of his revelation in ecstatic trance, or an alternate state of consciousness (Rev. 1:10; 4:2; 17:3; 21:10). In two of these instances, he journeys to the sky (4:2) or to a very high place (21:10) to see the cosmos from God's vantage point. God's designs are recorded in the constellations. For instance, the Lamb standing as if slain, that is, looking as if dead but quite alive (Rev. 5:6), is the constellation Aries with its head looking back at Taurus, the next constellation in order. Many ancient cultures recognized Aries just as John describes it.

Which constellation, therefore, does John label as the Dragon in the South? (The red color locates this constellation in the southern sky.) It can't be Draco (= Dragon), which is near the North Pole. A likely candidate would seem to be Scorpio, which at that time was a much larger constellation since it was a combination of Scorpio and Libra. (The Greeks separated Libra from Scorpio.) Scorpio always stands for darkness, death, and evil, hence it fits John's presentation of a malevolent dragon. The scenario John describes contains a Pregnant Woman (Constellation Virgo), with the traditional head (which later became Claws, and ultimately to this day is Libra) of the Dragon (ancient Scorpio) at her feet awaiting the birth of her offspring. The "red" snake or dragon depicted on the Ishtar Gate at Babylon may be a constellation, just as Tiamat, the stormy abyss symbolized by a dragon, seems to summon constellations (Viper, Dragon, Great-Lion, Scorpion Man, etc.; see *Ancient Near Eastern Texts*, 62) to assist in the battle against Marduk, the creator-God.

Then in John's report follows the sky war known from Israelite tradition when Michael defeated God's enemies. In the Mediterranean world, Orion (= Light) is the constellation that traditionally battles the evil Scorpio (= Darkness). According to Isaiah 13:10 in the Greek version (LXX): "For the stars of the sky and Orion and the whole array of the sky will not give light: and it will be dark at the rising of the sun, and the moon will not give its light." Thus, in the Hellenistic world, Orion stands ahead of and apart from the rest of the celestial army, while in the Israelite view of the world, Michael, God's sky servant, holds this position. Michael's battle with the Dragon at the dawn of creation is the Israelite interpretation of the well-known battle between Orion and ancient Scorpio.

Conclusion

Revelation 12 probably is based on two sources: one describing a conflict between a woman with child and a dragon (vv. 1-6 and 13-17), and another describing a sky war (vv. 7-9). They may have been composed by members of the house of Israel to describe the heavenly Israel, the spouse of God. John edited the material, made additions, and suggested another interpretation. As the decrees to the churches make quite clear (Rev. 2–3), there is intense concern about loyalty and deception among the churches. John the astral prophet seeks to allay believers' fears and unmask the deception plaguing them by revealing what he sees and experiences of God's will in the constellations of the sky. This has been established by God from the very beginning and is completely reliable and trustworthy. Blessed is the one who can see and understand.

6. Mirrors and Glass

"Black am I, and beautiful, O Daughters of Jerusalem, like the tents of Qedar, like the pavilions of Solomon. Do not stare at me because I am blackish, for the sun has burned me" (Song 1:5-6, trans. Roland E. Murphy in *Hermeneia*). How does this woman know she is beautiful? Is it because her lover (among others) has told her: "your voice is pleasant, and your face lovely" (Song 2:14)? Did she discover this herself by looking in a mirror? A brief survey of mirrors and glass in the ancient world suggests that she believed the word of others. Glass mirrors did not yet exist when this woman sang her song.

Mirrors

As he concludes his praise of love *(agapē)*, Paul writes: "For now we see in a mirror *(esoptrou)* dimly, but then face to face" (1 Cor. 13:12 RSV). This rendition is common in the majority of current English translations. Modern readers find it difficult to understand how one sees dimly in a mirror unless the lighting is very bad. A widely used Greek-English lexicon of the New Testament (Danker) explains that dimly or indirectly means "one sees not the thing itself, but its mirror-image." Knowing how modern mirrors can make a room seem larger so realistically that people sometimes walk into the mirror, this comment doesn't help.

The Douay-Rheims English translation (1582) from Jerome's Latin reports: "We see now through a glass *(speculum)* in a dark manner." It is echoed in the King James translation (1611) from the Greek: "For now we see through a glass, darkly; but then face to face." The English word "glass" in these translations is anachronistic. Even though glass was known since about 2500 B.C.E., mirrors from ancient times even to Paul's day were made of highly polished metal (silver, gold, copper or bronze; see Pliny the Elder's *Natural History* 33.9). It would be preferable to use the phrase "metal mirror" in modern translations.

The bronze basin and its bronze base for the tabernacle (and later in the temple) were made from the metal mirrors of the women who ministered at the door of the tent of meeting (Exod. 38:8). The Hebrew word for mirrors here *(mar'â* also designates the "visions" of Jacob (Gen. 46:2), Ezekiel (1:1), and Daniel (10:7). Given that the image viewed in highly polished metal is not as clear as in modern-day mirrors, we surmise that what the ancients saw in visions was similarly fuzzy, requiring careful refocusing and interpretation after the occurrence. Thus in the story of Jesus' transfiguration (Luke 9:30), it seems that the disciples saw in a vision two male figures whom tradition (or they) at first interpreted to be angels but subsequently interpreted to be Moses and Elijah (Pilch 2011).

Another Hebrew word translated as mirror *(rĕ'i)* describes the sky. Elihu asks Job: "Can you, like him, spread out the skies, hard as a molten mirror?" Clearly a molten mirror is metal. From the many occurrences of the word "sky" in the Bible, it is almost impossible to tell its shape. All agree that the sky is a (metal) vault that separates the waters above from the waters below. The stars are attached to this vault, and the sun and moon travel across it.

Metal mirrors became rather common in the first century. They had a round shape, and some had a handle of bone, ivory, or wood. The handle was very often carved in the form of Hathor, the Egyptian goddess of love, mirth, and joy, usually having the head or ears of a cow. With this concept of a metal mirror, we can better understand the observation of James (1:22-24) about those who hear but do not act upon the word they hear. "Such is like a man who observes his natural face in a [metal] mirror; for he observes himself and goes away and at once forgets what he was like." The image in a metal mirror (even highly polished) is not as memorable or impressive as that in modern-day mirrors. What can one remember from staring at one's image in the top of a tin can?

Ancient Glass

There are only a handful of references to glass in the Bible, and information about its discovery is obscure. Soviet archaeologists discovered smelters from around 2500 B.C.E. at the foot of Mount Ararat. This prompted some scholars to conjecture that the Sumerians derived their knowledge of glass from this site. Pliny (*Natural History* 36.191) reports that glass was discovered casually through the melting of the sand at the seashore under a fire at a place not far from Ptolemais (Acco, Acre).

Historians agree that the Phoenicians were the first to practice the art of making glass. Their basic technique was core forming, that is, bonding glass rods around a core of clay which would create a hollow vessel when the core was removed. Other techniques included casting, that is, pouring glass into a mold, or cold cutting, that is, carving from a solid block of glass. The object was often further decorated by grinding. The Egyptians after the Amarna period (1364 B.C.E.) became familiar with and fond of glass. Glass beads, trinkets, and various ornaments are commonly found in Egyptian graves. It is not clear whether these items were native or imported. The Egyptians appear to have copied the Phoenician technique of core-forming glass.

Around the seventh century B.C.E., the art of glass making spread into the eastern and central Mediterranean, chiefly to Rhodes, Etruria, and the end of the Adriatic Sea where Italy borders on Istria. The most widely used technique was core forming. The vessels produced were used mainly as unguent and scent containers, decorated with colored trails and one or two blobs. It is important to remember, however, that this glass was always colored and never transparent. Nevertheless, these products were the precursors of Roman blown glass, which was transparent.

Roman Glass

The Romans appear to have discovered and developed the art of blowing glass. The molten material is inflated on a blowpipe and then given its final shape either by manipulation on this blowpipe, or by blowing the material into a plain or patterned mold. This was indeed a revolutionary change in glass making. The process took a fraction of the time of older methods mentioned above. Since glass are could now be produced so quickly, glass domestic ware soon became very common in a market hitherto dominated by pottery and metalwork. The fact that glass, just like glazed pottery, could be cleaned and reused contributed to its wide popularity.

The skill of the Syrian workers who set up workshops in Italy, particularly at Rome early in the Augustan period (27 B.C.E. to 14 C.E.), was so great that within twenty or thirty years they developed nearly all the inflation techniques still in use 2,000 years later. Visitors to contemporary glass centers in Venice, such as Murano, can still see these techniques in use. Scholars point out that even the finest achievements of modern glass blowers do not surpass the products of those Roman workshops of antiquity.

Crystal

The Hebrew word *zĕkôkît*, usually translated "glass" in the Old Testament, occurs just once in the Bible: "Gold and glass cannot equal [wisdom], nor can [wisdom] be exchanged for jewels of fine gold" (Job 28:17). The word derives from the Hebrew verb meaning "to be bright, clean, and pure" (quite likely also the source of the name, Zacchaeus, the well-known "Mr.

Clean" who encountered Jesus near Jericho in Luke 19:2). Since the author of Job pairs glass with gold, scholars have concluded that the Hebrews considered glass a semiprecious item.

Moreover, the pairing of gold and glass persuades some scholars to suggest that "crystal" might be a better translation than glass. Natural quartz crystals were highly prized in antiquity. In the contemporary United States, crystal is commonly seen dangling from rearview mirrors of automobiles whose drivers frequently value these gems as powerful amulets.

The Hebrew word sometimes translated "crystal" actually means "ice" or "frost" (*qeraḥ;* see Gen. 31:40; Job 6:16; 37:10; 38:29; Jer. 36:30; and notably Ezek. 1:22: "Over the heads of the living creatures there was the likeness of a firmament, shining like ice, spread out above their heads" [RSV has "crystal" for ice]).

Crystal and the Sea of Glass

In Revelation (4:6), John the Prophet observes that "before the throne [in the sky] there is as it were a sea of glass, like crystal." Because crystal is a solid, it seems reasonable to interpret the sea as a transparent solid rather than a liquid. Since ice is water in a transparent solid form, John describes what he sees in a manner similar to the way Ezekiel reported what he saw. Both were looking at the same reality: the firmament, appearing like ice, a transparent solid. John sees the throne above the firmament, while Ezekiel sees the living creatures hovering below the firmament. Enoch describes the floor beneath God's throne (as also the throne itself) as crystal (*1 Enoch* 14:18).

If with John the Revealer the reader understands the throne of God as a constellation in the sky, there is ample evidence in the Mesopotamian and other sky traditions of the existence of enormous celestial starry "bodies of water." Egyptians knew of the heavenly ocean, a concept also known to the Greeks. It is out of this sea that John sees the sea beast (Tiamat, Yamm, Tehom) rise with its ten horns and seven heads (Rev. 13:1)

How did these water-crystal-ice images develop? Some scholars conjecture that the image of a "sea of glass like crystal" might have been suggested to a native Palestinian familiar with the Sea of Galilee reflecting upon its waves both the fiery glow of sunset and the snow-capped peak of Hermon. The Qur'an (27:44) reports a similar impression made by the throne of Solomon upon the Queen of Sheba during her visit (1 Kings 10). The glass floor before the throne of Solomon was so clear that she mistook it for water and bared her legs to wade toward him. Since the firmament separates the waters above from those below, images associated with other water would quite naturally be transferred to those waters.

In Revelation, the light of the heavenly city (21:11) and the river of the water of life (22:1) are both described as "crystal" clear. Coupled with the image of the sea of glass, like crystal (4:6; see 15:2), it would seem that the Greek word *krystallos* had resumed its original meaning of ice in these contexts, rather than the derived meaning, crystal. It would also seem that in the book of Revelation, references to glass do indeed point to true transparent glass, the impressive products of the Roman art of glass blowing.

Conclusion

In the world famous Corning (N.Y.) Museum of Glass there is first-century gladiator cup in which beverages were sold at the games (Harden 1987: 169). The purchaser kept the cup, decorated with images of athletes, as a souvenir. The survival of such artifacts demonstrates how relatively inexpensive and common glassware was for the ordinary people. The very few references to glass in the Bible do not contradict this judgment. This simply illustrates once again that the Bible is a high context document, that is, it presumes that people are so familiar with glass objects that it is not necessary to mention them often. On the other hand, the images associated with mirrors (polished metal) and glass (ice, crystal) reveal how our ancestors in the faith perceived and interpreted the world in which they lived.

FURTHER READING: EARTH

Baggati, Belarmino, O.F.M. 1971. *The Church from the Circumcision: History and Archaeology of the Judaeo-Christians.* Publications of the Studium Biblicum Franciscanum, Smaller Series 2. Jerusalem: Franciscan Printing Press.

Clottes, Jean, and David Lewis-Williams. 1996. *The Shamans of Prehistory: Trance and Magic in the Painted Caves.* Text by Jean Clottes. Translated from the French by Sophie Hawkes. New York: Harry N. Abrams, Inc.

Danker, Frederick William, ed. and revisor. 2000. *A Greek-English Lexicon of the New Testament and Other Early Christian Literature.* 3rd Edition (BDAG). Chicago and London: The University of Chicago Press.

Goodman, Felicitas D. 1994. *Jewels on the Path.* Volume 2. Santa Fe: Cuyamungue Institute.

Harden, Donald B., et al. 1987. *Glass of the Caesars*. Milan: Olivetti.

Jones, Brian C. 2009. "Wilderness." *New Interpreters' Dictionary of the Bible* 5: 848-52.

Murphy, Roland E., O.Carm. 1990. *The Song of Songs*. Hermeneia Commentary. Minneapolis: Fortress.

Murphy-O'Connor, Jerome, O.P. 2008. *The Holy Land: An Oxford Archaeological Guide from Earliest Times to 1700*. Fifth Edition, Revised and Expanded. Oxford: Oxford University Press.

————. 2011. "The Transfiguration of Jesus: An Experience of Alternate Reality." Pp. 124-45 in *Flights of the Soul: Visions, Heavenly Journeys, and Peak Experiences in the Biblical World*. Grand Rapids and Cambridge: Eerdmans.

Rollefson, Gary O. 2007. "Desert." *New Interpreters' Dictionary of the Bible* 2: 102-3.

Taylor, Joan E. 1993. *Christians and the Holy Places: The Myth of Jewish-Christian Origins*. Oxford: Oxford University Press.

Part Three

PERSONS

Western culture is admittedly highly individualistic. What members of this culture neglect to realize is that such personality types represent but 20 percent of the population on the face of the planet. The remaining 80 percent is collectivistic. Members of such cultures feel so strongly embedded in their group that they do not want to stand out as individuals. The Bible is all about collectivistic individuals, which explains the importance of groups, the frequency of stereotyping by group, and the lack of names or their unreliable facticity when a name is reported. We also reflect upon concepts such as citizen, nation, visiting strangers, resident aliens, and the like, which are quite familiar in our experience but are anachronistic labels when applied to the ancient Middle Eastern world. Such are the topics we consider in this chapter.

1. Citizen

In the Acts of the Apostles, Paul boasted of his citizenship in Tarsus, "no mean city" (Acts 21:39), and in Rome. On this basis, he demanded the privileges afforded by his Roman citizenship: exemption from scourging and other humiliating punishments (Acts 16:37-38; 22:25-29; 23:27) and legal rights in juridical matters (Acts 25:10-12). However, contemporary scholars doubt that Paul was a Roman citizen and now consider Roman citizenship a Lucan spin on Paul (Stegemann and Stegemann 1999: 302). In contrast, Jesus had no citizenship at all, since he was not born in a city. He came from Nazareth, a hamlet at most, subject to a monarch. Residents of monarchies were subjects, not citizens. Therefore Jesus had no entitlements and was unable to escape humiliating punishment and injustice meted out by a kangaroo court in Jerusalem. What meaning did citizenship have in the ancient world?

The Word: Citizen

The contemporary understanding of the term "citizen" derives from eighteenth-century political events such as the United States Declaration of Independence (1776), the United States Constitution (1789), and the French Constitution (1791). The term describes a member of a state or a nation (two terms that have modern connotations totally lacking in the ancient world) who owes loyalty to that respective abstract entity in return for guaranteed basic rights. Something like that understanding of citizen first developed among elite city residents in what we call Greece, but it was generally lacking in the ancient Near East, where residents were subjects. Even in Greece, however, one was not a citizen of Greece but rather of some Greek city. Thus the ancient understanding of citizen is tied to a place, to what Greek speakers called a *polis*, a city.

Misleading Translations

The Revised Standard Version uses the word "citizen" 35 times, and the NRSV just 27 times. Both translations impose upon the ancient texts meanings which the vocabulary in specific texts simply cannot bear. For example, the Greek word usually translated "citizen" *(politēs)* appears in only five passages (Luke 15:19; 19:14; Acts 21:39; Eph. 2:19; Heb. 8:11). In the Revised Standard Version, however, "citizen" translates Greek words or phrases which in Greek literally say "Roman man" (Acts 22:25) or simply "Roman" (Acts 22:26, 27, 28, 29; 23:27). Clearly these passages not only do not translate the Greek accurately, but they unwittingly impose upon these texts eighteenth-century meanings which they cannot possibly bear in the ancient world. How can we improve our understanding of what the sacred authors are trying to say on this matter?

Citizen = Inhabitant or Resident

At root, "citizen" in the Bible means simply inhabitant or resident. The Hebrew Bible reflects this primitive understanding when it refers to the inhabitants of a particular place in a very generic way with the word *ba'al*. While this word can mean owner (Exod. 21:28) or husband (Gen. 20:3), when used with a place-name it means inhabitant or leader (or lord; see Josh. 24:11; Judg. 9:2, 46, 47, 51; 1 Sam. 23:11). To translate this Hebrew word "citizen" without qualification is anachronistic. Thus Judges 9:51 should correctly be translated "all the people [inhabitants] of the city, all the men and women" (as in the RSV) or "all the men and women and all the lords [leaders] of the city" (as in the NRSV and NAB).

Civic Rights = Entitlements of Birth

Any entitlements that derived from birth in a specific place belonged to freeborn males. To call these entitlements "rights" in the modern sense of the word is also anachronistic. Nevertheless, ancient Hebrew laws recognized and sought to safeguard some basic entitlements. Chief among these was freedom or liberation from slavery if that should occur (Exod. 21:2ff.; Lev. 25:39-41) and recovery of ancestral property (Lev. 25:25-28; Deut. 15:12-18). These laws suggest that most [if not all] of the people born in that specific place are blood relatives (or fictive kin, like slaves of the household). This explains the bias toward kinship in biblical laws and the discrimination toward those who are not kin (see Lev. 25:44-46).

Resident Aliens

Following the ancient understanding, any nonnative, that is, anyone located elsewhere than in the place of birth, was a foreigner. In ancient Israel, a non-Israelite was a foreigner *(ben nēkār)* and had no entitlements whatsoever (Exod. 12:43). There are two kinds of foreigners. A sojourner *(tôšāb)* was a transient, a temporary and dependent inhabitant (Lev. 22:10; 25:6), while a resident alien *(gēr)* was a more permanent inhabitant who enjoyed some entitlements, none of them inherited, and was bound by certain obligations (Gen. 19:9, Lot).

In biblical literature, animal imagery plays a significant role in describing Israelites and outsiders. Hamor the Hivite and his son, Shechem, were outsiders who wanted to become insiders, that is, Israelites in order to marry Israelite women (Gen. 34). The Hebrew word *ḥămôr* means "ass." The ass lives among the flocks and herds but is unlike them. It is a work animal. The English-language humor may not have been absent in Hebrew contexts. The resident alien who tries to become an insider is like an ass (Eilberg-Schwartz 1991: 126-28).

The resident alien was entitled to Sabbath rest (Exod. 20:10; 23:12; Deut. 5:14) and redress in the judicial system (Deut. 1:16). Through Ezekiel God proposed that the resident aliens and their children were entitled to an inheritance among the tribes of Israel (47:22-23). On the other hand, the alien was also obliged to refrain from eating leavened bread during the feast of unleavened bread (Exod. 12:19). If he wanted to observe the Passover of the Lord, he and all his males were required to be circumcised (Exod. 12:48-49).

What appears to be good news for resident aliens in ancient Palestine, however, needs to be balanced with the repeated exhortation that Israelites be kind to them (Lev. 19:33-34). Their situation may not have been as rosy as the texts suggest. Sometimes the resident alien is mentioned in parallelism with the poor (Lev. 19:10; 23:22) and the fatherless and widows (Deut. 10:18; 14:29; 24:19-21) in circumstances that suggest that they may not have had adequate clothing or sustenance. There are also repeated prohibitions against oppressing the aliens (and the widows and the fatherless; Exod. 22:21-24; 23:9; Deut. 24:14, 17) and a curse against anyone guilty of that (Deut. 27:19).

The presence of such prohibitions indicates that resident aliens did not fare well in ancient Israel (or in subsequent history [see below]; nor perhaps anywhere, ever). Seeking to motivate Israelites to kindness toward aliens by reminding them to remember their own former status and experience as aliens (Lev. 19:34; Deut. 10:19; 24:22; etc.) was ineffective. Prophetic threats and condemnations point to Israel's failures (Jer. 7:6; 22:23; Ezek. 22:7; Zech. 7:10; Mal. 3:5). After the exile, treatment of aliens worsened (1 Chron. 22:2) until all people of foreign descent were formally excluded from the community (Neh. 13:3).

The Hellenistic Period

During the postexilic period in Israel (post-537 B.C.E.), citizenship in certain Greek cities involved special privileges but was quite restricted. For example, only a person born of two freeborn Athenians was considered a citizen of Athens in the fifth century B.C.E. Roman citizenship was somewhat easier to gain. The child of a Roman father was automatically a citizen. Sometimes residents of a foreign city were granted citizenship in the city of Rome en masse as a reward (e.g., Philippi). But the Roman citizen, outside a patronage context, actually counted for nothing. In the Hellenistic period citizenship acquired technical, political significance.

Nevertheless, it still remains difficult to interpret the meaning of citizen in English translations of individual biblical texts. For instance, Ptolemy is reported to have allowed those Judeans living in Egypt who were "initiated into the mysteries" to be "on the same footing as the citizens of Alexandria" (3 Macc. 2:30). Josephus insists that this was full-citizen status (*Antiquities* 12.1; 10.5.2), but scholars recognize that various grades of citizenship existed in Alexandria. If some Judeans attained full citizenship, it was as individuals and not by reason of being of Judean heritage. In any case, entitlement is associated with the ranking. Moreover, entitlements, as mentioned earlier, meant that Paul could be exempt from humiliating punishment and seek political redress. Jesus, who was a subject and not a citizen, had no entitlements.

Jesus-Group Members as Resident Aliens

Though travel in the ancient world was considered deviant, tragedies such as famine, war, and feud caused many to migrate. First Peter was a letter sent by a group in Rome (Peter, Silvanus, and Mark) to fellow Jesus-group members in Asia Minor identified as "visiting strangers" (1:1; 2:11) and "resident aliens" (2:11; 1:17). Like travelers and immigrants of all times, these displaced persons were targets of discrimination and disadvantage who found protection, support, and acceptance by seeking out fellow travelers or forming clubs of fellow ethnics or fellow craftsmen or fellow believers (Elliott 1981).

The resident aliens who received and read this letter had already found fellowship in local Jesus groups. Peter, Silvanus, and Mark assure them that they were reborn (1:2, 23; 2:2) children (1:14; 2:10) of a heavenly Father (1:2, 3, 17), united into one household of God (2:25; 5:1-4). Through their suffering, they enjoyed fellowship with Jesus (4:1, 12-13; 5:1).

Conclusion

As scientific biblical scholars know, the Bible does not offer all the direct answers for living. The Bible has no real equivalent to the modern understanding of citizen and citizenship. Moreover, the distinctions that did exist in the ancient world and are reflected in the Hebrew and Greek texts of the Bible are blurred in modern translations.

63

One commonality between biblical and modern cultures is a basic distinction people make between insiders and outsiders, us and them. A citizen is an insider in the country of birth but an outsider everywhere else. Every traveler or migrant has experienced outsider status at border crossings even between friendly nations. Faith communities in general profess to ignore these differences and welcome everyone, even those who do not share the community's faith. Here there should be no strangers and sojourners but rather kin ("fellow citizens") in the household of God (see Eph. 2:19-22). There is no substitute for citizenship, but treating foreigners like kin can ease those deficiencies.

2. People Are Not a Nation

Modern times have experienced a flood of new English translations of the Bible. This results not only from the discovery of new manuscripts such as the Dead Sea Scrolls but also from the fact that the meanings of English words and the realities they represent change over time. Still, reading an English translation is not as easy as it might seem. Often, one English word like "people" translates a variety of Hebrew and Greek words in the Bible: *'am, gôyim,* and *bene* (Hebrew); or *ethnos* and *laos* (Greek). Even the same Hebrew or Greek word, for example, *'am* or *ethnos,* by itself is ambiguous.

Accurate translation and respectful interpretation require sensitivity to the historical period and cultural setting of a particular biblical text. For instance, Numbers 23:9, which speaks of "people" not dwelling among the "nations," dates from after the Babylonian exile, 537 B.C.E., but the event it is relating (Balaam's prophecy) occurred during the exodus, around 1200 B.C.E. For this reason among others, Liverani observes that "the current idea that [ancient] Israel was a 'Nation' (in its modern sense) is doubtful and in any case the subject for specific research" (*Anchor Bible Dictionary* 4: 1031).

How is a modern reader to understand the word "people" when it occurs in the Bible? Why should it not be translated as "nation"? As interpreters have frequently repeated, the best commentary on the Bible is the Bible. What information does the Bible yield about "people?"

Elements in the Concept "People"

In antiquity, people were identified by birth (Simon bar Jonah, Matt. 16:17; Jesus, son of Mary, Mark 6:3), geography (Jesus of Nazareth, John 19:19), and gender (Zacchaeus, a son of Abraham, Luke 19:9; daughters of Jerusalem, Luke 23:28). A person derived privilege from being born of a certain family and in a certain place. This information helps a reader to notice that the concept "people" in the Bible appears to contain two basic elements: kinship and authority.

From the perspective of kinship, people seems to describe a group that is mutually related. One common Hebrew word for people, '*am*; '*ammîm*, probably derives from a verb meaning "to be united, connected or related." A similar Hebrew word for people, '*ummâ*; '*ummîm* (Ps. 117:1; also "tribes" in Num. 25:1, 6), may relate to the Hebrew word for mother ('*em*). Anthropology would confirm what etymology suggests: "people" are those who are consanguineous, that is, have a common ancestor, or are connected by other bonds that make them just like blood relatives (fictive kin), such as living in the same geographical location.

In Psalm 117:1 the Hebrew word for people ('*ummîm*) is parallel to and thus practically synonymous with the Hebrew word *gôy*, usually translated "nation" in the first part of that verse. The parallelism of these words raises a question about the distinction sometimes urged between '*am* (people) as a social and cultural term and *gôy* (nation, referring especially to non-Israel) as a political term. It seems preferable to understand these parallel words as reflecting a common distinction in group-centered, Middle Eastern culture between "us" and "them." Today's English Version of Exodus 19 reflects this understanding. God commands Moses to tell the "house of Jacob//sons of Israel = Israelites" (19:3) that he will make them a holy people (*gôyim*, v. 6) among all the people ('*ammîm*, v. 5; see also 1 Pet. 2:9). The same distinction produces a different reading of Numbers 23:9 in which God speaking through Balaam describes Jacob//Israel as "a people ('*am* = "us," the "in-group") dwelling alone" and not reckoning itself among "the nations" (*gôyim*, "them," the "outgroup"). Notice the questionable use of "nations" in this translation.

A second element derives from the perspective of authority: Who is in charge? An analysis of the context in which the Hebrew word translated "people" occurs in various biblical accounts suggests that this word "people" designated those who have authority over or are in charge of the place where they live. Narratives relating to the patriarchal period use the word people ('*am*) or people of the land ('*am hā'āreṣ*) to designate the non-Israelite inhabitants of Canaan. The Hittites who lived in Hebron were people of the land (Gen. 23:12-13) in contrast to Abraham, who was a resident alien at that time and who therefore had to negotiate with the Hittites for a burial place (Gen. 23:4). When Moses and Aaron sent spies to reconnoiter Canaan, the Amalekites, the Amorites, the Hittites, and the Canaanites (Num. 13:28-29; 14:9) who lived there were described as people of the land in contrast to the community of Israelites (Num. 14:2; literally, "sons of Israel" incorrectly translated as "people" in the RSV). The former groups were in charge; the Israelites were not.

Israel, a People

In his classic study of ancient Israel, de Vaux (1965) highlights three different meanings of the word "people" (1:70-72) in three different historical periods. To appreciate this evolving concept throughout history, we can apply a cross-cultural model developed by Benedict Anderson and refined by Bruce Malina (Malina 1994). The model helps analyze the historical experience of people from the biblical period to modern times. The way in which "people" lived and interacted through human history is what the model highlights.

1. Face to Face In antiquity, face-to-face relationships dominated. This is certainly the case in the patriarchal and patrilocal family and the tribal setting. Abraham negotiated face to face with Ephron and the Hittites for his family's burial place (Gen. 23). King David dealt with Saul's descendant, Mephibosheth, and his servant, Ziba, face to face (2 Sam. 9). Even ordinary subjects dealt with King Solomon face to face (1 Kings 3:16-28).

As de Vaux observes, prior to the return from exile, "people of the land" are a group of males with authority that contrasts them with the king or prince (Ezek. 7:27), the king's servants (Jer. 37:2), the priests (Jer. 1:18), and the prophets (Ezek. 22:24-29). The people of the land had authority for capital punishment for certain offenses (Lev. 20:2-4). In all instances, there is face-to-face interaction among all people: ordinary folk and leaders (de Vaux 1965: 1:70-72).

2. Face to Grace Ancient empires from the Assyrian to the Roman represented a mode of social interaction one step above face to face, namely, face to grace. Grace means favor, and favor/favoritism belongs to the Mediterranean institution of patronage featuring intermediaries (brokers) between sources of power (patrons) and those who need their help (clients).

Artaxerxes II, king of Persia (404-358 B.C.E.), permitted Ezra the priest to take with him to Jerusalem any of the people, priests, or Levites who wanted to go, and empowered him to appoint magistrates and judges there (see Ezra 7). De Vaux points out that after the return from exile, the phrase "people of the land" begins to shift in meaning to designate those who oppose the reconstruction of the temple, or the mixed-breed people who met the returnees from exile (Ezra 4:1-5)

In New Testament times, Herod the Great and his successors (these are imperial bureaucrats = brokers) dealt with geographically separated groups (villages; various ethnic groups) by means of local elites (landowners; toll collectors), therefore, face to grace; but sometimes they interacted face to face (see Luke 23:6-12, Jesus before Pilate and Herod). Herod and others like him occasionally related face to face with the emperor.

De Vaux's third category of people of the land as a pejorative term beginning with rabbinic Judaism after 90 c.e. is also part of face-to-grace interaction. The antipathy of rabbinic Judaism toward the people of the land reminds a reader that "grace" in this phrase does not carry a positive meaning.

3. Face to Mace In the medieval period, specifically in European feudalism, face-to-mace (power, force) social interaction replaced face-to-grace interaction. People now had only indirect contact with authority, which became centralized and played a social role. People dealt with agents of the centralized authority, networks of agents that often overlapped. Thus the bishop's agents might conflict with the local lords or monarchs. An abstract concept of space emerges, so that Israel ceases to be a people occupying a land and becomes transformed into the land itself. Israel is the land.

4. Face to Space The final form of human interaction, that is, how people relate to other people, is face to space. This is a modern mode of social interaction that emerged with the nation-state, which itself began to emerge in the eighteenth century. Currently, humans interrelate via technologies such as the telephone, telegraph, radio, TV, or the Internet. There is no direct contact with authority. Distant or localized strangers feel or imagine "community" through these technologies, as if the President of the United States on TV were speaking personally to this viewing family in its living room.

Conclusion

A professor at a Bible college in the Metro, D.C., region gave his students a list of questions about the Bible which they were to pose to college and university professors in the area. One question was: "Can an individual trust the Bible to lead them toward an intimate relationship with God?" This question suggests a similar one for our topic: "Can a reader of the Bible learn from it how to relate to 'people' or 'nations'?" The reflections on that word in this article would indicate that there is no simple answer to the question (nor to the question posed by students at that Bible college).

The idea of "people" will differ among contemporary readers. Travelers and emigrants from Western nations possess a strong sense of nationality (common language, history, etc.) and feel comfortable with the impersonal face-to-space relationships that prevail in modern nations. Bureaucratic hassles are annoying but tolerable because that's the way life is. For such, the Bible and its examples are irrelevant.

Travelers or emigrants from face-to-face or face-to-grace cultures (e.g., circum-Mediterranean countries, including democratic states) will be stymied and frustrated by the impersonal and unfeeling relationships experienced in the West. They cannot understand an impersonal "system" and would prefer the "personal touch" of friendship or clientelism, that is, patronage, flattery, bribery, and the like, as in the biblical world. For such, the Bible can be a source of comfort. An astute teacher or preacher will know how to resist making fundamentalist applications of biblical texts yet also know when to draw helpful analogies for travelers and emigrants accustomed to face-to-face and face-to-grace relationships, as in the Bible.

3. "Visiting Strangers" and "Resident Aliens": Insights from 1 Peter

One of the most marked characteristics of U.S. society is the great mobility of its population. From earliest colonial times, this has been a nation on the move. Wave upon wave of immigrants has peopled various parts of the country. There has been and continues to be a varied movement among U.S. citizens: from farm to city, city to suburbs (and exurbs), north to south, center to periphery, and many other locales.

For generations, U.S. residents have changed homes at a relatively fast pace. Even though the pace of residential mobility in the United States has been dropping over the last century, it is still high by international standards. Overall, about 20 percent of the U.S. population changes its place of residence each year.

The consequences of such a relatively high rate of mobility are many.

People change work associates, family visiting circles, children's school and play groups, participation in organizations such as congregations, and relationships with kin. Geographical mobility in this society is a cultural process that frees the individual from social control and encourages anonymity and independence. This fits well with the cultural emphasis on individualism and explains the correlative difficulty members of this culture have in forming and maintaining "community" except in times of crisis.

This rapid mobility also has an interesting effect on the perception and understanding of neighborhoods in the United States. Since the 1920s, the automobile has had an incalculable influence in this regard. U.S. residents accustomed to rapid and wide-ranging mobility have difficulty drawing "lines" or "boundaries." Are the next-door neighbors inside or outside our private worlds? How long must a newcomer live in a neighborhood to become an old-timer? How different can a new resident be — in color, age, physical capacity, economic status, and the like — and still be one of "us?" Where does the community's right to control new residents end and individual rights begin?

Despite the challenges that accompany mobility, experts in the social-scientific analysis of U.S. culture agree that geographical mobility is indeed a major characteristic of this culture that has enormous effects — not necessarily totally deleterious — upon a great many important aspects of the social system.

The Mediterranean World

As anyone sensitive to cultural differences might expect, people in the ancient Mediterranean cultural world had a different attitude toward geographical mobility. The migrations that did take place were often prompted by famine, war, feuds, or other such events. The destruction of the Jerusalem temple occasioned a great migration. By and large, however, a family fortunate enough to possess ancestral land was honor bound by the culture to preserve and protect it and remain on it in perpetuity. Naboth refused his king's offer to exchange land or money for his vineyard with this explanation: "The LORD forbid that I should give you the inheritance of my fathers" (1 Kings 21:3).

Moreover, family land was usually in the possession of a rather large, extended family. There was little reason to leave this land, for no one outside one's family could be trusted. Venturing beyond one's family and its land was a dangerous risk. A traveler leaving the home village hastened to kinsfolk for lodging. Only here could steadfast loving-kindness be expected. Otherwise, a traveler had to rely upon the hospitality of gracious hosts. In the ancient Mediterranean world, hospitality was granted mainly by men and only to strangers (Gen. 19). Traveling strangers kept their fingers crossed.

"Visiting Strangers" and "Resident Aliens"

John H. Elliott (1981) has demonstrated that 1 Peter was sent by a group in Rome (Peter, 1:1; Silvanus, 5:12; and Mark, 5:13) to fellow Jesus-group members in Asia Minor who are identified as "visiting strangers" (1:1; 2:11; RSV "exiles") and "resident aliens" (2:11; cf. 1:17). Some scholars prefer to give "spiritual" interpretations to these two phrases, but Professor Elliott convincingly argues that they are intended to describe the real-life political situation of this letter's original recipients.

In the ancient world, anyone who left the home setting for a different setting was a stranger. Being unknown in the new setting, strangers were both feared and contemned. Their peculiar accents, puzzling customs, and suspicious behaviors were naturally perceived to be threats to established peace, order, and well-being. Strangers were viewed as more than humorous and eccentric; they were considered to be dangerous. As such, strangers were normal targets of unofficial or everyday expressions of discrimination and disadvantage.

In Asia Minor, strangers who belonged to Jesus groups were identified by an insulting term which might best be translated something like "Christ lackeys" (1 Pet. 4:16). The native population knew that these strangers believed that a person called Jesus or the Christ had proclaimed a god who intolerantly forbade allegiance to or worship of any other god. These strangers foolishly followed the advice of Jesus. For this reason, members of Jesus groups were reviled (3:9) and unjustly slandered (2:12; 3:16) as immoral or criminal wrongdoers (2:12, 14; 3:17; 4:15). They were threatened with harm (3:13) and reproached for their allegiance to Christ (4:14).

In contrast, resident aliens were strangers who settled in the land; they were no longer just passing through. Still, resident aliens formed a class of people considered by the native population to be inferior to them, hence they were granted only very limited legal and social rights. Resident aliens live among a people who are not kinfolk and to whom the alien does not naturally belong. Other biblical characters who were resident aliens include Abraham among the Hittites (Gen. 23:4), Moses in the land of Midian (Exod. 2:22), and the Israelites in Egypt (Gen. 15:13).

Restrictions upon aliens affected whom they could marry, the types of business they could conduct, the holding of land and succession of property, the right to vote, the formation of associations and guilds, and more. In addition, they had to pay higher taxes and tribute. In effect, these people had no political rights. They were excluded from popular assemblies and subject to more severe forms of civil punishment.

Though some of these strangers and resident aliens lived in the cities of Asia Minor, the majority resided in the rural regions of the interior. The social discrimination they experienced encouraged them to form clubs and labor guilds for the purpose of mutual protection, support, and acceptance. Often these associations involved shared religious belief and worship as well. This was particularly true of the Christians who were converts from Judaism and paganism.

The Household or Family of God

One of the two major social institutions of the ancient Mediterranean world is kinship, whether real or fictive. (The other major institution is politics.) Real kinship is rooted in blood ties. Fictive kinship is "like" real kinship. It results from a variety of strategies, for instance, sharing the same wet nurse, participating in certain ritual meals, following a common faction leader whose goals all members of the faction share, and so on.

The resident aliens to whom 1 Peter was addressed had accepted Jesus as Messiah and recognized Jesus groups as a form of human community that provided the social unity and acceptance that were not available to them in society at large. Much more than this, however, the resident aliens recognized that they had received the favor and acceptance of the God of Israel.

These converts recognized that they were reborn (1:3, 23; 2:2) children (1:14; 2:10) of a heavenly Father (1:2, 3, 17; 4:17), united into one household of God (2:5; 4:17) or family-like community (2:17; 2:18–5:5; 5:9; 5:12-13). They perceived themselves to be members of the flock of God (2:25; 5:1-4). They enjoyed fellowship with Christ through their suffering (4:1, 12-13; 5:1).

Clearly the one thing that resonates throughout this letter is a contrast between the feeling of "homelessness" experienced by a visiting stranger and resident alien in society at large, and the feeling of "at home-ness" experienced by these same folk within the household of faith. This letter is definitely a consoling and encouraging word for Jesus-group members suffering as a result of social discrimination and alienation. It urges readers to resist pressures for social conformity but rather to stand fast in faith, hope, and love.

The Modern Believer

Many years ago, my late wife and I were forced by economic circumstances to migrate from the midwestern United States to the eastern region. Fortunately, we managed to sell our midwestern home and purchase a new home in the East, but the day of the move proved both welcome and terrifying.

After selling our home and removing its furnishings on Monday, we suddenly realized that we no longer owned a piece of land or a home. We no longer had any roots anywhere. Though scheduled to purchase our new home on Wednesday clear across the country, we had still not received word that our mortgage was approved. (That word did not arrive until the moment we sat at the table to purchase the new home on Wednesday evening!)

Traveling across the country, we truly felt like visiting strangers wherever we stopped. Fortunately in our culture credit cards, motels, letters of introduction, and formal patterns of culturally specific etiquette help to ease this disorienting experience. Our ancestors in the faith had to rely on the hospitality of strangers.

We were grateful to arrive in our new city, to finalize the purchase of our new home, and to move in. Yet for a long time, we felt like resident aliens. Our accents, our different origins, our customs, our expectations, everything simply didn't fit in here! State bureaucracies and their minions reinforced the feelings. "I work for the state that you are *trying* to move into!" "If you don't like the way we do things here, why don't you move back to where you came from?"

Moreover, differences in the ways in which Catholic Christianity expresses itself and is practiced across the United States also contribute in a strange and surprising way to a transplanted believer's feeling like a "resident alien." Reading First Peter in a contemporary life-setting like this helps a modern believer to appreciate the consolation and encouragement that our ancestors in the faith who were visiting strangers and resident aliens in first-century Asia Minor must have experienced upon receiving this letter.

Even so, the high value placed by U.S. culture on individualism (a value almost totally lacking in the Mediterranean world) makes weak community support and even mild persecution easier to tolerate or dismiss in the United States than in the Mediterranean world. A love for geographic mobility and novelty in a country as large as the United States makes it always feasible for U.S. individualists to seek greener pastures elsewhere.

4. Jesus and the Samaritans

Matthew's Jesus sees his mission exclusively to the lost sheep of the house of Israel (Matt. 10:5; 15:24) and explicitly prohibits his disciples from going among the Samaritans (Matt. 10:5). In contrast, John's Jesus interacts with a Samaritan woman (John 4), while Luke's Jesus not only interacts with a Samaritan (Luke 17:11) but tells a parable about a Samaritan who risks his very life tending to a nearly dead stranger who is surely a member of the house of Israel (Luke 10:33). Who are these Samaritans? How can a reader understand these two views of Jesus' attitude toward and interaction with them?

Origins

Knowledge of the Samaritans is sketchy, often contradictory, and in many instances simply nonexistent. Contemporary Samaritans claim that they have directly descended from the Northern Israelite tribes of Ephraim and Manasseh. According to them, when the Assyrians invaded and destroyed the Northern Kingdom in 721 B.C.E., only a small group — the elites — were deported. An inscription of Sargon II (*Ancient Near Eastern Texts,* 284-85) records the number as 27,290. The majority remained and continued to identify themselves as Israelites. In anthropological fieldwork and historical research, self-identification must always be respected and taken seriously.

The Deuteronomic Historian, in contrast, relates that the Samaritans descended from colonists who were relocated in regions of Samaria from lands that the Assyrians had conquered: Babylon, Cuthah, Avva, Hamath, and Sephar-vaim (2 Kings 17:24). When God sent lions to attack these aliens, Assyria repatriated an Israelite priest who settled in Bethel and instructed the colonists how to live properly in "the fear of the LORD" (2 Kings 17:25-28). This view is also reflected in Josephus (*Antiquities* 9.277-91).

The Samaritan self-identification insists that the majority of them have always been and still are loyal to Israel's God and to Israelite traditions. A small group exists to this day near Nablus! They have remained loyal to their group. However, the identification given by the Bible and Josephus places Samaritan faith and loyalty to God in doubt. Indeed, the biblical record describes these colonists as henotheists, worshipers of Yahweh, true, but also of other gods brought with them to Samaria from their lands of origin or former residence. This difference of viewpoint colors the rest of the biblical record, even though Samaritans are mentioned very few times in the Bible.

The Second Temple (520 B.C.E.)

According to the biblical record (Ezra 4), the Samaritans at first rejoiced to learn that those returning from Babylonian exile were charged with rebuilding the temple. But when their offer of assistance was rejected by the returnees, the Samaritans opposed and sabotaged that project (Ezra 4:4-5, 25) as well as the rebuilding of the walls (4:17-23). Persia was satisfied that this mutual hostility would prevent the people from uniting in revolt against its new conquerors. The point to notice is that the customary tendency of this Middle Eastern culture toward factionalism had continued for two hundred years since the Assyrian invasion and would continue into New Testament times.

Whether or not Samaritans ever built their own temple on Mount Gerizim is a point of scholarly debate. Archaeological remains of such a temple have eluded excavators, prompting scholars to hypothesize that rather than a temple the Samaritans constructed a modest shrine or tabernacle.

Greek Period (ca. 300 B.C.E.)

The Samaritans rallied behind Alexander the Great, while members of the house of Israel remained loyal to Persia. When Alexander destroyed Samaria, the Samaritans obviously became wary of the Greeks. But at this time, differences of opinion about Jerusalem and Mount Gerizim as centers of worship continued to be a major element that kept members of the house of Israel and Samaritans apart. Be that as it may, anti-Samaritan sentiment reached a peak in 128 B.C.E. when John Hyrcanus, governor and high priest in Judea, destroyed the Samaritan sanctuary at Gerizim.

Roman Period (63 B.C.E.)

Josephus reports two events about the Samaritans that help a modern reader understand the anti-Samaritan sentiment evident in Matthew (10:5; 15:24) and elsewhere (e.g., Luke 9:54; John 8:48). Sometime during 6-9 C.E., a group of Samaritans secretly joined some Judean pilgrims on their way to Jerusalem for Passover. They scattered human bones in the porticoes and sanctuary of the temple, thereby defiling it very seriously. Anyone who touched a corpse or human bone would be unclean for a day and would be obliged to purify themselves with a ritual bath. In response, the priests excluded everyone from the temple (*Antiquities* 18.29-30). No doubt the gossip network spread this news throughout the entire land. If the teenaged Jesus was not himself among the Passover pilgrims, he surely heard the news in Nazareth. It is not difficult to imagine the reaction of any devout Yahwist to this insulting sacrilege. Imagine the effect on an impressionable teenager. It would certainly never be forgotten!

The second event took place around twenty years after Jesus died (ca. 51 C.E.). Indeed, it was a major cause of the first Judean revolt against Rome (66-70 C.E.). Josephus offers two versions (*Jewish War* 2.232-35; *Antiquities* 20.118-36). The basic report is that Samaritans living in Gema, on the border between Galilee and Samaria, murdered one (or many) Judean pilgrims on their way to Jerusalem for the festival of Passover. In retaliation, Judeans from Jerusalem came and massacred the inhabitants of Gema. The chain of events after this becomes complicated. Simply told, the Samaritans managed to keep the sympathies of the local Roman representatives on their side. These Romans imprisoned and murdered Judeans. The Judeans remained persistent and eventually had the entire affair moved to Rome, where Caesar ruled favorably in behalf of the Judeans and ordered that the Samaritans be punished. Complex as this issue is, it nevertheless demonstrates that the seven hundred years of hostility between the Samaritans and the house of Israel since 721 B.C.E. showed no signs of abating.

New Testament

Regarding the Samaritans, whose representation of Jesus carried greater plausibility: Matthew's? or Luke and John's? Posed another way, can one imagine that Jesus was a fair and open-minded person to all people whom Matthew subsequently misrepresented in his gospel? Or was Jesus a typical, group-centered Middle Easterner who is fairly if unflatteringly (to modern sensibilities) represented by Matthew but subsequently presented in a more flattering light by Luke and John?

Group-centered cultures (who represent about 80 percent of the current population of the planet) tend to stereotype. Recall John's comment: "For Judeans have no dealings with Samaritans" (John 4:9). Could these people ever imagine an exception to this view? Does John's report about Jesus and the woman constitute such an exception? Or it is plausible that a Samaritan with a seriously polluting skin condition might possibly if accidentally find himself in the company of nine similarly afflicted Judeans who encounter Jesus and experience healing? Would that skin condition make "friends" out of "enemies" (Luke 17:16)?

John's reported stereotype is positive in nature (John 4:9). This means that it does not carry a negative connotation. It simply reports a cultural generalization. Many such cultural generalizations appear in the New Testament, especially stereotypes that identify people by their illness rather than by their name: a leper, a paralytic, a man with a withered hand, and the like. When a stereotype includes a negative judgment, it becomes a prejudice. There are three elements in a prejudice: a negative evaluation; this evaluation or judgment is based on ethnicity (behavior) or race (biology) rather than an individual's personal qualities; and this evaluation or judgment is rooted in an organized predisposition to react negatively (Pilch 1994). Prejudice seems to be reflected in Matthew. Jesus' directive not to go among the Samaritans (Matt. 10:5), his initial response of ignoring the respectful requests from a Canaanite woman on behalf of her daughter (Matt. 15:23) followed by a direct insult (Matt. 15:26), and his labeling a recalcitrant fellow member of the house of Israel as a "Gentile and tax collector" (Matt. 18:18) depict Jesus as a very typical, group-centered Middle Easterner. He seemed to accept his cultural stereotypes. Perhaps Jesus even went to his death with such unweakened group loyalty. Some scholars translate his final, postresurrection directive in this way: "Go therefore and make disciples of [the members of the house of Israel who are dispersed among] all nations, baptizing them . . ." (Matt. 28:19). This would tally with Jesus' avowed intention of reinvigorating theocracy ("the reign or kingdom of God") in Israel.

Samaritan Admirers

Evidence indicates that after Jesus' resurrection, Samaritans responded enthusiastically to the apostles' preaching and were eager to join the community of believers in Jesus who were chiefly of the house of Israel (e.g., Acts 8:4-8). It would be difficult to do so and attract still other Samaritans to someone who in his lifetime was opposed to ministering to them. Moreover, given the centuries-long hostility between Jerusalem and Samaria, Samaritans who accepted and believed in the risen Jesus might refuse to render any loyalty or respect to Jerusalem leaders. Luke's intriguing ploy of saying that the Samaritans had only been baptized in the name of Jesus but had not received the Spirit (Acts 8:16) is very clever. Jesus received the Spirit at his baptism, and so did all who submitted to baptism in his name. The Samaritans very likely received the Spirit at their baptism in the name of Jesus, but Luke singles out the Jerusalem apostles, Peter and John, as the ones from whom the Samaritans received the Spirit (Acts 8:14-15, 17). Had it not been for Luke's report, who knows but that the Samaritans would have remained believers in Jesus quite independent from the Jerusalem pillars?

John also cleverly juxtaposes Nicodemus (John 3) and the unnamed Samaritan woman (John 4) in contrasting scenes. Nicodemus is a leader in the house of Israel; the Samaritan is viewed as a miscreant half-breed. Nicodemus comes to Jesus at night; the woman meets Jesus at high noon. Nicodemus fails to understand Jesus' pun on a Greek word that can mean "from above" or "again." Jesus keeps insisting one must be born from above, while Nicodemus continues to understand that he must somehow undergo a "rebirth" process. In her dialogue with Jesus, the woman progresses from ground zero of no respect (she calls Jesus a Judean but with a tone of contempt) to respect: sir, prophet, and eventually Messiah in seven statements. When Nicodemus departs from Jesus, he is still "in the dark." When the Samaritan woman departs from Jesus, she is fully enlightened about his identity. John's point? Samaritans are welcomed into this believing community by Jesus himself (reinterpreted decades later, of course).

Lake Wobegon

Garrison Keillor is a familiar, American-born Norwegian who has lived much of his life in Minnesota. In his weekly radio program, Keillor delivers a monologue about completely fictional characters who inhabit a completely fictitious place in Minnesota: Lake Wobegon. Anyone consulting a map of Minnesota or calling its tourism bureau can verify that such a place simply does not exist. But no listeners are offended, even residents of Minnesota, at what Keillor develops week after week Indeed, no one turns the radio off because of this total fiction. Rather, people tend to listen more closely so as not to miss any of the nuances in Keillor's story.

Our high-context ancestors in the faith readily understood the reports they heard about the Samaritans or about Jesus and the Samaritans in the different accounts of the evangelists. These ancestors were quite aware of the cultural elements that a preacher or evangelist such as Luke or John would be skewing one way or another to make a point. We who live in a very different culture must exert more effort to gain the understanding that came so easily to them. Contemporary Samaritans can offer some assistance. In the final analysis, what do you think? Was Jesus anti-Samaritan? or pro-Samaritan? or sometimes one and sometimes the other? How will you decide?

5. Individuals? or Stereotypes?

A Christian minister in Africa once asked a mixed group of Africans and European missionaries to tell him the main point of the story of Joseph (Gen. 37–50). The European missionaries all noted how Joseph, as an individual, remained faithful to God no matter what happened to him. In contrast, the Africans observed how Joseph never forgot his family no matter how far he traveled away from his homeland or what he had to endure from his brothers. How do you read the story of Joseph? Is Joseph a rugged individualist who can take care of himself no matter what the odds? Or is Joseph an irreformable, family-oriented person who can never abandon them nor ignore their plight no matter what they may have dished out to him?

The differing interpretations of this story highlight two kinds of human relationships and human behaviors which flow from distinctive personality types: individualist and collectivist. The vast majority of the people described in the Bible represent collectivist personality types. Individualist personality types are rather rare in the Bible and in Mediterranean culture in general.

Individualist Personality Types

The social analyst Geert Hofstede points out that individualism as a personality type is represented among only 20 percent of the current population of this planet (Hofstede 1980; 1994). This percentage is higher than it has ever been in human history. The individualist personality type believes that each person is unique and distinctive. In the United States, for example, no Social Security number has been or ever will be reused, at least according to current plans. Individualists believe that their primary responsibility is to themselves and to their individual potential. The legal system in the United States has already acknowledged the right of a minor child to "disown" or "divorce" her or his parents if they threaten her or his well-being or individual potential.

Individual worth is based on individual achievements or individual possessions. Hence, one's personal status is achieved. One can be born on the wrong side of the tracks yet still change one's personal status through personal efforts and successes documented on a resume, displayed on diplomas and certificates on a vanity wall, and recorded in obituaries. Thus, achieving and competing are motivational necessities and the norm in individualistic societies.

Individualists value independence very highly and put a premium on uniqueness. Individualists seek autonomy from social solidarity. If they join a group, it is on the basis of an implicit renewable contract. Whether it be a support group like Weight Watchers or a church, individualists remain with the group only as long as it suits their purposes, or they lose interest or motivation. In this view, a group is simply a collection of individuals. The individual self is perceived as an entity separate from other persons and the physical world. Any personal decision is made by the self alone even it is not in the group's best interests. Individualists are interested in personal autonomy, self-reliant achievement, and personal satisfaction. Experts have called the commitment to individualism an "isolating" belief system. Excessive dependence upon any group is discouraged and frowned upon

While individualists read the Joseph story as that of another individualist like themselves, Joseph the ancient Middle Easterner was not at all an individualist. Few if any people in that culture were or are individualists. They were, rather, "collectivists."

Collectivistic Personalities

Hofstede's research discovered that the collectivistic personality type is represented among 80 percent of the current population of this planet. This percentage was quite likely much higher in antiquity. Such people prefer to be identified by the major group to which they belong rather than

be recognized as individuals. This is why appellations based on family belonging, such as "son of Jonah," are so common in the Bible. Consider also
how few Pharisees are named in the gospels. References usually are just to
"a Pharisee." For this reason, collectivistic personalities are also called
sociocentric or group-centered personalities. They see their primary obligation to others in a group and are committed to the development of the
group (2008: 17-35).

As a result, the individual or personal worth of a collectivistic personality is rooted in familial status, social position, status, or caste. Hence, personal status is ascribed, that is, it derives principally from being born into a
given family. Such a child immediately inherits all the family's honor built
up over generations, as well as all the family's enemies! This is the point of
genealogies in antiquity. They were ordinarily constructed only after a person died and became famous. Jesus, who died a shameful death but was
raised by God, received two different genealogies (Matt 1:1-17; Luke 3:23-
38), each by an evangelist intending to document Jesus' honorable status
and reputation.

In this context, inner-group achievement and competition are viewed
as disruptive. Recall the occasion on which the mother of the sons of
Zebedee requested from Jesus places of honor for her sons in his kingdom
(Matt. 20:20-21). On the face of it, one might think this a fair request in
pursuit of honor. But life in the Mediterranean world is a zero-sum game.
If someone gains honor, others have lost it. It is hardly surprising that
when the ten heard of this request, they became indignant (Matt. 20:24).
This is not because the mother beat these ten to an honor they would have
sought for themselves. Rather, their indignation demonstrates how disruptive and harmful to the group is the desire of any member to excel over
others. The discussion of the apostles at the Last Supper (Luke 22:24)
about who should be regarded as the greatest is not really competition. It is
rather an argument about evaluating their respective honor ratings. Their
society recognized some statuses as more honorable than others (see Sir.
38:24–39:11).

Collectivistic personalities reject independence in favor of group-
specific interdependence. Instead of cultivating uniqueness, they emphasize conformity. They seek ever deeper integration into social reality.
Group membership in collectivistic societies is not an option; it is an obligation. Group membership results from one's inherited social and familial
place in society. Thus every group is viewed not just as a collection of individuals but as an organic unit, inextricably interlocked. Any personal deci-

sion is made in consultation with the group and often in obedience or deference to its will. When Joshua challenges the Israelites to choose whether they want to serve Yahweh or other gods, he is not soliciting personal decisions. Notice his own judgment: "As for me and my house, we will serve the LORD" (Josh. 24:15). This was not the result of a democratic vote by members of that household. One can see the same collectivistic behavior with Lydia, who "was baptized, with her household" (Acts 16:15), and the jailer at Philippi, who also "was baptized at once, with all his family" (Acts 16:33).

Collectivists are interested in corporate solidarity and strong family-based identity. Experts have called this a "congregating" or "integrating" belief system. People in this culture are socialized to be dependent especially upon kin (real and fictive), to join or build networks and coalitions, to support and repeat community wisdom, to be no better than anyone else but rather to be just like others in the group.

Stereotypes

Because collectivistic personalities are generally not interested in individuals, they tend to accept stereotypes as authentic and trustworthy assessments of people. If one were to read Mark's gospel and jot down the names of the people Jesus healed, only one appears: "Bar Timaeus" (Mark 10:46). Yet this is not the blind man's personal name. It is rather his father's name, the patriarch's name. This designation of the blind man reports his relationship within that family circle. All members of the household, the entire group, will be identified by the patriarch's name. Similarly, Jesus' clients are identified by their ailment: "a man with an unclean spirit" (Mark 1:23); Simon's mother-in-law, "sick with a fever" (Mark 1:30), "a leper" (Mark 1:40), and so on. To know one in a category is to know all others in that category.

Similar stereotypes attach to places and the people who inhabit them. "[All inhabitants of the island of Crete] are always liars, evil beasts, lazy gluttons. This testimony is true!" (Titus 1:12-13). Recall Nathanael's reaction when he learns that Jesus is from Nazareth: "Can anything good come out of Nazareth?" (John 1:46). Or again the editorial comment in the story of Jesus meeting the Samaritan woman at the well: "For Judeans have no dealings with Samaritans" (John 4:9). The stereotype is not always pejorative. When he identified his place of origin, Paul said, "I am a member of the house of Israel, from Tarsus in Cilicia, a citizen of no mean city" (Acts

21:39). Trading on his city's reputation, Paul, like all its inhabitants, could claim similar honorable status.

Psalm 22

The classic studies of the psalms identify "individual" psalms of praise and "individual" psalms of lament as two categories. These are contrasted with group or national psalms of praise or laments. Scholars recognize Psalm 22 as an individual psalm of lament. On a superficial reading, the words seems to make that very clear: "My God, my God, why have you forsaken me. I cry. . . ." Upon a closer reading, however, it becomes clear that this person is not an individualist but rather a collectivistic personality. He hides behind "our fathers" (v. 4), who are obviously Abraham, Isaac, and Jacob. The composer of this psalm is living long after those "fathers," but he makes no reference to his own father. He aligns himself with the patriarchs. Allusions to Second Isaiah (41:14; 52:14; 53:3) in verse 6: "I am a worm, and no man; scorned by men, and despised by the people" reveal a person more at home mouthing the words of one of Israel's greatest poets than in formulating something fresh and new, personally crafted. A collectivistic personality can hardly imagine improving on the group's collective wisdom. Claiming "there is none to help me" (v. 11) indicates how bad off this collectivistic person really is even before he begins to describe his physical condition. Where is his "next of kin," his "redeemer," his "avenger" (all synonyms; Sir. 30:6; Num. 35:9-15; Lev. 25:25), who are culturally obligated to rescue him? Suppose the unimaginable in this culture has actually happened to him: His entire family and household have died. Where, then, are his friends? Has he made no friends in life? We begin to realize that his physical condition, bad as it is, may not be the biggest problem in his life.

In the first thanksgiving verses (22-26), the collectivistic sentiment continues to shine through. The lamenter will publicize his blessings in the midst of the community and urge them all to praise God. The Lord has not despised him (v. 24: "poor" or "afflicted" in the singular) because all the "poor" or "afflicted" (v. 26, plural) can count on God's help. This shift from singular to plural further illustrates the thinking and behavior of a collectivistic personality. I am not really different from the others in the group.

Denying Self

No doubt Jesus' exhortation to the multitude and disciples, that if anyone wanted to "come after me, let that person deny self, take up the cross, and follow me" (Mark 8:34-38//Matt 16:24-28//Luke 9:23-27) is familiar to many Bible readers. Surely, one would think, this is an individualistic exhortation to individuals. Matthew (10:37-38) and Luke (14:26-27), however, repeat the exhortation in a different context which helps the Bible reader to avoid the trap of imposing an individualistic interpretation on texts that require a collectivistic cultural perspective. In these two instances when Jesus exhorted listeners to take up their cross and follow him, he urged denial of the family (Matthew: who loves family more than me; Luke: one must hate family). In other words, when a collectivistic personality hears the words "self," or "me," or "I," such a person does not think of an individual "I" but rather of an "I" who is so strongly embedded in a group such as a family as to be almost invisible. Bruce Malina noted that when Francis of Assisi heard the words of Jesus in Matthew 16:24, he summoned his family to the village square, returned all his clothes to them, and obeyed the command to deny self by denying his family. He was then accepted by the Bishop into a new family, the church. Francis understood that to deny self meant to deny family. This is a collectivistic interpretation of a biblical passage that reflects collectivistic (and not individualistic) cultural values (Malina 1996: 67).

Conclusion

Specialists in cultural studies recognize that all people are so enculturated in their own native culture that they find it very difficult to think that other cultures view life very differently. Of all the cultural differences between modern Western believers and their ancient, Middle Eastern ancestors in the faith, this concept of collectivistic personality is extremely difficult to understand and appreciate. Grasping this concept, however, will provide the Western reader with a better understanding of other concepts in the Bible like "community" and the Church as the Body of Christ.

6. Status by Gender and Age

In every society, a person needs to know his or her proper place. In technical terms, a person needs to know his or her status. This knowledge is important because status determines one's role in society. If one knows one's personal status, then one knows what is expected and how one ought to behave. Some status is ascribed, that is, a result of birth, over which one has no control. Gender and age are two additional determinants of ascribed status. Other status is acquired, that is, a person can improve his or her standing in society. A person, for example, can learn to be a carpenter, and if one's carpenter skills continue to improve, one's reputation as a craftsperson also improves. In this article, we focus on ascribed status, that is, one's standing in ancient Mediterranean society, which derives from gender and age.

Gender

Anthropologists distinguish societies on the basis of how lineage is determined. Matrilineal societies trace lineage to a common ancestor through women, while patrilineal societies trace lineage to a common ancestor through men. Matrilineal societies tend to be found where centralized political organization is lacking, and where much of the productive work is done by women. One matrilineal society is the Hopi Indians of the Southwest United States. Matrilineal societies are not matriarchal. Genders of the same age are considered more or less equal; thus gender in this society has little to no bearing on status. Yet even though men cannot be dominated by the women in this society, they cannot do anything of which women disapprove.

In patrilineal societies, women tend to be isolated from their kin because they move into the husband's home, which is located in or near his father's compound. They must defer to the dictates of all the men in the husband's household. Women in such a setting must show great resourcefulness to protect their self-interests. In the Mediterranean world, a key female strategy for advancing self-interest is to pit one man against another. While the Middle Eastern mother usually bonds strongly with the firstborn son, Rebekah has oddly bonded with the younger, Jacob. Esau's behavior and decisions in the story line (e.g., Gen. 25:27-34) suggest that Rebekah realized that Jacob would be better "social security" for her old age than Esau. So she pits Jacob against his brother Esau, and Jacob against his father, Isaac. Rebekah is a classic example of how women in a patriarchal culture manage to get their way almost all the time (Gen. 27). Her behavior also helps to understand the advice a Queen Mother gives to her son about the power of women (Prov. 31:3). She knows full well how she has trained her own daughters.

It is, in point of fact, precisely such a strategy of pitting one male against another that Paul reflects in his letter to the Israelite community in Rome. This is the point he makes relative to his fellow ethnics when he notes: "by their trespass [that of fellow Israelites], salvation has come to the non-Israelites, so as to make Israel jealous" (Rom. 11:11, my interpretation). A strategy used by Middle Eastern mothers in raising their sons is to give a gift to the favored but nonreciprocating son, then take it away and give it to another son in order to make the favored son jealous. Thus does Paul apply to God's behavior what he may have experienced — personally or vicariously — in his own life with mothers. All God-talk (theology) is rooted in human experience (analogy), which is always culture specific. In those patrilineal societies which are also patriarchal, men are, of course, deemed to be of higher status than women (Sir. 42:14).

Age

In many societies but especially in patriarchal ones, older men are respected and valued more than younger males. In the 1980s a professor of social ethics visited Kenya and interviewed the Akamba people to learn how they would allocate scarce medical resources. He presented an actual case he had heard from a folk healer and was surprised by the answers. If the folk healer had only one dose of known effective Western medicine to dispense, she would give it to an old man rather than a young man, an older man with no children rather than a younger man with five children, and an older man who had no involvement in community projects rather than a younger man who was managing multiple projects that would improve the life of the community. In the final analysis, she would split the medicine knowingly, rendering it ineffective but demonstrating concern for each (Kilner 1984: 18-22). This report is not unlike St. Thomas Aquinas's judgment about whom a man must save in a fatal fire and in what particular sequence: father first, mother second, wife third, child last (*Summa Theologica* IIa-IIae, q. 26).

Patriarchal Culture

Patriarchs are always older males. It follows, then, that elderly males should be given greater respect and deference than the young. Moreover, the patriarch must achieve two key things if he expects to be respected: he must be able to impose his will especially on the males of his household,

85

and he must be able to count on loyalty from his sons. Of course, this is the ideal. Anyone familiar with Middle Eastern culture realizes that while the ideal is affirmed and acknowledged, it is often not observed in reality. This is why in many circum-Mediterranean cultures attractive appearances are preferred to repulsive reality. Let us consider some illustrations.

Sirach's advice to the elderly reads thus: "Speak, you who are older, for it is fitting that you should, but with accurate knowledge, and do not interrupt the music. Where there is entertainment, do not pour out talk; do not display your cleverness out of season" (Sir. 32:3-4). Some commentators say that this is advice for behavior at a banquet. If so, and if the advice was deemed necessary by the Sage, one conclusion seems obvious: The elderly must have behaved often in just this disruptive and annoying way at banquets. Moreover, Sirach's advice suggests that someone — perhaps the banquet master — told them to "shut up and listen!" When one reads Wisdom literature and notices the large number of admonitions directed at the elderly, it gives one pause. Were they esteemed more in the ideal than in reality?

As for the patriarch imposing his will on his sons, the father in Jesus' parable about the two sons (Luke 15:11-32) was a clear cultural failure. The younger son demanded and obtained his share of the property, which ought not to have been gained until his father died. The younger son's request was in effect a wish that his father were dead. Hardly respectful. The father should have responded immediately and harshly. Later, the elder son refused to join in the feast his father arranged for the younger son, who penitently returned from his disappointing adventure. He distanced himself from his younger brother by referring to him as "this son of yours," falsely accused him of immoral behavior, and then betrayed his true feelings toward his father when he said, "I have *slaved* for you these many years." He considered himself a slave rather than a son. Quite obviously, the father failed to impose his will on both of his sons.

In real life, the father should have killed the younger son on the spot. But if he did, he would have asserted his patriarchal authority but lost a son. What would that accomplish? So, as often happens in the Middle East, he makes the best of a bad situation because his alternative would be far less tolerable. The case is similar with the elder son. The father simply explains the reason for his behavior, but we never learn whether the elder son joined the feasting or not.

At the same time, the mother in Jesus' parable of the two sons is not mentioned; she is invisible. Using insights from Mediterranean culture to "fill in the gaps," a reader can plausibly guess that she bonded closely with the elder son, perhaps the firstborn. In this culture, the closest emotional bond exists between a mother and her son. The weakest exists between a husband and a wife, who routinely are patrilateral cousins. The mother could be presumed to be pleased that the younger — and obviously disrespectful, not to mention irresponsible — son is out of the picture. The elder son will inherit a double portion anyway (Deut. 21:15-17). He and his inheritance will be her "social security." She may have been as unhappy as her elder son at the return of and gracious welcome accorded to the younger upon whom some of his "double portion" was being expended.

The same is true of another familiar father of two sons in Jesus' parables (Matt. 21:28-31). He, too, failed to impose his will on his sons. By the values of Middle Eastern culture, the son who said he would work in the vineyard but had no intention of doing so actually fulfilled the divine commandment to "honor" father. He said what the father wanted to hear. He did not shame his father in public. The son who publicly refused to work in the vineyard shamed his father. In the Middle East, appearances are more important than the reality. Jesus, of course, did not ask a question about honor nor about appearances. "Which of the two did the will of his father?" His listeners knew and gave the correct answer. The son who made a shameful response to his father, but later went to work in the vineyard did his father's will. The audience, like all Middle Easterners, knows the reality. Appearances, however, are so much more comfortable.

Finally, Sirach's advice to young men reveals more cultural information: "Speak, young man, only when necessary, when they have asked you more than once" (Sir. 32:7 NAB). One semester when this passage came up in class, a student from Greece reported his frustration when he first arrived on campus. "When I came to Georgetown, I thought the students here were very rude. Friends would ask me whether I wanted to go to the movies with them. I would say no." Then, with exasperation in his voice, he added: "And they didn't ask me a second time!!!" The necessity of a double (or repeated) invitation is a cultural expectation in the Middle East and even in parts of Europe. When God calls Jeremiah to be a prophet, he demurs and says that he is too young. God must invite him a second time (Jer. 1:4-8). In the book of Job, the young man Elihu has listened quietly as Job's three friends strive to persuade Job that he must have offended God in some way. Finally, Elihu blurts out that he is tired of waiting to be invited to speak and contributes his view (Job 32:6ff.).

Conclusion

Like people in every culture, Westerners take their way of life so much for granted that they can't imagine a different way. Worse, people of every culture tend to believe that their way of life is the best way, the only way, so why seek another way, especially when it contradicts the established pattern. In fact, ever one should adopt this way. While the Middle Eastern view of gender and age as determinants of ascribed status strongly clashes with the Western view, that view makes good sense and keeps the culture functioning in a healthy way. Changing it can prove disastrous.

7. Names

Everybody knows that Saul, the "Hebrew born of Hebrews" (Phil. 3:5), had a life-changing experience of the risen Lord while traveling on the road toward Damascus, Syria. As a result and sign of this experience, his name was changed to Paul. However, Father Joseph Fitzmyer, among other Pauline scholars, points out that "there is no evidence that 'Saul' was changed to 'Paul' at the time of his conversion." Such knowledge about Paul and similar knowledge about other biblical narratives which "everybody knows" are excellent examples of "spurious familiarity." Information which "everybody knows" is all too often rooted in an oral tradition which has little if any contact with the evidence. Hence the assumed familiarity with the Bible in spite of never having read it is indeed spurious.

Why did Paul have two names? Why did Jesus give Peter a nickname: Cephas? If names are so significant, why does the New Testament rarely report the name of the people Jesus healed? A reflection on names in the Bible and its cultural world will help to answer these questions (Pilch 2008: 28-34).

Personal Names

A name is a word or phrase by which persons, places, or things are labeled in order to be known within a social system. There are personal names, geographical names, names for the deity, names of plants and animals, and so on. This article will focus mainly on personal names. In general, Israelite parents gave the newborn son his name on the eighth day after birth, when he was circumcised (Gen. 17:12). Sometimes God determined what that name should be (Matt. 1:21). Girls may have been named on the fifteenth day after birth (see Lev. 12:5). The name deriving from parents or God, however, can reflect a variety of things. In Hebrew, the name Saul means "asked for [from God]," which might suggest that his mother had difficulty in conceiving, or that his father wanted a son in addition to a daughter (Acts 23:16 refers to Paul's sister). Hannah, who also appeared to have difficulty conceiving, named her son Samuel, explaining her choice by saying, "I have asked him of the LORD" (1 Sam. 1:20). Literally, the name she selected derives from "Shem-el," meaning "the name of God" or "God's name is El."

Hannah's choice introduces a new consideration about names. If her explanation is what she intended, the boy's name should have been Saul. It appears that she was playing on similar-sounding words in Hebrew *(šā'ûl; šĕmûēl)*, a technique called homophony. It is not a common practice but offers one explanation for Hannah's choice. Homophony may also explain the association of the two names Saul and Paul, mentioned in Acts 13:9. Of course, we would still want to know why anyone would have two names.

Some names express parental gratitude for God's help (John 1:45: Nathanael = "God has given this child") or hopes for the child (Isa. 8:2: Jeberechiah = "May God bless this child") or parental beliefs and conviction (1 Kings 17:1: Elijah = "Yahweh is my God").

Other names reflect plant names (Gen. 38:6: Tamar = "palm tree") or animal names (Judg. 4:4: Deborah = "bee"; Jonah = "dove"; Num. 14:6: Caleb = "dog"). Among the people bearing animal names, Caleb's is difficult to interpret. The assumption is that a person in some way is similar to the namesake. Jonah, for instance, kept behaving like a homing pigeon instead of accepting the Lord's mission to travel to Nineveh. On the other hand, how was Caleb like a dog, and how would that be an appealing name? One explanation might be that though his report after scouting the land with Joshua represented a minority view, his positive judgment was as reliable as a good hunting dog might be. Calebite traditions told of a successful invasion from the south and settlement of the Hebron area by various groups associated with him.

Multiple Names

The types of multiple names familiar to us in the Bible and its cultural environment and the reasons for their acquisition vary extensively. It seems to be a common phenomenon of the Greco-Roman world (second cent.

B.C.E. to third cent. C.E.), which peaked in the second century C.E. In the New Testament, the author of Luke-Acts displays the greatest interest in double names. He seems to vary the formulae mainly for stylistic reasons.

In general, Romans had a three-part name: a given name *(praenomen)*, the name of the ultimate founder of that Roman family (the *gens*), and the family name (the *cognomen*). The given name was relatively unimportant. There may have been fewer than one hundred in use. Some common ones were Lucius, Marcus, Publius, Sextus, and Titus. The second, the name of the ultimate family founder (the *gens*), was the most important of these names. The typical ending was *-ius,* and it was often built from a place name or perhaps a cognomen. It designated the original clan (*Oxford Classical Dictionary,* 1970: "Names, Personal").

The *cognomen* served various purposes. It could designate the specific branch of a clan. Thus, Marcus Tullius Cicero belonged to the Ciceronian branch of the Tullius clan. Or it could signal some honor, as when Cornelius Scipio, who was victorious in Africa during the Punic War, had Africanus added to his name.

Women had only one name, usually the feminine form of the clan name. All of Cicero's daughters would be named Tullia. Slaves had only one name, either their given name or a name derived from their country of origin.

When we consider Paul, the Latin form, *Paulus,* appears both as a nomen and a cognomen in that world. Would this be the case for Paul? Such a cognomen seems unlikely for a born Hebrew. Luke describes him as "Saul, who is also known as Paul" (Acts 13:9), in a passage that marks a *change in his narrative.* As Saul, he worked among fellow Hebrews, but as Paul (the same person) he worked among Hellenized Hebrews in the Diaspora. This feature in the Acts of the Apostles might be the basis for the "spurious familiarity" about Paul's so-called name change mentioned above.

Luke's comment, however, deserves further consideration. Quite likely Paul's given name was Saul. Since the Hebrews used patronyms, that is, identified sons by their father (e.g., Joshua the son of Nun, Num. 14:6; or Simon bar-Jonah, Matt. 16:17), Saul might be carrying his father's or grandfather's name, both of which are possible. Recall the expectation that Elizabeth's son would be called Zechariah after his father, but she selected John, which the father confirmed (Luke 1:59-63). The name Paul could have been added to Saul in one of three ways. As already noted, it could have been a homophonic choice to create a pleasant, similar-sounding pair of names. Or it could have been something that began as an informal appellation within the family and among friends that eventually stuck as a second name, even before he was born. Scholars believe that Paul had both names already from birth (see Acts 22:26-29). In other words, Paul's double name might reflect his family's cultural assimilation. Israelites often adopted a Greek or Latin double name to demonstrate their affinity with Greco-Roman ways. This factor may explain Luke's fondness for using double names. He refers to "Simon called Peter" (Acts 11:13), and "John whose other name was Mark" (Acts 12:12), combining Hebrew with Greek and Latin names. It is difficult to claim that Peter was interested in cultural assimilation. Luke, on the other hand, strove to make the characters in his work appealing to Greco-Roman readers.

Nicknames

The nickname is another form of double name. Nicknames can fall into two general categories. Those that convey a neutral or positive image tend to be public and used in the presence of the persons involved. Luke introduces us to "Joseph, who was surnamed by the apostles Barnabas (which means, Son of encouragement) . . ." (Acts 4:36). Barnabas may have originated as a positive nickname. Here is an upbeat person characterized by his ability to encourage and motivate others. In this instance, it is his contribution to the community that gives encouragement.

Tradition indicates that Jesus gave Simon the nickname Peter = "Rock" (Mark 3:16). The nickname and pun, however, work best in Aramaic (*kêpā/kêpā*; see Matthew's Greek rendition [16:15-18]: *petros/petra*). The Aramaic word means "rock," "stone," or "crag." The Greek form is Kephas. It was Paul's habitual name for Peter (1 Cor. 3:22; 9:5; 15:5; Gal. 1:18; 2:9, 11, 14). Though each evangelist uses the nickname to suit his purpose, what might Jesus have intended in his association with Peter?

The nickname is like a parable: something else and other is meant. In the Middle East, saying one thing and meaning another is a common strategy in communication. It is difficult to imagine "the Rock" betraying and abandoning Jesus in his hour of greatest need, except as a parable. Perhaps this explains Jesus' nickname for Peter. He was not really a rocklike personality, so Jesus gave "Rocky" an ideal to strive for. By Paul's time the nickname had already stuck, but perhaps Paul used it sarcastically. The "pillar/rock" should not collapse or give in to pressure (as Gal. 2:11-14 suggests about Cephas) but should measure up to the nickname's image.

Naming someone or something ordinarily indicates having power over that person or thing. In Genesis 2, the first earthling names all the creatures. This is one way the earthling has dominion over creation (Gen. 1:28). In Genesis 3:28 the earthling names his wife Eve, mother of all living. In this instance, he shows that he understands her nature and distinctiveness and names her appropriately. To give a nickname is to change a person's name. Nicknaming someone demonstrates power and is also an effective means of social control.

A nickname with a negative connotation which conveys invidious personal characteristics is used to this day in the Middle East as an effective means of social control. It is definitely not an image which one would want to live up to. This might be the force of the nickname Jesus gave to James and John: "sons of thunder" (Mark 3:16). Loud and brash as thunder, they made no secret of their ambition to seek privileged places in Jesus' eventual honor (Mark 10:37). How could the ten hear them and not become indignant (Mark 10:41)? On the other hand, if one remembers that thunder in this culture is commonly understood as the voice of the deity or other suprahuman beings (see John 12:28-29), this nickname could have a positive connotation: "echoers of the voice of God." It would help explain why Jesus included these two in his select group.

Collectivistic Personality

It is easy for a Western reader to be misled by the distinctive and colorful names and nicknames that appear in the Bible. One could erroneously conclude that people with such names were individuals like modern Western people with unusual names or common names in an unusual spelling (e.g., Jon for John; or Garry for Gary). The fact is that 80 percent of the current population of the planet are collectivistic personalities. This means that they derive their identity from their focal group, chiefly the family but also the extended family, tribe, nation, and the like. Collectivistic personalities try to hide in the group rather than stand out from it.

One feature of collectivistic personalities like those who populate the pages of the Bible is to present different sides of their personalities to different people. Nabal was a wealthy man with three thousand sheep and a thousand goats, and a man blessed with a beautiful and intelligent wife, Abigail (1 Sam. 25). When David requested provisions from him, Nabal insulted David's emissaries, prompting David to plot revenge. Abigail secretly provisioned David and his men and explained to David: "Nabal is his name, and folly is with him" (v. 25). He acted foolishly in this instance, and perhaps on many other occasions, since he is described as "churlish and ill-behaved" (v. 3). But Fool, which is what Nabal means, may well be the name tradition bestowed on this collectivistic personality, who may have had another name.

Collectivistic personalities tend to stereotype others, identifying them by a generalization. The people Jesus healed are rarely named in the gospels. They are rather stereotyped by their ailment. To know one leper is to know them all! What need of a name or Social Security number? Bar-Timaeus (Mark 10:46) is not the blind man's name. It is a patronym identifying his father. He is the son of Timaeus.

Conclusion

Names are complex realities. Naming and nicknaming people, stereotyping, and calling people names (labeling) are only a few elements of this complexity. And each of these elements is itself subject to nuance. As someone once observed, to every problem or question there is an answer that is direct, simple, and wrong! Explanations of biblical names like those of Paul and Peter that derive from "spurious familiarity" certainly fall into this category. The best remedy for such spurious familiarity is to actually read the Bible and never lose sight of its Middle Eastern cultural context.

8. Photina: The Samaritan Woman

The story of Jesus' encounter with a Samaritan woman at the well of Jacob in Sychar is well known to readers of the Bible (John 4:1-42). It is read on the third Sunday in Lent in Year A of the liturgy for those who use the Common Lectionary. Since this set of readings is associated with the Catechumenate, it is often read also in Years B and C, replacing their own assigned readings. Prior to the nineteenth century, the story was interpreted as a factual report from the actual life of Jesus. Even so, others gave it a symbolic allegorical meaning (e.g., Origen), a sacramental perspective (e.g., Cullmann), or some other spin.

Contemporary biblical scholars recognize that the account is well crafted by the evangelist to make a point in the course of his gospel. In John, the Samaritans represented by this woman quickly come to understand the authentic identity of Jesus (Messiah, Savior of the world). They and the Samaritan woman stand in stark contrast to Nicodemus (John 3:1-21, the story immediately preceding), a ruler of the Judeans and a man of very high status. The woman meets Jesus at high noon. Nicodemus comes to Jesus at night and carries on a conversation with him in which he completely misses Jesus' point and play on words ("again" and "from above").

The dialogue between Jesus and the woman is noteworthy. It proceeds along the lines of a pattern that is repeated frequently in John: statement, misunderstanding, clarification. Jesus makes a statement (e.g., in v. 7 Jesus asks for a drink of water), his conversation partner misunderstands him (in v. 9 the Samaritan woman thinks that he means well water), Jesus clarifies (in v. 10 he says, "I can give you living water"). Moreover, Jesus and the woman each speak seven times. The woman's seven statements proceed from ground zero (an insulting response to Jesus: "Judeans and Samaritans do not interact"; v. 9) to recognition of his identity as Messiah (vv. 25, 29). At the conclusion of the story, the community recognizes him as "the Savior of the world" (v. 42). The sophisticated quality of this literary composition, along with the recognition that centuries-long hostility between Samaritans and Judeans would not be so easily and readily set aside, caused interpreters to read the story somewhat skeptically. Notre Dame biblical scholar Fr. John Meier writes: "All this makes one wary of claiming that behind this magnificent theological composition, foreshadowing as it does the Christian mission to the Samaritans, lies a particular event from the life of the historical Jesus" (Meier 2000: 228-29).

The Eastern Tradition

Recently the Polish biblical scholar Swietłana Wiśniewska published the Eastern Church's interpretation of the Samaritan woman (*Ruch Biblijny I Liturgiczny*, 2004). To begin with, this tradition accepts John 4 as a factual report of an event in the life of Jesus. The woman's name is Photina (in Polish: Swietłana; in Russian: Svetlana), derived from the Greek word for light *(phōs, phōtos)*. The Lord himself is thought to have given her this name, which means "enlightened one" or "the one shining with light." She is said to have had two sons, Joseph (or Josiah) and Victor (also known as Photinus or Photides), and five sisters: Anatolia, Phota, Photida, Parasceve, and Kyriaka.

Tradition says that Photina lived with her younger son, Joseph, in Carthage, where she preached the gospel. Victor, the elder son, was in the

Roman army. As a reward for success in battle, Emperor Nero promoted Victor to a leadership role in the military and assigned him to a city where a certain Sebastian was the official functionary ("mayor"). The emperor also instructed him to persecute Christians there. Sebastian, who knew that Victor was a Christian, advised him to obey the emperor and to cease proclaiming his faith publicly. In the event Victor encountered some untoward event, Sebastian pledged to rescue his mother and brother in Carthage from persecution.

Victor refused this advice and preferred to die rather than to obey Caesar. At this, Sebastian began to threaten Victor and his family. As punishment, God blinded Sebastian for three days and three nights and struck him mute. Regaining his voice at the end, Sebastian loudly acknowledged Christ as the one true God. Victor baptized him and his household. Many fellow citizens followed Sebastian's example, and eventually the news reached Nero, who summoned them all to Rome for judgment, that is, martyrdom. Christ appeared to the entire gathering as they traveled to Rome and pledged that he would remain with them in their imminent suffering for the faith. Victor also received a new name from Christ: Photinus, "because many enlightened by you will turn to me."

At the very same time, Photina, her son Joseph, and all the Christians of Carthage were on their way to Rome in reply to a summons from Caesar. Photina had already learned from God of their imminent suffering. When the group entered Rome, the entire city was stricken by her appearance. Everyone wondered who this woman might be. She was, of course, also accompanied by her five sisters, of whom she was the oldest.

All the Christians refused to obey Nero's command to deny the faith. He sentenced them to harsh torture, but after a few hours it produced no results. They did not even feel any pain. So the family was cast into prison (Photina, her two sons, and Sebastian), but they continued to preach and convert prisoners. The most noteworthy of Photina's converts was Domnina, Nero's daughter. This resulted in further torture, which finally ended in their deaths. Photina spit in Nero's face and, laughing at his stupidity, said: "Oh you profligate blind man, you erring person without a smidgeon of understanding. Perhaps you consider me to be just like yourself, since you wish that I would renounce Christ and offer sacrifice to those blind idols who resemble you?" For this remark, she was drowned in a well.

The Versions

Differing and conflicting versions of the story of Photina, her family and companions are found in many sources but especially the martyrologies. It seems that initially these were drawn up by local congregations and featured persons known to or cherished by each congregation. The Roman martyrology mentions the names of Photina, her sons and sisters, and Sebastian. Their feast was observed on March 20 in the Western church. The eminent historian, Cardinal Cesare Baronius (1538-1607), identified her with the Samaritan woman in John 4. A Greek tradition (around 984 C.E.) noted that Victor was sent to Galilee (another tradition says Gaul, i.e., France; still another, to a place in Italy) to kill Christians there. This martyrology describes their tortures: some are imprisoned with poisonous snakes, some have their eyes plucked out or have their hair pulled out, still others have their male members cut off or are crucified. Victor was torn in two, having been tied to two bent trees, but Photina died in prison. These notices testify to the cultural acceptance of violence and human torture in the ancient Mediterranean world.

Sorting It Out

In the sixteenth century, John Bolland, a Jesuit, was asked to complete the work previously begun by a Dutch colleague to critically evaluate information available about the saints. Bolland resolved to use the work of his predecessor and thought he could complete the task alone and in a short while. When it became overwhelming, he recruited assistance from fellow Jesuits, who eventually became known as the Bollandists. The first critical evaluation of sources (*Acta Sanctorum,* or *Lives of the Saints*) was published in 1643, and the process continued through a bumpy history. In the nineteenth century, the project was oriented along more strictly scientific lines, particularly in line with new philological methods, and it continues until today. The Bollandists presently play a role in "vetting" candidates for canonization. Relative to St. Photina, the Bollandists sorted through the data and concluded that it was spurious and unreliable.

Significance of the Story

Cultural scholars recognize that 80 percent of the current population of the planet are collectivistic personalities living in collectivistic cultures.

They stand in contrast to individualists who seek to stand out from any and every group to which they belong. Individualists relish distinctive names, and even if they carry the same name as their father or grandfather, they are careful to indicate which place in the series they hold, for example, John Smith IV. Collectivistic personalities prefer to be identified by their family (the blind "Bar-Timaeus"). They are also identified by their city ("Jesus of Nazareth") or often stereotyped by some characteristic ("a leper," "a possessed person"). This, of course, is "real life," "how it really is."

Story is different. In traditional storytelling, either the author or the audience will eventually name any anonymous personage. The name is an essential aspect of the human personality, as much as the body, soul, or double counterparts *(doppelgangers)*. In storytelling, the name either has a clear-cut and self-evident meaning (this is certainly true of Photina), or it has an implied, allusive, puzzling, or ambiguous meaning. This latter may be true of the nickname which Jesus bestowed on Simon ("Rock"), since in the gospels Simon is anything but as solid as a rock.

In the story of the Samaritan woman at the well, her name, Photina — whoever may have given it to her — seems to have derived from the context of the story (John 4) and the dyadic relationship she has with Jesus there. Scholars note that in this brief story, she is the most intensely catechized character in the New Testament. She is enlightened personally by Jesus, and she in turn enlightens the townsfolk. In the Byzantine tradition, a Troparion (a chant) of St. Photina, the Samaritan woman, proclaims: "Thou wast illumined by the Holy Spirit/and refreshed by the streams of Christ the Saviour./Having drunk the Water of Salvation/thou didst give copiously to the thirsty./O holy Great Martyr Photina,/Equal-to-the-Apostles, entreat Christ our God that our souls may be saved." Thus it is a small step from the significance of her name to creating a mission of evangelization for her in Carthage. The Bollandists correctly suspected the authenticity of this assignment since she was probably already an adult woman when she met Jesus and would have had to have lived more than sixty years longer to carry on such activity. Such longevity was rare if not impossible in that time and place. Moreover, the Bollandists also find no evidence that Nero had a daughter.

With a name, a character acquires individuality. Photina is no longer a cipher for the Samaritan people, but rather she now holds a place in the social system. She is no longer a woman of puzzling reputation but rather a mother, an elder sister, and even an evangelist. Thus, the name establishes for her a personal identity. And since homonymous names indicate a sharing in another's identity, the woman named Photina bears a very special relationship with Jesus, "the light of the world" (John 8:12; 9:5).

Conclusion

Though largely unfamiliar in the Western tradition, the story of St. Photina carries rich significance in the Eastern Church. Cardinal Baronius included Photina in the Roman martyrology because he was influenced by the tradition that the head of Photina was preserved in the church of St. Paul's outside the Walls in Rome. In the Orthodox tradition (which celebrates her feast on April 2), she is recognized (along with five others) as a powerful intercessor against the demon of lust. Yet another tradition recognizes her efficacy in the healing of trembling or shaking diseases. And so, the story crafted by John the evangelist to make a point in his gospel was detached from that gospel. As a free-standing literary unit, it took on a life of its own and continues to inspire the faithful according to their needs. As honorable as the ancient Eastern tradition may be, the challenge to the Western tradition is to square such pastoral creativity with the 1964 Instruction of the Pontifical Biblical Commission on the Historical Truth of the Gospels to "those who instruct the Christian people in sacred sermons. . . . When they narrate biblical events, let them not add imaginative details which are not consonant with the truth" (par. XIII). The advice would serve all Bible readers in good stead.

9. Naming the Nameless in the Bible

In the previous article, we learned how the nameless Samaritan woman who met Jesus at Jacob's well near Sychar eventually received a name, a family, a vocation to evangelize, and finally a martyr's death. There are many unnamed persons in the Bible who eventually received a name and identity either elsewhere in the Bible or in a tradition or document outside the Bible. At the same time, some biblical documents omit the name of a person identified in another biblical document. The process moves in both directions. We shall present a few examples and propose some plausible explanations.

Adding and Omitting Names in the Bible

The defender of Jesus in the dark Garden of Gethsemane who is nameless in the Synoptics (Mark 15:47, a bystander; Matt 26:51//Luke 22:50, one of Jesus' company) is specifically identified as Peter by John the evangelist (John 18:10), who also identifies the Synoptics' nameless servant of the high priest as Malchus. Thus, the attempt to identify nameless persons in the Bible begins in the biblical tradition itself. Recalling that Peter does not figure honorably or prominently in John's gospel until the very last chapter (an appendix), one might conclude that by naming Peter as the impulsive wielder of a sword in a dark garden, John deliberately chose to reveal yet another unflattering element about Peter. Long considered an intimate associate of Peter's, the evangelist Mark in contrast would understandably want to suppress Peter's senseless behavior. Current scholarship, however, doubts the reliability of Eusebius's report concerning the close relationship of Peter and Mark, hence it is difficult to determine whether or why Mark omitted the name that John reveals.

The reverse process, that is, omitting the name of a previously identified person, is illustrated in the report of the dying/dead daughter of a synagogue official helped by Jesus (Matt. 9:18-21, 23-26//Mark 5:21-24, 37-43//Luke 8:41-42, 49-65). Mark identifies this synagogue ruler as Jairus. Luke repeats the name and office, but Matthew omits it and makes his office generic ("ruler") by also omitting reference to the synagogue. It is futile and speculative to seek an explanation for Matthew's intentional manipulation of his source, Mark's report on these points.

Noah's Nameless Wife

Noah's nameless wife (Gen. 6:18 and throughout) undoubtedly holds the record for names assigned by tradition. Scholars have tallied 103 names from "A" (Abbatissa, Amizra, Amor'a, etc.) to "W" (Wa'ileh, Waliya)! (Though it is the last letter of the English alphabet, "Z" is the 7th of 22 letters in the Aramaic [i.e., Hebrew] alphabet and the 6th of 24 letters in the Greek alphabet). The names of the nameless wives of Noah's sons are not as numerous as those of their mother-in-law, but they add variety to the various lists. An eighth-century manuscript, "*Inventiones Nominum* (Findings of Names)," collected persons mentioned in various parts of Scripture bearing the same name (James 1902-3). The purpose of this handbook was to help students of the Bible to discriminate among them.

The manuscript exists in a few forms, and one (the Albi) adds some detailed notes on the identity of some biblical persons. Regarding the wives of Noah's sons, the manuscript drew on the *Jubilees,* Eutychius, and Epiphanius, among other sources. Later sources such as the Anglo-Saxon *Salomon and Saturn,* the Master of Oxford's *Catechism,* and the Anglo-Saxon *Heptateuch* presented still other names.

Where did these names come from? Francis Lee Utley (1941) proposed a variety of explanations, but five general views prevail. First, varying methods of transliteration from Hebrew to Latin account for half the list of 103 names. Such transliterations were made ages before the establishment of the International Phonetic Alphabet (IPA, 1933), which standardized phonetic laws and symbols. Language students and singers in particular are familiar with the IPA. Secondly, scribal errors — even intentional tampering! — account for a similarly large number of names. Thus Ham's wife was named Nachalatha and/or Nahalath, while Japheth's was Aradshisha and/or Arisisah. The similarity of these names makes it clear that scribal error is probably to blame.

A third source of names is the Bible itself or biblical *onomastica* (a list of names having similar characteristics). What better source for names than the Bible? The similarity of Hebrew names such as Naamah (Gen. 4:22) or Milcah (Gen. 11:29) to Noah's Hebrew name was sufficient to list these as names for Noah's wife. Similarly, the trio of similar-sounding names in the Vulgate such as Oola, Ooliba (Ezek. 23:4), and Oolibama (Gen. 35:25 Vulgate; 36:25 RSV) recommended them as names for the wives of Noah's sons. The main criterion, it seems, was for the name to have good Hebrew form.

A fourth source, classical parallels, would have been especially appealing to Hellenistic Israelites or Christian apologists. Thus the names of Pandora, Rhea, Cybele, Venus, Vesta, and Pyrrha appear in a number of lists for Noah's wife.

Finally, etymological fitness is a fifth source, as we have previously seen in the case of the unnamed woman at the well (John 4). She was called Photina (Svetlana in the Eastern tradition) because she became "enlightened." A number of the names assigned to Noah's wife seem to be etymologically suitable.

Three other explanations — besides pure invention! — are worth considering: aetiology, magic, and ascribed character. Aetiology is a story that tells how something originated. Matthew and Luke offer two different explanations of how the "Field of Blood" in Jerusalem came to be identified with this name. In Matthew the field refers to the blood of Jesus (Matt. 27:8); in Luke (Acts 1:19), the field refers to the blood of Judas. *Jubilees* (7:14-17; around 161-140 B.C.E.) explains that three cities were named after the wives of Noah's sons: Naeltamauk (the wife of Ham), Adataneses (wife of Japheth), and Sedeqetelebab (wife of Shem). We know nothing of the existence or location of these cities nor of Mount Lubar near which the cities were built and where Noah was buried. Nor can we be certain that these are the real names of the wives.

Since he lived in an age when human beings walked and talked with God, Noah was considered to be a person with extraordinary knowledge and power. Hence he was associated with ("good") magical practices, while his son Ham became associated with the devil and black magic. According to *Jubilees* (10:10-14), an angel taught Noah the healing art especially by means of herbs. Noah in turn shared this knowledge with Shem, his firstborn, whom he loved more than all his sons. Since names are very important in the practice of magic, this could help explain the multiplicity of the names of Noah's wife. Her name(s) would be important elements of magical formulae.

Finally, Noah's wife gained the reputation of a wicked woman in tradition. She was associated with Eve, Delilah, Naamah, Wahela (Lot's wife), Pandora, and Semiramis, whose names were also attached to her. Like Eve, Delilah, and Lot's wife, she betrayed her husband to the devil. It was through her (in the legends) that the devil learned that Noah was building an ark and tried to thwart his efforts. She helped the devil to enter the ark and gnaw a hole in the bottom. Like Eve, she used wine to corrupt her husband. All this evil resulted from Noah's wife — also like Eve — having been seduced by the devil (see 4 Macc. 18:7-9).

Naming Other Nameless Men

Everyone knows that the unnumbered and anonymous magi who visited Jesus at his birth (Matt. 2:1-12) are now fixed at three and named Caspar, Melchior, and Balthasar (Metzger 1980: 79-85). On the other hand, the Eastern tradition — especially in Syria — knows that they are twelve in number. Less well known are the names of the shepherds (Luke 2:8-20). Byzantine churches in Cappadocia (about 900 C.E.) name them Sator, Arepo, and Teneton, based on the famous Sator-square (a rebus of five words, as old as 79 C.E. since it was found in the remains of Pompeii). The thirteenth-century Nestorian *Book of the Bee* names seven shepherds:

Asher, Zebulon, Justis, Nicodemus, Joseph, Barshabba, and Jose. A wood-cut in the fifteenth-century French book of devotions (*Heures,* by Simon Vostre) identifies the shepherds as two women — Alison and Mahault — and four men — Aloris, Ysanber, Gobin le Gay, and le beau Roger.

While the Synoptic gospels name twelve disciples selected by Jesus (Mark 3:13-18//Matt. 10:2-4//Luke 6:12-16), Luke alone mentions 70 (or 72) unnamed others (Luke 10:1). The church historian Eusebius (4th cent.) admits that no list of these seventy exists, but he has heard five names: Barnabas, Sosthenes, Cephas, Matthias, and Thaddaeus. About fifty years later, Epiphanius adds to these five the seven "deacons" from Acts 6:5: Stephen, Philip, Prochorus, Nicanor, Timon, Parmenas, and Nicolaus. He also includes Matthias (Acts 1:23), Mark, Luke, Justus, Barnabas and Apelles, Rufus, Niger, and the rest of the seventy-two (*Panarion* 4:3-4). A seventh-century document (*Chronicon Paschale*) covering history from Adam to 629 C.E. presents a complete list, drawing the names from New Testament sources (e.g., Rom. 16; Luke 24:18; etc.). This results in some duplication because the same name appears in a few places (e.g., Tychicus in Eph. 6:21; Tit. 3:12). Nevertheless, the imaginative compiler believed that he was relying on a very trustworthy source.

Naming Other Nameless Women

The Canaanite (Matt. 15:22) or Syrophoenician (Mark 7:25) woman who petitioned Jesus on behalf of her unnamed daughter was Justa, according to the mid-third-century *Pseudo-Clementine Homilies,* and her daughter was Bernice (also spelled Berenice and Beronice). This name is of Macedonian origin and was widely used in the Middle East after the Ptolemies (300 B.C.E.). A fourth-century document (*Gesta Pilati* vii = The Gospel of Nicodemus) claims that the woman suffering from severe menstrual irregularity who was healed by Jesus was named Bernice (Matt 9:20ff.//Mark 5:25//Luke 8:43). Eusebius claims that he saw a bronze statue at Caesarea Philippi that reminded him of this story. The statue depicted a woman kneeling with arms outstretched as if in prayer opposite an upright figure who looked just like Jesus (*Historia Ecclesiastica* 7.18.1-2). Yet according to Arabic sources (*Apocryphal Gospel of John* 26), her name was Yusufiyah or Josiphiah.

Pilate's nameless wife (Matt. 27:19) attracted a Roman-sounding name: Procla. The name of the nameless widow of Nain whose nameless son Jesus raised from the dead (Luke 7:1) was Lia (Leah) or, in the Arabic tradition,

Barsaʿah, daughter of Yuwaʾil (Joel). As for the daughter of Herodias (Matt. 14:6), the *Book of the Bee* reports two traditions: some say that she was called Boziya, but others say that she had her mother's name: Herodias.

Conclusion

The reflections in this article were based upon the meticulous research of the esteemed biblical scholar and text-critic, Bruce Manning Metzger. He published his article ("Names for the Nameless in the New Testament") in 1980 to honor an equally renowned and respected scholar, Johannes Quasten. Metzger concluded that the more-than-two-thousand-year non-stop effort to supply names for the nameless in the Bible is a tribute to two things. On the one hand, there is the remarkable "fertility of pious imagination." On the other, there is an unwillingness to respect the silence and gaps of the biblical narratives. The union of these two elements resulted in a general tendency for traditions to continually emerge and multiply in an effort to leave no nameless person in the Bible unnamed.

As noted above, Francis Lee Utley, the scholar who in 1941 tallied and investigated the 103 names assigned to Noah's wife, offered plausible reasons to explain how the "pious imagination's" effort to supply names for the nameless goes about its task. Both scholars would likely agree that even in our time, nothing has happened to change this human compulsion. The popularity of Mel Gibson's *The Passion of the Christ* and Ron Howard's translation to film of Dan Brown's novel *The Da Vinci Code* attest to the unfailing fertility of pious imagination to flesh out sketchy, high context information, whether in the Bible or in other sources. For the contemporary believer, in each case (tradition and modern film), the result should be humorous and entertaining. Historical facticity will be very meager if it exists at all.

FURTHER READING: PERSONS

de Vaux, Roland. 1965. *Ancient Israel*, vol. 1: Social *Institutions*. New York and Toronto: McGraw Hill.

Eilberg-Schwartz, Howard. 1991. *The Savage in Judaism*. Bloomington: Indiana University Press.

Elliott, John H. 1981. *A Home for the Homeless: A Social-Scientific Criticism of 1 Peter, Its Situation and Strategy*. With a New Introduction. Minneapolis: Fortress.

Fitzmyer, Joseph A. 1990. "Paul." *The New Jerome Biblical Commentary* 79: 1-54.

Hobsbawm, E. R. 1990. *Nations and Nationalism since 1780.* Cambridge: Cambridge University Press.

Hofstede, Geert. 1980. *Culture's Consequences: International Differences in Work-Related Values.* Beverly Hills: Sage Publications.

————. 1994. *Cultures and Organizations: Software of the Mind: Intercultural Cooperation and Its Importance for Survival.* London: HarperCollins.

James, M. R. 1902-3. "*Inventiones Nominum* (Finding of Names)." *The Journal of Theological Studies* 4: 218-44.

James, Paul. 1992. "Forms of Abstract 'Community': From Tribe to Nation and State." *Philosophy of the Social Sciences* 22: 313-36.

Kilner, John F. 1984. "Who Shall Be Saved? An African Answer." Pp. 22-27 in *Choices and Conflict: Explorations in Health Care Ethics.* Edited by Emily Friedman. Chicago: American Hospital Association Publishing, Inc. Reprinted from *Hastings Center Report,* June 1984. Pp. 18-22.

Liverani, Mario. 1992. "Nationality and Political Identity." *Anchor Bible Dictionary* 4: 1031-37.

Malina, Bruce J. 1994. "Religion in the Imagined New Testament World." *Scriptura* 51: 1-26.

————. 1996. "The Mediterranean Self: A Social Psychological Model." Pp. 67-96 in *The Social World of Jesus and the Gospels.* London and New York: Routledge.

Meier, John P. 2000. "The Historical Jesus and the Historical Samaritans: What Can Be Said?" *Biblica* 81: 202-32.

Metzger, Bruce M. 1980. "Names for the Nameless in the New Testament: A Study in the Growth of Christian Tradition." Pp. 79-99 in *New Testament Studies: Philological, Versional, and Patristic.* Leiden: Brill.

The Oxford Classical Dictionary. 1970. Second Edition. Edited by N. G. L. Hammond and H. H. Scullard. Oxford: Oxford University Press.

Pilch, John J. 1994. "Illuminating the World of Jesus with Cultural Anthropology." *The Living Light* 31.1: 20-31.

————. 2008. *Stephen: Paul and the Hellenist Israelites.* Paul's Social Network: Brothers and Sisters in Faith. Collegeville, MN: Liturgical Press.

Stegemann, Ekkehard, and Wolfgang Stegemann. 1999. *The Jesus Movement: A Social History of Its First Century.* Minneapolis: Fortress.

Utley, Francis Lee. 1941. "One Hundred and Three Names of Noah's Wife." *Speculum* 16: 426-52.

Wiśniewska, Swietłana, 2004. "Postać Samarytanki (J 4, 1-42) w tradycji Kościoła wschodniego" ("The Figure of the Samaritan Woman [John 4:1-42] in the Tradition of the Eastern Church"). *Ruch Biblijny i Liturgiczny* 58: 237-47.

Part Four

FAMILY

Every reader of the Bible certainly knows what a family and family issues are. The reader never pauses to consider that this knowledge is culturally specific. All cultures recognize the family as a basic social institution, but each culture has a peculiar understanding of family. A father and mother are basic to every family because they are involved in procreation, in bringing children into the world. However, cultures differ in their understanding of father and mother and children. Some cultures place the father at the center (patriarchal), while other cultures place the mother at the center (matriarchal, or matrifocal).

In this part, we reflect upon the Middle Eastern family and related questions: virgin, marriage, adultery, rape, family, death, and final words. However, our reflections compare cultures: at the very least, Middle Eastern and Western. In some reflections, we introduce information from yet other cultures. The point to note is that while the culture of the people of the Bible is indeed distinct, it is but one culture among many. Other cultures see and interpret the same realities differently. Thus, when Paul says that adulterers will not enter the kingdom of heaven (1 Cor. 6:9-10), what are we to make of cultures which condone it? A larger question arises: Does the God who presumably occasioned the rise of other cultures (Gen. 11:1-9) remain culturally specific? Does God privilege one culture above all others? These are the questions that the social sciences can help address.

1. Virgin

Abraham sent his servant to find a wife for Isaac from among his kin in his own country (Gen. 24:1-4). The culturally preferred marriage partner for a boy in the Middle East is a parallel patrilateral cousin, that is, one's father's brother's daughter (FBD). Thus, the servant went to the city of Nahor (Abraham's brother, Gen. 22:20) in Mesopotamia. He sought God's help in making the right selection, and God responded immediately. Hardly had the servant finished telling God the strategy he would rely on to find the appropriate partner, Rebekah, "who was born to Bethuel, the son of Milcah, the wife of Nahor" (Gen. 24:15), came to the well where the servant rested with his camels. If a reader attends to the information in Genesis 22:20, it would seem that Nahor had no daughters, but his son Bethuel did. Thus, in modern terminology, Rebekah is a first cousin once removed. Not only is she the proper marriage partner, but she is also beautiful and a virgin "whom no man had known" (Gen. 24:16). Why does the sacred author add that description to the word "virgin?"

Virgin

Lexicographers observe that the Hebrew word *bĕtûlâ* and its Semitic cognates in the Ugaritic, Aramaic, Akkadian, and Arabic languages, which are often translated as "virgin," refer primarily to a stage in life, or an age, mainly the age of puberty or just after puberty begins. In other words, the focus is on a young girl of marriageable and childbearing age. Initially the word never contained a reference to physical integrity or virginity as generally understood in the modern, Western world. This understanding of virginity tends to be spelled out in a negative statement in the Hebrew Bible ("whom no man had known").

When the Lord instructed Moses to avenge the people of Israel on the Midianites, the warriors he sent to do this spared the women and children. Moses chided them for this and said: "Kill every male among the little ones, and kill every woman who has known man by lying with him. But all the young girls who have not known man by lying with him, keep alive for yourselves" (Num. 31:17-18). The Hebrew word for young girls in this passage does not necessarily imply virgin in the modern understanding, hence the phrase "not knowing man by not lying with him," that is, "who have never had intercourse," serves that purpose. This phrase is used with the words for women (Num. 31:35), young girls (Num. 31:18), Lot's daughters

(Gen. 19:8), and three times with *bĕtûlâ* (Gen. 24:16; Lev. 21:3; Judg. 21:12), giving specific meaning to that Hebrew word.

Bĕtûlâ Meaning Virgin

There are three occurrences of *bĕtûlâ* without qualification which clearly mean virgin in the sense of physical integrity. The high priest is required to marry a *bĕtûlâ* of his own tribe, and not a widow, or a divorcée, or one who has been shamed (defiled), or a prostitute (Lev. 21:13-14). The context indicates physical integrity. Ezekiel repeats this advice and adds yet another candidate for bride of a priest: "They [levitical priests, sons of Zadok] shall not marry a widow, or a divorced woman, but only a virgin *(bĕtûlâ)* of the house of Israel, *or a widow who is the widow of a priest*" (44:22). Ezekiel's addition of yet another possible marriage partner for a priest, namely, the widow of a priest but not the widow of a layman, strongly suggests that the meaning of virgin is cultural more than purely biological or anatomical.

The third occurrence is the discussion of "[tokens of] virginity" in Deuteronomy 22:13-21. The context is the occasion of a wedding in which the couple is expected to produce a blood-speckled sheet as "proof" either that the bride was indeed physically intact at that time of consummation, or that menstruation occurred shortly before the consummation of the marriage. This second interpretation points once again to the understanding of "virgin" as one who is of marriageable, that is, especially of childbearing age. The issue in this case is economic rather than sexual. In Deuteronomy 22:13-21, the husband may have been attempting to recoup the bride price if his charge that she was not a virgin when they married could not be refuted. Or he may have been trying to make certain that he could retain her irrevocably if his charge was refuted. Thus even where physical integrity seems to be clear, other meanings are not far removed.

Bĕtûlâ Meaning Young

There is one instance where the word *bĕtûlâ* standing alone definitely does not mean virgin in the sense of physical integrity. "Lament like a virgin girded with sackcloth for the bridegroom of her youth" (Joel 1:8). The entire community is exhorted to lament and turn again to the Lord. Once again the reference is to the woman being young. This is similar to the twelve or so passages in which *bĕtûlâ* is paired with another Hebrew word meaning young man *(bāḥûr):* "Praise the LORD! . . . Young men *(bāḥûrîm)* and maidens *(bĕtûlôt)* together, old men and children!" (Ps. 148:12). Clearly the two words together mean the same thing: young people. Physical virginity does not enter the picture at all.

Other Meanings

The Greek word *parthenos* that often translates *bĕtûlâ* has a similarly wide array of meanings. Essentially the word describes a maid, maiden, virgin, or girl. "If a girl *(parthenos)* marries, she does not sin" (1 Cor. 7:28). When used in the masculine form (e.g., Rev. 14:4), it may mean an unmarried man, or a man married only once (but see below). The emphasis is thus on a state of life (not married) and not on a sexual condition. Paul also uses the word in this sense (unmarried, a female marriageable teenager who is not a widow): "Now concerning the unmarried *(parthenon)*, I have no command of the Lord . . ." (1 Cor. 7:25). The five appearances of the word in 1 Corinthians (7:25, 28, 34, 37, 38) each carry different meanings, reflecting different perspectives. Luke uses the word *(parthenoi)* to describe the four unmarried daughters of Philip the evangelist (Acts 21:9). Matthew's report of one of Jesus' parables refers to ten maidens or wedding attendants *(parthenoi,* Matt. 27:1, 7, 11), some of whom came prepared and some who didn't. Luke describes the prophetess Anna as an old woman, "having lived with her husband seventy years from her virginity *(parthenia)*" (Luke 2:36). Clearly the word is best understood as marriage or entry into marriage.

Other epitaphs at Rome clearly identify as *parthenoi* some young married women who bore children but who died in youth. Again, the emphasis is on age rather than sexual condition. From such inscriptions, Josephine Ford suggests that the word might indicate being married only once. The importance of being married only once figures prominently in the Pastoral Epistles (e.g., 1 Tim 3:2 — bishop; 5:9 — widow).

The 144,000 "virgin" males *(parthenoi)* mentioned in Revelation (14:4) who did not defile themselves with women are in all likelihood those "sons of God" who did not cross cosmic species boundaries to take human wives and produce the notorious giants that existed before the Flood as their deviant colleagues did (Gen. 6:1-4). Human sexual intercourse does not entail defilement since both male and female are of the same species. The undefiled sons of God, on the other hand, did come to earth but did not intermingle with humans. They were not liars and deceivers as were their celestial colleagues. God's reward for remaining faithful to the divine purpose and plan was to restore them to their rightful honorable status ("re-deem them"). The emphasis is not so much on their sexual condition or activity as on their remaining faithful to God and God's plan.

The Virgin Mary

Only Matthew and Luke associate the word *parthenos* with Mary, the mother of Jesus. At the very end of his report of events attending the birth of Jesus, Matthew (1:23) cites the Greek translation of Isaiah 7:14, "Behold, a virgin [Greek *parthenos;* Hebrew *'almâ*] shall conceive and bear a son, and his name shall be called Emmanuel." Matthew interprets the events concerning Mary as fulfillment of this prophecy. Of course, prophets spe-cialized in learning and proclaiming the will of God for their here and now. Isaiah could not see seven hundred years into the future. He was speaking of a young girl of marriageable and childbearing age whose son-soon-to-be-born would continue the Davidic line jeopardized by the fool-ishness of King Ahaz. The very Hebrew word Isaiah used connotes these ideas. Scholars point out that that passage in Isaiah never referred to a vir-ginal concept before the New Testament sacred writers used it. Even though the Septuagint, the Greek translation of the Old Testament, ren-ders *'almâ* by *parthenos,* this latter word in the Septuagint often means quite simply "girl" or "young woman." For early believers, including Mat-thew, however, this Greek quotation strengthened their already existing belief that Mary's conception of Jesus was the work of God's Spirit.

Luke, who did not know Matthew's report, says that God sent the angel Gabriel "to a virgin *(parthenos)* betrothed to a man whose name was Jo-seph, of the house of David; and the virgin's name was Mary" (Luke 1:27). Taken by itself, this statement and the word "virgin" mean that she is not yet married but is betrothed. By itself, it makes no reference to physical in-tegrity. It is rather the fuller context which provides an equivalent to the statement that appears with *bĕtûlâ* in the Old Testament: "How shall this be, since I have no husband?" The marriage between Joseph and herself has already been arranged, and it is very likely going to take place. So Mary's statement in effect declares her physical integrity.

Conclusion

The precise origins of the belief in the virginal conception of Jesus by Mary are difficult to identify from a historical point of view. What this brief review of the use of some Hebrew and Greek words for virgin indicates is that in no case do these words *alone* mean virgin in the sense that we understand this word today. However, precisely such an interpretation with regard to Mary the mother of Jesus emerged quickly, it seems, in the believing community to underscore Jesus' conception as the work of God. That is reflected in the Infancy Narratives of Matthew and Luke from the end of the first century C.E.

Even so, in 1978, an ecumenical group of twelve biblical scholars (including Catholics, Episcopalians, Lutherans, a German Reformed, and a Presbyterian) reviewing the presentation of *Mary in the New Testament* recorded an interesting conclusion. Completing their study of Matthew 1:25 in context (that Joseph "knew her not until . . ."), the scholars suggested that "a likelihood arises that (according to Matthew's understanding) Joseph did come to know Mary after Jesus' birth and that they begot children" (Brown et al. 1978: 87). An exhaustive investigation by John Meier reviews that and subsequent studies and concludes that "the most probable opinion is that the brother and sisters of Jesus were true siblings" (Meier 1991: 332). The notion of Mary's perpetual virginity did not become common teaching until the latter half of the fourth century. Over time, this understanding developed further and is of course a central belief in many Christian churches today. The value of our cultural reflections and historical insights is that they help us appreciate that we are heirs of more than two thousand years of investigation guided by the Holy Spirit. It wasn't always the way we understand it now.

2. Marriage

Quite often the most familiar of human experiences is difficult to define. Anthropologists define marriage as a socially recognized bond between two persons of opposite sex, with culturally variable implications, including economic cooperation, the transfer or sharing of property rights, sanctioned sexual intimacy, and the legitimation of children resulting from the union. Through marriage, sexuality and procreation are given specific cultural meanings. Husband and wife, mother and father, son and daughter are culturally defined roles that are largely determined by that culture's interpretation of the genders. Status, or relative standing in a given society (higher, lower), is linked with gender and age and through them with roles associated with each gender and age. Moreover, these roles include mutual rights and responsibilities, but specialists find it difficult to define a consistent set of rights or statuses established by marriage in all cultures. That explains why some experts offer a simple definition of marriage as a "bundle of rights."

Marriage in the Hebrew Bible

These experts further observe that marriage as a recognized category of social relationship is not a universal phenomenon. A good number of languages, including biblical Hebrew, have no word for marriage! In the Hebrew Bible, the typical phrase is "to take (or give) a woman or daughter as wife" (Gen. 19:14; 28:1; 34:8; etc.). Another phrase is "to give a woman a dwelling"; woman here would be understood as wife (Neh. 13:27). The word translated as "intermarry" in Ezra 9:14 derives from the verb "to circumcise." It is an action by which a male "makes himself a son-in-law" or "selects a certain man as his father-in-law" from among the people of this land. The reference is the practice by which fathers-in-law sometimes circumcised the bridegroom just before the wedding.

The phrase "to take/give" a woman as wife situates the process in this culture within the context of gaining a possession, a new property. The groom's family pays a price (Heb. *mōhar*, bride-price) to acquire the woman for him as wife (Gen. 34:12; Exod. 22:16-17; 1 Sam. 18:25). As a result, the groom becomes the *ba'al* (translated "owner" or "lord"), and the woman is the *bĕ'ulat-ba'al* (Deut. 22:22, translated as "wife"). Of course, in the larger cultural picture the woman is more than property, and a simplistic view of the matter is untenable. Marriage in the Bible, thus, is not a religious event. It is essentially an agreement between two families to unite their families through these two representatives. The intended result is to strengthen both families. Only twice in the Bible is marriage referred to as a covenant. Ezekiel describes God's acceptance of Judah with this word: "I plighted my troth to you and entered into a covenant with you, says the Lord GOD, and you became mine" (Ezek. 16:8; see also Mal. 2:14). The concept of covenant is a subdomain in the linguistic semantic field of association. Particularly in tribal cultures a covenant is a very significant human bond. Sometimes it lasts a lifetime and might entail willingness to die for that relationship. Clearly in the Israelite interfamily context it was a two-sided bond, a result of negotiation and perhaps even compromise. (A written contract is mentioned for the first time in Tob. 7:14). In Israelite ideology, the covenant of God with Israel originated by divine initiative.

Forms of Marriage

Anthropologists analyze marriage patterns by studying the rules governing recruitment of marriage partners and the structure of the family unit. There are two general sources for marriage partners: within the group (endogamy or inmarriage) and beyond the group (exogamy or outmarriage; http://anthro.palomar.edu/marriage/marriage_2.htm). In general endogamy appears .to have prevailed in the patriarchal period (http://www .umanitoba.ca/faculties/arts/anthropology/tutor/case_studies/hebrews/ patriarchs.html). The most common preferential pattern in endogamy is cross-cousin marriages, for example, one's mother's brother's daughter, or one's father's sister's son, or variations. Isaac receives Rebekah as his bride (Gen. 24). She is the daughter of Bethuel, who was a son of Nahor, Abraham's brother, thus a first cousin once removed (Gen. 22:20; 24). Jacob finds his wives among the daughters of Laban (i.e., cousins), the brother of Jacob's mother, Rebekah (Gen. 28:2; 29:12).

But endogamy and exogamy are not mutually exclusive. In India, one must marry outside of one's lineage (lineage exogamy) but within one's caste (caste endogamy). Joseph married an Egyptian (Gen. 41:45). Moses married a Midianite (Exod. 2:21)/Cushite (Num. 12:1). Bathsheba, an Israelite woman, was married to Uriah the Hittite (2 Sam. 11:3). From the monarchy forward the endogamous pattern seems to have been gradually replaced by exogamy. At the time of the exile, Ezra and Nehemiah concluded that exogamy (marriage with non-Israelites) was in large measure the cause of the exile. God punished exogamy and preferred endogamy. Hence Ezra called for a return to endogamy (Ezra 9–10; Neh. 13:23-27).

The modern concern that endogamous marriages contribute to serious health problems was seriously challenged in the *Journal of Genetic Counseling* (Bennett et al. 2002). Research indicates that the incidence of birth defects among children of such unions is only two to four percentage points above the average. The researchers concluded that there is no need to offer genetic testing on the basis of consanguinity alone. Moreover, the cultural advantages of endogamy seem to outweigh the risks. Families have greater certitude about the qualities of prospective marriage partners, and family solidarity is strengthened.

Family structure also varies. Clearly, the patriarchs were polygamists along the lines of polygyny. In this setting, the women are all of equal status, as is clearly the case in sororal polygyny where Jacob married the sisters, Rachel and Leah (Gen. 29:1-20). A polygamous family structure tends to produce rival wives (e.g., Sarah and Hagar, Gen. 16:1-6; Hannah and Peninnah, 1 Sam. 1; etc.; compare Prov. 30:23). The proverbs concerning contentious wives are quite likely about such rival wife situations (Prov. 19:13; 21:9, 19; 25:24; etc.). Given the gender-based division of space in such cultures, it is not the men with whom these women contend but rather with each other in the women's quarters. David had seven named wives (1 Sam. 18:17-30; 25:38-43; 2 Sam. 3:2-5), and Solomon had many more than that (1 Kings 3:1; 11:3).

Lest a reader draw an erroneous conclusion from the extravagances of David and Solomon, it is important to remember that polygyny is a way of producing many sons. At the beginning of the twentieth century in the United States, a woman had to bear 6.1 children just to reproduce herself. Mortality rates were even higher in antiquity. Thus, not only did polygyny produce a large and necessary workforce, but it made the family strong. "Sons are guns" (Ps. 127:3-5). There are no instances of polyandry in the Bible.

Arranging the Marriage

As already noted, the purpose of marriage in many cultures of the world including ancient Israel is to strengthen two families by uniting them. Fathers made the arrangements (Gen. 24:2; 38:6; Deut. 7:3). Since women (by whom the boys were raised until the age of puberty along with the girls; see 2 Tim. 1:5) knew the potential partners far better, they proposed the appropriate partners to the fathers, who made the arrangement public and formal. Since children are God's gifts and not simply something parents produced on their own (Ps. 127:3), the match arranged by the parents is also God's doing: "What therefore God has joined together, let not man put asunder" (Matt. 19:6).

At the proper time, most likely the occurrence of the girl's menarche, the couple was betrothed. This is not equivalent to engagement in the modern world. Engaged couples select one another as partners. Betrothed couples are matched by their families usually without input or approval of the partners. The Israelite tradition did not distinguish between a betrothed and a married woman. The couple was obliged to marital fidelity, and infidelity at this time was a punishable crime (Deut. 22:23-29). This, of course, was part of Joseph's dilemma when he learned of Mary's condition (Matt 1:18-19). Was Mary unfaithful? Would he have to punish her as the Torah required, or would he pretend that he was guilty and look like a cuckold to the village? Not an enviable dilemma. Usually some time elapsed between the betrothal and the time at which the man took the woman into his home in the patriarchal compound. This "taking of the woman" into his home is what is called "marriage" in the Bible (recall that this is the phrase ["taking of the woman"] commonly used in the Hebrew Bible).

The Marriage

During the betrothal period, each partner continues to reside in the father's compound. In a patriarchal culture, the father lives with all his sons, single and married, and the unmarried daughters in a large compound. Men never move out. The women leave their paternal home and move into the compound of the husband's father. The couple will have their gender-divided "home" in this compound. This is the appropriate cultural context for understanding Genesis 2:24: "Therefore a man leaves his father and mother and cleaves to his wife, and they become one flesh." It would be social suicide for a son to remove himself from the patriarchal compound. Not only would he be abandoning the source of meaning and subsistence in his life, but he would find all life-sustaining networks severed as well. This passage in Genesis does not really serve as a warrant for monogamy. That would be reading into it something the author and his culture could not have intended. That would be eisegesis.

At the prearranged time (required for arranging the feasting that would accompany the event), the groom went with "the friend of the bridegroom" (John 3:29; see Judg. 14:20) and other close boyhood friends to the home of the bride's father in order to fetch her. It seems that in ancient Judea there were two such "friends" (one from the groom's side and one from the bride's), but in Galilee this was not common. Indeed, the "steward of the feast" (John 2:8) at Cana appears to have played the role of "friend of the bridegroom" there.

The essence of "marriage" was "taking the woman" from her father's household to the compound of the groom's father (Tob. 7:13; Matt. 25:5-6). An oath might have been pronounced (Ezek. 16:8, "pledging troth"), and perhaps a blessing was spoken (Gen. 24:60; Tob. 7:12). But the family and the entire village waited patiently and enthusiastically for proof of the consummation (Deut. 22:13-21). "Tokens of virginity" were the blood-speckled sheets that "proved" the bride had been a virgin and remained faithful until this moment. It was also "proof" that the groom was capable of being a father. The whole purpose of this union was to join two families and to strengthen them. Strength will come to the patriarch's family from more children but especially sons. Girls will bring strength to the family if they can be matched at the right time with a partner from another strong family. Imagine the pressure such a public expectation placed on the groom.

Divorce

Since marriage in Israel (and in other circum-Mediterranean cultures, e.g., Greece) is the fusion of the honor of two families, divorce is the rupture of this union. It is the painful and shameful separation of these two families. This is no simple matter and can carry serious consequences. Divorce will lead to feuding, which may escalate to violence and might erupt into a bloodshed. If this happens, there will be a blood feud between the families forever. From this perspective, it is hardly surprising that Jesus was opposed to divorce (Matt. 19:1-9//Mark 10:1-12). That would be disastrous. It is also for this reason that Jesus termed "mediators" truly honorable (Matt 5:9; commonly translated "peacemakers"). On another occasion, he himself was honored to be invited to mediate between two feuding brothers. However, noting that the request was rooted in greed, Jesus declined the invitation (Luke 12:13-15).

The more serious concern for Jesus groups was remarriage (presumably after the death of a spouse), that is, second marriages. The Pastor proposed that candidates for the leadership position in a community be married only once (1 Tim. 3:2). Young widows posed a special concern because the family might remarry them. Hence, a "true" widow was one who was at least sixty years old and married only once (1 Tim 4:9). In contemporary China, there is a similar concern on the part of children concerning a widowed parent. Some threaten suicide if the surviving parent should remarry. The basis of the concern, of course, varies from culture to culture. Scholars are not agreed on the basis upon which the Pastor based his concern.

Conclusion

With the passage of time after Jesus' death and resurrection, Jesus groups had to face the challenge of living after the pattern of the life of Jesus in a different (and sometimes hostile) environment. As the first six chapters of Daniel offered such advice to Israelites living in Maccabean times, so too did the sacred writers of letters which include "tables of household rules" (Eph. 5:21–6:9; Col. 3:18–4:1; and 1 Pet. 2:13–3:12). These "rules" were intended in part to help families live exemplary lives in Greco-Roman culture by adopting certain values of that culture.

Believers who do not live in Mediterranean culture of the past or present hold different beliefs about marriage and observe very different customs. No matter where a believer lives, the challenge is to shape those beliefs and customs according to Jesus' teaching about the will of God on this subject. A literal imitation of biblical practices in the matter of marriage would not only be impossible apart from that cultural setting. It would be disastrous if attempted. Thus, the scholarly practice of beginning to analyze a human problem in all its cultural complexity and then turning to Scripture heuristically makes very good sense. Understanding one's own culture on its own terms and appreciating the Mediterranean culture of our ancestors in faith help a believer begin to build a bridge between the two.

3. Family

Like marriage, family is a notoriously difficult word to define. The anthropological definition of family is "a core group of closely related, cooperating kin, encompassing two or more generations, whose members (affines excluded) are prohibited from sexual relations." (Affines are in-laws.) Anthropologists further observe that such a family, that is, a two-generation (also called nuclear) family, is a "universal human social grouping" which provides four indispensable functions: sexual, economic, reproductive, and educational. These could be viewed as four major roles that are shaped by the respective status of each family member: father, mother, and child. Father and mother participate in all four roles, but the child only in economic (as a pair of working hands) and educational roles (as the learner of skills and values).

Euro-American custom has tended to view the family unit as based upon the conjugal bond (husband and wife). In Euro-American experience, marriage and family are inseparably linked, but this is not a universal phenomenon. Many societies place primary emphasis on blood ties as the focal symbol in structuring the family unit. This most certainly is the case with ancient Israel. Remember that they marry endogamously, or blood relatives. Indeed, the Bible uses a wide range of Hebrew words to describe kinship relations. These are often translated in English as "family," but clearly the family envisioned in these texts is not at all like the Western grouping that the English word "family" brings to mind.

Family in the Hebrew Bible

In antiquity, the social organization of Israel's neighbors involved a stratified hierarchy (social and economic) with kings and elites at the top (2 to 10 percent of the population) and a huge peasant population that supported them at the bottom. In contrast, Israel emerged along the lines of tribal kinship groups (tribes, clans, families) initially without a monarchy, that is, a hierarchical centralized power-wielding elite core. We date Abraham to 1800 B.C.E., and Saul the first king to just before 1000 B.C.E.

The three main words associated with "family" in biblical Hebrew (and often translated by that word) are *šēbeṭ* (tribe), which includes *mišpāḥâ* (clans, referring to territory as well as to families), and *bêt 'āb* (house or household of the father-patriarch, i.e., the extended family). Examining the roles of members of the clan and family gives interesting insight. Biblical scholar Norman Gottwald (1979) has described the clan *(mišpāḥâ)* as a "protective association of extended families." Its socioeconomic role was chiefly *restorative*. This means that the clan exercised a set of emergency behaviors or actions that were intended to restore member families in the clan to autonomy when the family itself was unable to do this.

The chief player in this scheme of things was the *gō'ēl*, the next-of-kin or kinsman-redeemer, who fulfilled a variety of such restorative roles. Sirach praises the father who raises a son properly with appropriate physical discipline, because such a son will be "an *avenger*, a *gō'ēl*, a next-of-kin, a kinsman-redeemer, against his [father's] enemies, and one to repay the kindness of his [father's] friends" (Sir. 30:6). Such sons are like arrows in the hand of a warrior (Ps. 127:3-5). Thus, the kinsman-redeemer was expected to avenge the murder of a relative (or rape of a sister; Num. 35:9ff.), to raise a male heir to his brother who died childless (levirate marriage; Deut. 25:5-10), to redeem land lost within the clan (understood as territory; Lev. 25:23-28), and to maintain (= support) a fellow kinsman and/or his dependents or redeem them from debt (Lev. 25:35-55). The military role of clan members was to provide men for the army in time of war. The Hebrew numeral translated as "one thousand" *('elep)* also served as a synonym for *mišpāḥâ*, thus reflecting this clan obligation.

Family as a Small Unit

The *bêt 'āb* (literally, "house of the father"; but usually translated family) was the most important small unit among the people from whom the collectivistic individual Israelite drew identity. Collectivistic personalities characterize 80 percent of the cultures on our planet at the present time. The percentage was definitely much higher in antiquity. In the collectivistic Israelite family, a member felt included without reservation, a member to be protected in any need, and in turn the member developed a strong sense of responsibility to others in the family. This was a large, extended family that included all the male descendants of the still living patriarch/ancestor. The *bêt 'āb* described the family as well as the housing compound in which they lived. Perhaps as many as fifty to one hundred persons could live in this compound. The reconstructed model of "Peter's house" in Capernaum, which can be viewed at the Museum of the Studium Biblicum Franciscanum, at the Second Station, Via Dolorosa, in Jerusalem, is a good illustration of such a compound. One can see in this model Jesus' dwelling (Mark 2:1), to which he relocated after he left Nazareth. It was located in the compound of Jonah the patriarch, father of Simon and Andrew, who also lived there with their siblings and families. Such a "nuclear extended family" and its members played four important roles: economic, judicial, didactic, and covenantal.

The *bêt 'āb* possessed its own ancestral land, with which it could be economically self-sufficient. This land was inalienable; it might not be sold (1 Kings 21). The Jubilee Year, although never actually implemented in Israel, was established to make sure that ancestral land that had somehow been lost would be returned to the original *bêt 'āb* (Lev. 15). This family was also the basic judicial forum deciding matters of marriage (Gen. 27:46–28:5) and divorce, and discipline of sons (Prov. 13:24; 19:18; 22:15; 23:13-14). The case of the rebellious son (Deut. 21:18-21) indicates that only when internal resources failed was the matter brought before the elders. Here, too, these elders were senior males of each household who gathered at "the gate" and adjudicated cases brought before their group (Deut. 22:19; Prov. 22:22; etc.).

The family was also the first school of the child. Here gender-linked obligations were taught and the traditions, stories, myths, laws, and so on were passed on by the head of the house (Deut. 6:4-9; 11:18-25; 32:46-47). The firstborn son played a very special role in the family (Exod. 13:2, 12-15; 22:29) because he linked each family with Yahweh, who smote the firstborn of the Egyptians but spared the Hebrew firstborn as a pledge of protection through all generations (Exod. 12). Finally, the family was central in the covenant relationship of Yahweh to all of Israel. The prophetic preaching against the usurpation of family land was in large measure due to concern that loss of the patrimony would break that covenant relationship (e.g., Isa. 5:8-10; Mic. 2:1-3).

Individualistic and Collectivistic Families

It would surely seem that a key role for men and women in families of all cultures could be derived from the biblical notion of clan as a "protective association of extended families." Scholars point out that Western value systems associated with individualism are divisive and isolating. Moreover, such individualism characterizes only 20 percent of the current population of our world! The overwhelming majority of the world's cultures are collectivistic, group-centered, and group-oriented cultures. Their value system is unifying or conjunctive, as is evident from what was said above. Individual hopes, aspirations, and endeavors are always subordinated to a concern for preserving the well-being of the group. That's what distinguishes a "collectivistic individual or person" from an "individualistic individual or person."

Collectivistic groups defer to "tradition" and accept it as valid and normative. The author of 2 Thessalonians exhorts believers to "stand firm and hold to the traditions which you were taught by us, either by word of mouth or by letter" (2 Thess. 2:15). Tradition is the handing down of established and time-proven wisdom collected by the group. This tradition both grounds and includes identification with the culture (Exod. 10:2; 12:26; 13:8; Deut. 4:9; 6:7, 20-25; 32:7, 46). Tradition roots and nourishes family structure, which in its turn perpetuates tradition. The process is circular.

Status and Roles

Tradition and group orientation highlight the importance placed upon authority at every level of biblical society. It is God who ascribes statuses and roles. The thinking in collectivistic society is that since God alone determines gender, and society determines the status associated with each gender, God determines an individual's status. The same is true of roles, since no status in any culture can ever be separated from a role. Thus in the basic institution of family, parents are to be honored (Mark 7:10) since

God assigned that status to this specific couple. Yet culture assigns different roles to these statuses. The majority of anthropologists understand roles as the full set of *actual* behaviors that go along with a status. This is also known as "role performance," that is, the complete enactment of the rights and duties of one's status.

Roles are reflected in the "codes of household duties," which begin to emerge in the traditions of later Jesus groups (Eph. 5:21–6:9; Col. 3:18–4:1; and 1 Pet. 2:13–3:12). Scholars believe that these "codes" originated in the Hellenistic discussions about household management. Surprising as it may seem to many, Mediterranean culture in general and the biblical world in particular were indeed concerned with order and harmony. The questions faced by later Jesus groups was how to live out their new life in Christ within the framework of the natural and social orders recognized by the society in which they found themselves. Thus it was of great importance to teach and practice loyalty and faithfulness. Sons must honor and obey fathers; slaves should obey their masters. Even Jesus was praised for his faithfulness to God (Heb. 3:1-3) and his unswerving obedience (Heb. 5:8; Rom. 5:14-21).

Conclusion

As is evident in the biblical examples given above, if a single family is unable to meet any of its needs, the broader association of extended families is ever ready to lend a helping hand. Thus, a primary role within the family for men and women in collectivistic cultures would be to reflect upon the unifying features of their value systems and work at further developing and strengthening them. Group orientations urge individuals not to seek their own good, their own individualistic objectives and plans, but always to "seek the good of the neighbor" (1 Cor. 10:24). Promoting one's own interests, whether by an improper marriage as in 1 Cor. 5:6-8 or by eating proscribed foods as in 1 Cor. 8:1-2, 7-11, rejects a sense of accountability to the group. Yet precisely such accountability lies at the heart of group-centered cultures. Promoting and affirming such accountability is important in families, from which that sense will also extend to the broader, group-centered society.

A second conclusion that suggests itself from our reflection on family in the Bible is to initiate or reinvigorate the "redeemer's" roles available to men and women in any given culture. From the perspective of a collectivistic, that is, group-centered society, the answer to Cain's question,

"Am I my brother's keeper?" (Gen. 4:9), is a resounding "Yes!" Modern versions of protective associations of families might be the village or the city neighborhood, or something similar. It need not be formal. In fact, most often it isn't. Such a concern for others, which is rather customary in group-centered culture, is often lacking in individualistic cultures. There, such a concern would be considered an unwelcome intrusion into other people's affairs. Bible readers from individualistic cultures should feel challenged rather than comforted by the examples of their collectivistic ancestors in the faith. Individualist cultures have much to learn from group-centered cultures. Now would be a good time to begin building the bridge between the two types of cultures.

4. Adultery

According to Paul, adulterers — one category of people unconcerned with the honor of others — will not inherit the kingdom of God (1 Cor. 6:9-10). Who in fact are adulterers? What is adultery? Given many basic differences between Middle Eastern and Western cultures, one needs to pose the question in a different way. Some proper questions to ask are: "What sort of behavior was labeled adultery in first-century Israel?" "What did the label 'adulterer' mean at that time?" The answer is that adultery in the biblical world meant dishonoring a male by having sexual relations with his wife (or one of his wives). By this understanding, only a male could commit adultery! As such, it is an exclusively male activity. A woman, whether willing or not, could be caught in adultery but was incapable of committing it. Notice that in Middle Eastern culture, adultery is not about sex or sexual infidelity. It is about shame: one male shames another by taking advantage of the woman that male is supposed to protect.

In the patriarchal social system of ancient Israel, adultery was only one of a set of male actions that dishonored or shamed other males. The cultural obligation of a shamed or dishonored male is to defend his honor and to take revenge either personally or through the kinsman-redeemer. Adultery thus inevitably leads to feuding. Just like the rest of the "thou shalt not's" of the final five of the Ten Commandments, the prohibition of adultery looks to prohibiting attacks on male honor that would end in in-group feuding. The Ten Commandments are concerned with inner Israelite peace and harmony by prohibiting behaviors that would lead to ongoing feuds.

Of course, the inevitable problem with exporting biblical morality to people whose social system is alien to that of ancient Israel is that of what sense the culturally specific moral injunctions of ancient Israel might have for members of other cultures. For example, one anthropological study of 112 societies discovered that in 56 percent of them, husbands are not officially condemned for adulterous liaisons, while only in 12 percent of these same societies is such behavior on the part of a wife tolerated. This reflects a discriminatory, gender-based standard in many cultures that extends over millennia. Men are excused much more often than women (Broude 1994: 275).

At the extreme, ethnographic information about the Lesu, a Melanesian society in New Ireland (part of an archipelago belonging to Papua New Guinea), indicates that husbands and wives are not only allowed but expected to have sexual liaisons with persons other than those given to them in marriage! Exclusive sexual relations with one's marriage partner(s) in this society, particularly among the young, is considered abnormal (Broude 1994: 275). Are such people committing adultery? Are such people doomed not to inherit the kingdom of God?

Adultery

To understand the meaning of adultery in the Bible, one must begin with the meaning of marriage. At an abstract level, cross-culturally, marriage is the process of binding or bonding two or more parties with a view to producing offspring and mutual support (see the discussion on marriage in Part Two above). This definition is rather vague since each of its parts allows for a range of applications. For example, is the process of binding or bonding a contract, a customary agreement, a temporary arrangement (until children are grown), or what? And who are the parties to the marriage? An individual male and one female? Or an individual male and multiple females? Or does the marriage join two extended families with one providing a male and the other providing a female to symbolize the union? Are the individual male and female(s) in the marriage expected to "belong" to each other? Or does each one adhere to the particular family of origin? Or is the male or female expected to adhere to the family of the male or female? And to whom do the offspring belong? To the husband, to the husband's family, to the wife, to the wife's family, to both husband and wife together, to the larger clan? These questions derive from information learned by anthropologists through their study of diverse societies. As these questions indicate, it is best to treat marriage as a culturally specific set of behaviors rather than some abstract universal human institution. What these questions point up is that while all peoples on the planet have the institution of marriage, the meanings ascribed to marriage are culturally specific. Hence instead of speaking about "marriage," it is more useful and more precise to speak of U.S. mainstream marriage, ancient Mediterranean, Roman, Greek, or Israelite marriage, and the like.

The same is true of "adultery." While in the United States this word usually refers to deviant marital behavior, for example, "extramarital sexual relations," whether by the husband or the wife, such is not the case in ancient Israel, as noted above. To take another example, while our U.S. definition of marriage refers to a bond between two persons of opposite sex, among some groups in East and South Africa sometimes both partners are female (Shapiro 1997: 304-7). One female assumes certain aspects of the male role, though obviously a surrogate genitor is needed to produce a child. This female "husband" is recognized as such by everyone locally. She is acknowledged as a true partner in this union and not simply as a woman acting as a man. This cultural example explains why specialists agree that "marriage" and "adultery" (if it exists in a given culture) must be viewed and interpreted within the context of extremely varied roles for women and men in the variety of kinship forms.

A Variety of Marriage Strategies

Since marriage in the Old Testament was neither a religious nor a civil institution but rather the fusion of the honor of two families determined by the respective patriarchs, any discussion of divorce or extramarital sex must also take place within the context of the Middle Eastern understanding of honor. There are a number of common features in ancient Middle Eastern marriage, but perhaps the most notable is that the female of one family is embedded in a male of another family, namely, her husband (and his family). The wife's social standing is henceforth intimately bound up with the honor of the husband (and his family). Divorce was the disembedding of the female from the honor of the male (and his family) together with a fresh redistribution and return of the honor of the two families involved, often with endless recriminations against the female's family and feuding. Extramarital sexual relations in this same context and from this same perspective were sometimes acceptable and sometimes unacceptable, depending in particular upon the changing perceptions of women. Malina has outlined these perceptions in his review of the variety of marriage strategies that can be identified in the biblical period (Malina 2001: 134-60). The strategies are conciliatory ("I the husband permit extramarital sex if it is to my benefit"), aggressive ("I struggle with you to gain supremacy over you, hence I will capture your women but protect mine"), or defensive ("I will ignore the women of other groups and stay only with the women of my group").

The Patriarchal Period (1800 B.C.E.): Conciliatory Strategy

The preferred marriage partner for a boy in the Middle East has for millennia been a patrilateral parallel cousin, a father's brother's daughter. For example, according to Genesis 24:15, Isaac married Rebekah, the daughter of his first cousin, Bethuel, who was the son of Nahor, brother to Abraham, who was Isaac's father. One needs a chart to keep the relations straight, and it is very advisable to do that while reading these passages in the Bible! However, wives and daughters were used to the patriarch's advantage when necessary. This is a conciliatory strategy. Abraham readily offered his wife Sarah to the Pharaoh to preserve his own life (Gen. 12:10-20). Even in the presence of their prospective husbands (Gen. 19:14), Lot offered his virgin daughters to the angry men of Sodom (Gen. 19:8) in his attempt as a good host to protect his guests. As he behaved with the Pharaoh, so did Abraham behave with Abimelech (Gen. 20:2-18). Indeed, he instructed his wife Sarah to say of him: "he is my brother" (Gen. 20:13). While this is undeniably true (see Gen. 20:12), it is clear that in this and the other instances, sexual hospitality or extramarital sex is considered acceptable. The social norm was to offer women especially to men of higher social status if it contributed to the controlling male's advantage.

The Israelite Period (1000 B.C.E.): Aggressive Strategy

This strategy is best illustrated in the many wives of David (1 Sam. 25:39-43; 27:3; 2 Sam. 3:2-5) but especially Solomon (1 Kings 11:1ff.). The idea is to keep our daughters exclusively for ourselves but to take the women of other groups. In return, the men of the other group receive patronage, power, or protection from us. In such a cultural setting, sexual hospitality (extramarital sex) is interpreted as shameful behavior because the woman is deeply embedded in the honor of her husband (Exod. 20:14, 17; Deut. 5:18, 21). This extramarital sex now called adultery is a very serious trespass into the space of an honorable fellow Israelite male. Such an action is a negative challenge and requires revenge as a riposte.

Moreover, since the mutual honor of the families is involved, these arrangements must be honest and devoid of the deception so prevalent in Middle Eastern culture. The law concerning the "tokens of virginity" (Deut. 22:13-21), for instance, is but one means of guaranteeing honesty and preventing feuding and vengeance that could escalate to blood feud. But the symbolism of blood in this matter is even greater. Marriage is not simply a contractual relationship. It is also a blood relationship. The "stranger" wife joins the husband's patriline, and if she dishonors him, she should rightly be put to death (Deut. 22:20-21). Permitting the husband to divorce such a wife (see Deut. 24:1) is very likely a compromise solution.

The Postexilic or Judean Period (537 B.C.E.): Defensive Strategy

The word "Judean" (preferable to the anachronistic term "Jewish" in this historical period) describes the behavior and customs of those who lived in Judea after the exile (587-537 B.C.E.). This historical period includes the activities at Qumran as well as at the time when Jesus was alive. The defensive strategy is illustrated in Nehemiah 10 and Ezra 9–10, which report the decisions made by priests and accepted by themselves and the Judean elites who were returning to their preexilic homeland. Essentially, from the time of those priests' decisions, marriages with women born within the covenant with Yahweh were to be kept, and marriages with outgroup women were to be avoided. Those outgroup marriages that already existed had to be dissolved. Hence the decision to divorce all wives drawn from non-Israelite families (along with their children) and to take instead partners from pedigreed Judean families. The "divorce" which God hates in Malachi (2:16) is that between fellow Judeans and not between Judeans and outsiders as decreed in Ezra-Nehemiah. Such a decision leads to monogamy, which clearly stands in contrast to the aggressive strategy of the preceding Israelite period. It is within the context of this union (becoming "one flesh," as the Yahwist describes it in Gen. 2:24; compare Sir. 25:26) that the Priestly author reports God's command to the first couple to "be fruitful and multiply." Malina (2001: 151) notes, "It is this defensive marriage strategy coupled with the perception that embeds female sexual purity in male honor that lies at the bottom of the sexual behavior found in the Priestly writings of the Old Testament" (mainly Leviticus, a postexilic collection of laws). This strategy also serves as the appropriate context for understanding discussions of marital and sexual behaviors in the Qumran documents and statements of Jesus reported in the gospels.

Adultery in this period (537 B.C.E. to 70 C.E.) means sexual relations with a fellow Judean's wife. In this period and cultural context such adultery not only challenges a Judean male's honor but is also "an abomination before the LORD" (Deut. 24:4). Even though the sexual exclusivity of the wife for her husband is routinely presented in terms of a material possession, the notion of monogamy and concomitant prohibition of extramarital sex are solid and constant. Sexual hospitality or sacred prostitution is now both shameful and forbidden (Lev. 19:29). Sexual body fluids render a person unclean, whether it be the male experience of involuntary emissions (Lev. 15:16-18, 32) or the female experience of menstruation (Lev. 15:19-30). All these postexilic laws reflect concern for purity or holiness, which amounts to ways of keeping "us" separate from "them." That is what God desires above all.

The gospel tradition reports five statements of Jesus relative to adultery but not within the context of marriage. Rather, Jesus' statements take place within the context of divorce. Scholars recognize Luke's as quite likely the authentic, primitive saying of Jesus: "Everyone who divorces his wife and marries another commits adultery" (Luke 16:18a). Since adultery at that time meant dishonoring a fellow Judean male by taking sexual advantage of his wife, this statement makes little sense as a moral directive. Rather, it has the quality of a parable since it would be totally puzzling to a first-century Middle Eastern listener. A man cannot commit adultery against himself. What, then, is this parable's foundation in reality? Quite likely the notions first expressed by Hosea and then repeated in other prophets. Hosea presents the relationship of God and God's people in the analogy of marriage. When God's people abandon God in favor of other deities (idolatry), this behavior is termed adulterous. Such thinking is clearly rooted in the defensive marriage strategy in which the partners become "one flesh" (Gen. 2:24). They share a blood relationship that is impossible to shed. God is shamed by such behavior and will seek to restore divine honor.

Post-Jesus groups beginning with Luke (85 C.E.) tried to make sense of Jesus' parable by turning it into a viable moral directive. Luke added, "and he who marries a woman divorced from her husband commits adultery" (Luke 16:18b). Only if a divorced woman is still considered somehow yet embedded in her husband could the new marriage be viewed as adultery. Luke also bases his addition/interpretation on the notion of marriage as a blood relationship.

Another discussion of adultery involves Jesus' response to questions about divorce (Mark 10:2-9). He tells a parable about divorce in the context of adultery (Mark 10:10-11) to clarify the meaning of "what therefore God has joined together, let not man put asunder" (v. 9), which is an obvious reference to the cultural practice of families (patriarchs) arranging the marriages of their male and female children. Since God selected the parents, God through these same parents joins their children in a blood relationship ("one flesh," Gen. 2:24). In his turn, Matthew explains divorce/adultery (Matt. 19:9) with the parable about eunuchs "for the sake of the kingdom," which many scholars believe does not refer to celibacy but rather to a wronged partner in a blood relationship faithfully waiting for the return of an errant blood relative/partner (Matt. 19:11-12). This notion of a blood relationship is also the idea behind "two becoming one" (Mark 10:8; Matt. 19:5-6).

The Pauline Interval: Modified Defensive Strategy

Since Paul rejects the Second Temple and the Torah interpretations associated with it, he dismisses Israel's legal tradition in favor of developing, distinctive Jesus-group customs. These customs, however, by which post-Jesus-group members are to live out their interpersonal relationships derive from the Spirit, the activity of God's power, within their various communities. Thus it would be fair to call Paul's notion a charismatic defensive strategy. While this strategy continues to maintain the separation of "us" from "them," Paul insists that post-Jesus group behavior should at least be as good as the best in surrounding cultures (see, e.g., 1 Cor. 5:1).

Paul refers to Jesus' parable about divorce (see the discussion above) now adopted as a group norm (1 Cor. 7:10, 11). Concerning marriages that existed before one or the other or both partners became Jesus-group members, Paul urges that these continue (1 Cor. 7:17). Yet if there is an unbelieving partner who poses a problem, peace is more important than preserving the marriage (1 Cor. 7:15). With regard to new marriages (or remarriages), Paul clearly reflects the defensive strategy by insisting that these should take place "in the Lord" (1 Cor. 7:39; 2 Cor. 6:14–7:1) quite likely with other members of the Jesus group.

Conclusion

Filipino anthropologists observe that prior to the Hispanic period (sixteenth century) sexual hospitality was common in that culture. Extramarital sex by the woman was not viewed as misbehavior. The lover had to pay a fine. Despite very different cultural values and understandings of marriage, contemporary Western marriage therapists rank extramarital sex behind eight other factors in the breakup of marriages, such as poor communication, unrealistic expectations, and power struggles (Francoeur 1994: 10). The challenge for modern believers is how to resonate with New Testament marriage ideals that took root in a culture so alien to U.S. experience. How can U.S. Christians actualize the New Testament understanding of marriage as a metaphorical blood relationship that renders extramarital sex as reprehensible as incest in contemporary U.S. culture?

5. Rape

What did Shechem really do to Dinah (Gen. 34)? Bibles and commentaries usually identify this story as "the rape of Dinah." Translations of the specific verse in question (Gen. 43:2) differ, though in general the sense is the same. He "lay with her by force" (NAB; NRSV), "raped her" (TEV; CEV), "raped her, and so dishonoured her" (JB), "forced her to sleep with him" (NJB), "lay with her and dishonoured her" (NEB), "lay with her and defiled her" (KJV), and "violated her" (NIV; NKJV). The literal translation of the Hebrew — "humbled her" (found only in the Jewish Publication Society translation of the Tanakh, 1917) — gives pause and raises questions about the other renditions.

Rape in Anthropological Research

Social scientists define rape as the action by which one person forces sexual intercourse upon another. Ethnography shows that across cultures, only the rape of women by men is reported. This does not mean that women do not rape men. Lot's daughters forced themselves on their inebriated father (Gen. 19:30-38). The contemporary Siuai of Oceania view the woman as the more aggressive gender (Broude 1994: 251-55). One explanation of why rape by women is not reported is the difficulty in some cultures of distinguishing between rape and coyness. Among the Ifugao in the Philippines, it is a scandal if a girl does not resist. The community never knows for certain whether her resistance was genuine or the culturally expected strategy for preserving her reputation, her honor. Another reason why rape by women is not reported is that in some cultures the line between consensual sexual intercourse and rape can be blurred. For instance, the Lakher of South Asia do not consider it a rape if a man successfully has intercourse with a woman while she is asleep. This is considered stealth and not force. Moral theology textbooks from before the Second Vatican Council (1962-65) reported a similar principle: "qui dormit, non peccat — one who is asleep cannot sin."

Ethnographers identify two kinds of rape: normative, which is condoned by society; and nonnormative, which is not condoned but rather considered wrong or a crime (Broude 1994: 251). Both of these kinds of rape together form a cultural universal. This means that rape is a characteristic of human life that can be found in all cultures. Nevertheless, in some cultures rape is very rare. One such culture is the Cuna of Panama, who force a briar up the rapist's organ and leave him to die.

In a study of 38 societies, 37 percent viewed rape as normative. This means that rape in these societies is accepted, ridiculed, or ignored (Broude 1994: 252). The Mundurucu of Brazil use rape to punish a woman who violates certain rules. Common victims are unfaithful wives or girls who play hooky from school. Men in this society view gang rape as humorous and love to recount tales of their experiences publicly in order to make women anxious (Broude 1994: 253).

This same study identified 63 percent of the societies that disapproved of rape (21 percent mildly, 42 percent strongly). In these societies, rape is viewed as nonnormative and punished. In Rwala the rapist is killed, and if the victim becomes pregnant her baby will also be killed. Without kin, especially a male, the baby has an anomalous and ambiguous status in the community.

Rape in the Ancient World

It is important to note that the context in which rape is discussed in the cuneiform law codes is adultery (Westbrook 1992: 552-53). Thus, these laws consider the status of the victim and her lack of consent. Three statuses are distinguished: an unattached woman, a betrothed woman, and a married woman. If the victim is unattached, her father can demand that the rapist marry her with no possibility of divorce, but the rapist will have to pay one third more than the standard bride-price (*Middle Assyrian Laws* A 55; compare Deut. 22:28-29). If the rapist is married, the father of the victim may rape the rapist's wife.

If the woman is betrothed, the rape is punishable by death. "If one citizen rapes a woman who is marriageable and is engaged to another citizen, then the sentence is death" (*Code of Ur-Nammu*, art. 6; compare Deut. 22:23-24; Ur-Nammu was a ruler around 2000 B.C.E. in Sumer, contemporary southern Iraq). If the woman was married, the penalty is also death. "If one citizen forces himself on the wife of another when she is outside her house and says, 'Have intercourse with me,' and has intercourse with her, even though she resists him and does not consent, regardless of whether he has been caught in the act or has been accused by witnesses, the man is executed. The woman is not guilty" (*Middle Assyrian Laws* A 12; compare Deut. 22:23-27).

Rape in the Bible

The Hebrew word telling what happened to Dinah is the same one that appears in the Deuteronomy passages cited above (Deut. 22:23-29) and in other places, too. Shechem "humbled her" (Gen. 34:2). That meaning (based on the Hebrew verb stem [piel] that indicates intensity, repetition, causation, or a privative idea) appears in other occurrences of that Hebrew word in the context of "rape." Thus, the warrior who took a captive woman to wife may free her later but not sell or enslave her because "he humbled or humiliated her" (Deut. 21:14). The old man of Gibeah who provided hospitality to the Levite and refused to accede to the townspeople's demand that the old man allow them to "know" the Levite ("know" in the sense of sexual penetration is a way of humiliating the stranger) offers instead his own maiden daughter or the Levite's concubine, whom they might humble or humiliate instead (Judg. 19:24, 25; 20:5). The word occurs four times in the story of Amnon's humiliation or shaming of his sister, Tamar (2 Sam. 13:12, 14, 22, 32). Through the prophet Ezekiel, God excoriates Jerusalem males for humiliating women during their menstrual period (Ezek. 22:10; see Lev. 18:19) or for humiliating their sisters (Ezek. 22:11; recall Amnon).

The anonymous author of Lamentations affirms the cultural plausibility of the interpretation "humble" or "humiliate" when he uses the same word in the same verb stem to describe a common practice in ancient warfare. "The wives in Zion were ravished (= humiliated) by the enemy, the maidens in the cities of Judah" (Lam. 5:11). Women in the ancient world were obliged to be protected by their fathers, brothers, or husbands. Some man was always responsible for them. Rape in this context is not primarily about sexual gratification, nor even exerting power over a woman, so much as it is a shaming strategy. Males are shamed for not protecting their women, and the woman is shamed by not having a solicitous male kinsperson. The legislation in Deuteronomy (21:10-14) concerning the captive woman seeks to prevent a second humiliation (sale or enslavement). Yet without kin in that society, the freed captive woman still remains in a precarious situation.

The Humiliation (Rape) of Dinah

Scholars admit that this is a difficult story to analyze and interpret. There are inconsistencies that have prompted some scholars to identify three different stories pieced together in our biblical account. What seems most clear is that this story is rooted in two interrelated but very complex issues from the period of proto-Israelite existence (around 1000 B.C.E.). One issue is Shechem, a Canaanite city, which was simultaneously a safe and dangerous place in premonarchic Israel. This is where Joshua gathered the tribes to renew the covenant (Josh. 24) but also where Dinah was humiliated (raped). A second issue relates to marriage practice: endogamy (marrying within the group) versus exogamy (marrying outside the group). Marrying outside the group has advantages, such as expanding territorial possessions. Yet it also poses the danger of introducing alien values that will disrupt the group in a serious way. Our reflection seeks only to understand the humiliation (rape) and the brothers' final comment: "Should our sister have been treated like a harlot?" (Gen. 34:31).

A Reading Scenario for the Story of Dinah

Dinah is the only female child of Jacob explicitly mentioned, though there probably were others (Gen. 46:15). Her birth is announced (Gen. 30:21), but no explanation is given for her name as for those of her twelve brothers. This is probably because she is not associated with an eponymous tribe as are her brothers. Dinah is Leah's seventh and final child. She next appears four chapters later in this story about her humbling or humiliation (Gen. 34).

Dinah is introduced as the daughter of Leah, one of only seven such identifications through the mother in the Bible (Gen. 34:1; 2 Sam. 3:3, 4 [2x]; 1 Chron. 24:26 [2x]; Esth. 9:29). Individuals are commonly identified by their father, for example, Simon son of John (bar Jonah; see John 21:15-17 [3x]). After this association with her mother in v. 1, Dinah is consistently associated with Jacob and her brothers (vv. 3, 5, 7, 13, 19, 27, 31). That she went to visit some women of the land immediately raises a cultural question: Why did she go alone, unaccompanied by any other women? An unaccompanied (unchaperoned) woman in the ancient world was suspected of being of loose virtue, deliberately placing herself in jeopardy. Women normally moved around in clusters with other women and children (including boys younger than the age of puberty). Even if this was a short walk, the audience hearing this element of the story would be troubled.

Shechem, a Canaanite, saw her, seized her, and humbled or humiliated her. A few interpretations are possible. Perhaps she was a loose woman. But no evidence supports that. An unchaperoned woman (married or not married) in public offers the opportunity for one man to shame the man or men with whom this woman is associated (father, brothers, husband). Since the next verses indicate that Shechem loved her and sought to marry her, this interpretation also is not plausible, even though he has indeed humiliated both her and her male kin.

A third interpretation is that Shechem used this strategy for gaining Dinah as his wife (see above, *Middle Assyrian Laws* A 55; compare Deut. 22:28-29). His action was likely driven by lust, similar to the behavior of some of the sons of God toward the daughters of men (Gen. 6:2 RSV). But still wanting to marry her, he strove after the deed to win her affection. Literally, "he spoke upon the heart of the girl" (v. 3), a phrase that occurs ten times in the Bible, usually following a sense of guilt or repentance (Gen. 34:3; 50:21; Judg. 19:3; etc.). Like Samson, Shechem directs his father, Hamor, to get this girl for him as wife (v. 4). Hamor in turn presents his case on behalf of his son, Shechem, and explains the benefits of exogamy to Jacob and his sons. Shechem pledges to pay the bride-price no matter how high it might be set (see Exod. 22:15-16; Deut. 22:29).

The Brothers' Response

When they learned what happened to their sister, the brothers were shocked and outraged. Shechem's behavior was indeed an outrage in Israel. (Israel as such does not yet exist in Jacob's day, so it might mean an outrage to Jacob = Israel.) The Hebrew word translated "outrage" (*nĕbālâ*) occurs thirteen times in the Hebrew Bible, eight of which relate to sexual misdeeds (e.g., Deut. 22:21; Judg. 19:23; 2 Sam. 13:12; etc.). "Such a thing ought not be done!" (v. 7; see 2 Sam. 13:12). It is culturally unacceptable.

The brothers realize that all the family males have been remiss and left their sister unguarded. This is their fault, but they have a new obligation now. As next of kin, as redeemer-kinsmen, the brothers must avenge the family's honor, which has been seriously damaged (Sir. 30:6). They must kill the rapist. While Jacob may have been inclined toward forgoing revenge and establishing exogamous marriage because of its obvious advantages, the brothers devise a deceptive plan. Before they can allow Dinah to stay with Shechem, he and all the males must be circumcised (a premarriage ritual not covenant related). Three days later, while they were still in pain, Simeon and Levi massacred all the males and rescued their sister. The other brothers sacked the place to avenge Dinah's humiliation, taking wealth, women, and children. In reply to Jacob's worry about retaliation, the brothers retort: "Should our sister have been treated like a harlot?" To forgo revenge would leave the impression that Dinah was not a virtuous woman. Thus, the humiliation of Dinah by Shechem shamed Jacob's family, which had no other recourse than to avenge the family's loss of honor by killing the rapist and his entire group. To improvise upon a familiar saying: "In the Middle East, honor isn't everything. It's the only thing!"

Conclusion

Though the basic action in rape is that one person (whether male or female) forces sexual intercourse upon another, it is interpreted differently across cultures, as noted above. In the Hebrew Bible, that action is reported as humiliating or humbling another person. Recalling the significance of honor and shame as core values of circum-Mediterranean cultures, humiliation is major shame. Primarily it is the men responsible for seeing to the safety of the woman who are shamed (father, brothers, husband). Secondarily the victim is shamed because no appropriate male took pains to watch over her. Shame must be avenged, which explains Dinah's brothers' decision. Yet revenge initiates a cycle of violence beginning with retaliation for the revenge, which explains Jacob's preference for forgoing revenge. Viewed in this cultural context, life in the Middle East not easy.

6. A Noble Death

In an interview with Dan Rather of CBS (February 2003), Saddam Hussein rejected any idea of going into exile to avoid war. He said: "We will die here. We will die in this country and we will maintain our honor — the honor that is required . . . in front of our people." Saddam and his translators or spokespersons were the only ones in the ongoing Iraq scenario to use the word "honor" in speeches. It may well be that the other discussion partners neither recognized nor understood this core Middle Eastern cultural value. Saddam's comment about death reminds a Bible reader of the death of Eleazar (2 Macc. 6:18-31).

Eleazar the Scribe

Scholars date the story of Eleazar's execution in the time of Antiochus Epiphanes, about 167 B.C.E. They generally agree that the basic account is factual, even though the name Eleazar is common and is found in a number of hero martyr stories. A close reading of the account cannot help but notice the repetition of words associated with the semantic field of "honor," the core cultural value in the ancient and contemporary Middle Eastern world. Eleazar, a scribe in high position, of noble appearance, preferring death with honor, had the courage to refuse the easy way out, made a high resolve worthy of his years and dignity of his old age, and so on, and so on. A core value is one that drives human behavior. Since a value conveys meaning wrapped in feeling, it is easy to understand the power of core values. Eleazar's story illustrates this well.

Honor is a claim to worth or value which is socially, that is, publicly acknowledged. Public agreement is critical. Honor usually surfaces when three characteristics of a person come together: authority, gender status, and respect. Authority is a person's ability to control the behavior of others. Authority is not physical force. It is a symbolic reality. At least in part, Eleazar's authority stems from his status as "a scribe in high position" (v. 18). Since only 2 (but not more than 10) percent of the ancient population was literate, a scribe, that is, someone who could read and write, possessed powerful authority. Even the simplest of scribes, that is, those who wrote only one kind of document (e.g., a bill of sale for a specific item or a limited number of items) was able to control the behavior of the buyer and the seller. The authority of such a scribe could hold both parties to the contract. Moreover, by modifying his writing from contract to contract, a scribe could make it impossible for his illiterate clients to learn how to write their own bills by imitating what they saw. As "a scribe in high position," Eleazar was obviously much more competent. Since he was willing to give an example to the young of "how to die a good death willingly and nobly for the revered and holy laws" (v. 28), one can surmise that he might have been a scribe who copied the Torah. This would give him very great authority (Sir. 38:24–39:11).

Gender status derives from the obligations and entitlements associated with gender. In the Middle East, males have higher status than females simply because they are males (Sir. 42:12-14). Older men have higher status than younger ones (Sir. 32:3-8, but notice the caveats about older men). Eleazar is ninety years old (v. 24), which was a rarity in antiquity. Moreover, men with gray hair possess added stature. "The glory of young men is their strength, and the dignity of old men is gray hair" (Prov. 20:29). Further, gray hair is the result of leading an honorable life. "Gray hair is a crown of glory; it is gained by virtuous living" (Prov. 16:31).

Finally, respect is the attitude one must have toward those who control one's existence. In the biblical world, God is ultimately in control of all existence. The respect due to God is typically called "fear" in the Bible. "The fear of the LORD is the beginning of wisdom" (Ps. 111:10; see also Sir. 19:20; 21:11; and elsewhere). When advised by his friends among the torturers to pretend to eat the swine and deceive everyone into believing that, Eleazar "declared himself quickly, telling them to send him to Hades" (v. 23). At his death Eleazar reminds everyone that the Lord knows he suffers gladly and willingly "because I fear [= respect] him" (v. 30). The sacred author presents Eleazar as a quintessentially honorable person because he fears the Lord. This honorable reputation is both ascribed (by virtue of his gender) and achieved (by virtue of his status as scribe and his respect toward God rather than toward his oppressors). Whether factual or hyperbolic, this story in which the intersection of his noble status as scribe, the esteem his advanced age demands, and the respect he shows to God all converge, is quite remarkable. The convergence places Eleazar in a very honorable position.

Eleazar Rejects Deception

In the ancient and contemporary Middle East, honor is so important that secrecy, deception, and lying are acceptable and legitimate strategies one might use to protect and even attain it. In small villages where everyone knows everyone else's business, people pay close attention to how those who find themselves in shameful predicaments will "preserve" their reputations, or at least put up a good front (see Deut. 22:13-21). Even notorious liars are closely watched because this activity offers satisfying entertainment in an otherwise rather drab world.

The old friends of Eleazar advise him to deceive the king by substituting food he could lawfully eat for the forbidden food of the sacrifice commanded by the king (v. 22). This deception would spare his life, and his old friends would take care of him. Surely everyone who knew this man well would recognize the deception and would appreciate his cleverness and success in fooling the king. This deception would be at least as entertaining or perhaps even more so than witnessing his violent torture and death, itself a popular form of entertainment in the ancient world.

Eleazar's reason for rejecting the suggested deception is interesting. He deems it unbecoming to his age (v. 24). Why? Though he may not have been ninety years old, Abraham engaged in deceit to save his life (Gen. 12:13; 20:12). At the instigation and insistence of his mother, the young Jacob deceived his father, Isaac (Gen. 27), and stole his brother's birthright. Perhaps Eleazar never engaged in deception and didn't want to begin now. This would be quite implausible in the Middle Eastern world. On the other hand, the sacred author may be presenting Eleazar as an idealized hero, who would be very plausible in the Middle Eastern world where appearances are more important than reality. Image is the most important element of honor. The public perception is what counts. Italians call it *figura*, specifically, *bella* as opposed to *bruta figura*. Moreover, the sacred author has already intimated a long, blameless life by reference to Eleazar's gray hair.

Further, Eleazar doesn't want to create a false impression of abandoning his religion for another to many young men who would be led astray. This would "defile and disgrace" his old age (v. 25). This is somewhat plausible, but modeling is not significant in the Middle East since one is always "making oneself out" to be someone, whether one truly is such a person or not. Moreover, modeling is also not a Middle Eastern strategy for raising young boys. Physical discipline is the preferred biblical stratagem for making a man out of a boy (Prov. 13:24; 19:18; 22:15; 23:13-14; 29:15, 17; Sir. 30:1-13). What might be driving Eleazar's response to his dilemma: to deceive and save my life? Or to refuse to obey the king and die a noble, manly death? He chooses the latter (vv. 27-28), and the sacred author does indeed identify Eleazar's death as a model "not only to the young but to the great body of his nation" (v. 31). But does not this behavior also demonstrate that he was well trained by his father to endure physical pain, indeed death itself, fearlessly? In other words, he dies like a man in this culture is expected to die.

The Seven Brothers

The very next chapter (2 Macc. 7) reports how seven brothers followed Eleazar's example in choosing to die manfully (honorably) rather than preserving life by acting shamefully. "The brothers and their mother encouraged one another to die nobly" (2 Macc. 7:5). When the king makes an appealing offer to the youngest surviving son, the mother encourages him to remain steadfast in his resolve. "Do not fear this butcher, but prove worthy of your brothers. Accept death, so that in God's mercy I may get you back again with your brothers" (2 Macc. 7:29). The mother was the last to die. While the collocation of these reports about Eleazar and the seven sons are presented as a model which is diligently followed, both stories confirm that the respective fathers followed the advice of the Sage who wrote Proverbs and raised their sons accordingly.

Dying Honorably

Saving or preserving life is a cardinal value in the biblical tradition. "I have set before you life and death, the blessing and the curse. Choose life, then, that you and your descendants might live . . ." (Deut. 30:19; compare Mark 3:4; Luke 6:9). Yet as Moses completed that sentence, he explained: "loving the LORD your God, obeying his voice, and cleaving to him; for that means life to you, and length of days, that you may dwell in the land which the LORD swore to your fathers, to Abraham, to Isaac, and to Jacob, to give them" (Deut. 30:20). Eleazar, the seven sons, and their mother understood this perfectly well.

True honor is that which God acknowledges. It sometimes (often?) differs from the human estimate of honor. "For even if for the present I should avoid the punishment of men, yet whether I live or die I shall not escape the hands of the Almighty," said Eleazar (v. 26). The brothers, too, placed their hope in God and recognized that they might be suffering for their sins. To eat the pork would dishonor the God who established this law for Israel (Lev. 11:6-8). Such a dishonor to God would certainly merit divine retribution, which they all understood full well. Eleazar decides that by "manfully giving up my life now, I will show myself worthy of my old age. . . ." The end result of his virtuous living will honor God and leave an impressive example to youth and to the whole nation (vv. 27-28).

Conclusion

These reports about martyrs who accept death rather than betray God are impressive and worthy of emulation. Saddam Hussein was not at all in the same category. The only point of comparison between him and these biblical stories is the core Middle Eastern value of honor, and how it drives human behavior in reasonable ways incomprehensible in other cultural contexts. Christians know of similar stories from the time of Roman torture and persecution in the first century c.e.

The story of Eleazar, however, is cast in a new light by Luke's story of Peter's vision (Acts 10:9-16). Shortly after Jesus died and was raised, a hungry Peter fell into a trance while praying and saw a sheet descending from the sky with all kinds of four-legged animals, reptiles, and birds. A voice commanded him: "Rise, Peter; kill and eat." Peter refused, saying he had never eaten anything common or unclean. The voice replied: "What God has cleansed, you must not call common." This happened three times, and the vision ended. Only God could abrogate God's own law recorded in Leviticus 11 concerning clean and unclean foods.

The Conservative and Orthodox Jewish traditions which still observe the laws of Leviticus 11 continue to see a model worthy of imitation in the deaths of Eleazar and the seven brothers with their mother. Yet, in the United States, some follow alternative options. When discussing this issue in class, a Jewish student from New Orleans said that her Conservative congregation held an annual shrimp boil as a fund-raiser. Members of the Congregation were willing participants in the event.

Christian tradition respects the reports about these martyrs but is rightly puzzled by God's apparent change of mind. Though it is not in the same category, the twentieth-century abrogation of the prohibition of eating meat on Fridays for Catholics (a church rule, not God's) caused similar puzzlement. With regard to our passage about Eleazar and the seven brothers, is it possible to die honorably for the wrong reasons? How would one know? If the significance became clear only long after the fact, what would that say about the deaths? Life's choices and their consequences are never simple. Thanks be to God for being an understanding God.

7. Final Words

My late wife, Jean, used to write articles explaining the cultural background of the scripture selections in the Lectionary readings for Sundays.

For her, readings from John's gospel were "crabgrass in the lawn of life." The style of that gospel is so repetitive that it seems to go around in circles. The author seems to say the same thing over and over again, often using the same words. The significance of this kind of language escaped her (and me, too, when she asked for my advice). We now know that this is antilanguage peculiar to an antisociety such as John's community. The basic purpose of such language is not to communicate ideas but rather to imbue interpersonal relationships with ever deepening emotional anchoring.

Antisociety

An antisociety is a group that is set up within a dominant society as a conscious alternative to it. In a sense, it is a resistance group, but the resistance can be passive (get along with the main group, without making trouble) or active (exercise hostility toward the main group perhaps with the intention of destroying it). The dominant society which John's community, an antisociety, resisted was "the world." For the most part, "the world" in John's gospel is Israel, or, more specifically, the Judeans (anachronistically translated "Jews"; see 8:23; 9:39; 12:25, 31; 13:1; 14:30; 16:11; 18:36). For example, "Jesus answered him [the high priest]: 'I have spoken openly to the world; I have always taught in synagogues and in the temple, where all Judeans come together; I have said nothing secretly'" (John 18:20).

Antilanguage

In order to set itself apart from the dominant society and other competing groups (e.g., "sheep not of this fold"; John 10:16), an antisociety develops an antilanguage as a form of resistance. Antilanguage usually consists of two elements: new words for realities not usually known by these words; and many words for items of central concern to the antisociety.

Literally in Greek, John speaks of "believing *into* Jesus" (e.g., John 1:12; 2:11, 23, 24; 14:1, 12; 16:9; 17:20; etc.), where the more common expression is "faith or believing *in* Jesus."

John uses a new phrase, "believing into," one that he seems to have coined, instead of the more commonly accepted phrase, "believing in." Moreover, John uses a broad range of words and phrases to say the same thing. Thus, phrases that have the same meaning as "believing into him" are following him, abiding in him, loving him, keeping his word, receiving him, having him, or seeing him. In our modern experience, this is similar to the language used by gangsters (gangsters being an antisociety with our dominant society), which has many words for a gun: heater, Smith and Wesson, .45, gat, piece, and so on.

Antisociety Is like a Family

In the Mediterranean world, an antisociety is rooted in and built upon the same foundation as the family. It is obvious that the family model characteristic of the Mediterranean is built around a central father figure, the patriarch. In an environment of harsh geographic and climatic extremes (90 percent of the land is desert with hot temperatures), there is safety and security in numbers. Hence the family tends to be very large. Such a large family needs a strong leader, a patriarch, who in turn wants to have as many sons as possible. These sons will reside with the father even after they are married.

Boys and girls are reared almost exclusively by the women in the women's world. Here, boys are favored and pampered. At the age of puberty, when they are transferred without benefit of a formal rite of passage into the male world, boys encounter a more harsh reality and rigidly hierarchical relationships. It is a reality which they must accept, for the stability and effectiveness of the family depend upon it. This explains in part why physical discipline for boys is routinely promoted in the Wisdom literature (Prov. 13:24; 19:18; 22:15; 23:13-14; 29:15, 17; Sir. 30:1, 12).

The patriarch must ensure that the boys are socialized to be loyal to their family of origin. The family's reputation depends upon such loyalty. The so-called prodigal son in Jesus' parable (Luke 15:11-32) shames his family of origin, and one wonders whether the father failed to discipline him appropriately in his younger years (see Sir. 30:7-13). The son's demand displays a low (perhaps no) level of loyalty to the family. His request and behavior shame his family in the village and set a bad example for other sons in the village. The entire village will eventually seek to do what the father is unwilling to do.

Obviously, the successful patriarch is one who is able to impose his will not only on sons but on members of the entire family. Sirach cautions the patriarch about the dangers posed by headstrong daughters (29:10-12; 42:11) and urges sons to serve their parents as masters — a telling image (3:7). The two sons commanded by their father to work in the vineyard contrast the values of honor and loyalty (Matt. 21:28-31). Honor can exist without loyalty, as appearance does not have to square with reality. The son who says what his father wanted to hear honors his father. Loyalty, however, is inextricably bound up with honor. The son who eventually went to work in the vineyard after his initial shameful response to the father remained loyal and reaped honor. Loyalty was and continues to be a central value in Mediterranean families. Without it, the family will collapse.

Farewell Speeches

In the Bible, key figures made "farewell speeches" (or spoke "final words") before dying: Jacob (Gen. 49), Moses (Deut. 31–34), Joshua (Josh. 23–24), Samuel (1 Sam. 12), and David (1 Kings 2:1-9), among others. It is possible to consider these final words as similar to a "last will and testament" for their survivors, which included their children. Indeed, there is a collection of literature known as the *Testaments of the Twelve Patriarchs* (the twelve sons of Jacob).

In the modern Western world, where economics is the prevailing social institution, a last will and testament ordinarily assigns inheritance. In the West, the main theme of the last will and testament is disposition of property and wealth. Western culture does not usually have special considerations for the firstborn as does Mediterranean culture (see Deut. 21:15-17; compare Luke 12:13-15). In ancient Israel, of course, this was not just culture; it was God's very own law (Deut. 1:3).

In the Mediterranean world, kinship is the dominant social institution. At the death of the patriarch, the family is concerned about its impending loss. What will happen now? Will the family fall to pieces? Who will lead it? What dangers lie ahead? Moreover, in the Mediterranean world, people at the brink of death are believed to know what is going to happen to persons who are near and dear. Because the dying person is closer to the realm of God than to the realm of human beings, that person is thought to become prescient. After all, human knowledge is limited, but God knows all things, even the forthcoming.

With the final words, the last will and testament, a dying person strives to give advice about how to keep the family together, how to strengthen the loyalty of all its members. He or she gives good wishes and expresses concern for the ongoing well-being of the group. This is true of Jesus' farewell speech (John 13–17). Jesus can foresee forthcoming difficulties, offer advice on how to avoid them, strengthen the bonds of his fictive group, and more.

141

The Jesus Group in His Lifetime

Just as in the Synoptics, so too in John, the first followers of Jesus leave their blood-family behind (at least for a while, one dry season from May to September) and form a surrogate or fictive family with Jesus at the center. Andrew, one of the first called by Jesus (John 1:40), then summoned his brother, Simon Peter (1:41). The next day Jesus called Philip (1:43), who in turn called Nathanael (1:45). John's story line relates how these and other followers bonded with Jesus as he taught, preached, and worked signs (John 2–12).

How closely knit was the fictive kinship group that Jesus gathered in his lifetime? Unlike the reports of Mark (14:50) and Matthew (26:56) in which all the disciples fled when Jesus was arrested, John's Jesus asks the arresting cohort that the disciples be dismissed (John 18:8). Only Jesus is arrested (18:12). Luke says that there were male disciples with the women at Jesus' cross (23:49). In John, the "other disciple" managed to gain access for himself to the court of the high priest, and the disciple whom Jesus loved (same as the "other disciple") stood with the women at the foot of Jesus' cross. Therefore, at least some of Jesus' fictive kin group remained loyal to him.

Yet, it is important to keep in mind that John is writing long after Jesus died and was raised. Perhaps to a degree greater than in the Synoptics, John's story line has its chief focus on the risen Jesus still present in the community of those who "believed into" him. Information from the actual life of Jesus is filtered through this perspective. In the actual life of Jesus, he and his group were not an antisociety. Jesus was interested in reforming Israel and preparing for the forthcoming theocracy that he proclaimed. His mission was to call the lost sheep of the house of Israel (Matt. 10:6) to a change of heart so that they could be an integral part of that forthcoming theocracy.

Evidence to support the idea that Jesus and his disciples did not seem to be an antisociety in his lifetime is clear in John. Jesus came to his own (either family, or Israel, or both; 1:11), but they did not "receive" him. They did not show hospitality to him with whom they ought to have held a relationship of solidarity (see 3:11; 4:44; 5:43). Those who did receive him became his kinsfolk ("children of God"; 1:12). In his final hours, those who ought to have recognized Jesus' true identity said: "We have a law, and by that law he ought to die, because he has made himself the Son of God" (19:7). Many years later, the John the evangelist's community and those who believed into him recognized that this was more than a claim. The resurrection proved that Jesus was indeed acknowledged by the Father as Son.

The Messianist Group in John

The final words of Jesus in John (chaps. 13–17) aim principally at strengthening the loyalty of the Messianist Group to Jesus. The Messianist Group consists of those who after his resurrection accepted and believed into Jesus as Messiah. The concern about disloyalty (of Peter) and betrayal (by Judas, 13:18-20) in Jesus' lifetime after his resurrection becomes concern about the contemporary group loyalty and group solidarity. The exhortation to mutual love is an exhortation to become more solidly attached to one's family, village or city quarter, fictive kin group, yes, even to God! Such attachment must be demonstrated externally, as by supporting the well-being of the group even to the point of dying for other members.

The vine imagery (chap. 15) depicts the close interpersonal relationship between the risen Jesus and individual group members. This in turn serves as the basis for closely embedded relationships between group members. Just as love means group attachment, so hate means disattachment from the group.

Perhaps the most significant of Jesus' final words is "I will see you again and your hearts will rejoice, and no one will take your joy from you" (16:22, in the context of vv. 16-24; also 17:24, in the context of vv. 20-26). The loss of a loved one is difficult enough in our individualistic culture. It is almost unbearable in a collectivistic culture (which represents 80 percent of the contemporary population of our planet). How do they cope with loss?

Because collectivistic personalities rely on a connectedness with others and value the opinions of others in order to make sense out of life, they imagine and believe that the connectedness continues even after death. That connectedness helps them to maintain contact with deceased loved ones. According to contemporary psychiatric research, approximately 90 percent of the contemporary population of the planet experience deceased loved ones in alternate states of consciousness (trance, dreams, ecstatic experiences, and the like). The experience can last for as long as ten years and longer. It would seem that the original recipients of John's gospel experienced the risen Jesus in this way whenever they gathered. Even outsiders knew this, as evidenced by the request by Israelite émigrés returned to Jerusalem for a pilgrimage. They said to Philip, "Sir, we wish to see Jesus" (John 12:21). During the life of Jesus, this episode has one meaning. But during the time of John's community, it surely points to their ability to meet the risen Jesus during their gatherings. Matthew's community also sensed the presence of the risen Jesus as they gathered to hear and resolve legal cases (18:20: "where two or three are gathered in my name, there I am in the midst of them").

The farewell words of Jesus were consoling affirmations to those who knew Jesus of Nazareth in his earthly life. In the Messianist groups, these farewell words became instructions for newcomers on what to expect in the group (the presence of the risen Jesus), and why (Jesus promised it), and how (by remaining embedded in the group, related in mutual love = attachment, and the like). Since these kinds of experiences were normal in the family, they would be normal in the fictive kinship group, which is "just like family." John's antisociety, which embraced Jesus as Messiah and Son of God, had no choice but to distance itself from "the world," that is, Israel, which rejected Jesus as Messiah and Son of God. As a consequence, John's antisociety could experience Jesus in alternate reality while the dominant society could not.

Conclusion

The word that we translate "faith" actually means faithfulness or loyalty in Middle Eastern culture. The central issue for family and surrogate family alike is for all members to remain faithful and loyal to the group and to one another. In the Middle East, a dying person's final words strive to strengthen and sustain that loyalty.

FURTHER READING: FAMILY

Augsburger, David W. 1986. *Pastoral Counseling across Cultures*. Philadelphia: Westminster.
Bennett, R. L., A. G. Motulsky, A. Bittles, L. Hudgins, S. Uhrich, D. L. Doyle, K. Silvey, C. R. Scott, E. Cheng, B. McGillivray, R. D. Steiner, and D. Olson. 2002. "Genetic Counseling and Screening of Consanguineous Couples and Their Offspring: Recommendations of the National Society of Genetic Counselors." *Journal of Genetic Counseling* 11: 97-119.
Bloch, M. 1988. "Death and the Concept of Person." Pp. 11-29 in *On the Meaning of Death: Essays on Mortuary Rituals and Eschatological Beliefs*. Edited by S. Cederroth, C. Corlin, and J. Lindström. Uppsala Studies in Cultural Anthropology 8. Stockholm: Almqvist & Wiksell.

Broude, Gwen J. 1994. *Marriage and Family Relationships: A Cross Cultural Encyclopedia.* Santa Barbara: ABC-CLIO.

Brown, Raymond, Karl P. Donfried, Joseph A. Fitzmyer, and John Reumann, eds. 1978. *Mary in the New Testament.* Philadelphia: Fortress, and New York/Mahwah: Paulist Press.

Bullough, Vern L., and Bonnie Bullough. 1994. *Human Sexuality: An Encyclopedia.* New York and London: Garland Publishing, Inc.

Campbell, Joan Cecelia. 2007. *Kinship Relations in the Gospel of John.* CBQMS 42. Washington: The Catholic Biblical Association of America.

Deacy, S., and K. F. Pierce. 1997. *Rape in Antiquity: Sexual Violence in the Greek and Roman Worlds.* London: Duckworth.

Ford, Josephine M. 1967. "Betula, Parthenos, and Virgo." Pp. 8-22 in *A Trilogy on Wisdom and Celibacy.* Notre Dame, IN: University of Notre Dame Press.

Francoeur, Robert. 1994. "Adultery." Pp. 8-12 in *Human Sexuality: An Encyclopedia.* Edited by Vern L. Bullough and Bonnie Bullough. New York and London: Garland Publishing, Inc.

Gottwald, Norman K. 1979. *The Tribes of Yahweh.* Maryknoll: Orbis.

Levinson, David. 1989. *Family Violence in Cross-Cultural Perspective.* Frontiers of Anthropology, vol. 1. Newbury Park: Sage Publications.

Levinson, David, ed. 1995. *Encyclopedia of Marriage and the Family.* New York: Macmillan and London: Simon & Schuster.

Malina, Bruce J. 2001. *The New Testament World.* Third Edition Revised and Expanded. Louisville: Westminster John Knox.

Malina, Bruce J., and Richard L. Rohrbaugh. 1998. *Social Science Commentary on the Gospel of John.* Minneapolis: Fortress.

Meier, John P. 1991. *A Marginal Jew: Rethinking the Historical Jesus.* New York: Doubleday.

Pilch, John J. 1997. "Family Violence in Cross-Cultural Perspective: An Approach for Feminist Interpreters of the Bible." Pp. 343-63 in *A Feminist Companion to Reading the Bible: Approaches, Methods, Strategies.* Edited by Athalya Brenner and Carol Fontaine. Sheffield: Sheffield Academic Press.

Shapiro, Warren. 1997. "Marriage Systems." *The Dictionary of Anthropology.* Oxford: Blackwell.

Stewart, Edward C., and Milton J. Bennett. 1991. *American Cultural Patterns: A Cross-Cultural Perspective.* Yarmouth: Intercultural Press.

Talbert, Charles H. 2006. "Miraculous Conceptions and Births in Mediterranean Antiquity." Pp. 79-86 in *The Historical Jesus in Context.* Edited by A. J. Levine, D. C. Allison and J. D. Crossan. Princeton: Princeton University Press.

Van Hasselt, Vincent B., Randall L. Morrison, Allan S. Bellack, and Michel Herson, eds. 1988. *Handbook of Family Violence*. New York/London: Plenum Press.

Westbrook, Raymond. 1992. "Punishments and Crimes." *Anchor Bible Dictionary* 5: 546-56.

Winthrop, Robert H. 1991. *Dictionary of Concepts in Cultural Anthropology*. New York: Greenwood, 1991.

Part Five

LANGUAGE

On December 15, 2005, the U.S. Department of Education published the results of its study, "National Assessment of Adult Literacy" (http://nces.ed.gov/naal/). The study evaluated three kinds of literacy: prose (ability to understand a continuous text, e.g., a book of the Bible), document (ability to understand a noncontinuous text, e.g., the "J" or "P" document in the Pentateuch), and quantitative (ability to use numbers embedded in printed materials). In general, while quantitative literacy had improved since 1992, prose and document literacy had dropped. Relative to college students, that drop was significantly different from 1992!

Even so, we in the Western world take literacy, that is, the ability to read and write, quite for granted, and perhaps rightly so. Technology, such as the computer or the iPhone, may be weakening this ability somewhat. The slow demise of newspapers might be an indication of that. Still, Western readers of the Bible quite likely never reflect on the fact that literacy in the ancient world may have been as low as 2 percent of the population. Still, the predominantly oral culture managed remarkably well. In this part, we examine aspects of language in the Bible, including literacy, the Ten Commandments, insults, curses, and nonverbal communication such as touch and casting the evil eye.

1. "How Do You Read?"

Studies of the ancient world propose that not more than 10 percent of that population could read and write. Some scholars think that that select group may have been as small as 2 or 3 percent of the population of ancient Israel. If Jesus read from the scroll of Isaiah in his village synagogue (Luke 4:16-17), did he belong to an elite minority? Where did he learn how to read (see John 7:15)? If he could read, did he know how to write? Who were the "scribes" with whom Jesus was often in conflict? What did they write? These questions do not have simple answers, but we know enough about literacy in antiquity to offer some educated guesses.

Varieties of Literacy

UNESCO's definition of an illiterate person as "one who cannot with understanding both read and write a short, simple statement on his everyday life" reflects its own contemporary goals more than the cultural context of contemporary or ancient peoples in non-Western cultures. According to Professor Lucretia Yaghjian, the processes of oral and written communication in antiquity — and their overlap! — require modern researchers to distinguish various kinds of abilities (Yaghjian 1996: 206-20).

Many people were "hearing-readers" (auraliterate). They could remember and understand what was read aloud to them. Matthew's Jesus seems to consider his disciples "hearing-readers" when he reminds them of what they had heard when others read the Torah to them (5:21, 27, 33, 38, 43). Confident that they understood what was read, Matthew's Jesus was able to present a new perspective on these sections of the Decalogue. "You have heard . . . , but I say to you."

Perhaps an equal number were "repeating-readers" (oraliterate). Such people could remember, understand, and repeat substantially if not literally what someone had read to them. Scholars recognize that when the Pharisees challenged Jesus about his disciples plucking ears of grain on the Sabbath (Mark 3:23), Jesus justified their behavior by alluding to David's similar deed of assuaging hunger in the house of God (1 Sam. 21:1-6). "Have you never read what David did . . . ?" (Mark 2:25).

The modern reader who consults 1 Samuel is embarrassed to see that Mark's Jesus has misidentified the high priest: it was not Abiathar as Jesus claims, but Ahimelech! Abiathar was high priest when David was king (2 Sam. 15:35). Ahimelech, his father, was priest when David ate the consecrated bread. How could Jesus have made such a mistake? Perhaps he did not remember accurately what he heard (or personally read). Perhaps Mark was responsible for reporting the wrong name. Whoever made the mistake (Jesus or Mark) was not reading from a text, nor was the text literally memorized. The allusion to that event very likely was made on the basis of a memory of that passage which was heard when another person read it.

Reading

Understood in a restricted sense, reading is the ability to decode linguistic symbols by *looking* at a written text. People learn alphabets and words. Then they learn how to communicate orally by combining the words in patterns that are intelligible to others. Some also learn how to identify the letters, words, and patterns in written communication, thus gaining an understanding of what the writer or author intended to say and actually meant. Because in the modern world opportunities to learn how to read are widespread and reading materials are affordable and easily accessible, people forget what a complex skill this is.

Three passages in the New Testament seem to indicate that Jesus could read and write. In the case of the woman caught in the act of adultery, Jesus is reported to pause in the conflict to bend down and write with his finger on the ground (John 8:6). Speculation about what he might have written covers a wide range of guesses, but the most plausible explanation is that he doodled. Mediterranean men under stress often doodle in an attempt to buy some time in order to come up with an appropriate sarcastic comeback, or to avoid losing one's temper and doing something regrettable, and so on. Moreover, this particular story was not originally part of John's gospel; sometimes it is reported in Luke's gospel. Some even think that it is a much later creation. If it preserves a reliable tradition about Jesus' writing at all, doodling has the highest degree of plausibility in the cultural world of the Middle East.

Only Luke among the evangelists presents Jesus as "truly" literate or, more specifically, "oculiterate," that is, capable of linguistically decoding what he reads with his eyes from a written text. Matthew and Mark portray him as a "repeating reader," one who repeats what he heard others read. In that famous scene in his village men's community center ("synagogue" in translations; Luke 4:16-30), Jesus *reads* from the Isaiah scroll. More, he *interprets* the passage for the listeners. Scholars are divided about the facticity of this passage. The information about Jesus actually reading from and interpreting Isaiah may be a later addition. The verses that Jesus reportedly read and reported by Luke are a jumbled mixture of Isaiah 61:1a, b, d; 58:6d; and 61:2a. What scroll would contain this arrangement? Despite its promise, this passage, too, is not helpful for understanding the Jesus of history.

In the third passage (John 7:15), when Jesus began to teach in the Jerusalem temple, the men asked: "How is it that this man knows his letters when he has never studied?" This question leads us to a consideration of "formal education" that results in scribal literacy.

Scribal Literacy

Scribal literacy is the ability to read AND to interpret a document. In the case of the Hebrew scriptures, this would entail not only the ability to read a Hebrew text (even long after Hebrew was commonly spoken by and familiar to the majority of the population) but also to grasp the Israelite traditions. Only in this way could the "scribe" read and relate the document under question to other elements of the tradition, identify allusions, and the like.

The scribe, a person who could read and write in antiquity, was truly in the minority of the population. Many people who could write were unable to read. They had the ability of recognizing and copying each letter of a word, but they could not read or understand the word. Knowing the alphabet does not mean that a person can read words. The problem is even more complicated when we remember that in antiquity the manuscripts had no spaces between words. The Sinaiticus manuscript has leaves that measure 15 inches by 14 inches. The letters were written in brown ink, four columns per page, with 48 lines to a column, and usually 12-16 letters per line. The text was written on the ruled lines in *scriptio continua* with some punctuation (high and middle points and colon). Some letters are crowded in a smaller size at the end of a line. Often, sections of text end in mid-line; a new section starts at the beginning of the next line and is moved into the margin slightly.

Because this skill of writing gave the scribe an elevated status in society, one can understand why such a person would not be willing to teach that skill to others. A close examination of documents written by scribes in antiquity indicates that they deliberately made changes in similar documents (e.g., bills and contracts). A person who regularly had to pay a scribe to produce the same kind of document (e.g., a contract) would not be able to learn how to imitate it from the many presumably identical documents he had seen. The scribe's deliberate variations in many reproductions of the same kind of document would befuddle even the most clever of imitators.

Clearly this was the lowest of level of scribe: one whose knowledge was limited to writing bill, contracts, and the like.

Scribes who were able to copy the Scriptures worked with a higher level of ability. They could copy long documents which had a rich vocabulary, complex grammatical structures, and the like. Because each copy was expected to be a faithful reproduction of the original, this kind of reading and writing was a highly regarded skill. It was not just the ability to remember what one heard read, or what one had once seen and could repeat from memory, with excusable variations. Rather, it was the ability to be precise and accurate.

At the next level, an accomplished scribe could also interpret what he had read and copied. This kind of scribe is described by Ben Sira (38:24–39:5). The Sage first contrasts this person with the farmer, the craftsman, the smith, and the potter (Sir. 38:25-32). All of these are necessary for civilization, but none have the status of the scribe (Sir. 38:33–39:5). He not only preserves the discourse of notable figures (writes), but penetrates the subtleties of parables (interprets). Sirach's observation is valuable. Consider the fact that Jesus often not only beats scribes in verbal conflict but leaves them utterly bewildered in verbal jousting. They admire his mysterious ability to interpret the tradition. "How is it that this man has the ability to read and interpret Scripture, when he has never studied?" (John 7:15). Of the three passages, perhaps this one is most suggestive of Jesus' ability to read and write, though scholars are not agreed.

Coins

Because modern Western culture is dominated by economics and economic considerations, readers in this culture often miss the significance of coins in antiquity. As numismatists insist, coins in antiquity were predominantly a means of communication rather than a medium of exchange. They were mass-produced texts! Coins were designed with a reading audience in mind, an audience with a rudimentary reading skill. One didn't need perfect eyesight to see the iconography on the coin, and not too great a reading skill to see what was inscribed on the coin. When Jesus responds to opponents who question him about paying taxes to Caesar, he asks: "Whose likeness and inscription is this?" (Matt. 22:20). Any peasant could answer that question.

Coins of inconsequential value reminded the possessor of the current ruler's identity and appearance. This was the person who was really in charge of the peasant's life. With his question, Jesus entraps the Pharisees who sought to entrap him! The entire episode demonstrates that each person involved had this basic reading ability whether he read the inscription of the coin personally, or whether someone had read it to him.

The Ethiopian Eunuch

The story of Philip and the Ethiopian eunuch give us yet another glimpse into reading in the ancient world (Acts 8:26-40). This minister to Candace, Queen of the Ethiopians, is reading the scroll of Isaiah as he rides in his litter. The fact the Philip hears him reading indicates that in antiquity reading meant reading aloud, whether to oneself or to an audience.

Philip asks: "Do you understand what you are reading?" (v. 30). The eunuch's reply gives us another insight into the ancient experience of reading: "How can I, unless someone guides me?" (v. 31). Those who could read were a minority indeed. And those who could understand and interpret what they read were perhaps an even smaller minority.

Jesus

What, then, can we say about Jesus? It seems that he could indeed read Aramaic, the language of his time. Luke suggests that he could also read Hebrew. Some would argue that he knew Greek as well. All suggestions are plausible. Perhaps the more important consideration is that he could also interpret! He had a grasp and understanding of his traditions that was impressive. Indeed, it was awesome! His antagonists in the Fourth Gospel are astonished (John 7:15, quoted above). His ability to interpret and interweave tradition is amazing. This was always — even to this day — a sign of true manhood in the Middle East: that one not only knows the written tradition, but can quote it appropriately and interweave it creatively for the contemporary situation.

Conclusion

At a "Pops" concert played and sung by the Baltimore Symphony Orchestra and Chorus, Marvin Hamlisch brought into magnificent sound the music and lyrics of Cole Porter. In his commentary before each composition, he told the audience about events in the life of Cole Porter that helped understand what that composer and lyricist actually wrote, and what he meant to say by his music and lyrics. To be sure, all the musicians on stage can read the music they play and sing. They can also interpret it with varying degrees of skill and success. Conductors, however (like Hamlisch), who know the rich tradition in which that music stands, who know what the composer wrote and intended to communicate, can dispel misunderstanding, enhance the enjoyment, and put the listener in touch with the composer and his living heritage. Jesus the Scripture reader did this for the listeners of his day. Preachers and teachers ought to do the same in our day.

2. The Ten Words

Pollsters report that more Americans believe in the Ten Commandments than do people in other Western countries. Yet only a small percentage of Americans are able to name all ten! Modern psychology explains that the human brain can juggle only seven items, give or take two, at one time. Short lists are easier to remember. These same respondents valued each commandment differently. Ninety-three percent of 1,200 Americans randomly interviewed agreed with the commandment, "Thou shalt not kill" (most important of the ten), but only 57 percent agreed with "Thou shalt keep holy the Sabbath" (least important). Though this data derives from a 1982 study sponsored by the Center for Applied Research in the Apostolate (CARA), American preferences remain similar even today. Americans are increasingly concerned with death by violence (homicide), yet church attendance in general remains low. Still, the Ten Commandments tend to surface regularly as a discussion point in all elections and many other discussions. How did our ancestors in the faith view the commandments?

Two Reports

The Ten Commandments appear as such in Exodus 20:1-17 and Deuteronomy 5:6-21. Since they are not numbered in the Bible, it is not easy to identify the ten in each report. Indeed, the numbering familiar to modern believers differs according to traditions. For Roman Catholics, the sixth commandment deals with adultery (Exod. 20:16; Deut. 5:18). In the Protestant enumeration, this prohibition is the seventh commandment.

Moreover, there are obvious differences in each report. Compare Exodus 20:8-11 and Deuteronomy 5:12-15 concerning the motives for observing the Sabbath. Scholars agree that the versions presently in our Bibles are probably postexilic (post-537 B.C.E., very likely around 400 B.C.E.) developments of traditions that originated much earlier. Nevertheless, scholars are reluctant to trace the commandments in their present form to the Mosaic era. What the biblical tradition emphasizes is the divine origin, the completeness, and the finality of this collection of laws (Deut. 5:22). Following the Catholic listing, the first three commandments insist on maintaining and respecting God's honor. The fourth, Sabbath rest, reflects God's being. By insisting on respect and support for parents, the fifth looks to maintaining the social fabric. The rest of the "Thou shalt nots" look to preventing feuds in Israelite society, or, in other words, the maintenance of harmonious social relations (see Ps. 133).

Biblical References

The two lists of commandments (Exod. 20; Deut. 5) are never repeated verbatim *in toto* in the Hebrew Bible or in the New Testament. There are allusions to some commandments (e.g., Hos. 4:2; Jer. 7:9; Ps. 50; 81) and references to commandments that interpolate other materials (Matt. 5:21-48), or simple references to some (Rom. 13:8-10; Jas. 2:8-13), or reports that are out of sequence (Mark 10:19//Luke 18:20).

Many statements in the Wisdom literature echo the commandments without citing them specifically. "A man who bears false witness against his neighbor is like a war club, or a sword, or a sharp arrow" (Prov. 25:18; see also 6:19; 12:17; 14:5; 19:5, 9) reflects Exodus 20:16 and Deuteronomy 5:20. Did God's prohibition need reinforcement from human wisdom, or did the commandment develop out of human experience? "He who does violence to his father and chases away his mother is a son who causes shame and brings reproach" (Prov. 19:26) is a situation that strains the imagination in the light of the only commandment which includes a reward for its observance (Exod. 20:12; Deut. 5:16). While a casual reader might consider the reward as coming from God, it may well be the gift of his parents. A son daring to attempt violence against his parents can expect to be killed by his father or father's brother. This proverb raises the possibility that such behavior was not rare in spite of the commandment.

Another Viewpoint

In *Antiquities* (3.5.4; Whiston translation), Josephus reports that Moses did indeed write on two tablets the precepts spoken by God. Josephus further observes that "it is not lawful for us to set [these precepts] down directly, but their import we will declare." In other words, as the translation notes indicate and scholars recognize, the list of commandments, like the sacred name of God (YHWH), was not to be recited or stated directly in the order in which the commandments were found in the Torah. For instance, notice how Matthew reports Jesus listing the commandments: "And he said to him [an unidentified petitioner], 'Why do you ask me about what is good? One there is who is good. If you would enter life, keep the commandments.' The petitioner said to him: 'Which?' And Jesus said, 'You shall not kill, You shall not commit adultery, You shall not steal, You shall not bear false witness, Honor your father and mother, and, You shall love your neighbor as yourself'" (Matt. 19:17-19).

This cultural practice relative to citing the commandments is dictated by concerns for secrecy and concealment, two major strategies for safeguarding honor in cultures where honor is a core value. According to tradition, God first disclosed the divine name to Moses (Exod. 3:13-15). To know the name of someone is to possess the ability to control that person. To know God's name allowed a person to summon the deity for assistance. Thus the name itself was presumed to have controlling power over the deity whose name it was. Consider your experience when a car salesperson whom you do not know at all addresses you by your first name. The salesperson enters your personal social and psychological space and attempts to manipulate you. This is quasi-magical power. If it works this way in your life, it will work in relationship to God as well. Hence in order to obviate any attempt to manipulate God (which is idolatrous behavior), one is not allowed to say God's revealed name at all. The name stood for a living person, gave access to that person, and had an effect on that person.

While people called upon the name of God (Gen. 4:26; a tradition that differs from Exod. 3:13-15) and blessed it (Ps. 72:18-19), one of the commandments (Exod. 20:7; Deut. 5:9) forbids abusing the name of God. The customary interpretation of this commandment is that it prohibits calling upon God to witness a lie or to use God's name in a curse. But considering that lying in this culture, like secrecy and deception, is a legitimate strategy for defending honor, it is more plausible to see the prohibition as safeguarding against attempts to manipulate God. The tradition is clear that such behavior could have disastrous consequences (Num. 22–24, 31; Acts 8:14-24). The custom of not pronouncing God's name can be plausibly explained as an effort to safeguard God's honor or not shame God (see Lev. 26:14-45).

The situation with the two lists of commandments in the Bible is similar. Dictated, as it were, by God, these words possessed the power of the deity. Josephus says that Moses brought the people to God in order that they might hear the words directly, "that the *energy* of what should be spoken might not be hurt by its utterance by that tongue of a man, which could but imperfectly deliver it to their understanding" (*Antiquities* 3.5.4). In the ancient world, it would be foolhardy to toy with such power. The power belonged to God alone, and concealment or secrecy is a means by which power is maintained. Thus, when people avoid repeating these powerful words directly and literally, they safeguard and sustain the power of their deity, who surpasses all other deities.

Secrecy and concealment also rest on a premise of distrust. One cannot trust others with certain information. One does not know what they will do with the information, nor how they may react to the information. The Israelites would be concerned above all that no one (either among themselves or, worse yet, among their enemies) should aggravate God and thus incur divine displeasure. Better not to take any chances; don't trust anyone with these powerful words.

Surrogate Commandments

The phrase "ten commandments" derives from Exodus 34:28: "And he [Moses] wrote upon the tables the words of the covenant, the ten words." This is the literal translation of the Hebrew; English translations say, "ten commandments." This verse has prompted scholars to conclude that perhaps the original form of the commandments was the negative Hebrew particle *(lo)* and a verb. In the light of Josephus's comment, however, it is also possible that the ten words were an abbreviation created deliberately in order not to risk repeating the powerful words of God with complete exactitude.

Scholars have also discovered lists of "disguised ten commandment lists" in the Bible. The earliest forms appear to be personal protests of innocence (or personal confessions). The prophet Samuel addresses Israel: "Here I am; testify against me before the LORD and before his anointed. Whose ox have I taken? Or whose ass have I taken? Whom have I oppressed? Or from whose hand have I taken a bribe to blind my eyes with it? Testify against me and I will restore it to you" (1 Sam. 12:3).

By the first century c.e. and even earlier, this personal confession had evolved into a depersonalized form of protest that served as a rhetorical device to define and describe qualities. Notice that in this depersonalized form, the listing generally includes ten items: "Do you not know," writes Paul, "that the unrighteous will not inherit the kingdom of God? Do not be deceived: neither fornicators, nor idolaters, nor adulterers, nor male prostitutes, nor homosexuals, nor thieves, nor greedy exploiters, nor drunkards, nor slanderers, nor robbers will inherit the kingdom of God. And such were some of you; but you were washed, you were sanctified, you were justified in the name of the Lord Jesus Christ and in the Spirit of our God" (1 Cor. 6:9-11). Notice that each of the ten categories of people listed here is preceded by a negative, a rather obvious imitation of the ten words in abbreviated form.

Jesus and the Commandments

The Matthean Jesus appears to know about interpreting and "disguising" his references to the commandment lists according to the custom Josephus identified. In the Sermon on the Mount, Jesus notes that whoever "relaxes one of the least of the commandments" shall be called least in the kingdom (Matt. 5:18). Later, in declaring that which defiles a person, Jesus repeats the same selections from a commandment list "in disguise" or in abbreviated form (Matt, 15:19). This latter list matches the sequence in the Sermon on the Mount. Thus in Matthew 15:19, Jesus speaks of murder (Matt. 5:21-26), adultery/fornication (Matt. 5:27-30), divorce/theft (Matt. 5:31-33), false witness (Matt, 5:33-37), and slander (Matt. 5:38-42). The context in Matthew 5:38-42 is civil law and safeguarding rights. Lawsuits routinely involved lying and deceit (see Prov. 25:7c-10, 18). So, while cautioning against slander, Jesus apparently approves Proverbs 20:3 when he urges litigants to settle before their case gets to court (Matt. 5:25-26).

Conclusion

In traditional scholarship, these disguised commandment lists have been included in virtue and vice lists. A rich body of research has gathered and analyzed these lists. They were indeed very widespread in the ancient world and existed in polytheistic, Judaic, and Jesus-group literature. This article helps to explain what nearly all these researchers have noted but failed to explain, namely, the close relationship to the Ten Commandments which some virtue and vice lists in Judaic and Jesus-group literature exhibits (Rom. 1:29-32; 1 Tim. 1:9-11). Josephus's passing comment offers important insight for understanding these disguised commandment lists but also the central importance of the ten words. Indeed, Philo arranged the 613 commandments recognized in the Pharisaic tradition according to the list of the Ten Commandments. Our ancestors were similar to Americans in holding the ten words as central to their lives. Unlike modern Americans, though, our ancestors did not rank-order the commandments in any of their disguised lists. Their selective attentiveness was guided rather by the concerns of the moment and the prohibition against citing the list verbatim *in toto*.

3. The Art of Insult

The Middle Eastern cultural emphasis on manliness is familiar to many readers of the Bible. One way to demonstrate manliness is to endure physical pain without screeching or crying (Pilch 1995; 1993). This is exactly how Isaiah describes the Servant of the Lord: "he was oppressed, and he was afflicted, yet he opened not his mouth; like a lamb that is led to the slaughter, and like a sheep that before its shearers is dumb, so he opened not his mouth" (53:7). Fathers socialize their sons toward such manliness by physical punishment (see Prov. 13:24; 19:18; 20:30; 22:15; 23:13-14). For the author of Hebrews, Proverbs like these (3:11-12) explain why God the Father treated Jesus his Son as he did (5:5-10; 12:3-11).

There is another equally important way to demonstrate manliness. Mastery of language and the ability to turn a good phrase are other marks of a true man in the Middle East. Humor, puns, and wordplays are examples of mastery of language (Pilch 1999: 92-97). Insults are another display of mastery of language.

Push and Shove

In the Mediterranean world, people engage many times daily in a game of "push and shove." The game relates to honor, the core value of this culture. The pushing and shoving are attempts to besmirch the honor of the other in some effective way. Specialists give this game a technical name: challenge and riposte. A challenge can be a gift, an invitation, and very often a question. There is no neutral question in the Middle East because it is always possible that the one to whom the question is posed will not know the answer.

The word "riposte" belongs to the sport of dueling and describes a sharp, swift thrust made after parrying an opponent's lunge. A lie and an insult are two very appropriate and fitting ripostes to any question. Telling a lie ends the exchange, but insulting the questioner ups the ante as the game continues. Only the definitive shaming of one of those involved ends the game.

David and Goliath

The familiar story of David and Goliath is one example of push and shove peppered with insults. Goliath is nine feet nine inches tall (1 Sam. 17:4), quite extraordinary for that time according to physical anthropologists. He hurls a challenge at the Israelite army to select a warrior to do battle with him, one on one (17:8). He adds insult to underscore the challenge (17:10).

David pleads with King Saul to send him to battle. Saul points out the obvious: David is too young to battle with a seasoned warrior. He is not an equal to Goliath, and only equals can play the game of push and shove. Furthermore, David is a shepherd, and this is a despised occupation in the culture. It would be insulting to send him up against a warrior. Moreover, David doesn't even come close to Goliath's height. David defends himself as very powerful and up to the task. He recounts how he killed lions and bears in defending his flocks. Besides, he argues, God is on his side. It is important to remember God's place in the honor scheme of the Israelites. God's reputation as kin-God of the Israelites is always at stake when enemies come to do battle. If Israel loses, God is shamed. The gods of the enemy are perceived to be superior to Israel's kin-God.

Saul offers his armor to David, but it doesn't fit. David is weighed down by equipment to which he is unaccustomed. He approaches Goliath in his shepherd garb, taking five smooth stones in his pouch and holding his sling in his hand. Compared to Goliath with his uniform and equipment (17:5-7), David looks naked. Moreover, he is too young and inexperienced to play in this game. His good looks similarly testify that he is not battle scarred. No wonder Goliath disdained David (17:42). He shouldn't be playing the game. Were it not that Goliath perceives that David is not his equal, Goliath would be insulted. But an inferior cannot insult a superior.

So Goliath does the equivalent of trying to flick away a pesky mosquito. "Am I a dog that you come to me with sticks?" (17:43), he asks, and he curses David by his gods. Goliath's words can be seen as a dismissal of David, or a foolhardy person (like David in Goliath's eyes) can interpret them as a challenge and move the game forward.

David's eloquent response (17:44-47) makes Goliath's blunt challenge look tame by comparison. David is clearly a master of words. Indeed, he has already been described as such (16:18). He taunts Goliath ("come to me") and tells him that his weapons will not spare his life, for David intends to make of Goliath food for the birds of the air and beasts of the field. Already David has bested his opponent in one dimension of manliness.

The rest is anticlimactic. David rushes forward to meet Goliath. With a powerful shot from his sling, David kills him, then beheads him with Goliath's own sword. This shameful end for Goliath ends the game of push and shove between himself and David. Note well that the war of words in the Middle East is as important if not more so than actual physical combat. And everything is, indeed, about honor.

Jesus, Master of Words

Mark (15:39) indicates that the manly centurion who drew execution duty that day was impressed by the manly way in which Jesus died. He hung on the cross from nine in the morning to three in the afternoon, apparently without saying a word. Only at the end does he whisper a prayer, shriek, and breathe his last. This was similar to the way in which Eleazar and the seven brothers died as reported in 2 Maccabees 6–7, and certainly similar to the Servant described by Isaiah (Isa. 52:13–53:12 [53:3, 7]).

But Jesus also demonstrated his manliness by his mastery of language. He seems to have enjoyed punning, and he told some impressive parables. Remember that with a parable, a speaker says one thing but means something else. This is a common Middle Eastern way of communicating. The stories about sowers and seeds, vineyards, their owners and workers, and stewards are not really about agriculture, viticulture, or employer-employee relations. They are about something else entirely. These stories are about God, how God behaves with those in his theocracy, and how life should be conducted in that theocracy ("kingdom or reign of God").

Jesus, Master of Insult

Since no question in the Middle East is perceived to be an innocent request for information, it is interesting to observe how Jesus answers questions. Quite often he insults the questioner or responds with his own question. Those who study rhetoric recognize the latter strategy as "parry with a query."

One of Jesus' favorite insults is the word "hypocrite." In Matthew's gospel, the word is found only on Jesus' lips. It is directed only to the Pharisees or describes them (6:2, 5, 16; 7:5; 15:7; 22:18; 23:13, 15, 23, 25, 27, 29; 24:51). The word in Greek does not have quite the same meaning as the English word. In Greek, the word means "interpreter, expounder, actor." If a reader were to replace the English word "hypocrite" with "actor" in Matthew's gospel, two things would emerge. Jesus truly considers his opponents, the Pharisees, to be like actors. Torah may be the lines they quote, but it is not the script by which they claim to live. This helps understand why Jesus says: "practice and observe whatever they tell you, but not what they do; for they preach, but do not practice" (Matt. 23:3). They are actors.

The second observation is that Jesus appears to know a lot about theaters and acting. Where might he have learned that? Three and a half miles north of Nazareth, about a one-hour walk, lies a place called Sepphoris. It was the principal residence of Herod Antipas ("that Fox," according to Jesus' insulting identification) until the years 19-20 C.E. In recent years, archaeologists excavated a magnificent theater there. The speculation is that it was probably under construction when Jesus was a teenager. It would seem plausible that a village artisan like Joseph and Jesus, his dutiful and obedient teenage son who would take up his father's trade, might find an outlet for their skills in the building projects of Herod Antipas. Mary would pack a lunch for them, perhaps even snacks. They might even have worked on constructing the theater. Moreover, in that period there were theaters in Jerusalem, in Sebaste, and in Caesarea — it would be difficult not to learn about theaters, acting, and actors even if one never attended the theater.

Other Insults

Jesus appears to have known well how to aim his insults appropriately. When he deals with learned people, he asks derisively: "Have you not read?" or "Can't you read?" Thus, when a lawyer (Torah expert) asks him: "What shall I do to inherit eternal life?" (What can anyone do to inherit anything?) Jesus retorts: "How do you read?" (Luke 10:25). We learn from the lawyer's response that he knew the answer all along. He could and did read very well. When dealing with illiterate people (in Jesus' day about 95 to 97 percent of the people could not read or write), Jesus would ask: "Have you not heard?" (Matt. 5:21, 27, 33, 38, 43), or did you sleep during discussions and presentations of Torah?

Perhaps the most memorable illustration of mastery of language and insult occurs in the story of the woman not of Jesus' ethnic group who wanted a favor from him (Pilch 2002: 18-20). Matthew reports that a woman, a Canaanite, addressed Jesus respectfully and requested him to do something about the demon that plagued her daughter (Matt. 15:21-28). Since she is a woman, and a foreigner, she is not Jesus' equal. There are two strikes against her. She cannot insult or affect him, and at first he does the proper thing. He ignores her!

But as she persists and begins to make a scene, the disciples urge him to snip this in the bud. Jesus answers that it's none of his business because he was "sent only to the lost sheep of the house of Israel." Matthew's Jesus, of course, is consistent in this. The worst thing he can call somebody is a Gentile (18:17), that is, a non-Israelite, not one of his own kind.

Since no one whispers in this culture, the woman has clearly heard the words Jesus spoke in her direction if not directly to her. She turns up the pressure, kneels before Jesus (thereby blocking his progress), and begs with amazing, continued respect: "Lord, help me." Then Jesus winds up for perhaps the best insult of his entire career: "It is not fair to take the children's bread and throw it to the dogs." By any calculation and interpretation, insinuating that this woman is [like] a dog is certainly not flattering or honorable. Any lesser person might have figuratively put tail between legs and fled for safety.

But this woman stands her ground: "Yes, Lord, but even the dogs at least get to eat crumbs from the table!" This is the only person in all the gospels who has beaten Jesus in the game of push and shove until his trial. Her quick wit and ready riposte gained the favor she wanted from Jesus. It was the least he could do to save face in the face-losing outcome of this game.

Conclusion

It is challenging to attempt to match Matthew's Jesus who identified himself as "gentle and lowly in heart" (11:29) with Matthew's Jesus as master of insult. Perhaps it helps to recognize that Jesus was a truly representative male in his culture. The cultural obligation to demonstrate manliness is incumbent on every male. Anyone who didn't measure up would be ignored and fail to get a hearing. David could be violent as a warrior but gentle with his friend Jonathan, as Jesus was violent in the temple fracas but gentle with fellow ethnics in need. There is a proper time for all the cultural values, including insult.

4. The Power of the Curse

Picture the scene. A devout Israelite accustomed to visiting the temple to praise God is now met there by an accusing crowd gathered to judge him. The accusers are people the Israelite loved, that is, to whom he was staunchly loyal. This is, after all, a collectivistic culture where people are closely bonded with one another. What are the charges? "He did not remember to show kindness, but pursued the poor and needy and the brokenhearted to their death" (Ps. 109:16). The charges are mingled with a long string of curses because, as the accusers say, "This man loved to curse" (v. 17).

The Israelite believes that the charges against him are lies (v. 2). There is no basis for the accusation (v. 3). How will he plead? Innocent, of course (vv. 20ff.)! But before he enters his plea, he turns the table on his accusers. The singular subject in verses 6 to 19 ("he") stands in contrast to the plurals in the verses that precede and follow ("they"). What the devout Israelite does is turn the curses and charges against him back at his accusers. He says in effect: "The same to you, buddy/buddies!" Keep in mind that this is a very public event. The purpose of such "trials" is not to weigh evidence and determine guilt or innocence but to determine how to shame the person. As this psalm indicates, it was a shaming (and cursing) contest.

This psalm is but one of a number of "curse psalms" in the Bible (see Pss. 69; 79; 83; 5; 6; 7; 10; etc.). This devout Israelite does not surprise Bible readers who remember God's promise to Abraham: "I will bless those who bless you, and him who curses you I will curse" (Gen. 12:3). Paul cursed anyone who would dare to preach a gospel different from his (Gal. 1:8-9). Why all this cursing? How is it that even God curses? What is a curse and why does it permeate the Bible (Brichto 1963)?

The Curse

The American belief that "sticks and stones will break my bones but names will never hurt me" is unusual among the cultures of the world. In the majority of the world's cultures, human beings realize that words spoken cannot be retracted. Apologies are inadequate. Hurtful spoken words will inevitably produce serious and undesirable consequences like revenge. Words are as powerful as deeds. It is this basic belief that gives the curse its force. A curse is a form of communication (word, gesture, symbolic action) intended to direct damage, harm, trouble, disaster, even death toward a person or object.

163

In the Bible, curses entail two key elements. One is the irrevocable mysterious power of words, as described above. The second element is the curse's involvement of the deity. Whereas in many cultures the words of the curse themselves carry power, thus overlapping with magic, in the biblical world the deity named in the formula is the one who makes the curse effective or ineffective. As Balaam protested: "How can I curse whom God has not cursed? How can I denounce whom the LORD has not denounced?" (Num. 23:8). From this conviction evolved the "curse prayer" (prayer of imprecation), that is, a form of communication attempting to persuade the one with power to make the curse effective to act on the petitioner's behalf. In this framework, the curse is removed from the realm of magic.

God and the Curse

Scholars observe how blessing and curse structure the book of Genesis. The Priestly story opens with blessing upon all of humankind (Gen. 1:28). The Yahwist's story introduces a series of shifts between curse (from God on the first earthling and his consort, and on Cain) to blessing (on the survivors of the Flood). Curse reappears in the Tower of Babel story, but blessing returns in Abraham and culminates in Jacob's (and God's) blessing of the twelve sons.

Remembering the principle that everything human beings know and say about God is based on human experience, which in turn is culturally shaped ("all theology is analogy"), a reader can appreciate why the God described in the Bible is quite Mediterranean in character and not at all transcultural. When God's creatures disobey, they dishonor or shame God. Blasphemy by definition is dishonoring or shaming God. In a world where these are the core values, a superior shamed by an inferior is bound to extract satisfaction (sometimes known as revenge). Hence God has no choice but to curse disobedient creatures.

Consider the curses in Genesis 3. The serpent who had legs (= dragon, leviathan; see Rev. 12:9) must now crawl (v. 14). The ground will yield its produce only to exhausting toil (v. 17). This last word, "toil," is exactly the same in the sentence addressed to the woman. Carol Meyers (1997: 29) has therefore proposed a more culturally plausible rendition of that verse: "I will greatly increase your toil and pregnancies,/[along] with travail shall you beget children" (v. 16).

The parallelism in these verses indicates that the woman will work the resistant soil along with her partner, and due to miscarriages and deaths in early infancy she will experience many pregnancies just to reproduce herself. Pain is not mentioned in the text. At the turn of the nineteenth century in the United States, a woman had to bear 6.1 children to reproduce herself. The situation was far worse in antiquity.

A sharp pair of eyes might perceive that God's curse was brought on by those who suffer it. The modern Western accusation about "blaming the victim" is entirely implausible in the ancient Middle East. In the game of honor and shame, everyone knows the consequences of failing. Among humans, the penalty is frequently death! In the larger honor scheme, God can inflict death too, but the record indicates that that is something of a last resort. God has other ways of attaining the requisite satisfaction.

Human Beings and the Curse

Defense Whether viewed as magic (i.e., impersonal causality) or as effected by the deity (i.e., personal causality), the power of the curse was a legitimate means of defense in a variety of situations. Sarcophagi found in Egypt, Phoenicia, and Greece contain curses to protect the deceased against grave robbers and violators. In Babylonia and Israel such a curse was commonly placed on boundary stones to guard against theft of land. "You shall not remove your neighbor's landmark . . ." (Deut. 19:14). "Cursed be the one who removes the neighbor's landmark," pronounced by Moses (Deut. 27:17) in the passive voice, suggests that God is the one who will do the avenging. The passive voice is a respectful way of talking about God without mentioning God in situations where no human agent is in sight.

Self-defense People who perceived that they had no other means of protecting themselves (e.g., by lying or slander) would have recourse to a curse. "Do not slander a servant to his master, lest he curse you, and you be held guilty" (Prov. 30:10). Consider Proverbs 11:26: "People curse him who holds back grain, but a blessing is on the head of him who sells it." Western interpreters often view this verse anachronistically as an injustice in terms of a free-market economy. Middle Easterners identify in this verse a person of means who is refusing to be a patron. A patron is one who can obtain for a petitioner benefits that could not be gained by personal initiative, or on terms better than one could gain by personal initiative. The man in Jesus' parable with the bumper crop who refused to be a patron but hoarded his surplus for his retirement received the ultimate curse from God: "Die, you fool!" (Luke 12:13-21).

Sirach's (4:5-6) caution is well advised: "From one in need turn not your eyes, give him no reason to curse you; for if in the ache of bitterness he curse you, his Maker will hear his prayer." The Sage reported folk wisdom on the same topic from a slightly different perspective: "Like a sparrow in its flitting, like a swallow in its flying, a curse that is causeless does not alight" (Prov. 26:2). A righteous person need not fear a curse.

Sanction of a Promise Since lying and deception were approved cultural strategies for preserving honor, one could never be certain of statements made by people unless they swore to its truth with an oath: "Amen, Amen, I say to you" or "Truly, truly, I say to you." These phrases are equivalent to a modern "curse": "Cross my heart and hope to die, I am indeed telling the truth." Similar oaths would be "by my father's grave" or "by my mother's womb," meaning "may he not rest in peace" or "may she become sterile."

Abimelech and the commander of his army make Abraham swear by God to be honest and never deal falsely with him or his posterity. Abraham answers: "I swear." This is equivalent to a curse on one's self, "May God deal with me and avenge you if I do not keep my bargain, promise, etc." (See also Ruth 1:16-17.) A similar "curse" appears when Abraham sends his servant to his kin to find a wife for Isaac and makes the servant swear by putting his hand under Abraham's thigh (a euphemism for the genitals; Gen. 24). The idea is that if the servant in any way does not keep his promise to Abraham, the servant's source of fertility will dry up and become ineffective. In a culture where family (kinship) is the central social institution, threatened loss of fertility is a strong incentive to keep one's promise.

While the commandments are familiar to most readers of the Bible, the sanctions are less so. If Mediterranean human beings bind each other to their promises by means of curses, God does the same in spades. To assure that the twelve tribes will adhere to their commitments and keep their covenant responsibility, the Levites ceremoniously pronounced twelve curses which the people confirm: "Amen" (Deut. 27:15-26; also Deut. 27–32; Lev. 26). The curses are God's sanctions to insure that the people will obey the commandments. Given the number of times exhortations to obey the commandments are repeated in the Bible, it is fair to surmise that even the threat of sanctions was not always an effective motivating factor.

People Who Should Not Be Cursed

A deaf person must not be cursed because the inability to hear means that the person is unable to protect against it (Lev. 19:14). Other curses like this one that deserve the penalty of death include cursing one's parents (Exod. 21:17; Matt. 15:3-4) or God's anointed (2 Sam. 16). For a younger son to seek his inheritance before his father has died is equivalent to wishing his father dead, to cursing his father (Luke 15:11-32). That that father did not kill his son on the spot is just one of the many cultural anomalies in Jesus' parable (see above).

Jesus and the Curse

Jesus challenged the strategy of "the same to you, buddy!" by exhorting his followers to bless those that curse them (Luke 6:28). Moreover, according to Paul (Gal. 3:10ff.) Jesus freed those who believe in him from the generic curse laid on those who do not observe the Torah perfectly (Deut. 27:26). By taking on the specific curse associated with crucifixion (Deut. 21:23) — in Paul's not entirely clear interpretation — Jesus took the place of those upon whom the generic curse fell and freed them from its consequences.

The concluding chapter of Revelation (Rev. 22:3) echoes the prophet Zechariah (Zech. 14:11) in describing the new Jerusalem as a place where nothing cursed will exist. Those still deserving God's curse will be cast out (Rev. 22:15).

Conclusion

American culture prefers civility and diplomacy to cursing. It tries not to offend. The impact of this perspective on theology is to explain away cursing in the Bible. Commentators emphasize Jesus' prohibition of cursing as reversal of a cultural trait. They tend to explain Old Testament practices as uninformed. Whatever the value of such interpretations, it is important not to lose sight of the power of the curse in that world even to this day. Words are more powerful than nuclear weapons.

5. No Thank You!

The lone Samaritan among the ten cleansed from a polluting skin condition who returns to thank Jesus is the only person in the New Testament to do this. Middle Eastern readers easily understand why. To say "thank you" in the Middle East signals an intention to end a relationship. Since "Judeans have no dealings with Samaritans" (John 4:9), this Samaritan was likely in the "wrong place at the right time." He received healing from God through Jesus' mediation, and he knows that he is hardly ever likely to encounter Jesus again. The realistic Samaritan praised God from whom his healing came and then returned to end his relationship with Jesus (Luke 17:11-19). Jesus says nothing of the gratitude or lack of it among the other nine. Why do Western commentators, teachers, and preachers invariably misunderstand and misinterpret this story?

The Meaning of "Thank You"

Gratitude is a human response to kindnesses experienced or favors received, but it takes different forms in different cultures. It also carries different meanings. In parts of India, there exists no expression for "thanks." The culture of those regions has not required its invention. Beneficent social acts toward others are viewed as the fulfillment of an obligation. If someone gives a gift, the recipient believes the gift is the result of an obligation and therefore deserved. No verbal acknowledgment is necessary. In fact, an overt expression of "thanks" places a finite value on the gift received and reduces its significance. Moreover, in these parts of India, "thanks" implies the termination of a social relationship. Not only is that unkind, but it is also foolhardy. How can one know that one won't need the help of this donor again at some time (Stewart and Bennett 1991: 94-96)?

In another part of the world, an Arab proverb reports: "Don't thank me; you will repay me." The cultural context here is clearly one of informal dyadic contract. I give you a gift or do you a favor, and by accepting it, you owe me a gift or favor in return. When you repay my favor, I owe you another gift or favor. The process usually continues without end. Clearly, the context in this culture, as in India, is one of social obligation. The consequence of such a cultural pattern of behavior is an ongoing strengthening of a human relationship.

In contrast to these cultures, according to anthropologists, Americans seek to minimize incurring social obligations in their social life (Stewart and Bennett 1991: 94). For Americans, saying "thank you" expresses gratitude but does not include or even imply an obligation to reciprocate. Americans do their best to avoid personal commitments to others. They do not like to get involved, but if they do, they prefer to do it anonymously as in a pooling of donations to assist the needy in a crisis. (The same exists in the case of gift-giving — birthdays, wedding showers, etc. — in the offices of corporate America). This way, the individual donor remains anonymous and obligation free, and the individual recipient is similarly obligation free. No beneficiary of United Way benefits feels at all obligated to United Way or to those who contribute. The beneficiaries, of course, are grateful.

This kind of behavior is extraordinary among the cultures of the world. Anthropologists observe that everywhere else in the world outside the United States, a human relationship that does not involve obligation is simply not significant. An anonymous gift in other cultures is nonsense, meaningless. If the gift does not deprive or inconvenience the donor, it holds less significance for the recipient. In Japan, for instance, the American penchant for spontaneous (and short-lived), individually bound, and obligation-free social relations is viewed as a social ornament rather than the substance of the social system. In Japan, social relations are based on dependence and a recognized and respected hierarchical social structure. Thus, giving and receiving gifts in Japan are rooted in a deeper cultural pattern of binding human beings to create and sustain a web of human relationship. The American ideal is to maintain the individual inviolate.

Thanksgiving Psalms

Hermann Gunkel, the pioneer of psalm research, identified a category of psalms which he called "Individual Songs of Thanksgiving." Later scholars identified a category of "Communal Songs of Thanksgiving." In many instances, these sentiments of thanksgiving were expressed after recounting a tragedy or misfortune from which the individual or group was rescued. In other words, the thanksgiving followed a lament. Lists of these psalms vary, but Kselman and Barré offer the following in *The New Jerome Biblical Commentary* 34:9: individual thanksgiving psalms — Psalms 9–10; 30; 32; 34; 41; 92; 103; 116; 118; 138; communal thanksgiving psalms — Psalms 2; 21; 45; 110.

Searching English translations for the word "thanks" or "thanksgiving" in the Bible in general or psalms in particular confirms the truth of an Italian proverb: "Traduttore, traditore" — Every translator is a traitor! Serious Bible students often consult at least five translations in order to see where serious problems may exist in the original text. Of 161 occurrences of "thank, thanks, thanksgiving" in the NRSV, 53 are found in Psalms.

"I will give thanks to the LORD with my whole heart" (Ps. 9:1). "Sing praises to the LORD, O you his saints, and give thanks to his holy name" (Ps. 30:4). "It is good to give thanks to the LORD, to sing praises to your name, O Most High" (Ps. 92:1). "O give thanks to the LORD, for he is good; his steadfast love endures forever!" (Ps. 118:1). "I give you thanks, O LORD, with my whole heart; before the gods I sing your praise" (Ps. 138:1).

The Hebrew word usually translated "thanks" or "thanksgiving" (*tôdâ*, which in modern Israeli Hebrew means "thank you") is a noun deriving from a verb *(yādâ)* that basically means "to throw, or to cast." In one of its tenses (hiphil) this verb is thought to mean "to give thanks, laud, praise." Scholars are not agreed as to how that meaning relates to "to throw, or to cast," but they surmise that it may derive from gestures that accompanied the public expression of gratitude.

If we trust the report of cultural anthropologists about the significance of saying "thank you" in many cultures of the world, including the Mediterranean world, then we must suspect that lexicographers are mistaken in assigning the meaning "give thanks" or "thanksgiving" to these Hebrew words. It is by far preferable and indeed culturally more plausible to translate these words as "give praise" or something similar. Indeed, noted biblical scholar Claus Westermann suggests that the Hebrew verb *yādâ* should be translated "praise" rather than thanks. His culturally correct insight would result in renaming Gunkel's "Individual Psalms of Thanksgiving" as "Narrative Praise of the Collectivist Individual."

Only a fool would want to end a relationship with God. A beneficiary of God's benevolence is indeed grateful. In the Middle East and the circum-Mediterranean world, the proper response to benefits received, the proper expression of gratitude, is to broadcast the virtues and generosity of one's donor, or patron. Such clients can never reciprocate the gift, but singing the praises of the donor expresses a sense of indebtedness and enhances the donor's honorable reputation. This is what healed or rescued suppliants did in the temple when they recounted their misfortune and then reported how God rescued them from it. To thank God would be to end that relationship, equivalent to suicide! To praise God, in public, far and wide, would be exactly what God, conceived in Mediterranean terms, desires.

The New Testament

According to Danker (*Greek-English Lexicon of the New Testament and Other Early Christian Literature,* p. 415), the Greek word translated "thank you" *(eucharisteō)* shows that one is under obligation. As an English translation, he suggests: "be thankful, feel obligated to thank." This word is related to another, *charis* (often translated "favor," "grace," "benefaction," etc.), which, according to Danker (p. 1079), also involves a sense of social obligation so bound up with the reciprocity that characterizes Mediterranean cultures. In the Semitic world, this sense of obligation stands out strongly in the phrase "steadfast loving-kindness" *(ḥesed)*.

It is therefore no surprise that, in the New Testament, "thanks" are directed to God in most occurrences. The phrase "thanks be to God" is common in Paul and elsewhere (e.g., Rom. 6:17; 1 Cor. 15:57). Jesus gave thanks before distributing food to the crowds (Matt. 15:36; John 6:11) and again when he was at table with the Twelve (Mark 14:23; Luke 22:17, 19; etc.).

Yet the simple translation "thank you" does not adequately reflect what the New Testament is reporting. People are not terminating a relationship with God (which is what "thank you" signals in the Mediterranean world). Rather, they are expressing indebtedness to God, a sense of obligation to acknowledge God publicly as beneficent beyond imagination.

Translations

Specialists recognize two kinds of translations: literal (word for word, or technically "formal correspondence") and literary (meaning for meaning, or technically "dynamic equivalence"). As our knowledge of Mediterranean culture deepens and improves, it seems to become increasingly difficult to achieve a literal translation. In this present discussion, it would seem to be wrong to retain "thank you" and related words in modern English translations. Even if this is what dictionaries propose, the cultural significance of "thank you" would indicate that only in the story of the healed Samaritan recounted by Luke (17:11-19) is that phrase appropriate and correct in its Mediterranean cultural meaning. In all other instances, the notion of obligation and indebtedness is the primary meaning communicated in expressions of gratitude. Somehow, either in the translation or a footnote, that would have to be noted.

Conclusion

Some scholars suggest that Luke modeled the story of the ten "lepers" on the story of the single one reported by all the Synoptics (Mark 1:40-45//Matt. 8:2-4//Luke 5:12-16). They also note that in the story of the ten, Jesus did not command those healed "to make an offering for your cleansing" (Luke 5:14) because that would have been impossible for the Samaritan, who was barred from entering the Jerusalem temple. If indeed Luke had been that sensitive to the Samaritan among the ten, it is equally plausible that he realized that the Samaritan had no choice but to end this blessed but brief relationship with Jesus by saying, "Thank you."

6. "Who Touched Me?"

One day as a crowd pressed around him, Jesus asked: "Who touched me?" (Mark 5:30; Luke 8:45). His astonished disciples reminded Jesus of the facts of Mediterranean culture. People in Mediterranean cultures are comfortable standing as close as six to eight inches from each other, while people in Western culture tend to keep a space of twelve to sixteen inches between each other. Moreover, in the Western world, people do not touch each other as spontaneously or readily as did people in the Mediterranean world. Human touch serves different functions and sends different messages in different cultures.

Touch

Touching is a symbolic means of communication that signals the nature of various human interactions (Malandro, Barker, and Barker 1989). The amount of touch one will receive and give is determined, at least in part, by culture, sex, age, status, and personality. The Western cultural preference for avoiding touch is especially evident on elevators or when a person takes a seat next to or between travelers on public transportation. On elevators, Western people attempt to "shrink" into themselves to avoid touching others. On public transportation, travelers similarly "shrink" their bodies in order not to touch fellow travelers as they edge themselves into a seat. Things are very different in the Mediterranean world, as the disciples reminded Jesus.

Functional Categories of Touch

Specialists have identified five basic categories of touch. The functional-professional category is characteristic of physicians (e.g., measuring the pulse, taking blood pressure), barbers, and beauticians, among others. In Western culture, visiting the beautician is sometimes a covert means for getting touched when it is lacking in one's life. In the ancient world, healers often touched clients as part of therapy. Jesus touched those afflicted with a repulsive scaly skin condition (so-called "lepers") as he declared that they were made clean (by God, of course; e.g., Matt. 8:3 and pars.). Modern observers call this "therapeutic touch." We shall explore it in more detail below.

A second category of touch includes social-polite gestures. The handshake or taking someone by the hand fits into this category. A handshake establishes or confirms friendship. When Peter takes the lame man by the right hand and raises him up (Acts 3:7), that action is not part of the healing process. It is a caring touch, that is, it lends physical support to someone who needs it to stand or move along. It is also a signal of friendship.

A third category of touch includes gestures that communicate friendship-warmth. In the Mediterranean world in general, male friends frequently hold hands in public while walking. Judas selects the gesture of a kiss (a kind of touch) as a sign of friendship (Mark 14:44-45) to identify Jesus in the dark garden for those who came to arrest him.

A fourth category includes touching gestures that pertain to love and intimacy. The Song of Solomon mentions many of these gestures. The final and fifth category is related to this, namely, touch intended for sexual arousal. Paul's statement, "It is well for a man not to touch a woman," can be translated more explicitly as "It is well for a husband not have to sexual relations with his wife," or better: "It is well for a married couple not to have children" (1 Cor. 7:1; see also Gen. 20:6; Prov. 6:29; Malina and Pilch 2006: 86). We don't know the reason for Paul's statement, but it could be the Israelite tradition that babies born at the end time would be malformed monsters (cf. Luke 21:23).

Messages of Touch

Touch communicates at least five different kinds of messages. Perhaps the most obvious message is emotion, as in greetings and farewells. The beloved fantasizes in Song of Solomon (8:1): "If I met you outside, I would kiss you." Of course, this kind of gesture even between married partners is simply not acceptable in the public sphere of ancient Middle Eastern culture. Moreover, the kiss of greeting differs from the kiss of lovers. It consists of kissing the other person on each cheek. Paul exhorts letter recipients to greet each other with a holy kiss (1 Thess. 5:26; 1 Cor. 16:20; 2 Cor. 13:12; Rom. 16:16; 1 Pet. 5:14). Hosts greeted guests with a kiss (Luke 7:45). The kiss of farewell is more emotional than the kiss of greeting (Acts 20:37).

The kiss was also prominent in Eucharistic celebrations (Justin, *Apology* 65.2) and prescribed in the *Apostolic Constitutions* (8.11; also 2.57) whereby clerics kiss the bishop, laymen other men, and women other women. Apparently, kissing was also open to abuse. Tiberius issued an edict forbidding general kissing (Suetonius, *Lives* 3.34.2). Pliny *(Natural History* 2.1-3) describes a facially disfiguring disease to which male nobility seemed to be subject and which was transmitted by a kiss.

A second message communicated is status. Thus, the person who initiates the touch is generally considered to be of a higher status. The initiator controls the interaction because touch increases the immediate closeness of persons. Variations of this kind of touch include the handshake, which occurs between persons of a real or pretended equality of power relations, and supplication, in which the initiator temporarily assumes a position of inferiority. John (4:47) says that the royal aristocrat "begged" Jesus to come and heal his son. This term describes the process by which one seeks a favor from a patron. The process often included kissing the hem of the patron's garment, and it is plausible to imagine that the royal petitioner did this as well.

A third message communicated by touch is the expression of body-contact needs. Many historians think that group sleeping used to be the worldwide norm (see Luke 11:7). As that custom passed away, human beings resorted to at least fourteen tie signs to gain body contact. A body contact tie sign is a behavior that indicates a wish to be held. Some examples are the arm link, the shoulder embrace, the waist embrace, the caress, and so on. The handshake is a very obvious tie sign, as is the kiss. Historically, the primitive handshake indicated that no weapons were concealed. In the Roman world, the hand-to-chest gesture sent the same message. In the Roman Empire, the handshake took the form of a clasping of the forearms. In modern Western culture, the handshake is a gesture of welcome. The palms interlock, signifying openness, and the touching signifies union or oneness.

The body guide is another interesting tie sign. Here one places one's hand on another person's back to guide that person in a certain direction. It is a very old parent-to-child behavior which conveys love but also the notions that "I care" and "I am in control." It is conceivable that Jesus may have sometimes used this gesture with his disciples, perhaps even when he sent them out two by two (Matt. 10:5).

A fourth message of touch expresses the need or wish to be held. Cuddling and other forms of body contact provide feelings of security, protection, comfort, contentment, and love. Finally, some touches express the need for self-intimacy. Putting one's hand to one's head after slamming a door and realizing that the keys are locked inside is a gesture that performs the contact one might expect from an imaginary sympathetic companion.

Healing Touch

Touch in general is closely related to status, especially in male-to-male contact. Adult male status includes self-control and self-empowerment. Males are expected to retain or obtain control over their individual selves. Of course, Mediterranean males are permitted to lose self-control when overpowered by emotion, but friends are expected to restrain them and prevent them from doing damage to self or others. When the man calms down, he is puzzled by how he lost control. One can only wonder why Jesus' disciples did not intervene to restrain him when he caused a disturbance in the temple (see John 2:13-15). Thus gesture and deportment reveal and contain status. This consideration plays a role in what is known as the "healing touch."

Modern observers define the healing touch as an action whereby a healthy person touches a sick person to soothe that person's pain or alleviate that person's suffering. Healing touch is not mentioned in the Hippocratic corpus, but the gesture does occur in Greek tragedy and in the Bible. While male friends in the Mediterranean world readily touch each other even in public, the case is somewhat different for touching gestures between strangers. Male members of two different households must work out a face-saving strategy in the public sphere. Usually this strategy involves transforming the relationship into kinship, which is extremely important given the range of meanings that touching can carry.

Touch between males not biologically related has a potentially emasculating force. It can imply or demonstrate moral weakness, servility, homoerotic interest, or feminization, all of which damage the claim to adult male status. On the other hand, a male who is ill loses self-control (e.g., the lame, the blind). Moreover, loss of bodily strength and desperate and verbal reaction to pain feminizes a man. Jesus' six hours of silent suffering on the cross culminating in a final shriek only before he died made a powerful impression of his manliness on the centurion who stood guard (Mark 15:25-39). In contrast, Jesus' self-presentation as a mother hen who would gather the citizens of Jerusalem under her wings could be a slightly embarrassing hint of gender ambiguity remaining from having been raised with the girls until the age of puberty by all the women of the family. The intention is clear, but he (or his evangelist) might have selected an image more suited to male touching patterns.

Touching children incurs no loss of status but rather communicates the power and control of the one who does the touching. Those who brought children to Jesus that he might touch them recognized his healing power (transmitted through the hands) and no doubt hoped that his touch might protect the children from the "evil eye" of others who had lost children in childbirth or at an early age (Luke 18:15; Mark 10:13; see also Mark 5:41, where the death might have resulted from the "evil eye" [= destructive envy] of villagers — see the next chapter).

Touching non-related males in the private sphere is permissible, but again the relationship must be redefined. Touching between males not of the same household can be polluting. Most often the relationship is transformed into friendship, or into a fictive-kin relationship, where the touch can be understood as filial duty. When Jesus touches Peter's mother-in-law (Matt. 8:15), the gesture occurs in the private sphere. Moreover, men and women are not equals, hence there is no loss of status on Jesus' part. Recall the woman who knew that because of her menstrual irregularity her touch would pollute Jesus but did it anyway (Mark 9:20). She had nothing to lose but much to gain. Jesus also extended a healing touch to the so-called lepers (Matt. 8:3), to blind persons (Matt. 20:34), and to the deaf and mute (Mark 7:33), but these clients appear to be inferiors because of their illness.

Conclusion

The basic human need for touch is heavily interpreted and controlled by culture. Simple as the gestures mentioned above may be, each one needs to be carefully analyzed (Pilch 2000a). Even in a culture where people are accustomed to standing very close to each other and touch each other more often than in other cultures, one must knows the rules of touch by which one protects and maintains one's honor. Jesus seems to have worked well and effectively within his culture's rules.

7. The Evil Eye

Alessandro Ciammarughi, a native of Rome, Italy, designed the scenery and costumes for the Baltimore Opera Company's production of Giuseppe

Verdi's *Il Trovatore* in October 2003. The story is set in Biscay, Spain, and begins on a dark night during which the soldiers of Count di Luna attend their master while he lingers beneath the balcony of Leonora, the woman he loves. To keep themselves awake and alert, they ask Ferrando, their leader, to tell them once again the story of the Count's brother.

Ferrando describes how an old gypsy woman bewitched (Italian *ammaliato*) the infant who suddenly became ill with a fever. Suspected of foul play, the gypsy was burned at the stake. The infant disappeared, but later an infant was found in the ashes at the stake. The gypsy's daughter, Azucena, was believed to have taken revenge in this way on di Luna's father for her mother's punishment. The old witch, however, was believed to assume many forms (a crow, an owl, but especially a civet rat) each night as she returned to continue working her witching ways. As Ferrando finishes the story, the back wall of the dark set is illumined to project a large human eye, open wide, staring at and frightening the Spanish soldiers to run off stage but also staring beyond them at the audience. At four performances, the American audiences found this scene amusing yet puzzling. A Spanish (or Italian) audience would be as frightened as the actors! A Mediterranean audience would cross themselves, avert their eyes from the set, or caress the amulet they wear to ward off this evil. They would do this because the stage set reproduced the gypsy's evil eye (*mal ojo* in Spanish; *malocchio* in Italian). That of course is exactly what Alessandro, the Italian set designer, intended. That same fright is what Verdi's librettist, Salvatore Cammarano, wrote into the lyrics of the opera. That fright also is what Verdi composed in his music.

The Evil Eye

According to ethnographic studies in the Human Relations Area Files at Yale University, approximately 36 percent of their total world sample (186 societies) believe in the power of otherwise good persons to inflict harm upon other persons, animals, and things by a mere glance of the eye directed toward them. Sometimes this glance can even cause the death of an otherwise healthy person. Belief in the maleficent power of the eye is rooted in its link with the heart, the location of a person's innermost attitudes and desires. Thus a greedy or envious person desires the possessions of another, but since he or she can't gain it, such a person wishes it to be disfigured or destroyed.

The Sage distinguishes between a person "good of eye" (Prov. 22:9) and one "evil of eye" (Prov. 23:6; 28:22). In Proverbs 23:6, for example, it seems that an uninvited guest has come to the banquet of an otherwise generous person who pretends to be graciously hospitable but has been forced by this intruder into a negative attitude. Thus, while the host outwardly encourages the guest to "eat and drink," his heart is not in his exhortation. The heart will communicate its true sentiments through the eye to the food and the guest (e.g., Prov. 21:4). The late Fr. Roland Murphy translated the obscure Hebrew of Proverbs 23:7 thus: "For it is like a hair in the throat"; RSV: "he is like one who is inwardly reckoning"), which will cause the uninvited guest to vomit (Murphy 1998: 172, 175). While this last statement might be metaphorical, medical literature documents the fact that people who live in cultures that believe in the efficacy of the evil eye do sometimes become ill and even die if they believe that an enemy has cast an evil glance at them.

Who Can Cast the Evil Eye?

One obvious characteristic of a person who could cast the evil eye was some ocular irregularity. A person whose eyes were not perfectly centered would be a prime suspect. Pope Pius IX had a "lazy eye" (one eye looked to the side while the other eye looked directly at an object), and when Italian pilgrims knelt to kiss his ring, they would use appropriate hand gestures to counteract any possible evil influence from his glance. Another characteristic would be joined eyebrows. *The Acts of Paul,* an apocryphal work, describes him as a "man small of stature, with a bald head and crooked legs, in a good state of body, with eyebrows meeting . . ." (3:2). Even if this is an idealized rather than a factual description, the joined eyebrows might lead one to conclude that some people thought Paul had the power to cast the evil eye. That the Galatians did not "spit" at the sight of him (Gal. 4:14 literally; "scorn or despise me," RSV) suggests that the Galatians did not consider him to possess the evil eye. The author of *The Acts of Paul* is explicit: "Paul, who had eyes only for the goodness of Christ, did them no evil, but loved them greatly" (*Acts of Paul* 3:1).

Protecting against the Evil Eye

Obviously, a basic form of protecting oneself against the evil eye is not to look dangerous people in the eye. Another is to conceal valuables from the sight of all. In contemporary Italy where male children are envied by those who do not have sons, some parents dress their young sons as girls to thwart any possibility of the child being subjected to the evil eye from other envious parents. Cultures who accept the reality of the evil eye also rely on a variety of objects to ward off the "glance" or "the fierce look," as the Arabs refer to it. Scarlet and blue and similar hues are favored colors. Notice the blue and purple and scarlet color (Exod. 35:35) in the garments for Aaron and his sons (Exod. 31:10). A priest can't be too cautious when coming into close contact with the realm of God and of the spirits. Strings of knots were also popular (see Num. 15:38 — notice the color purple; Deut. 22:12; Matt. 9:20). Various amulets painted with eyes as well as crescents were worn to protect by distracting the gazer and causing his or her gaze to bounce the evil intent back on himself or herself (see Judg. 8:21, 26; Isa. 3:19-23).

Jesus and the Evil Eye

Jesus wore on his cloak the tassel as prescribed in Numbers 15:38 (Mark 6:56), though not as large as those of the Pharisees (Matt. 23:5). It served not only as a reminder to keep the commandments, but the violet cord that bound the tassel protected against evil spirits and the evil eye. Four times in the New Testament, Jesus is reported to have made explicit references to the evil eye. In Matthew 6:22-23 (and Luke 11:33-34), Jesus notes that the one who has an evil eye is totally evil. The first hired in Matthew's parable of the workers in the vineyard give the evil eye to the owner because he behaved generously toward the last hired but kept his contract with the first hired (Matt. 20:15). They wish to destroy the owner's property and wealth. Since the parable is really about God and not about just wages, or employer-employee relationships, those who would want to hold God to a contract dare to give God the evil eye in retaliation for God's generosity toward others who don't make contracts with God but simply trust in the deity. It would seem that by placing this parable into its proper cultural context, its point cuts much deeper.

In a private instruction to his disciples after a conflict with opponents, Jesus reminds them that the evil eye and its intentions spring from the heart (Mark 7:22). The reader will not find the phrase "evil eye" in English translations of all these passages but rather the word "envy" or "greed," or something similar. One should not be misled by the ordinary meaning of this English word. The Mediterranean social system requires a different interpretation of greed and envy as thus far explained.

Evil Eye: A Culture-Bound Syndrome

A syndrome is a group of signs and symptoms that occur together and are recognized as characterizing a particular health abnormality. The physical syndrome consisting of fever, sore throat, perspiration, and/or chills usually indicates a cold or the flu or something similar A culture-bound syndrome points to an abnormality that is distinctive to a specific culture because the interpretation of the signs and symptoms is primarily social or cultural rather than biomedical (Pilch 2000b: 152; Simons and Hughes 1985). As a young singer, opera diva Denyce Graves took a German-born friend to her Faith Bible church in Washington, DC, her hometown, one Sunday. "She had no idea what she was in for," said Ms. Graves. "People falling out, speaking in tongues, shaking, shouting. . . . The girl asked: 'Denyce, is everybody O.K.?'" The dictionary defines "falling out" as a disagreement or quarrel, but that is not what happened here. Falling out is a culture-bound syndrome which to others might seem like a fainting spell, a convulsion, or a host of other physical ailments. It is rather a culturally specific and culturally learned response to an experience during a Pentecostal worship service, a charismatic experience.

In other words, culture-bound syndromes are folk-conceptualized disorders that include changes in customary behavior and experiences in their symptomology. The consequences experienced by someone who believes that he or she has been given the evil eye, or whose friends and relatives hold that belief, is another culture-bound syndrome. One effect of the evil eye could be death. Medical studies of Mediterranean ethnic populations frequently report the death of a healthy person and list the death as due to a conviction that an enemy cast the evil eye upon him or her. While mortality rates in the ancient world were high, and many if not most deaths were due to serious disease, the evil eye could account for other deaths. Some estimates place infant mortality rates at 30 percent, with another 30 percent dead by the age of six, and 60 percent by the age of sixteen. The twelve-year-old girl whom Jesus restored to life (Mark 5:42) might indeed have died from disease. Yet given the high mortality rate among children and adolescents, this perhaps otherwise healthy young lady could also have been the envy of many in the village who would not and perhaps did not hesitate to cast an evil eye on her to cause her death. Why, in their minds, should that girl be alive when their sons and daughters had already died?

Some reports of Jesus' healing activities indicate that his saliva was part of the therapy. He used spittle in the healing of the deaf mute (Mark 7:23) and again in the healing of two blind men (Mark 8:23; John 9:6). Pliny (23-79 C.E.) observes that spittle has special curative powers (*Natural History* 27.75). Tacitus (55-120 C.E.) reported that a blind man sought to regain his sight by applying the spittle of Emperor Vespasian (9-79 C.E.) to his eyes (*Historiae* 4.8). As already indicated above concerning Paul's experience among the Galatians, saliva (spitting) in the Mediterranean world was considered especially effective protection against the evil eye. Blind people were among those who were considered capable of casting the evil eye upon others, so Jesus' use of spittle in these instances is both an apotropaic measure (for self-protection against the evil eye) and a therapeutic strategy.

Conclusion

In opera, the scenery designer, the stage director, and the conductor are each like a preacher who knows the text and music very intimately, who understands what the librettist and composer intended to communicate, and then proceeds to guide the musicians, singers, and actors to perform accordingly. The task is always to be faithful to the composer/librettist and to what they have transmitted on paper. The challenge is to bring all of that to life. When I last sang in *Il Trovatore* with the Milwaukee Florentine Opera in 1977, the production did not come to life as realistically and authentically as in Baltimore in 2003. Verdi and Cammarano, composer and librettist, were surely as thrilled by these four Baltimore performances as Jesus and his evangelists would be by homilies in which similarly gifted and faithful preachers might interpret the gospels.

FURTHER READING: LANGUAGE

Brichto, Herbert. 1963. *The Problem of "Curse" in the Hebrew Bible.* SBLMS 13. Philadelphia: Society of Biblical Literature.

Danker, Frederick William, ed. and revisor. 2000. *A Greek-English Lexicon of the New Testament and Other Early Christian Literature.* 3rd Edition (BDAG). Chicago and London: The University of Chicago Press.

Elliott, John H. 2012. *Beware the Evil Eye: The Evil Eye in the Bible and the Biblical World.* Eugene, OR: Wipf & Stock.

Esler, Philip R. 2012. "Ancient Mediterranean Monomachia in the Light of Cultural Anthropology: The Case of David and Goliath." In *The Idea of Man and Concepts of the Body: Anthropological Studies on the Ancient Cultures of Israel, Egypt, and the Near East.* Oriental Religions in Antiquity. Edited by

Anjelika Berjelung, Joachim Friedrich Quack, and Jan Dietrich. Tübingen: Mohr Siebeck.

Malandro, Loretta A., Larry L. Barker, and Deborah Ann Barker. 1989. *Nonverbal Communication*. Second Edition. Reading: Addison-Wesley.

Meyers, Carol. "The Family in Early Israel." Pp. 1-47 in *Families in Ancient Israel*. Edited by Leo G. Perdue, Joseph Blenkinsopp, John J. Collins, and Carol Meyers. Louisville: Westminster John Knox.

Murphy, Roland E. 1998. *Proverbs*. Word Biblical Commentary 22. Nashville: Thomas Nelson.

Pilch, John J. 1993. "'Beat His Ribs While He Is Young' (Sir. 30:12): A Window on the Mediterranean World." *Biblical Theology Bulletin* 23: 101-13.

———. 1995. "Death with Honor: The Mediterranean-Style Death of Jesus in Mark." *Biblical Theology Bulletin* 25: 65-70.

———. 1999. *The Cultural Dictionary of the Bible*. Collegeville, MN: The Liturgical Press.

———. 2000a. "Gestures." *The Eerdmans Dictionary of the Bible*. Grand Rapids: Eerdmans.

———. 2000b. *Healing in the New Testament: Insights from Medical and Mediterranean Anthropology*. Minneapolis: Fortress.

———. 2002. *Cultural Tools for Interpreting the Good News*. Collegeville, MN: The Liturgical Press.

Simons, Ronald C., and Charles C. Hughes. 1986. *The Culture-Bound Syndromes: Folk Illnesses of Psychiatric and Anthropological Interest*. Boston: D. Reidel.

Stewart, Edward C., and Milton J. Bennett. 1991. *American Cultural Patterns: A Cross-Cultural Perspective*. Yarmouth: Intercultural Press.

Yaghjian, Lucretia B. 1996. "Ancient Reading." Pp. 206-20 in *The Social Sciences and New Testament Interpretation*. Edited by Richard L. Rohrbaugh. Peabody, MA: Hendrickson.

Part Six

HUMAN CONSCIOUSNESS

In the last two decades or so, cognitive neuroscience and related disciplines have made giant strides in understanding the human brain and how it works. Much of the progress has been made by studying brain-impaired subjects. The results of such studies have helped to illumine the research reports by specialists in psychological anthropology who have long been aware of the common human capacity for experiencing more than thirty different levels of consciousness or awareness on a very regular basis. Human beings wander in and out of different levels many times a day: sleep, waking consciousness, daydreaming, road trance, fantasy, and so on.

In this part we reflect on biblical reports which are best understood as experiences in alternate states of consciousness: dreams, Jesus' walking on the Sea, the resurrection appearances, the ascension of Jesus, Paul's call to be an apostle, Paul's (and others') trips to the sky, and the like.

1. Dreams

"Here comes this dreamer," said Joseph's brothers derisively (Gen. 37:19). At this point in the story line Joseph has dreamed that eleven bound sheaves bowed to his sheaf, which stood upright in the field where they all were working. In another dream, the sun, moon, and eleven stars were bowing to him. Joseph was very imprudent for sharing his dreams. What is noteworthy, however, is that the dreams he had were immediately interpreted with ease by his brothers and his parents, who were understandably upset by their content. Joseph himself later interpreted the dreams of the chief butler and chief baker when he was in prison with them in Egypt (Gen. 40). While modern readers are inclined to give dreams Jungian or other psychological interpretations, the ancients followed a different path (Artemidorus 1990). To understand our ancestors in the faith, it would help to begin with an overview of our modern understanding.

Human Consciousness

Dreams take place in human consciousness, a rather complex dimension of the human person. While we have learned very much about human consciousness, there is much more that still eludes and puzzles researchers. Anthropologists who study and compare many cultures point out that the state of consciousness that we in the West consider "ordinary" or "normal" is actually a construct, not a fixed fact of existence. Indeed, our "ordinary" state of consciousness is, in many ways, quite arbitrary. In other words, human consciousness is capable of a wide horizon of potentials that each culture shapes into a fixed and stable "state." This state of consciousness adapts the individual more or less successfully to survive in her/his culture's consensus reality. Long before we came into existence, our respective culture evolved to an agreement on how to view and interpret reality. It is not a democratic enterprise on which each member votes or chooses to agree or disagree. We are enculturated into our culture's consensus reality. In the Bible, we encounter an ancient, Middle Eastern culture's consensus reality. In that culture, spirits are a normal part of consensus reality; in Western culture, in general, they are not.

One anthropologist, Crapanzano (2001: 632-33) has enumerated more than thirty-five states of consciousness: dreams, daydreams, nightmares, incubation dreams, directing imagings, hallucinations, *dédoublements de conscience*, illusions, visions, depersonalization, derealization, bodiliness, the stare, fugues, sexual ecstasy, mystical ecstasy, prayerfulness, inspiration, furor, aesthetic contemplation, *Ergriffenheit* (being seized), being charmed, transported (in the French sense of *transporter*), entranced, hypnotic trance, possession trance, television trance, distractions, soul loss, soul flight, shamanistic trance, nirvana-like experiences, *susto* (sudden, overwhelming fear), near-death experiences, and many drug-induced experiences. These, of course, are in addition to "normal" or "waking" consciousness.

Dreams in the Ancient Mediterranean

How did the ancients think about dreams? Plato (*Laws* 909E-910A) was skeptical about the supernatural nature of dreams. He noted that "all women especially" and "sick folk everywhere, and . . . those who have been in peril or distress" as well as those who have had a "slice of good fortune" are wont to build shrines or found temples on the basis of dreams. Aristotle denied that God communicated to anyone in dreams, since ordinary people dream, and God doesn't speak to ordinary people. "It is absurd to hold that it is God who sends such dreams, and yet that he sends them not to the best and wisest, but to any chance persons" (*On Prophecy in Sleep* I [462b]).

Classics scholars remind us, however, that in Hellenistic times there was no single authoritative theory about dreams. Aristotle, Plato, even the well-known Artemidorus (see below) had little influence. It was the Homeric writings that remained the classic sources on dreams and their interpretation. Indeed, for Greek culture, Homer comes close to being "sacred scripture."

In contrast, the sage, Jesus ben Sira, encourages paying attention to visions "specially sent by the Most High" (Sir. 34:6). Yet this opinion is very much the exception because, in general, ben Sira says that only the "senseless" and "fools" (v. 1) take dreams seriously. He further believes that "divination, omens, and dreams are unreal; what you already expect, the mind depicts" (v. 5; Anchor Bible translation). Literally in Greek, the word translated "unreal" means "idle, foolish, meaningless." The word "unreal" is an inappropriate translation because it contradicts not only Mediterranean cultural consensus reality but also the insights of psychological anthropology. Clearly Joseph and his family did not consider dreams unreal, nor even idle, foolish, and meaningless. On this point, Sirach probably reflects a segment of Hellenistic consensus reality of his time and place.

Artemidorus

In his famous book on dreams, *Oneirocritica*, Artemidorus (1990) was interested in dreams as a key to the future. He considered them to be primarily predictive. In contrast, the modern, post-Freudian world views dreams as keys to the unconscious, mirrors of the self. Artemidorus distinguished three kinds of dreams, all dealing with external matters of fact. First, the symbolic dream, which is full of metaphors that need interpretation. The Pharaoh's chief butler and chief baker who were in prison with Joseph

(Gen. 40) each had symbolic dreams. The butler dreamed of a vine with three branches whose grapes he squeezed into the Pharaoh's cup for him to drink. Joseph said that after three days the Pharaoh would restore the butler to grace. The baker dreamed he had three cake baskets on his head. The uppermost had baked foods for the Pharaoh, but the birds were eating it. Joseph interpreted it to mean that after three days the Pharaoh would hang the butler, and birds would eat his flesh (Gen. 40:8).

A second kind of dream is the vision (Greek *horama*), which preenacts a future event. Peter's dream (Acts 10:9-16, called *horama* in v. 17) in which he saw a great sheet filled with all kinds of animals and was commanded to kill and eat to assuage his hunger at that moment is an example of this kind of dream. Peter objected to eating unclean food, and the voice countered: "What God has cleansed, you must not call common." It happened three times. In Peter's subsequent encounter with Cornelius, the God-fearing centurion, whose dream/vision instructed Cornelius to summon Peter to his home, Peter grasps the significance of his dream. Experiencing the descent of the spirit upon Cornelius and his entourage, Peter realized that his dream was indeed predictive of this meeting and the resulting change in attitude of Judean believers in Jesus toward totally enculturated, "secular" Judeans who wanted to believe in and accept Jesus.

The third kind of dream is an oracle *(chrēmatismos)* in which the dreamer's parent, a priest, a god, or some other respected person reveals clearly a course of action for the dreamer, what the dreamer should do or should not do. This is the Greek word Paul uses (Rom. 11:4) to describe Elijah's encounter with God on the mountain (1 Kings 19:9-18). God instructs Elijah to anoint two kings (Hazael over Syria; Jehu over Israel) and to anoint his successor as prophet: Elisha. Clearly, in the Israelite tradition, God does communicate in dreams.

God and Dreams

"Hear my words," said the Lord. "If there is a prophet among you, I the LORD make myself known to him in a vision, I speak with him in a dream" (Num. 12:6). To Moses, however, God speaks "mouth to mouth, clearly, and not in dark speech." If dreams belong to "dark speech," they require interpretation. God interprets dreams (Gen. 40:8; 41:16; Dan. 2:28), and sometimes God grants this gift to special persons (Dan. 1:17; 5:11, 14).

As noted above, prophets and dreamers (prophecy and dreams) are usually paired. Samuel laments when he senses that God has ceased communicating with him "either by prophets or by dreams" (1 Sam. 28:15). God is understandably disturbed when prophets claim to have received communication in dreams from the deity, but God has not so communicated (Jer. 23:16-32). On the other hand, God uses signs and wonders in apparent confirmation of a dream to test the people's loyalty (Deut. 13:1-5). Hence determining whether a person had a dream or lied, and then deciding on the interpretation of the dream was a common occurrence but one fraught with the risk of making a mistake.

The New Testament

In comparison to the Old Testament, the New Testament reports far fewer dreams. Scholars sometimes distinguish between dreams (only Matthew uses the Greek word *onar*) and visions (Luke favors these words: *horama, optasia, horasis*), but anthropologists caution that one should not press the distinction, for they actually overlap and both belong to the category of altered states of consciousness experiences. An example of the overlap is Matthew's description of the transfiguration as a vision (17:9), which can also be a waking dream. In Matthew's gospel, Joseph (1:20-21; 2:13) and the magi (2:12) receive instructions for conduct in a dream, and Pilate's wife has an ominous dream involving Jesus (27:10). The author of Revelation receives information from God in a trance, yet another altered state of consciousness (Rev. 1:10; 4:2; 17:3; 21:10 — the English phrase "in spirit" in each of these verses is best translated "trance").

Early Christianity

Scholars observe that up until the fourth century C.E., Christianity did not favor visions of the deity. Yet a peculiar development took place. Through fasting and prayer and other ascetic practices, anyone could cultivate dreams and stimulate visions. On the other hand, official dream interpreters were forbidden; such were banned from baptism in the early Church. Synesius of Cyrene, a fourth-century convert to Christianity, said: "At twenty-four years of age, it is inexcusable for a man still to need an interpreter of his own dreams." It seems that this movement to promote dreams and visions among larger numbers of people was a response to the decision to close the biblical canon. Dreams and visions gave all persons a potential direct link with God, and unlike Scripture they did not require any but personal interpretation.

Tertullian (c. 160-230 C.E.)

The Church Father Tertullian wrote what is considered to be the first Christian treatment on dreams (*De Anima* 45–49). He believed that the majority of humankind came to know God through dreams (47.2). The reference is to the one true God of the Christians, though in Carthage he lived among men and women who were predominantly pagans.

Tertullian claimed that dreams came from three sources: God, the devil, or the soul (46-47). Jerome (c. 334-420 C.E.) reported his dream of being summoned before the Judge who asks: "Who are you?" When Jerome replies: "I am a Christian," the Judge answers: "You lie, you are a follower of Cicero, not of Christ." Then he received lashes of the whip and suffered pangs of conscience. How did he decide that the dream was real and was from God? He could feel the pain in his shoulders long after the dream ended (*Letter* 22.30).

According to Tertullian, most dreams came from the devil. Dreams of the heretics and schismatics, like those of the Gnostics and Montanists, surely came from the devil. Dreams can play a double role. On the one hand, they can establish and confirm a truth. On the other hand, dreams can overturn authority, which some say is why they were so important to schismatics and heretics.

Thirdly, following the Stoics, Tertullian says that dreams come from the soul. Sleep is for the body, but not for the soul. The body rests, but the soul does not, which is why we dream. Sleep is like death. In sleep, the soul was separated from the body, so that dreams allowed one to communicate with the dead or those who live in alternate reality. As such, dreams would be a perfect vehicle for divine revelation and frequently offered solutions to daily problems. Waking from a dream is like resurrection from the dead (*De Anima* 53).

Tertullian borrowed many ideas from Hellenistic sources but insisted that Christian dream interpretation must be different. It is first with Isidore of Seville, in the seventh century, that scholars recognize the birth of a specific Christian orientation to interpreting dreams.

Conclusion

The popularity of dream analysis in the modern world often leads enthusiasts to apply post-Freudian insights and interpretations to the Bible. It is well to remember that people in the Bible, like 80 percent of the current population of the planet, are collectivistic personalities. This means that they are not only nonintrospective but antiintrospective. The function of dreams in antiquity was that of all experience of altered states of consciousness: to impart new information (from God, of course, who alone knows everything) or to provide a solution to a problem in life (a course of action, a decision, and the like). Even so, we clearly see how our ancestors in the faith struggled to distinguish true dreams (authentic communication from God) from a lie (see Jer. 27–28).

2. Seeing God

A fifth-century patristic document, "The Sayings of the Fathers," reports that the abbot Olympius told how a pagan priest came to the monastery and spent the night there. When he observed the lifestyle of the monks, he asked: "Leading this kind of life, do you see anything of your God?" The abbot replied: "No." The pagan priest then said: "When we perform the sacred rites for our god, he hides nothing from us but reveals his mysteries to us. But you, after so many labors, vigils, periods of silence, and ascetic exercises, say 'we see nothing?' It would seem that if you see nothing, you keep evil thoughts in your hearts which separate you from your God, and because of this, he does not reveal his mysteries to you." The abbot reported the words of the priest to the elders, who marveled and said that it was so.

Seeing God

The biblical tradition tells us that Jacob (Gen. 32:30), Moses (Exod. 33:11; Deut. 34:10), and Gideon (Judg. 6:22) spoke with God "face to face." Indeed, the Israelites communicated with God "face to face" (Num. 14:14; Deut. 5:4). Paul and John the letter writer used the phrase "face to face" to declare how earnestly they yearned to see the recipients of their letters (1 Thess. 2:17; 3:10; 2 John 12; 3 John 14). On the other hand, the tradition also reports the belief that no one can see God and live (Exod. 19:21; 32:30; Judg. 13:22). Those who survived felt blessed (Gen. 16:13 [?]; Judg. 6:22-24). What are we to make of these apparently conflicting reports?

Speaking with God "face to face" and "seeing God," a common expression for pilgrimage to the temple, are concrete verbal expressions of an intense experience of God. We can deduce this from the nature of personal, face-to-face encounters in Middle Eastern culture. The meeting is indeed intense. In a face-to-face encounter, Middle Easterners stand six to eight inches apart, the normal parameter of personal space. Persons want to experience the breath of the conversation partner, the God-given breath by which a person has life. To withdraw that by standing further apart than six to eight inches is shameful. The degree of emotional exchange in this encounter accompanied by frequent touching is similarly intense.

To transpose this total human experience to an encounter with God certainly increases its level of intensity. It is definitely a human peak experience which can never last long, for it would be more than the human person could endure and survive! Thus, to experience God this intensely and live is wondrous indeed. Isaiah survived what he experienced as a cauterization of his lips with a burning coal (Isa. 6:5-7). Jeremiah felt God touch his mouth (Jer. 1:9). Ezekiel felt the very force of God enter into him when the deity spoke to the prophet. That force was so powerful that it stood Ezekiel on his feet (Ezek. 2:2; 3:24)!

Evil Thoughts

If we allow for the stylized form of the pagan priest's explanation of why the monks don't see God despite using all the right techniques, it is possible to clarify the meaning of "evil thoughts" that separate one from God. Modern researchers into human consciousness point out that the body is our common human, biological heritage. At the physiological level, every human body is constructed and "wired" the same way. While medical students still study the various systems in the human body separately (skeletal, muscular, endocrine, nervous systems, etc.), research indicates that these systems communicate with each another in ways we never realized before (e.g., Pert 1999).

Human consciousness also seems to have physiological underpinnings. Changes in levels of consciousness register differently on machines designed to test this. Thus if the human organism is not malformed or damaged, it has an incredible physiological basis for experiencing various states of consciousness. To phrase it otherwise, the human person is capable of experiencing its Creator in the very fiber of the human body, whether in emotions such as joy, fear, bliss, and the like, or in consciousness. Jacob was physically exhausted after encountering God. He felt as if he had wrestled the deity all night to a draw (Gen. 32:22-32)!

Research indicates that 90 percent of the people on the face of the planet use the biological basis for experiencing God or transcendence regularly, spontaneously (Pilch 2011b: 216-30). They embrace the ability to live life intensely, to plunge without restraint into the total living experience that opens human consciousness to its deeper levels. The other 10 percent are hindered by "evil thoughts." Contemporary Westerners, devotees of modern science, have developed a metaself, a critical observer who monitors and comments on experience. This metaself will not allow complete abandon, yielding of control, total absorption in lived and unmediated experience which is the essence of highly focused levels of consciousness through which God seems to speak most often to human beings. To use the words of the pagan priest, these "scientific" convictions are "evil thoughts" which hinder people from encountering God.

Perhaps it was not very much different with the ancients. When Samuel was ministering under Eli, the sacred author comments: "The word of the LORD was rare in those days; there was no frequent vision" (1 Sam. 3:1). Why did Eli not receive a word from the Lord? Eli's sons were worthless fellows who mistreated those who came to offer sacrifice. Eli learned of it and scolded them, but they would not listen. This suggests that Eli did not raise his sons properly, for it is the Middle Eastern patriarch's cultural task to make sure that he can impose his will on his sons and assure unswerving loyalty to himself. Eli's obvious failure as a father makes it very plausible that obsession with his sons' misconduct made it difficult for Eli to be open to communication from the Lord. While it is important to recognize that the initiative of communication lies with God, the petitioner must also be prepared for and open to the encounter.

Techniques

The pagan priest enumerated with apparent agreement the techniques which the monks utilized to prepare for an experience of God: labors, vigils, periods of silence, ascetic exercises. Modern research has identified techniques that appear to work physiological effects, which in turn trigger changes in consciousness (Gore 2009). One of these is drumming, that is, a rhythmic pattern of beats. Speeding up or slowing the rhythm produces different levels of consciousness and experiences. In his visions, Ezekiel "heard the sound of a great earthquake" (3:12). An earthquake I experienced in 1969 on the fifteenth floor of a graduate residence hall in St. Louis, Missouri, gave me the impression that some youngster was skipping rope in the room above mine. I was irritated, but the face of my visitor, who had experienced many earthquakes in Puerto Rico, registered terror. This rhythmic shaking was too familiar. In his vision Isaiah (6:4) felt the foundations of the temple thresholds shake.

Incense or scent is another common stimulant for changing levels of consciousness. Isaiah refers to the smoke that filled the temple (6:4), quite likely a combination of incense and smoke from burnt offerings (see Ps. 66:13-15). In his temple vision, Ezekiel (8:11) sees the seventy elders each holding a censer emitting "smoke of the cloud of incense." The volume and intensity of the smells in the temple would stimulate visions, thus assuring pilgrims and worshipers of an opportunity to see God.

The intense concentration that characterizes an altered state of consciousness can be achieved by fasting and similar practices. Daniel was mourning for three weeks. He "ate no delicacies, no meat or wine entered my mouth, nor did I anoint myself at all for the full three weeks." Then the vision occurred (Dan. 10:2). Jesus fasted for a longer period (Mark 1:12-13), and at the end his filial loyalty was tested in a trance experience (Matt. 4:1-11//Luke 4:1-13).

Seeing the Word

The word for "vision" (Hebrew *ḥāzôn;* Greek *horasis*) used in 1 Samuel also serves as the title of some prophetic books (Isa. 1:1; Nah. 1:1; Obad. 1). The visions of the prophets are familiar to readers of the Bible. In the visions, prophets sometimes see things (a boiling pot, Jer. 1:13; bones, Ezek. 37), but they always hear a message ("Thus says the LORD" or an equivalent; Jer. 1:14; Ezek. 37:5). More curious is this phrase: "the *word* which he [Isaiah, Amos, Micah] saw" (Isa. 2:1; Amos 1:1; Mic. 1:1), or "the *oracle* which he [Isaiah, Habakkuk] saw" (Isa. 13:1; Hab 1:1). How does one see spoken words or oracles? Is this prophetic "shorthand" for vision and message?

Psychological anthropologists who have investigated worldwide evidence concerning visions and other alternate states of consciousness point out that these experiences have no sound track. The visionary provides the sound track that reflects the visionary's culture. Thus, the prophets who saw visions (a boiling pot; bones; the constellation "throne") also provided a sound track that interpreted what they had seen. The sound track, of course, was inspired by God; it was indeed God speaking to the prophet. The two elements are so inextricably bound up in the experience of the visionary that it makes perfect sense to say that he saw the word or oracle of the Lord.

Seeing in Ecstasy

Dictionaries customarily list the passages mentioned above (word or ora-cle that he saw) as instances of "seeing as in an ecstatic state." This, of course, is quite correct from our modern, enlightened point of view. It very likely describes in modern terms quite correctly what the ancients experienced in these passages. But is this entirely fair to our ancestors? They do not seem to have distinguished the variety of meanings of "ec-stasy" identified in dictionaries. For example, the Hebrew dictionary (Brown-Driver-Briggs) describes the scene in which Moses, Aaron, Nadab, Abihu, and seventy of the elders of Israel saw God and ate and drank in his presence (Exod. 24:9-11) as a "theophany." How does this dif-fer from encountering God, and seeing (and hearing oracles) in an ec-static state? All these events are experiences in alternate states of con-sciousness. Many scholars now see the need for rewriting dictionaries along the lines of semantic domains, such as Louw-Nida's *Greek-English Lexicon of the New Testament Based on Semantic Domains*. Nearly all dic-tionaries reflect the social system of the lexicographer rather than the so-cial system of the people who spoke that ancient language. Hence the need for this new kind of dictionary.

The Greek word translated "ecstasy" *(ekstasis)* occurs twenty-nine times in the Greek Bible (Septuagint) and seven times in the New Testament. Paul fell into an ecstasy/trance (Acts 22:17) in which he received a directive from God dictating an immediate course of action: flee Jerusalem! Peter had an ecstasy/trance (dream) that gave new instruction from God con-cerning appropriate foods to eat (Acts 10:10; 11:5). These instances corre-spond to the general purpose of such experiences: to give new information or offer advice for a course of action. The other instances of *ekstasis* are translated "amazement": reaction to healings (Mark 5:42; Luke 5:26; Acts 3:10) and to the discovery of the empty tomb and the young man's message about Jesus (Mark 16:8). Yet it is also plausible that the ancients considered all these events (trances and healings) as amazing!

Conclusion

Felicitas Goodman, the anthropologist who, together with Erika Bour-guignon, conducted most of the pioneering research on altered states of consciousness grew up in the Hungarian region of western Rumania in a Lutheran setting. Throughout her youth, she regularly experienced altered states of consciousness. At her confirmation, she was advised to put away such childish things and behave now like an adult. When one of her friends entered the convent, Felicitas asked the same question of her that the pagan priests asked of the monks. Felicitas's friends gave her the same answer as those monks did (Goodman 1990: 3-4).

It seems that the Johannine community of adults regularly experienced God and the risen Jesus in alternate states of consciousness. That was the point and purpose of their liturgies. When John writes, "No one has ever seen God" (1:18), he apparently is denying claims of those outside his circle to have had that privilege. John's community retained a tradition we do well to explore and restore.

3. Jesus Walking on the Sea

Everyone is familiar with the gospel story describing Jesus walking on the Sea of Galilee. He is heading toward his disciples, who are in a boat (Mark 6:45-52; Matt. 14:22-33; John 6:16-21). The English phrase inspired by this event ("s/he [thinks s/he] walks on water") intends to describe someone who can accomplish the impossible with ease. Like many popular interpretations of the Bible, this one too misses the mark. All human beings actually do walk on water when it rains. To walk on the sea is an entirely different matter. Sea is a key word in this gospel story and in the entire biblical tradition. A clearer understanding of that word and reality suggests a new interpretation of this event in the life of Jesus.

The Sea

Many ancient cultures, including that of Palestine, personified much if not all of reality. The sea was no exception. In the Mesopotamian traditions, Tiamat is the primordial watery source of life, a goddess. Contemporary scholars now discount that Tiamat is the source for the biblical *těhôm* (deep, sea, abyss; see Gen. 1:2; 7:11; 8:2), but they correctly recognize that the basic ideas of these myths derive from a common and shared cultural perspective. The distinctive significance of the biblical tradition is that God controls this potentially unruly sea and does not gain his mastery as a result of a battle with it. Modern Bible readers must keep these personifications in mind to properly appreciate biblical narratives on their own cultural terms.

Seas Known to Biblical People

Keeping in mind that all theology is analogy, that is, everything human beings know and say about God is rooted in human experience which is always culturally interpreted, a reader wants to know which seas were familiar to biblical people. Even land-bound peasants knew of the Mediterranean. In the Bible it is often referred to simply as "the sea" (Hebrew *yām;* Num. 13:29), and sometimes "the Great Sea" (Num. 34:6, 7). The psalmist (29:3) presents a vivid description of how this body of water could turn violent and destructive. Because this watery presence loomed so large west of the land, this Hebrew word for sea also served as the designation for the compass designation "west."

Among other seas mentioned in the Bible, the Sea of Reeds (usually translated "Red Sea" as in Exod. 15:22), crossed by the ancient Hebrews in the exodus, is difficult to locate geographically. The sea located in the Arabah region south of Palestine is called the Salt Sea (Gen. 14:3), the Sea of the Plain (Josh. 3:16), or the Eastern Sea (literally, "in front of" a person facing east; see Ezek. 47:18). Its high concentration of salt and other minerals permits no life to exist in it, hence the name "Dead Sea." This name is deceptive, however, for though this sea is usually calm, occasionally severe and dangerous thunderstorms do develop. This is quite in keeping with the dense nature of this personified body of water.

Finally, the Sea of Galilee (see, e.g., Matt. 4:18) figures very prominently in the Synoptic gospels. Its most ancient name was Chinnereth (Num. 34:11), from the Hebrew word for "harp" (perhaps describing the shape of the lake or the sound of its waters). In the Hellenistic and Roman periods it was called Gennesaret (e.g., Matt. 14:34). John calls it the lake of Tiberias (6:1; 21:1). Situated about 640 feet below sea level, its size today is 13 miles long and 8 miles wide at its widest part.

Of special interest is the wind pattern on this sea. Two large valleys on the west side usher in strong afternoon breezes from the West, particularly during the dry season (end of April to the end of September). These can quickly churn up waves on the peaceful waters to a height of seven or more feet. In the winter, a similar wind pattern from the east can produce the same effect. No experienced fisherman would sail in such storms, and, if he were caught in a sudden squall, he would do everything to return to shore as quickly as possible.

Walking on the Sea of Galilee

The gospel report about Jesus walking on the Sea of Galilee toward his disciples in a boat has been variously interpreted. Some scholars consider it a "nature miracle," that is, an action that clearly surpasses the so-called laws of nature. While this might make sense to the modern, post-Enlightenment mind, the ancients lived by the simple perception that whatever happened actually happened. While it may have been a singular, rare, or infrequent experience, it wasn't contrary to anything. If they saw it, they believed that it really happened. If it was beyond customary human ability, it had to have some other-than-human but still personal explanation. Some person was responsible for it.

Other scholars consider this event to be an appearance of the risen Jesus that has been "retrojected" into his earthly life. They connect the story linguistically ("by/upon the Sea") particularly with John 21:1-14 and also with the literary form of other resurrection appearances. These scholars also deny any real parallels between Old Testament stories of walking on the sea (e.g., Job 9:8 LXX) and similar stories in pre-gospel pagan literature (e.g., about Orion, Poseidon, Poseidon's son by the human Europa, Euphemus, and others). They correctly note that none of these stories could have served as a model for the evangelists but neglect to take seriously the fact that such perspectives about certain kinds of persons coursing over the personified sea were quite common in the ancient world. Moreover, these scholars do not provide a satisfactory explanation of what the first readers or hearers of such a story would have gotten out of it. Invariably there is too hasty a segue to a theological interpretation linked with the risen Lord and the Eucharist.

Alternate Reality

Even the most current studies attempting to understand the Jesus of history generally take little cognizance of the fact that he became incarnate in the ancient Mediterranean world. Anthropologists who specialize in this region and its literary records point out that approximately 90 percent of world cultures and 80 percent of circum-Mediterranean cultures readily experience altered states of consciousness. From the biblical record alone, which is included in the anthropological data bank, it is evident that the people of this ancient culture were certainly among that 80 percent.

Studies of Moroccan Jews in Israel are particularly enlightening in this regard (Bilu and Abramovich 1985). When they were forcibly repatriated to Israel in the 1950s and 1960s, the Moroccan Jews carried with them not only their personal belongings but their beliefs, values, and traditions. They revitalized their practices and attached them to new sites and saints to substitute for those left behind. One of these takes place at the tomb of Rabbi Shimeon Bar-Yohai (2nd cent. c.e.) at Meiron near Safed. On the anniversary of his death, these devotees make a pilgrimage to his tomb, celebrate a picnic-like feast in the surrounding countryside, and expect to see him in a dream.

The dream pattern typically has four elements, common in ASC experiences. (1) Those experiencing the vision are initially frightened and (2) do not recognize the figure. (3) The figure offers calming assurance (e.g., "do not be afraid") and (4) identifies himself ("it is I . . ."). Then the figure offers information: clarification of identity or granting of a favor, for example, healing or a healing strategy. The purpose of the experience is to illuminate a puzzle in life (who is this man?) or to suggest or approve a line of conduct ("my beloved son; listen to him"; Mark 9:7). Notice that this is not a "literary" form. It is a pattern of human experience constructed by the culture rather than by someone's creative imagination.

The Disciples Experience Jesus in an ASC

Jesus and those who knew him were quite familiar with and adept at experiences of alternate reality. Accounts of Jesus' baptism, transfiguration, walking on the Sea of Galilee, and post-death or resurrection appearances readily fit into the common, Mediterranean cultural experiences of altered states of consciousness even when the experience is reported "incompletely" or "selectively."

When Jesus comes walking on the Sea of Galilee toward his disciples, (1) they are frightened (Mark 6:50; Matt. 14:26; John 6:19). (2) They do not recognize Jesus, thinking instead that they see a ghost (Mark 6:49; Matt. 14:26; nothing in John, but 6:20 suggests that they do not recognize him at all). (3) Jesus calms them ("have no fear" — Mark 6:50; Matt. 14:27; John 6:20) and (4) identifies himself: "It is I" (Mark 6:50; Matt. 14:27; John 6:20). So far so good for an ASC experience.

Matthew (14:28ff.) illustrates what happens when a person breaks the trance. Peter is not convinced that he is really seeing Jesus and demands: "*If* it is you, bid me come to you on the water." Jesus says "Come," and Peter progresses toward Jesus. But then the wind startled him, his fear (and skepticism) returned, and he began to sink, as will happen if one steps out of alternate reality back into consensual reality, out of the trance into a waking state. The trance experience will not continue in the waking state, just as a dream interrupted does not ordinarily resume after the interruption despite diligent attempts to fall back asleep again into the dream.

Meaning of the Report

True to the style of high context literature, the gospels of Mark and John do not report the meaning of this ASC experience. They presume that their intended audience knows it. While in Mark the disciples are "utterly astounded" and still puzzling over the breads, in John they are glad to take him into the boat. Matthew spells out the purpose — perhaps as he sees it — quite clearly: "Truly you are the Son of God." This trance experience provides the disciples with yet another insight into the identity of Jesus, a new piece of information or further confirmation of an insight known and gradually deepening.

Anthropological psychologists who specialize in ASC experiences emphasize that the content of these experiences is vacuous (hence Peter's doubt). It is the culture of the recipient that provides the information necessary to interpret the experience. This is where the cultural information from both the Old Testament and the pre-gospel pagan reports is relevant. Narrow concentration on literal correspondences to construct a literary form misses the forest for the trees. Both sources (OT and pre-gospel pagan reports) indicate that the activity of walking on the Sea demonstrates that such a person is superior to and in control of the personified Sea, whether riding a chariot on the waves or literally walking on the surface.

The Old Testament is particularly helpful because it echoes a motif that occurs frequently in the gospels. Jesus seems to do something that only God can do, in this case, walk on the Sea. It would be premature to conclude that therefore Jesus is God. Rather, the audience would recognize that Jesus is an extraordinary human being, one with a seemingly distinctive relationship to God, who normally behaves in this way. Jesus does things only God can do. In the Hebrew tradition, this cumulative evidence would continue to build Jesus' reputation as a "holy man," a *ḥasîd* or *ṣaddîq*, that is, one who has a special relationship to God with special benefits for fellow humans.

Seeing the Risen Jesus

Some concordances list the appearance of the risen Jesus in Luke 24:37 as a parallel to the story of Jesus walking on the Sea: "But they were startled and frightened, and supposed they saw a spirit." Actually, the elements of fear, lack of recognition, allaying of fear, and communication of new information or assurance of a course of action to be taken common to ASCs are quite normal in resurrection appearances, which are also experiences of a person's (Jesus') alternate reality. Recall that this is a culturally patterned experience, not a literary creation. It is inappropriate, therefore, to consider the ASC experience of Jesus walking on the Sea as a retrojected resurrection experience.

Conclusion

In recent years, it has often been repeated that the historical-critical method is dead. It has not delivered what it promised. Perhaps the real problem is that the historical-critical method has been neither sufficiently historical nor critical. Cultural insights about the pan-human experience of alternate states of consciousness would enhance literary and historical-critical studies. In this light, the historical Jesus stands out ever so clearly as a typical person of his first-century Mediterranean culture.

3. Resurrection Appearances

After the conclusion of a presentation to a Christian community on the resurrection appearances of Jesus, a member of the congregation replied: "I'm a psychiatrist. I treat people who hear voices and see things that aren't there." His comment was sincere and serious. It was also puzzling. Did he think these reports were mere literary creations? Were they simply symbols of something but nothing more than that? Or, to use psychiatric jargon, were they nothing but hallucinations? (In psychiatry, this word carries a pejorative meaning.)

The puzzlement arises because contemporary cognitive neuroscience has researched and described in considerable detail the function of the brain and nervous system in human consciousness in its many variations. The average human person changes levels of consciousness many times a day: sleep, waking time, daydreaming, road trance, and so forth. Human beings are capable of experiencing more than thirty-five different levels of consciousness. Further, ethnographic evidence indicates that perhaps as many as 90 percent of cultures on this planet experience many of these different levels of awareness on a routine basis. The technical term for this human experience is alternate states of consciousness or awareness. The resurrection appearances are just one example of alternate state of awareness that are reported throughout the Bible. Beginning with the "heavy, [divinely induced] sleep" in the first creature (Gen. 2:21; compare Isa. 29:10; 1 Sam. 26:12) and ending with the book of Revelation, which records the seer's "trance" experiences (Rev. 1:10; 4:2; 17:3; 21:10: "in spirit" = in trance), it is clear that alternate states of consciousness are a select moment during which God reveals Godself and important information for human beings (see Gen. 15:12; 1 Sam. 3:1; Job 4:13).

Resurrection Appearances

Drawing on her extensive cross-cultural research, anthropologist Dr. Felicitas Goodman identified four elements in an ecstatic trance experience. (1) The visionary is usually frightened by the experience and (2) doesn't initially recognize the person who is appearing or what is being seen. (3) The person in the vision offers calming assurance followed by self-identification: "Don't be afraid. It is I." If it is an object, the visionary seeks to identify the object: Is it a flying saucer? a saint? the face of Jesus? and so on. (4) Finally, the visionary receives (a) some useful information such as an answer to a concern, a solution to a problem, an insight for a new direction in life and the like, or (b) a commission.

In the resurrection appearances, the women are frightened by their experience (Mark 16:8; Matt. 28:8; Luke 24:5). The person appearing in the vision offers calming assurance to dispel the fright: "Do not be afraid!" (Matt 28:5, 10; see also Mark 16:6; Luke 24:37). At first, those who see him often don't recognize the risen Jesus, someone they knew when he lived and walked among them. Mary Magdalene mistook him for a gardener (John 20:15). The disciples on the road to Emmaus thought that he was a stranger (Luke 24:16). The disciples in Jerusalem thought they saw a ghost (Luke 24:37). The disciples on the Sea of Galilee saw a stranger on the shore who gave them advice about where to cast their nets (John 21:4).

Sometimes, however, the visionary does recognize the person appearing in the vision (Mark 16:5, a young man in a white robe; Matt. 28:5, the angel of the Lord; Luke 24:4, two men in dazzling garments, i.e., angels; John

20:20, 28; 21:7, Jesus). Finally, the experience offers new information (Mark 16:6; Matt. 28:6; Luke 24:6, Jesus has been raised [by God]; Luke 24:13-35, all that the Scriptures said must happen to Jesus; John 20:17, I am going to my Father). Sometimes it offers instruction (Mark 16:7; Matt. 28:7-10, go and meet the risen Jesus in Galilee; Luke 24:44-49, Jesus opens his travel companions' minds to understand the Scriptures). In other instances of seeing the risen Jesus, the visionaries receive a commission (Matt. 28:16-20, go preach to the lost sheep of the house of Israel dispersed among all the nations; Luke 24:48, you are witnesses; John 20:21-23, bring new members into the community; 21:15-19, Peter, feed my sheep). Thus characteristics of vision experiences identified by Dr. Goodman as existing in all cultures are quite evidently present in the New Testament accounts of those who saw the risen Jesus.

Cognitive Neuroscience

Relative to the resurrection appearances, cognitive neuroscience offers a helpful insight. Many scientists have performed electroencephalograms on people who signal when they have entered a different level of consciousness. For instance, neuroscientists have studied Franciscan religious women at prayer and a layperson practicing Tibetan meditation, and analyzed the electroencephalographic tracings carefully (Newberg, D'Aquili, and Rause 2002: 1-10). The subjects in such studies described their experiences with the scientists, who correlated their report with the tracings. Among the many things they learned about the function of the brain in these experiences was that the colors seen characterized different levels of consciousness or awareness. These colors, of course, were products of the technology rather than elements of the brain experience.

The anthropologist Dr. Goodman, however, has developed a similar insight and taught it at her Institute in Santa Fe, New Mexico. Using similar technological experience from experiments in which she participated in Germany, she interpreted the colors one might see in a trance. The sequence reflects neurological changes. To see white is a sign of being in a trance, in a different level of awareness. Orange means that the trance is weakening. Naturalistic colors indicate a still weaker level of trance. To see actual figures with clarity means that the trance is over. The visionary has returned to waking (so-called "normal") consciousness.

In the Israelite tradition, light (white) is the manifestation of God's honor or glory (Isa. 60:1; 62:1; Luke 2:9), that is, God's very self. The light sometimes takes the form of a cloud (Exod. 24:15ff.) or fire (Deut. 5:24) flashing brightly (Ezek. 1:4, 27-28; 10:4). The bright light from heaven (Acts 9:3; 22:6), even brighter than the sun (26:13), that Paul saw on the road to Damascus is typical of stage one of an ecstatic trance. (Anthropologists identify three stages in a typical trance experience.) Paul the Pharisee, who was familiar with light in the Israelite tradition, would be aware that he was entering a different level of awareness, a different "stage" of consciousness, or that some being from the realm of God might be initiating communication with him.

In the resurrection reports, the young man clothed in a white robe is plausibly a being from the realm of God (Mark 16:5). In Matthew, the angel of the Lord has an appearance "like lightning, and his clothing was white as snow" (28:4). Similarly in Luke (24:4), the two men in dazzling garments are angels, as they are also explicitly identified in John (20:12). In the resurrection reports, Jesus is never associated with the color white. (He is described in this way only in the transfiguration; Matt. 17:1-18 and par.) He is, however, frequently not recognized. From a neurological perspective, the white color signals that the visionaries are indeed in an alternate state of awareness. They are experiencing visitors from the realm of God and the spirits. The fact that they often don't recognize "the distinct face or figure" of Jesus also indicates that this is an experience in an alternate state of awareness.

Location of the Appearances

Where did the trance experiences of the risen Jesus take place? Six occurred near the tomb in which Jesus was buried. Two were experiences of Jesus himself (Matt. 28:8-9; John 20:14-18), while four were experiences of other beings (Mark 16:5-7; Matt. 28:1-7; Luke 24:1-11; John 20:11-13). Eight appearances were away from the tomb (Galilee; Emmaus: Matt. 28:8-10, 16-20; Luke 24:13-35, 36-53; John 20:19-23, 24-29; 21). Regarding the appearances near the tomb, the study of Moroccan Jews forcibly "repatriated" to Israel in the 1950s is enlightening. In Morocco, these Jews used to venerate a *murabit* (Arabic for holy man) with an annual pilgrimage to his tomb. There they picnicked, prayed, and sought healing in a ritual reminiscent of the Asclepian ritual. When they were moved to Israel, they transferred their devotional practices to the tomb of Rabbi Simeon bar Yohai (2nd cent. C.E.) at Meron near Zefat. Here they experienced their holy man (saint) in a vision as they did in Morocco, and obtained favors from him.

The important discovery of this study is that many cultures expect to experience a holy man in some altered form of consciousness at his tomb. In Mark's gospel, the very first title applied to Jesus is "Holy One of God" (Mark 1:24). Jesus was recognized as and lived and behaved according to all the criteria of a holy man identified and described by anthropologists in their cross-cultural studies. The major gift of a holy man to his people is to broker healing from God to those who need it. The firm expectation about a holy man in Israelite culture is that he would be raised to life in the world to come.

As for the experiences of the risen Jesus away from the tomb, once again psychiatric research contributes additional insight to anthropological information (Matchett 1972; Rees 1971). Many cultures, including that of ancient Israel, view death as a process rather than a punctiliar event, as does the West. Death certificates in the West record a specific time of death. In contrast, death as a process usually entails the transition from this world to the next, a transition from one mode of existence to another. Sometimes a journey is involved. In nearly all instances, a metamorphosis is key. "We shall not all fall asleep, but we shall all be changed" (1 Cor. 15:51). Viewing death as a process allows the survivors to continue to relate to a departed loved one for a significant time after the moment of expiration. Psychiatric research has documented that survivors of a beloved departed one continue to experience that person for many years, but most commonly within the first ten years after the loss. Thus, the fact that Mary Magdalene is mentioned in all the accounts of an alternate state of consciousness experience of Jesus and of other beings from the realm in which Jesus is now with God suggests that her relationship to Jesus may have had stronger emotional roots than that of all the others except perhaps the Eleven.

Significance of the Experiences

Peter's speeches in Acts present a reliable summary of the experiences of Jesus' followers. In his lifetime, Jesus of Nazareth was commended by God with mighty deeds, wonders, and signs that God worked through him. Some accepted Jesus, while others doubted and rejected him. Jesus' shameful death on the cross, a punishment reserved for criminals, caused his followers to wonder whether they had been deceived. If God was truly with Jesus, how could God allow this to happen?

But shortly after Jesus' death, his friends began to experience him transformed and alive in altered states of consciousness experiences (Pilch

2011a: 146-62). Since only God can raise a person from the dead, God must have been pleased with Jesus. God rewarded Jesus with resurrection, which the Israelite tradition recognized as the reward of the righteous. "God raised this Jesus; of this we are all witnesses. . . . Let the whole house of Israel know for certain that God has made him both Lord and Messiah" (Acts 2:32, 36).

Why did nonbelievers, even Jesus' enemies, not see him after his resurrection? Actually, a major skeptic and enemy of Jesus, Paul of Tarsus, did experience the risen Jesus (Acts 9; 22; 26). In another speech, Peter explains what anthropologists also know from their fieldwork: "This man God raised [on] the third day and granted that he be visible, not to all the people but to us, the witnesses chosen by God in advance, who ate and drank with him after he rose from the dead" (Acts 10:40-41). While human beings are neurologically "hardwired" for experiences of God and other beings in the realm of God, as neuroscientists describe this pan-human capability, the spirits determine if and when to interact with human beings.

Conclusion

The psychiatrist who observed that he treats people who hear voices and see things that aren't there is representative of some other scientists. One difference between DSM-III and DSM-IV (*Diagnostic and Statistical Manual of Mental Disorders,* a basic resource book) is that many religious experiences that were labeled as pathological in the former edition were omitted or recognized as "normal" in the latter one. Good science can help understand and appreciate the marvelous gifts to human beings from the Creator God so long as the creature doesn't reject or spurn them. "If Christ has not been raised, your faith is in vain" (1 Cor. 15:17).

5. Journeys to the Sky

The scholarly study of sky journeys was a significant dimension of the lifework of my dear friend and anthropological mentor, Dr. Felicitas D. Goodman, who died on March 31, 2005, at the age of 91. Born and raised as a Lutheran in Hungary, she was educated by the Ursuline nuns. As an adult, she trained first as a linguist and later as an anthropologist. Her research on glossolalia and on religious ecstatic trance experiences (alternate states of consciousness experiences) is the definitive work on these topics.

Eight years before her death, she published a brief reflection on what she expected to happen in death and her journey to the realm of God (Goodman 1997). She learned the substance of these reflections in trance experiences. The journey to the realm of God that she anticipated and described echoes similar journeys recorded in the Bible and other literature.

Sky Journeys

The Bible and related literature report two kinds of journeys to the realm of God. There are round-trip journeys made by people while they are alive, for example, John (Rev. 4:1-2), Paul (2 Cor. 12:2), Enoch *(1, 2 Enoch)*, and one-way journeys such as Jesus made after his death and resurrection (Luke 24:50-51; Acts 1:1-11). Some human beings who have made a one-way journey while still alive must still return in order to complete the round trip (e.g., Enoch, Gen. 5:24; Elijah, 2 Kings 2:1-12; Ezra, 2 Esdr. 8:19b). How are we to understand these journeys: Are they "real"? Did these characters only imagine that they were traveling? Or, in some instances, is the journey simply a literary fiction created by an author about an ancient personage?

Anthropological Insight

One anthropologist defines the shamanic soul flight or soul journey "as an ASC (altered state of consciousness) in which some aspect of the experient — soul, spirit, or perceptual capacities — is thought to travel to or be projected to another place, generally a spirit world" (Winkelman 1999: 411) It is important to notice that journeys by living persons to the realm of God are experiences that occur in alternate states of consciousness. Anthropologists and neuroscientists point out that the human sense of continuity of consciousness is illusory. The brain works hard at maintaining a sense of continuity though the experiences are quite disparate. Human beings actually have the ability to pass through more than thirty-five different levels of consciousness or awareness. They do this regularly and routinely each day. One wakes from sleep and dreams, begins the day and occasionally daydreams, fantasizes, takes catnaps, and perhaps experiences road hypnosis while driving. These are just a few examples of the different levels of human awareness.

A second element in this definition is that "some aspect" of the human person makes the journey. The traveler doesn't necessarily make the journey bodily. The clearest example occurs in the *Ascension of Isaiah* (2nd cent. B.C.E.–4th cent. C.E.). Though his companions "did not think that the holy Isaiah had been taken up" (6:14), the angel (spirit guide) who took Isaiah on his journey through the sky says, "You have to return into this body" (7:5; see also 8:11). Thus the author-visionary of this work claims that Isaiah's journey was similar to what contemporary anthropologists and psychiatrists would call an "out-of-body experience" (OOBE). Philo, the first-century Israelite "scribe" from Alexandria, speaks of "practitioners of wisdom" who make sky journeys: ". . . in mind and thought they share the ranging of the moon and the sun and the ordered march of the other stars fixed and planetary. While their bodies are firmly planted on the ground, they provide their souls with wings so that they may traverse the upper air and gain full contemplation of the powers which dwell there" (*Special Laws* 2.44-45, LCL). There is a sizeable scientific literature on this and the similar event known as a near-death experience (NDE).

A third element to note in this definition is the phrase "*is thought* [my emphasis] to travel or be projected." While some might interpret the italicized phrase as an expression of skepticism or disbelief concerning the journey, it rather reflects an anthropologist's respect for the visionary's report. Once the investigator establishes that his or her native informant is truthful and trustworthy, he or she reports the information communicated as truthful and trustworthy. The challenge is to understand it in the scientific terms known to the investigator. Thus the traveler (e.g., the author of the *Ascension of Isaiah*) makes it clear that some aspect other than the body has made the journey. Skeptical scientists have conducted experiments asking an admitted traveler to tell what is in an adjacent room. Few travelers are successful. Of course, the adjacent room is not alternate reality, which is quite different from consensual reality.

Human Experience

Biblical scholars in general tend to say that sky journeys, trips to the realm of God, have been imagined or are a literary device intending to convey some mysterious truth. There are, however, some biblical scholars who recognize that there is some basis in human experience behind these "fictitious" reports, even if they don't know what it might be or won't recognize OOBEs or NDEs as plausible candidates. Yet a distinct minority of scholars believes that these visionaries did indeed on occasion dissolve the boundaries between consensual reality and alternate reality and manage to reach the realm of God, the spirit world. This in fact is what Dr. Goodman believed she had learned in her research and experimentation and personal experience.

The biblical tradition knows of a hole in the sky through which beings from either realm can visit the other realm (Pilch 1999: 147-52). The hole is usually located directly over the earthly residence of the deity, who is believed to reside in the sky directly above. This place is viewed as the center of the world or the navel of the universe. Since there were a number of temples constructed over sites in the Middle East where the deity appeared, there were a number of such centers of the world, with corresponding holes in the sky. In early Israelite tradition, one such hole was over Bethel, where Jacob saw a ladder and spirits ascending and descending (Gen. 28:17). Another early Israelite tradition saw the center at Babylon (about fifty miles south of Baghdad, Iraq), where the tower of Babel allowed God to come to earth through the hole in the sky to visit Babylon (Gen. 11:5). In the Babylonian tradition, the sky above Nippur was the location of the hole. It was in this vicinity that Ezekiel experienced God in ASCs (Ezek. 1:1). Thus, holy persons like the patriarch Jacob and the prophet Ezekiel knew the location of the hole in the sky and could gain entry to or communicate with the realm of God.

Goodman's research and experimentation with her undergraduate students at Denison University (Granville, OH) discovered similar insights about travel to other realms of alternate reality. They explored the opening or passageway between consensual reality and alternate reality, which is equivalent to the ancient notion of a hole in the sky. But a much more important discovery was that, for these moderns, this opening was not so much a specific location as a requirement for the human traveler to attune the body for the journey and gain the ability to pass through the opening. This tuning of the body may well explain Paul's statement that "flesh and blood cannot inherit the kingdom of God. . . . We shall not all sleep, but we shall all be changed . . ." (1 Cor. 15:50-52). A change or tuning of the body is necessary to navigate the passageway between alternate reality and the realm of God. The change comes about with death, but it is possible to experience the change, temporarily, without dying.

Goodman drew her insight about changing the body from studying depictions on ancient pottery, but especially a particular painting of a man in the Lescaux cave in France. The painted figure was lying at a thirty-seven degree angle to the horizon. Half of his body was limp, but the other half rigid. Goodman hypothesized that there was a reason for this posture, and experiments confirmed that this was a key posture for making a sky journey in an alternate state of consciousness. Subsequent experiments with her students confirmed the hypothesis (Goodman 1990: 20-23, 71-75). Analysis of similar ancient depictions, especially on pottery, resulted in the discovery of over sixty different ritual body postures which tune the body for a variety of alternate states of consciousness experiences (Gore 1995). Given the many reports about alternate states of consciousness and sky journeys in the Bible and related literature, it is reasonable to hypothesize that our ancestors in the faith, just like other humans as far back as 100,000 years ago, knew that the body is a "control system" for changing perception, or levels of awareness. They knew how to tune the body in order to access the realm of God.

The Ascension of Jesus

Jesus' trip to the realm of God after his death and resurrection was a one-way journey to the realm of God. Everyone will take a similar journey after death. Luke is the only one who reports it (Luke 24:50-51; Acts 1:1-11), and rather sparsely at that. The disciples witness the event in an alternate state of consciousness. The word "stare" confirms this, since in the majority of instances in the Acts of the Apostles where the word occurs it is an element in an altered state of consciousness (Pilch 2004: 41, 75). Further, the vision of the white-robed men points to the same thing. "And while they were gazing [staring] into heaven [the sky] as Jesus went, behold, two men in white robes stood by them . . ." (Acts 1:10).

Given the centrality of the Jerusalem temple, the Israelites were quite certain of the opening or entryway from this reality to the realm of God over Jerusalem. That is the point from which the risen Jesus departs (concerning the opening, see 1 Kings 22:19; 2 Chron. 18:18; Ezek. 1:1; Mark 1:10; Matt. 3:16; Rev. 4:1). He could not have ascended in Galilee (nor does the tradition say that, e.g., Matt 28:16). While the many graves in the vicinity of Jerusalem have been explained by a tradition that claims that this is where the final judgment would take place, it is also possible that people wanted to be located as close to the hole in the sky as possible in order to facilitate their ascent.

The colors one perceives in an altered state of consciousness alert the visionary about whether or not s/he actually is in an ASC. The colors relate to neurological changes. To see black means that one is in "normal" consciousness. To see white means that the level of awareness is changed: one is in an ASC. The cloud that took Jesus "out of their sight" is white in color.

Moreover, in the Israelite tradition, the cloud symbolizes God's presence, power, or honor (Exod. 16:10; 19:9; 24:15-18; Ezek. 10:3-4; Ps. 18:11; Dan. 7:13; Luke 9:34-35; 1 Thess. 4:17; Rev. 11:12). The passive voice in Acts 1:9 ("he was lifted up") further confirms that God is the agent who took Jesus into alternate reality. Both Luke and the disciples knew this and could draw on their traditions to express their experience of Jesus' ascent.

Two men in white robes interpret the vision to the apostles (Acts 1:10-11). The white robes indicate that they are from the sky, from alternate reality, the realm of God. The apostles are still in an ASC. They tell the apostles that Jesus will return someday from the sky (compare 1 Thess. 4:16) and with the same attendant phenomena that accompanied his departure ("the same way you saw him go into the sky"). Human beings will witness his return in an alternate state of consciousness ("clouds" signal this; see Luke 21:27), and he will be accompanied by sky servants ("beings in white robes"). That Jesus reached the destination of his sky journey is confirmed by Stephen, who peered through the hole in the sky over Jerusalem and saw Jesus "standing at the right hand of God" (Acts 7:55-56).

Conclusion

As we have previously noted, the medieval theologians reminded us that all theology is analogy. Everything one can know and say about God is rooted in human experience. The late Dr. Goodman and her associates have richly explored a dimension of human experience that is common to more than 90 percent of the population sample studied in the ethnographic record. Thus it is an experience shared by many human beings currently alive on the planet. Moreover, the experience of ASCs and sky journeys can be traced back at least 100,000 years (Goodman and Nauwald 2003: 10-12). Filtering the biblical record through social-scientific insights does not rationalize the evidence so much as it enriches the theological perspective.

6. Paul's Call to Be an Apostle

The scene of Paul's experience on the road to Damascus reported by Luke three times in the Acts of the Apostles (9:3-19; 22:6-16; 26:12-18) is familiar even to those who have never read the Bible. Such familiarity is often "spurious" because details of the recollection find little to no support in Luke's version and even less in Paul's references to the same event (Gal. 1:15-16; 1 Cor. 15:8-9; 2 Cor. 4:6: Phil. 3:12). What really happened to Paul on that occasion?

Luke and Paul

Contemporary biblical scholars are generally agreed that the Acts of the Apostles is not a reliable source for factual information about Paul. In Acts, Luke has intentionally reshaped Paul into a different person than the one he actually was. The historical Paul was a citizen of neither Rome (Acts 22:25) nor Tarsus (Acts 21:39). If he had factually been a Roman citizen, it would have been impossible for Paul to receive as many beatings as he reports and of which he boasts (e.g., 2 Cor. 11:24-25). This and similar information about the historical Paul uncovered by contemporary biblical scholars is readily available in many studies and commentaries. What, then, can be said about Luke's thrice-told (and interpreted) report of Paul's experience on the road to Damascus?

The one common element in the reports of Luke and Paul is that Paul's call by God most definitely occurred in an alternate state of consciousness, something Paul experienced more than once in his life (see 2 Cor. 12:7). This is not surprising, since tradition notes that God routinely communicates with human beings in this way. "The word of the LORD was rare in those days; there was no frequent vision" (or experience of God in an alternate state of consciousness; 1 Sam. 3:1). Luke knew how Paul had learned about what the God of Israel was doing in Jesus of Nazareth (Gal. 1:15-16; 1 Cor. 15:8-9). What Luke did was to fashion a report that differed from Paul's which nevertheless accords perfectly well with the patterned human experience known as ecstatic trance, one of more than thirty-five different states of consciousness or awareness of which human beings are capable. Indeed, Luke reports more than twenty instances of group and individual experiences of altered states of consciousness in the Acts of the Apostles. He was obviously familiar with the experience, and knew how to report it according to the cultural paradigm (Pilch 2004).

Luke and the Stages of Trance Experience

Psychological anthropologists identify three stages in a trance experience. In the first or mildest level of an altered state of consciousness, the visionary perceives light and geometric patterns. The shift in consciousness is often induced by intense concentration. Those who drive motor vehicles are familiar with "road trance." Intense concentration on the journey and the route causes the mind to shift awareness to another level. The driver arrives safely at the destination having observed all the laws and having followed the correct route but doesn't recall the journey because his or her mind was thinking of something else.

After witnessing the murder of Stephen (Acts 7:58–8:1), Paul engaged fully in persecuting believers in Jesus Messiah. "Ravaging the church, and entering house after house, he dragged off men and women and committed them to prison" (Acts 8:1-3). On the road to Damascus, even if he was only walking (no beast is mentioned), Paul was "still breathing threats and murder against the disciples of the Lord" (Acts 9:1). There can be no doubt that the topic and person that intensely engaged Paul's mind was Jesus, whom he considered to be a fraud and, in light of his crucifixion, quite clearly not beloved or approved by God.

The bright light from heaven (Acts 9:3; 22:6), even brighter than the sun (Acts 26:13), is a sign of a shift in Paul's consciousness. Whether this happened as a matter of fact, or whether Luke is creating this element, the fact is that Paul's level of awareness is shifting, and Paul is aware of it. The light color indicates this shift to anyone familiar with trance experiences.

In the second stage of a trance experience, the visionary seeks to impose meaning on what she or he is seeing. In the Israelite tradition, light is associated with God, God's honor or glory, and/or the realm of God (e.g., Isa. 60:1). Paul the Pharisee knew that God or someone from the realm of God was attempting to communicate with him. In imposing meaning on the vision, the visionary also provides the "sound track." In other words, the content of the message will flow from the latent discourse of the culture.

Paul the Pharisee was so focused on the crucified, and therefore shamed, Jesus Messiah that the context was ripe for Jesus Messiah to communicate with him. Paul, "breathing threats" (Acts 9:1) and in "raging fury against [believers in Jesus]" (Acts 26:11), was certainly obsessed with Jesus and his deceived followers. Paul's activity was rooted in his Torah-based conviction that these fellow members of the house of Israel were not at all faithful to the God of the covenant. Thus, the dialogue between Paul and the risen Jesus emerges from Paul's emotional state and the circumstances of his commission to hunt down and imprison those who believed in Jesus.

Scholars note that the dialogue between the risen Jesus and Paul appears with little variation in all three accounts. Traditional biblical scholarship has identified this as a "dialogue with apparition literary form" with a very consistent and discernible tripartite structure. Basically there is the question of Jesus ("Why do you persecute me?"), the response of Paul ("Who are you, Lord?"), and the self-presentation of Jesus ("I am Jesus, the one whom you are persecuting"), following which Jesus assigns Paul a task or mission.

But is this literary form nothing more than a literary device serving to describe an encounter with God, an angel, or other beings from the realm of God? Once again, psychological anthropology suggests that, in addition to being a literary form, it is also a predictable, Mediterranean cultural pattern. This is how Mediterranean people have learned to react to such an experience. Every culture prescribes predictable behavior patterns in common human experiences. Thus Mediterranean culture, or its social system, prescribed the appropriate behavioral pattern by which shifts in levels of awareness, that is, alternate states of consciousness, should be experienced, interpreted, and reported.

The actual dialogue reported in Acts is quite likely not a verbatim report entrusted at some time by Paul to Luke. It is rather, as scholars note, facts with interpretation. Paul experienced the risen Jesus in an alternate state of consciousness (fact) and interpreted his experience for himself. Every visionary does this. Luke cast Paul's interpretation into the form of this dialogue. Of course, it is also possible that Paul reported his interpretation of his experience with others by means of this dialogue. However, his own comments in his letters never make any such reference. It is impossible to determine where in Luke's reports the facts end and the interpretation begins, but it is important to keep in mind that a factual event underlies his reports.

The upshot of Paul's experience is that he realizes how mistaken he has been. If Jesus speaks with him from the realm of God, then Jesus was approved rather than condemned or rejected by God. Jesus is indeed the Messiah. The result of the experience in each of these three reports is easy to see. First, a dramatic change takes place in Paul's understanding of Jesus. Second, Paul is entrusted by God with a new mission (or missions). These are two very common results of trance experiences in all cultures: the visionary receives new insight into a problem or an answer to a nagging question; or the visionary is enlightened about and empowered to take a new direction in life.

Paul's View of His Call

In his authentic letters, Paul understands himself as a "holy person" called by God to a specific task. Anthropologists have called such a person a "shaman," but this is just one cultural example of a holy person, a Siberian Tungus. However, the phenomenon of a holy person is found in all cultures. The process of becoming a holy person involves six elements.

1. A spirit contacts the candidate to possess or adopt him. Paul believes that God selected him already from conception. God "from my mother's womb had set me apart and called me through his grace" (Gal. 1:15). With allusions to Isaiah (41:1) and Jeremiah (1:5), Paul situates himself in the prophetic line and understands himself to have been selected for a prophetic ministry just as these prophets were.

2. Identification of the possessing or adopting spirit. It is clear in some of the opening greetings of his letters that Paul understood that it was the God of Israel who selected him for his ministry (Rom. 1:1; 1 Cor. 1:1; 2 Cor. 1:1; Gal. 1:1).

3. Acquisition of necessary ritual skills. Where and how did Paul learn to be a holy man? Certainly in part from his heritage as a Pharisee. ". . . in observance of the law a Pharisee," he wrote, "in zeal I persecuted the church, in righteousness based on the law I was blameless" (Phil. 3:5-6). Two kinds of holy people existed in the Israelite tradition: the ṣaddîq was one who sought to please God by keeping all commandments (the Pharisees identified 613), while the ḥasîd sought to go even beyond that. Paul appears to include himself in the first category, and quite likely the second as well.

4. Tutelage by both a spirit and real-life teacher. While Paul declared his independence of all human counsel (e.g., Gal. 1:12, 16-17), he does admit that he spent fifteen days with Kephas, himself a holy man by Israelite reckoning (Gal. 1:18). Some scholars think that Kephas not only taught Paul about the earthly Jesus whom Paul never met but perhaps also taught him the ritual skills which a holy person must master, for example, inducing and interpreting alternate states of consciousness experiences, healing, and exorcism. Others disagree, claiming that what Paul wanted from Kephas above all was acknowledgment that God alone was Paul's teacher (Malina and Pilch 2006: 189). The role of Ananias and Barnabas (Acts 9:10 and 27) is open to similar interpretation. Did they teach Paul anything? or did they rather confirm what Paul insisted on in his letters: God alone was his teacher.

Luke appears to confirm this view when he reports that the Spirit selected Barnabas and Paul for special ministry (Acts 13:2). Paul's spirit teacher is none other than God. Paul is convinced that God personally revealed the significance of Jesus to him (Gal. 1:15-16; 1:11). Paul does not relate the nature of that contact or that revelation. It may be similar to what Luke described in Acts, or it may be different. Yet God is clearly Paul's primary instructor.

5. Growing familiarity with the possessing or adopting spirit. In his communication with the community in Corinth, Paul refers to his "abundance of revelations" (2 Cor. 12:7). Since this letter is dated (57 C.E.) roughly twenty-three years after his call and commissioning (34 C.E.), Paul has had at least that many years of experience, thus a growing familiarity with God and others in the realm of God.

6. Ongoing trance experiences. As just indicated, Paul refers to an abundance of revelations (2 Cor. 12:7), not to mention sky journeys (2 Cor. 12:1-4), that is, trips to the realm of God with feet planted firmly on the ground, a common and documented experience of holy persons in all cultures. Indeed, the author of the book of Revelation explicitly admits that he took such journeys to the realm of God and other places from which he could see the cosmos from God's vantage point (e.g., Rev. 4:1-2; 21:10).

Conclusion

The event traditionally described as "the conversion of Paul" is more appropriately identified as "the call of Paul" or "commissioning of Paul" by God to a certain task. Paul did not convert from Judaism to Christianity since the latter did not yet exist. Rather, Paul learned that the God of Israel had done something new in Jesus of Nazareth, and God called Paul to communicate that to fellow Israelites, especially those living among non-Israelite people. Luke's reports seem to place Paul on par with eyewitness companions of Jesus, that is, the apostles. Paul seems to understand and locate himself in the context of the Israelite prophets, holy men, selected by God for specific tasks.

7. Paul the Apostle in Cultural Context

Everyone knows Paul as "the Apostle to the Gentiles." Peter and others were to work among fellow Israelites, while Paul believed that he was called to spread the good news among non-Israelites. Such knowledge is another example of "spurious familiarity," that is, information that is obvious and presumed to be known and accepted by everyone but difficult or perhaps even impossible to document. Anyone who reads Paul's letters even superficially has to be amazed and then puzzled by the complexity of his communications. They draw on traditions from Israelite sacred literature that would be rather unknown by and quite foreign to non-Israelites. The letters aren't any easier for modern believers to understand. Suppose Paul's call was to preach to Israelite minorities living among non-Israelite majorities in Asia Minor, Macedonia, Achaia, or elsewhere outside of Palestine. His letters and his activities would look quite different (Malina and Pilch 2006).

Paul's Call to Be an Apostle

In the previous chapter, I interpreted Paul's reports of his vocation (Gal. 1:15-16; 1 Cor. 15:8-9; 2 Cor. 4:6: Phil. 3:12) as an experience of God in an alternate state of consciousness. What did God communicate to Paul? That the God of Israel had done something new in Jesus of Nazareth crucified and raised from the dead, and that God was calling Paul to communicate that innovation to fellow Israelites, especially those living among non-Israelite people. The innovation that Jesus proclaimed in his lifetime was a forthcoming Israelite theocracy or the kingdom of heaven/God. The innovation that Paul should proclaim was that the God of Israel raised Jesus from the dead, thus revealing him to be Israel's Messiah (Christ) and cosmic Lord, with a view to the forthcoming Israelite theocracy (1 Thessalonians and elsewhere throughout the letters). The Messiah is an Israelite concept and expectation. Who other than Israelites would be interested or persuaded by Paul?

Paul the Apostle as Change Agent

In contemporary social-scientific terms, Paul is best understood as a change agent (Pilch 2009). A change agent is someone authorized by another (a change agency) to communicate an innovation (the change) to clients for their benefit. Jesus in the name of God authorized the Twelve as change agents (see Matt. 10). Pharisee groups often authorized Israelite scribes as change agents (see Matt. 22:16). But Paul insists that he was authorized by the God of Israel personally and not by any group (Gal. 1:1). This is why Paul, like Jesus (Matt. 11:2-6) and the Baptist (Matt. 11:7-15), often had to answer questions about the source of his authority or his authorization.

What was the message God wanted Paul to proclaim? God was about to institute an Israelite theocracy in Jerusalem and Judea. The first step was raising Jesus from the dead and constituting him Lord and Messiah. God was about to deliver redemption or restoration of honor to Israel. Those Israelites living outside of Palestine for whom this was a solution to a long-embarrassing problem would form a support group (local church) to assist themselves in behaving in a way that would express their trust in the God of Israel and adopting proper behavior toward one another and toward God. What was the embarrassing problem? Almost seven centuries of domination by foreign powers: Assyria, Babylon, Persia, Greece, and Rome! What kind of God is it who can't protect the people from conquest and domination by other powers? At last with the raising of Jesus, this God is about to assert rightful power and establish the long-awaited theocracy. This in a nutshell is the essential message of Paul's seven authentic letters.

Paul's Tasks as a Change Agent

Paul the apostle, viewed as a change agent, has seven tasks, all of which are reflected in his letters. The first is to develop a need for change. Not only does the apostle assess the audience's needs at this stage, but he also helps to create some. This occurred during a personal visit (usually the first) by Paul or other change agents such as Timothy and Silvanus (see 1 Thess. 1:1). Such a visit would establish credibility and trustworthiness between change agents and clients. It would also demonstrate the empathy of the change agents with local needs and problems.

The second task is to establish a relationship of information exchange. This, of course, is the purpose served by the letters but also by messengers. From Athens, Paul sent Timothy to check on the Thessalonians, who adopted the innovation they had earlier proposed. Paul rejoiced at the report Timothy brought upon his return (1 Thess. 3:1-6) and then wrote his letter.

Diagnosing the problem is a third task. (Note that other than the first and last tasks, the remaining tasks need not occur in the sequence presented here.) Problems inevitably occur for various reasons. Some members of the Israelite minority to whom Paul wrote might not have agreed with the innovation or those who adopted it. This caused dissension in the group. Or the innovation created problems unforeseen by the change agent when adopters applied it to new situations. The steady flow of information between Paul and the Jesus groups he founded facilitated this task for Paul. In his first letter to the Corinthians, Paul reacts to (quite likely oral) reports from Chloe's people (1 Cor. 1:9–6:20) and then replies to specific questions sent to him by the Corinthians (1 Cor. 7:1–15:58). For Paul or any change agent to be successful, he must view the situation empathetically, that is, put himself in the shoes of the uncomfortable. Paul appears to have been able to do that very well.

A fourth task is creating the intent to change in the client. Another name for this task is motivation: How does one get started on a desired course of action and, perhaps more important, how does one persevere in that determination? Perhaps a cross-culturally valid key to achieving this task is to appeal to the client's self-interest, different as that may be in individual cultures. With specific reference, however, to his task among fellow Israelites living outside Palestine and perhaps feeling disconnected from events occurring in Palestine, Paul made frequent reference to what God has done "for us" (e.g., Rom. 5:8; 8:31-32), reminded his clients that Jesus died "for us" (e.g., 1 Thess. 5:10), and described what the forthcoming theocracy holds in store "for us" (Rom. 8:31; 2 Cor. 1:3-6, etc.).

It would also be possible to motivate change by personal appeals or by references to the "the common good of the community." Knowing the controversy and dissension that Paul could and did stir in some communities, an exhortation such as "Be imitators of me, as I am of Christ" (1 Cor. 11:1) would have mixed effectiveness and in the long run would very likely lose its force. Nor would appeals to the greater good of the community be any more effective, as the Corinthian factions make clear (1 Cor. 1:10-17).

A fifth task, and perhaps the most daunting one, is the challenge of translating intent into action. As the ancient proverb observed: knowledge is not virtue. Simply being aware of good behavior is no guarantee that it will ever be put into practice. The change agent expects an action response from the clients. He looks for behavioral change. Basically, the change agent expects clients to live according to the program he advocates. The lists of virtues proposed by Paul illustrate the kind of behaviors he desired. "Live by the Spirit, I say, and do not gratify the desires of the flesh. . . . The fruit of the Spirit is love, joy, peace, patience, kindness, goodness, faithfulness, gentleness, and self-control" (Gal. 5:16, 22-23). This represents his program, behavior that is appropriate to the forthcoming theocracy.

As an illustration of how to do this, he unashamedly points to himself. He applauds the Thessalonians for doing just that: "And you became imitators of us and the Lord, for in spite of persecution you received the word with joy inspired by the Holy Spirit, so that you became an example to all the believers in Macedonia and in Achaia" (1 Thess. 1:6-7). Paul's governing principle, like that of all change agents, is the realization that actual implementation of a proposed lifestyle served to confirm the basis (knowledge) on which it was presented. The result is self-reliance and self-renewal in the client. Thus, works or deeds by Jesus groups would flow from faith. To focus exclusively on knowledge or motivation with secondary emphasis on implementation would result in temporary change. It would be faith without Jesus-group works or deeds.

A sixth task of the apostle as change agent is to stabilize change and prevent discontinuation of any part of it. Any reading of Paul's authentic letters reveals that the innovations he introduced to the communities had at least two results: dissonance bound up with accepting the new and rejecting the old; and challenges from other change agents (usually called "Judaizers"). The principal tool Paul used was directing reinforcing messages to those who adopted the change.

The letter to the Galatians is a good illustration. Paul begins (Gal. 1–2) with a vigorous defense of his call by God to be a change agent or apostle. The call is directly from God (Gal. 1:1). So, too, is the innovation from God (Gal. 1:6-12). God's innovation did not require circumcision (Gal. 5:2-12). It is important to understand that infant male genital mutilation known as circumcision did not become an Israelite marker until the Maccabean period, around 150 B.C.E. Contemporary Jewish scholars also note that it was just a nick rather than the removal of the complete foreskin. Complete removal did not become a requirement until about 150 C.E., after the Bar Kochba Revolt (132-135 C.E.). The nick could be and was easily undone in the Hellenistic era by those Israelites who wanted to acculturate as completely as possible in the lands where they lived as minorities. It would be fair and plausible to say that the Israelite males with whom Paul interacted outside of Palestine did not bother to have the nick. Like the people among whom they lived, they considered it barbaric mutilation. The so-called Council of Jerusalem (Acts 15) did not require it of the Israelites either. Hence Paul's anger with those Israelite change agents who followed him and contradicted his gospel. "I wish those who unsettle you would castrate themselves!" (Gal. 5:12).

The final task of a change agent is to end the relationship. The change agent's task is to introduce and stabilize innovation and then move on. This, indeed, was Paul's intention as well. He had miles to go so that he might introduce the innovation among Israelites living in the whole known world outside of Palestine. He would not be tied down and settle in one place until he had achieved his goal. Yet, the goal was not just to spread the innovation but to assure that those who accepted it would behave according to their new social identity until the coming of the Lord Jesus. "It is by your holding fast to the word of life that I can boast on the day of Christ that I did not run in vain or labor in vain" (Phil. 2:16). Or as a disciple of Paul explained more explicitly: "I have fought the good fight, I have finished the race, I have kept the faith. From now on there is reserved for me the crown of righteousness, which the Lord, the righteous judge, will give me on that day, and not only to me but also to all who have longed for his appearing" (2 Tim. 4:7-8).

Conclusion

What about the "real" Gentiles? The non-Israelites? Paul did not think highly of them, nor was he much concerned about them. He considered them to be branches cut from a wild olive tree and grafted, "contrary to nature," onto a cultivated olive tree (Rom. 11:24). The horticultural practice of the time was exactly the opposite, namely, to graft cultivated branches onto wild olive trees. A wild branch grafted onto a cultivated tree will produce bitter and inedible fruit. In typical Mediterranean fashion, Paul recorded for posterity a well-crafted insult for non-Israelites.

8. Divine Darkness

When Mother Teresa of Calcutta (1910-97) was beatified on October 19, 2003, many were stunned to learn or to be reminded that she had experienced a "dark night" in her relationship with God for nearly the last fifty years of her life (Kolodiejchuk 2007). During this time she felt a "terrible pain of loss, of God not wanting me, of God not being God, of God not really existing." Yet those familiar with her life insist that she is an example of a classic Christian mystic whose loyalty God tested and strengthened by this dark night. Does God behave like this? Is this concept reflected in the Bible?

Dark Night

Perhaps most readers associate the term "dark night" with the great Carmelite mystic, St. John of the Cross (1542-91), from whose Spanish poem, *Noche oscura,* this phrase derives. He speaks of the Dark Night of the Sense and the Dark Night of the Spirit (but never *of the Soul,* a common misinterpretation; Egan 2000). The poem was written in the context of love produced by union with God and achieved after a painful experience of purgation (the Dark Night). John's commentaries on his poem highlight the dryness, pain, and darkness of that purgation. "Both the sense and the spirit, as though under an immense and dark load, undergo such agony and pain that the soul would consider death a relief" (*The Dark Night* 2.5.6).

The Presence of God

To understand "dark night" as a metaphor for the perceived absence of God, it is important to begin with the notion of the presence of God. The Hebrew word most often translated "presence" of God is literally "the face" of God. When the man and his wife heard the Lord God in the garden, they "hid themselves from the presence [= face] of the LORD God . . ." (Gen. 3:8), that is, they tried to flee from God's presence. Of course, it is impossible to hide from the omnipresent God (Jer. 23:24). On the contrary, throughout the Bible God's people yearned for the divine presence and diligently pursued it. "'Come,' says my heart, 'seek God's face'; your face, LORD, do I seek!" (Ps. 27:8 NAB).

The Bible mentions other things that are associated with or indicative of God's presence. During the exodus, "The LORD preceded them in the daytime by means of a *column of cloud* to show them the way, and at night by means of a *column of fire* to give them light" (Exod. 13:21 NAB). But this did not last. God gave instructions for constructing an *"ark"* (Exod. 25:10-22), which served as God's footstool (1 Chron. 28:2). The column of cloud also stood at the entrance of a *meeting tent,* which Moses alone entered to communicate with God "face to face" (Exod. 33:7-11). The *temples* on Zion (the mythological temple of Solomon and the historical temples of the Persian period, 520 B.C.E., and that of Herod the Great, c. 40 B.C.E.–70 C.E.) were God's personally selected places of residence among the chosen people (1 Kings 8). Interestingly, God dwelt in darkness in the Jerusalem temple (1 Kings 8:12).

The Perceived Absence of God

Sometimes God was perceived as deliberately withdrawing the divine presence from the people as a whole or from individuals. The prophet Hosea reported God as saying, "I will go back to my place until they make reparation and seek my face [presence]" (Hos. 5:15). God's purpose in this instance is to stir the people to repentance. About two centuries later, Ezekiel wrote that God resorted to the same strategy once again: "The nations shall know that because of its sins the house of Israel went into exile; for they transgressed against me, and I hid my face from them and handed them over to their foes, so that all of them fell by the sword. According to their uncleanness and their transgressions I dealt with them, hiding my face from them" (Ezek. 39:23-24).

One psalmist personally begged God: "Do not hide your face from me, do not repel your servant in anger. You are my salvation. Do not cast me off; do not forsake me, God my savior!" (Ps. 27:9 NAB). Feeling as if one is cast off or forsaken by God while still believing one can converse with God surely describes a relationship with God in which God is not so much absent as perhaps purposefully ignoring the plight of clients or even abiding in a different place (see Ezek. 11:22-23). This seems to be the biblical experience of divine darkness.

Jeremiah

Perhaps the most poignant example of this kind of "perceived divine absence" in the Bible is those segments of Jeremiah identified by scholars as his "intimate papers" or "confessions" (scattered throughout Jer. 11–20). Jeremiah does not perceive divine absence, but rather that God is not delivering on divine promises to him. In response to Jeremiah's complaint that his wicked opponents are prospering (Jer. 12:1-4), God answers: "If running against men has wearied you, how will you race against horses?" (Jer. 12:5 NAB). Things will only get worse! When Jeremiah complains again about his suffering (Jer. 15:10-18), God says that he needs to abandon self-pity and repent (Jer. 15:19)! If Jeremiah does this, he will become the kind of prophet God expects him to be, and God will protect him (Jer. 15:20-21).

At his darkest moment, Jeremiah feels that God has duped him (Jer. 20:7-18). His pain is unbearable; his despair is black indeed. He curses the day on which he was born. More than that, he wishes he had died in the womb. Scholars recognize many textual problems in these "confessions of

Jeremiah," not the least of which is the surprising profession of confidence in God (Jer. 20:11-13) sandwiched between a lament (Jer. 20:7-10) and a self-curse (Jer. 20:14-18). While some scholars believe that these optimistic verses are misplaced, others point out that people who find themselves in this position don't think or speak logically. This interpretation is very plausible in a Middle Eastern cultural context where rules of Western logic don't apply. God is present in Jeremiah's divine darkness, but God behaves contrary to expectations.

Psalm 88

Another illustration of divine darkness is this gloomy Psalm 88. It is the whining lament of a very sick collectivistic personality whose tragic life situation was heightened by friends and companions who have abandoned him (vv. 9, 19). This only served to underscore his feeling of being abandoned by God as well (v. 15). Unlike other laments, this psalm contains no vow of praise. It ends on a note of apparent despair: "my only friend is darkness" (v. 19). Still, it is noteworthy that the psalmist directs his complaints directly to God and assumes that God hears them (vv. 2, 10b, 14). The psalmist thus demonstrates his belief that he still has a relationship with God. God exists. The psalmist is keenly aware that God is responsible for his suffering (vv. 7-9, 15-19 with the repetition of "you" and "your").

Despite this awareness of God's role in his life, the psalmist did not have the sensible awareness of God's presence for which he had hoped. "Why do you reject me, LORD? Why hide your face from me?" (v. 15). This is his experience of divine darkness. How does he attempt to remove it? By resorting to the most powerful cultural strategy available to him: The psalmist appeals to God's sense of honor. He sketches the shame that will sully the divine reputation if he dies. Dead men tell no tales, and they also can't sing God's praises for divine deeds and benefactions (vv. 11-13). It is difficult to determine whether God answered his prayer. One would expect an appended thanksgiving if the psalmist were rescued. On the other hand, some scholars think the praise of God is veiled in the verses we have. Another psalmist who was quite aware of an all-present God said: "Darkness is not dark for you, and night shines as the day. Darkness and light are but one" (Ps. 139:12). He also noted: "If I lie down in Sheol, you are there, too" (Ps. 139:8). Perhaps our psalmist thought along similar lines. For our psalmist, then, is there darkness? Yes. Perceived absence of God? Likely not.

Divine Darkness in History

Professor Carol Zaleski (2003) reminds us that divine darkness received many different interpretations in the history of Christian theology and spirituality. Theologians and mystics inspired by writings of the sixth-century Pseudo-Dionysius the Areopagite (mistakenly assumed to be the person named in Acts 17:34) affirmed that God dwells in inaccessible light. So strong is this light that it veils God in a dark "cloud of unknowing." But this describes God's transcendence more than a human feeling of abandonment.

In the twelfth century, William of St. Thierry rejoiced in the human incapacity to see that God is present. This, according to him, allowed love to play a great role, for love is the proper eye for seeing God. Later generations of Christians turned from this cheerful view to a more desolate darkness, such as John of the Cross described. Yet God is present in this darkness, purifying the soul and preparing it for divine union. Thus there is dark knowing and dark loving, and John rejoices in that night that joined Beloved with lover.

It seems that only in the modern period has the dark night been transformed into radical doubt about everything: one's own spiritual condition, God's promises, and even God's very existence, as Mother Teresa admitted. Professor Zaleski notes that in 1823, Abbot Chapman of the famed Downside Abbey wrote a letter to a nonmonastic friend on this topic. His advice was to dismiss these feelings and doubts. Instead, forge strongly ahead resolved to assure the Lord that one is ready to suffer whatever God sends. In other words, Professor Zaleski concludes, convert the feeling of abandonment by God into an act of abandonment to God. Faith, that is, loyalty to God in times when God seems to be absent, or when one has no sensible awareness of God's presence, is a good strategy against the contemporary experience of divine darkness.

Seeking God's Face

Searching the Bible for hints to remain in God's presence, we learn that God is close to those who walk with him, like Enoch (Gen. 5:24), Noah (Gen. 6:9-10), and the patriarchs (Gen. 48:15-16). So, too, are those close to God who actively seek the divine presence (Amos 5:4-6) and those who trust in God as their rescuer (Pss. 18; 34; Isa. 58:9). It goes without saying that those who do good and avoid evil will enjoy God's presence (Amos

5:14). If, despite these actions, divine darkness descends on a person, one can only respect the all-knowing God's intentions even if one doesn't know or understand them. What is important above all is to remain unswervingly faithful to God after the example of Jesus (Mark 14:35-35). That may not relieve the darkness (Mark 15:34), but it will eventually help one to attain the fullness of life intended by God (Matt. 28:1-10; 1 Cor. 15:50-56).

Conclusion

The biblical evidence indicates that our ancestors in the faith did experience divine darkness, or what later tradition termed the "dark night." They attributed the experience to a deliberate decision of the omnipresent God to withhold the divine presence from the people as a whole or from individuals. Yet even in this perceived absence of God, the deity was always available somewhere. Petitions and prayers could be and were directed toward God. Where God indicated a reason for this decision, it was usually intended to restore or strengthen the bond between God and the people or God and individuals. Biblical personalities did not seem to have the feelings of contemporary believers of "God not being God, or God not really existing." In the Bible, wicked people are usually characterized by the latter two traits, and their judgment is intentional. The tendency of biblical personalities to remain loyal to God no matter what (the authentic, Middle Eastern cultural understanding of "faith") appeared to be a common response to the experience of divine darkness. That would seem to be good advice for believers of all times and all cultures.

FURTHER READING: HUMAN CONSCIOUSNESS

Artemidorus. 1990. *The Interpretation of Dreams: Oneirocritica.* Translation and Commentary by Robert J. White. Second Edition Revised and Enlarged. Torrance: Original Books.
Bilu, Yoram, and Henry Abramovitch. 1985. "In Search of the Saddiq: Visitational Dreams among Moroccan Jews in Israel." *Psychiatry* 48: 83-92.
Bullkeley, Kelly, ed. 2001. *Dreams: A Reader on the Religious, Cultural, and Psychological Dimensions of Dreaming.* New York: Palgrave.
Crapanzano, Vincent. 2001. "The Etiquette of Consciousness." *Social Research* 68: 627-49.
Egan, Keith J., T.O. Carm. 2000. "Dark Night: Education for Beauty." Pp. 241-66 in *Carmel and Contemplation: Transforming Human Consciousness.*

Carmelite Studies. Edited by Kevin Culligan, O.C.D., and Regis Jordan, O.C.D. Washington: ICS Publications.

Goodman, Felicitas D. 1990. *Where the Spirits Ride the Wind: Trance Journeys and Other Ecstatic Experiences.* Bloomington and Indianapolis: Indiana University Press.

―――. 1997. *My Last Forty Days: A Visionary Journey among the Pueblo Spirits.* Bloomington: Indiana University Press.

Goodman, Felicitas D., and Nana Nauwald. 2003. *Ecstatic Trance: A Workbook.* Havelte: Binkey Kok.

Gore, Belinda. 1995. *Ecstatic Body Postures: An Alternate Reality Workbook.* Santa Fe: Bear.

―――. 2009. *The Ecstatic Experience: Healing Postures for Spirit Journeys.* Rochester: Bear.

Kolodiejchuk, Brian, ed. 2007. *Mother Teresa: Come, Be My Light: The Private Writings of the Saint of Calcutta.* New York: Doubleday.

Malina, Bruce J. 1999. "Assessing the Historicity of Jesus' Walking on the Sea: Insights from Cross-Cultural Social Psychology." Pp. 27-42 in *Authenticating the Activities of Jesus.* Edited by Bruce Chilton and Craig A. Evans. Leiden: Brill.

Malina, Bruce J., and John J. Pilch. 2006. *Social-science Commentary on the Letters of Paul.* Minneapolis: Fortress.

Matchett, William Foster. 1972. "Repeated Hallucinatory Experiences as a Part of the Mourning Process among Hopi Indian Women." *Psychiatry* 35: 185-94.

Newberg, Andrew, M.D., Eugene D'Aquili, M.D., Ph.D., and Vince Rause. 2002. *Why God Won't Go Away: Brain Science and the Biology of Belief.* New York: Ballantine.

Pert, Candace B. 1999. *Molecules of Emotion: The Science behind Mind-Body Medicine.* New York: Simon & Schuster.

Pilch, John J. 1999. *The Cultural Dictionary of the Bible.* Collegeville, MN: The Liturgical Press.

―――. 2004. *Visions and Healing in the Acts of the Apostles: How the Early Believers Experienced God.* Collegeville, MN: The Liturgical Press.

―――. 2011a. "Appearances of the Risen Jesus in Cultural Context: Experiences of Alternate Reality." Pp. 146-62 in *Flights of the Soul: Visions, Heavenly Journeys, and Peak Experiences in the Biblical World.* Grand Rapids and Cambridge: Eerdmans.

―――. 2011b. "Visions in Revelation and Alternate Consciousness: A Perspective from Cultural Anthropology." Pp. 216-30 in *Flights of the Soul: Vi-*

sions, *Heavenly Journeys, and Peak Experiences in the Biblical World.* Grand
Rapids and Cambridge: Eerdmans.

————. 2011c. "Paul, a Change Agent: Model for the Twenty-First Century."
Pp. 81-99 in *Celebrating Paul.* Edited by Peter Spitaler. Washington: The
Catholic Biblical Association of America.

Rees, W. Dewi. 1971. "The Hallucinations of Widowhood." *British Medical
Journal.* 4: 37-41.

Winkelman, Michael. 1999. "Altered States of Consciousness and Religious Behavior." Pp. 393-428 in *Anthropology of Religion: A Handbook.* Edited by Stephen D. Glazier. Westport and London: Praeger.

Zaleski, Carol. 2003. "The Dark Night of Mother Theresa." *First Things* 133
(May 2003): 24-27. Available online. Downloaded May 19, 2011. http://
www.firstthings.com/article/2007/08/the-dark-night-of-mother-teresa-42

Part Seven

GOD AND THE SPIRIT WORLD

The topics in this part are usually discussed by Christians under the topic of the Trinity: the mystery of three persons in one God. The concept of the Trinity took nearly a thousand years of reflection, acrimonious debate, and scholarly reflection and developed pretty much in the way familiar to contemporary Christians.

How did our ancestors in the faith understand God? A medieval theological principle accepted by St. Thomas Aquinas and all medieval theologians and philosophers is: All theology is analogy. Everything that human beings can know and say about God is rooted in human experience. An oft-neglected aspect of human experience is that it is culturally specific. In our previous reflection on the family, we noted that while a father and mother are essential to procreation and to families in every culture, cultures in their turn interpret and understand a mother and father very differently. In Middle Eastern culture, the loving father is one who heeds the advice of Proverbs 23:13-14:

> Do not withhold discipline from a lad,
>   if you beat him with a rod, he will not die.
> If you beat him with the rod
>   you will save his life from Sheol.

An American father who behaved like this would probably be arrested and jailed.

In this part we reflect on how the Middle Eastern culture of our ancestors in faith colored the way they understood God, Jesus, and the world of the spirits.

1. God in Middle Eastern Perspective

An article in a scholarly European theological journal observed in a footnote that a prestigious American University offered a puzzling course on "The Problem of God." According to that author, God is not the problem. It is human beings who have a problem understanding God! The author was referring to Georgetown University, Washington, DC, which offers approximately twenty-five sections of a course with this very title to help students fulfill the requirement of taking two theology courses. The catalogue describes the course in this way: "An examination of the religious dimension of human experience and consciousness in relation to a number of problems and challenges: the problem of knowledge; the relation of faith and reason; various historical, social and existential determinants of belief; the challenge of atheism and humanism; the impact of secularization on religion."

Apparently the European theologian was not only unaware of this course description but also unfamiliar with a series of lectures delivered by the late eminent American theologian, John Courtney Murray, S.J., at Yale University in 1962 and published by that press the next year as *The Problem of God*. These lectures were rooted in a request by the Maryland Province of the Society of Jesus to Fr. Murray in 1940 to "design a college theology curriculum for lay people which would aim at," in Murray's words, "conveying an intelligence of the Christian life, as a power for personal and social regeneration, especially in its relation to the contemporary culture of human society." When in the 1960s the Georgetown theology program was organized as a department, Murray's vision of a student-centered course was put into place and continues to this day.

In his Yale lectures, Murray stated "the problem," and his survey showed how it emerged in the Bible and then was restated and investigated in theology (especially patristic and medieval theology) and in his own contemporary period. In this article, I propose insights that the social sciences contribute to the contemporary discussion of God, particularly as God is presented in the Bible.

Theology Is Analogy

Scholastic philosophers coined an axiom about God-talk: "All theology is analogy." What that axiom condensed was the conviction that everything human beings could know and say about God was rooted in human experience. Thus if human beings are good, then God must be something like good human beings. But since God created human beings, God must be superior to them in everything. Thus God must surpass human beings in goodness, and so on. This of course was already noted by the biblical Sage: "If through delight in the beauty of these things men assumed them [fire, wind, stars, etc.] to be gods, let them know how much better than these is their Lord, for the author of beauty created them. And if men were amazed at their power and working, let them perceive from them how much more powerful is he who formed them. For from the greatness and beauty of created things comes a corresponding perception of their Creator" (Wis. 13:3-5).

What philosophers and the Sage were not aware of, it seems, is that all human experience is culture specific. For example, while all cultures acknowledge the role of a father for males and a mother for females, each culture specifies that role in a very different way. A Mediterranean father treats his sons quite differently than does a Western father. The author of Hebrews draws on the behavior of Mediterranean fathers toward their sons to explain how God behaves toward male creatures. "My son, do not regard lightly the discipline of the Lord, nor lose courage when you are punished by him. For the Lord disciplines him whom he loves, and chastises every son whom he receives [Prov. 3:11-12]. . . . God is treating you as sons; for what son is there whom his father does not discipline?" (Heb. 12:5-7). The Greek word translated "discipline" includes the notion of physical punishment, which is what the Sage prescribed as the proper way to rear a son (see Prov. 13:24; 19:18; 22:15; 23:13; 29:15, 17). The author of Hebrews simply reported the Sage's observations about God and how fathers raise their sons, and then "theologized" with them. A more accurate interpretation of Hebrews would be: "God is treating you as *a Mediterranean father treats his Mediterranean* sons. For what *Mediterranean* son is there whom his *Mediterranean* father does not discipline *with physical punishment?*" For the author of Hebrews, this is the proper cultural context for understanding the way God treated Jesus. Jesus prayed to God "to save him from death" (see Mark 14:32-42), and God heard that prayer. Then the author concludes: "Precisely because [commonly translated "although"] he

229

was a son, he learned obedience through what he suffered" (see Heb. 5:7; compare Proverbs, mentioned above). The fusion of love and violence in this understanding of God is undoubtedly repulsive to Westerners, whose culture suggests a different way of viewing the loving deity and that deity's loving behavior toward creatures. Notice the different cultural understandings of a "loving father."

God as Father

In order to be a father, a human being must obviously be of the male gender and possess male physical organs. God, however, is a genderless spirit who does not possess any physical organs. Hence it is less appropriate to refer to God as father than as "fatherly." This means that in the Scriptures, God is imagined by human beings as behaving toward creatures like a Mediterranean father behaves toward his own flesh and blood. The specific kinship term "father" doesn't explicitly appear in the Old Testament, though related terms do. Thus, Isaiah (43:6) reports God saying: "bring my sons from afar and my daughters from the end of the earth." And in Hosea (11:1), God exclaims: "Out of Egypt I called my son." The context is always election as God's special people. "You are the sons of the LORD your God" (Deut. 14:1). It is in the New Testament, and especially in Jesus' address to God, "Abba, Father . . ." (never "Daddy"; Mark 14:36; see Pilch 1999: 2-3), where this becomes an explicit appellation for God. Paul clarifies the case and confirms our point. According to Paul, God sent forth his Son, "that we might receive adoption as sons," enabling us to cry, "Abba! Father!" (Gal. 4:4-6). In other words, calling God Father is an analogous use of that word.

Now in the Mediterranean world of past and present, a person who is not the biological father of another person but who treats that person as if he were the biological father is known as a patron. The entire complex of interpersonal behaviors between such a person (a patron) and others treated by that person like flesh and blood (clients) is known as patronage. "The Godfather" series of films is a good contemporary presentation of how the social institution of patronage functions in the context of Italian culture in particular (or Mediterranean in general).

A patron is essentially a person of means or a person with surplus who is able to satisfy needs that another person is unable to fulfill by personal effort or when it is needed. A patron freely chooses clients from among those who need his benefactions or simply those upon whom he chooses to shower them. The same God who established the rights of the firstborn (Deut. 21:15-17) frankly admits: "I have loved Jacob [second born of twins], but I have hated Esau [the firstborn]" (Mal. 1:2-3). In Jesus' parable about God as a generous patron (Matt. 20:1-16), the first hired learn to their painful exasperation that they contracted with God while God elected to treat the others, including the last hired, like a generous patron, as if they were kin, with favoritism but without a contract. Patrons are not culturally obliged to be fair. Rather, they are obliged to share their surplus (see Luke 12:15-21; 18:18-27) in return for respect and a grant of honor from clients.

Give Glory to the Lord!

Contemporary believers, especially athletes after successful events, are fond of publicly "giving glory to the Lord!" Many of these believers exhort others to "Give the glory to God!" The prophet Isaiah exhorts the inhabitants of Sela: "Let them give glory [Hebrew *kābôd*] to the LORD" (Isa. 42:12). Matthew's Jesus advises his disciples to let others "see your good works and give glory [Greek *doxa*] to your Father who is in heaven" (Matt. 5:16). People healed by Jesus routinely gave glory or praise to God: "And immediately he received his sight [the blind man near Jericho] and followed him [Jesus], glorifying God; and all the people, when they saw it, gave praise to God" (Luke 18:43).

Glory in Middle Eastern culture is another word for honor, reputation, or good standing. Other ways of expressing "give glory" would be "praise," "acclaim," "honor," and the like. It is the core cultural value, which means that it governs people's behavior. If this is true of human beings, then it must surely be true of God. And, indeed, God in the Bible is presented in most honorable terms, and God behaves by the code of honor and shame. In Psalm 44, the psalmist first reminds God of past honorable behavior: God liberated the chosen people in the days of old. God gave the people victory. "In God we have boasted continually, and we will express our indebtedness to you forever" (Ps. 44:8). But in this moment, the enemy has gained the upper hand. God has made Israel a byword and laughingstock among peoples (Ps. 44:13-16). Though God has cast them off (Ps. 44:9), Israel has not forgotten God, nor departed from God's ways (Ps. 44:17-22). This is calculated to shame God, the Patron of Israel, into action. The psalmist concludes by exhorting God to wake up and deliver them (Ps. 44:23-26)!

Affronts to honor require vengeance or "getting satisfaction," which varies even across honor-based cultures. Dueling was one strategy for avenging an affront to honor between equals in such cultures. A study of dueling in the early modern historical period discovered that in Germany and other northern European countries nearly all duels ended with the death of one of the parties. In contrast, duels in Italy and other circum-Mediterranean countries ended with the injury of one of the parties. In each case, avenging honor had different results. On the other hand, Paul's mention of God's "wrath" is rooted in an analogy of getting satisfaction by a superior over a shaming inferior. The divine wrath is actually about God exacting the satisfaction required by a deity so as to maintain divine honor in the eyes of people who see God dishonored (Malina and Pilch 2007).

From the honor-based perspective of biblical culture, God possesses honor that is both ascribed (by essence) and achieved (by mighty deeds such as creation and redemption). Honor, of course, requires public recognition. God's honor must be acknowledged and recognized by all of creation. The psalmist assures us: "The heavens are telling the glory of God; and the firmament proclaims his handiwork" (Ps. 19:1). God is honored as is appropriate.

The Holiness Code (Lev. 17–26) concludes with divine promises and warnings about the blessings and punishments for honoring or dishonoring God. The word in traditional theology that describes acts dishonoring or shaming God is "sin." For this, there is "hell to pay," as the vernacular would have it. In Leviticus 26, God promises blessings: rain, abundant harvests, peace, victory over enemies, human fertility, and assurance of abiding divine presence (Lev. 26:3-13). But if God's people disobey (= shame) God, then God declares a progressive parade of punishments (Lev. 26:14-39). However, when they confess to shaming God and "make amends for their iniquity" (Lev. 26:41), God will reconsider and remember. This passage concludes with a simple declaration: "I am the LORD" (Lev. 25:45), and modern readers might add: "And don't you forget it!" When viewed through the lenses of analogies, God epitomizes the core cultural values in ways humans can hardly approximate.

Conclusion

Jerome Neyrey, S.J., illustrates in abundant detail what social-scientific insight adds to reflections on the God of the Bible from a Middle Eastern perspective (Neyrey 2004). The perspectives presented in this chapter summarize but two of the three major "lenses" that he uses to read the evidence. Neyrey's book is a worthy update for and complement to the reflections initiated by the Second Vatican Council peritus, John Courtney Murray, S.J.

2. God in the Parable of the Talents/Pounds

Every so often, newspapers report the story of a pastor who draws inspiration from Jesus' parable about the "talents" (Matt. 25:14-20//Luke 19:11-27). The pastor entrusts each family or head of household in the parish with ten dollars, exhorts them to "work with it," and awaits the result after a specified amount of time. Some do fantastically well and return a large amount to the church. A few keep the money with no intention of returning it. The results always please the pastor because the return is always larger than the sum distributed. The pastor then sings the praises of the industrious members of the congregation for their gospel-inspired behavior. Could the same person who said, ". . . lend, expecting nothing in return, and your reward will be great, and you will be the sons of the Most High" (Luke 6:36), make an about-face on another occasion and praise in parable those who lent with the deliberate intention of gaining interest (Luke 19:11-27)?

The Parable

Parables represent the typical Middle Eastern cultural practice of saying one thing but meaning another. Western listeners or readers must keep this foremost in mind. This parable is not about lending money and gaining interest. Such a practice is considered stealing (Exod. 22:25). It is forbidden by the Torah, except when dealing with foreigners (Deut. 23:20)! The parable is about God, and how God interacts with human beings. However, the parable presents a snapshot of some event or behavior set in the Middle Eastern world. Understanding this setting is central to interpreting the parable correctly.

All scholars agree that the parable as it appears in Matthew and Luke is heavily edited. Indeed, Luke's version adds allegorizing verses. What might Jesus' original parable have sounded like? It is possible to sketch an "originating structure" which is simply a list of the actions that the parable reports (Malina and Rohrbaugh 2003: 384-94). This parable has four such elements. First, as he is about to embark on a long journey, a master entrusts money to servants, returns, and demands an accounting. Second, some of the servants have increased the entrusted amount and return that augmented sum to the master, who rewards them. Third, one servant confesses that he was frightened and buried the amount entrusted to him in the ground so that he might return it intact to his master. Fourth, the angry master takes the money of the last servant and gives it to the first.

Thus pared down to what might have been Jesus' original story, the parable loses reference to diligence among those waiting for the Parousia. That was not Jesus' point. Further, true to its nature as a parable, the story contains no application or interpretation. It challenges the first-century listener to reflect on the possible applications in her or his own situation. Who were the listeners?

Jesus' Audience

Some parable scholars think that Jesus aimed his parables particularly at his opponents. From this perspective, the parable can be interpreted as a warning to leaders concerning their stewardship of resources (other than material) entrusted to them by God. This may indeed be true, but the audience was probably larger than that. It would also have included Jesus' disciples and very likely Galilean peasants since more than 90 percent of agrarian populations were rural farmers. What would the parable say to this larger group of listeners?

Modern readers, like pastors mentioned earlier, tend to give the parable a definite capitalistic interpretation. Would such a point bring joy to peasants who were taxed (= exploited) at levels as high as 40 percent of production? Would that be good news to peasants who, after such exploitation, had hardly enough left to live near or at subsistence levels? A modern reader needs to remember a few more ideas.

Limited Good

Peasants in all cultures view their world and all its goods (natural resources, manliness, honor, friendship, love, etc.) as finite in quantity and already distributed. No more is available where this came from, hence there is no way to increase quantities. Thus if someone somehow manages to obtain more of something, that necessarily means that someone else has lost this same material. We recognize this as a zero sum game, and that precisely is the peasant view of life. Such behavior is shameful. In this parable, the servant who was able to augment the sum of money that was entrusted to him behaved shamefully in peasant eyes. To augment that sum means that someone else was deprived of what was rightfully his. This can't be good news. Such an interpretation approves the exploitation that peasants experience all the time.

Money

Added to the difficulty of grasping the notion of limited good (since modern Westerners tend to think of limitless goods: there is always more — and better — where this came from!) is understanding the function of money in the ancient world. Peasant families were primarily consuming groups, that is, they consumed what they produced. There was precious little if any surplus after taxes (= exploitation), not to mention the risks of production. If they managed somehow to get money by selling a commodity, the money was used only to buy other commodities in order to satisfy family needs. Hoarding the money or using commodities and/or money to make a profit was an unnatural use of money according to Aristotle (*Politics* 1.9). Indeed, profit making was considered evil and socially destructive.

As St. Jerome phrased it: "Every rich person is either a thief or the heir of a thief" (*In Jeremiam* 2.5.2). In order to become rich, one has to accumulate more than one originally had. This means that one has to take someone else's share. Those with surplus are expected to share, to play the role of a patron. Jesus condemns saving surplus to satisfy personal interests (Luke 12:13-21). Indeed, such a person is greedy, and it is often possible in Bible translations to replace the word "rich" with "greedy."

The rate of return in the parable is truly astonishing. In Matthew's version, the two servants each gain 100 percent, and in Luke's version one gains 500 percent and another one 1,000 percent. Roman sources relevant to the first century indicate that the legal interest rate was 12 percent. The gains reported by Luke are quite likely exaggerated and would evoke gasps and vocal protests from any first-century Mediterranean audience.

Interpreting the Parable

The interpretation of the parable hinges on the perspective of the storyteller. Did Jesus tell this parable from the perspective of the rich, the master and the servants who acted dishonorably by colluding with the master in "stealing" from others, or the perspective of the last servant, who while presumably "disobeying" his master acted honorably by preserving the trust?

The master is described as "a hard man" (Matt. 25:24; harsh, cruel, merciless) or "a severe man" (Luke 19:22; strict and exacting). He admits to being someone who reaps where he has not sowed and gathered where he has not winnowed (Matthew), or taking up what he did not lay down, and reaping what he has not sowed (Luke). He is greedy to the core. He is a thief! He is the exact opposite of the rich man praised by Sirach: "Happy the rich man found without fault, who turns not aside after gain!" (Sir. 8:2).

In contrast, the third servant does the honorable thing by not seeking to augment the money entrusted to him. In Matthew, the servant buries it, which is what the Mishnah recommends (*Baba Batra* 4:8). Such a person would not be responsible for the loss of an entrusted amount. The servant in Luke wraps it in a cloth, which the Mishnah identifies as a riskier choice. In either case, the third servant refuses to participate in his greedy master's scheme to take money from others (interest) to which he has no right. Western interpreters generally view the third servant as a failure. He played it safe instead of taking a risk.

An Alternate Version

Eusebius the church historian reports a version of this parable which was known from the so-called *Gospel of the Nazoreans.* We have no manuscript of this gospel. All we have are quotations and allusions by some Church Fathers and in a few later writings. This gospel is customarily considered a second-century translation of Matthew from Greek into Aramaic. Only Eusebius preserves this fragment (*Theophania* 22):

> But since the Gospel [written] in Hebrew characters which has come into our hands entered the threat not against the man who had hid [the talent], but against him who had lived dissolutely —
>
> For he [the master] had three servants:
>
> > A one who squandered his master's substance with
> >   harlots and flute girls
> > B one who multiplied the gain
> > C and one who hid the talent
>
> and accordingly . . .

C′ one was accepted with joy
B′ another merely rebuked
A′ and another case into prison

I wonder whether in Matthew the threat which is uttered after the word against the man who did nothing may not refer to him but by epanalepsis to the first who had feasted and drunk with the drunken.

Eusebius seems to have been troubled by canonical Matthew's version. On the basis of the version that he knew from the *Gospel of the Nazoreans,* Eusebius identifies Matthew's first servant with the dissolute one from that gospel. For this behavior, he is thrown into prison. The second servant who only increased his master's money is merely rebuked. Yet neither the author of the *Gospel of the Nazoreans* nor Eusebius applauds this servant. It is rather the servant who hid the talent who is praised. He held fast to his beliefs despite fearing his master; he behaved honorably with the trust and returned it safe and sound to his Master.

In the final analysis, everything depends on how one views the master and the third servant's comments about him. Knowing the master to be an "exacting" man, the third servant reasoned that he had better act honorably than risk losing the master's money. Peasants hearing this story would applaud that servant's decision and behavior. Is the Master angry with the servant? Assuredly so. Is this appropriate? Elites in the audience would say yes. Peasants in the audience would say no. Peasants would say that Jesus is warning rich people about their unwarranted reactions to Torah-based peasant behavior. The Master in the parable did indeed condemn the third servant. But did Jesus?

Conclusion

This interpretation of the parable is based on the research and publications of Professor Emeritus Richard L. Rohrbaugh, of Lewis and Clark College, Portland, Oregon. Each time he has presented Eusebius's interpretation to a Western audience, people are incredulous. They find it difficult to accept. How could a capitalistic interpretation be mistaken when it stands out so clearly in the story? That interpretation, however, does not stand out so clearly for audiences in the Middle East where Professor Rohrbaugh has lived and visited for extended periods. Could it be possible that Eusebius and the *Gospel of the Nazoreans* were correct in seeing

Jesus' condemnation of the master's attitude in this parable? Could it be possible that Matthew and Luke failed to see that? Modern believers who live in capitalistic societies comfortably theologize from the parable about responsible stewardship of the gifts of grace or human talents which they interpret to be a highly desirable and profitable result — in the capitalistic sense — before the Master returns (Jesus' second coming). Peasants (even today) would draw a different conclusion. Could the peasants be right?

3. God and Lying Spirits

About four hundred prophets consulted by King Ahab assured him that his attack on Ramoth-gilead would be successful. "The LORD will deliver it over to the king," they said (1 Kings 22:6). One dissenting prophet, Micaiah ben Imlah, told Ahab: "The LORD has put a lying spirit in the mouths of all these prophets of yours; the LORD himself has decreed evil against you" (1 Kings 22:23). If you were King Ahab, whom would you believe? Does not the tradition say: "God is not man that he should speak falsely" (Num. 23:19; compare Titus 1:2)? Yet Ahab's army was routed, and he was killed by an archer who shot at random (1 Kings 22:34). Perhaps Micaiah spoke truthfully about the Lord after all. Presuming that he did, why did the Lord use lying spirits to cause harm to Ahab?

All Theology Is Analogy

It is an axiom in theology that everything human beings know and say about God is rooted in and based upon human experience. The good elements of human experience are ascribed to God in their most perfect dimensions. The bad or undesirable elements of human experience are absolutely denied to God. All human experience, however, is culturally interpreted. Thus the concepts of God presented in the Bible reflect the values of the Mediterranean culture shared by various biblical authors. The prevalent images of God as behaving in a fatherly fashion or even being called father are analogies based on the experience of Mediterranean fathers or father-like figures. A good Mediterranean father physically disciplines his son (Prov. 13:24; 23:13; etc.) in order to impose his will upon the son and to insure maintaining the son's loyalty. Physical discipline helps the son become a cultural hero (e.g., the faithful servant: Isa. 50:6; 53:7;

etc.), that is, a manly person who can endure suffering without flinching (read the story of Eleazar; 2 Macc. 6). The author of Hebrews presents God as treating Jesus in just this way (Heb. 5:7-10).

A Most Honorable God

The core value of Mediterranean culture is a concern for honor, a good reputation. Honor or good reputation derives essentially from birth, but it is also possible to gain honor by means of specific behaviors. People who have surplus wealth can gain honor by becoming patrons to needy clients. People who refuse to be patrons behave shamefully and are condemned by all, including a God conceived within this cultural context (Luke 12:13-21). Matthew's parable about the workers in the vineyard presents God precisely as an ideal patron (Matt. 20:1-16, esp. v. 15).

True Honor

By definition, honor or reputation derives from someone making a public claim to worth or value AND others publicly acknowledging and approving that claim. The claim can be either explicit or implicit. Pilate's question to Jesus, "Are you the king of the Judeans?" (Matt. 27:11), was seeking an explicit claim. To make an explicit claim to honor would be improper and risky since someone in the audience might have good information to challenge the claim. Hence Jesus' deflective and highly appropriate response: "That's what YOU say!"

An implicit claim to honor is one, for instance, that derives from status or role. Middle Eastern Bedouin interpretations of the father in Jesus' parable who asks each of his two sons, separately, to work in the vineyard are illustrative (Matt. 21:28-32). One son immediately says yes but never goes; the other son immediately says no but eventually does go to work. Bedouins explain that the son who said yes is the more honorable of the two for a number of reasons. A major reason is that he did not shame his father by publicly refusing to obey him as did his brother. He said what his father wanted to hear ("yes"). This is not a lie as the West understands lying. It is rather selective transmission of information. Saying what someone wants to hear is honorable behavior. It fulfills the commandment: "Honor thy father and thy mother" (Exod. 20:12; Deut. 5:16). That he did not actually go to work is irrelevant in these cultures where the ideal is preferred to the real.

Secrecy, Deception, and Lying

What about the father's indirect claim to honor in this story in which he publicly attempts to impose his will on his sons? That, in fact, is the explicit question Jesus asks: "Which of the two did his father's will?" (v. 31). Jesus' audience gives the correct answer: the one who publicly insulted his father but then (presumably without anyone knowing it?) actually went to work in the vineyard. Even though this audience, like every Mediterranean audience, knows the correct answer, they still prefer the ideal to the real, the appearances to the reality. Honor, reputation, is as much about appearances as it is about reality, which is sometimes too discouraging to be "honest" about (Pilch 1999: 46-51, 129-34).

Since honor claims depend on information available to those who should make the judgment, the less information they have the better chance of their acknowledging the claim to honor. Hence secrecy, deception, and outright lies are legitimate cultural strategies for preserving one's reputation or honor. Too much information threatens honor claims The son who had no intention of working in the vineyard needed to preserve his "apparent" reputation as an obedient son. In preserving his reputation, he also preserved his father's reputation as a successful father.

What about the Mediterranean cultural "rule" that one may never lie to one's family? It is acceptable and indeed desirable to lie (or engage in secrecy and deception) with all others and other families but not with one's own family (see Prov. 25:7c-10). Didn't the son lie to his father? Mediterranean people will reply that telling the father what he wanted to hear is not a lie. It is the right thing to do. Did the son deceive the father? Perhaps the father knew his sons only too well and realized he'd "win one and lose one." Perhaps the audience was deceived more than the father.

Ahab the Shameful

Ahab, king of Israel (869-850 B.C.E.), married Jezebel, daughter of Ethbaal, King of Tyre. While he possessed solid military power and maintained a strong and stable government, Ahab was judged negatively by the Deuteronomic historian. "He did more to anger the LORD, the God of Israel, than any of the kings of Israel before him" (1 Kings 16:33). He allowed Jezebel to sustain the cult of Baal and built a temple to him in Samaria (1 Kings 16:32). Beyond that he acquiesced in Jezebel's strategy for having Naboth falsely accused and then executed in order to obtain his vineyard, which Ahab wanted for himself, though he did repent of this (1 Kings 21:27-29). And that's the rub! If Ahab repented, why did God mislead Ahab's prophets so as to occasion his death? Why also does the Deuteronomic historian judge Ahab so harshly? The answer would seem to be Ahab's less than perfect loyalty to Yahwism, his willing tolerance of Baalism.

God Plays by Mediterranean Rules

As perceived by Mediterranean biblical authors and their audiences, God thinks, speaks, and behaves according to all the Mediterranean cultural rules. All theology is analogy, and the God-talk of the Bible reflects Mediterranean cultural values. The king rules in the name of Yahweh and ought to behave appropriately. A king who finds place for Baal alongside of Yahweh shames Yahweh and will pay the penalty. In the Mediterranean world, honor and shame are indeed matters of life and death. As the psalmist notes: "Toward the faithful you are faithful, toward the wholehearted you are wholehearted, toward the sincere you are sincere, but toward the crooked you are astute" (Ps. 18:26-27 NAB; also Hebrew; see also 2 Sam. 22:26-27). Other translations offer interesting versions of the last stich. "Toward the perverse you are devious" (NAB rev.; also Hebrew). "With the perverse, you are wily" (Ps. 18:26 NIV). "Cunning to the crafty" (Ps. 18:26 NJB). "With the crooked, thou dost show thyself perverse" (Ps. 18:16 RSV). The Mediterranean value is well expressed: when shamed, the shamed person will outdo the perpetrator in perversity and win! While a shamed human being may fail in taking revenge, a shamed but powerful God won't.

Prophets are spokespersons for the will of God for their here and now (e.g., Isa. 7:14 directed to King Ahaz in 734-733 B.C.E.). At the same time, prophets often seem to speak an ambiguous or cryptic message (e.g., the almond tree and boiling pot; Jer. 1:11-19). How can one trust the message or its interpretation? When it comes to pass, the Deuteronomist clearly asserts that God spoke that message (Deut. 18:18-22). But if a prophet speaks something God has not said, that prophet will die (Deut. 18:20; see Jer. 27–28).

To interpret our story of Ahab, perhaps it is best to work backward. He was mortally wounded in battle and died. How is one to explain this? Did he not consult the prophets and receive word that God approved and would grant success to his battle plans? Was the nay-sayer Micaiah ben Imlah not a perennial nay-sayer? Did not Elijah previously assure Ahab that God accepted his repentance for the death of Naboth? Would it not make sense for Ahab to trust the four hundred prophets against the one?

If prophets are spokespersons for God, and the four hundred claim to have received their message from God, then perhaps God was responsible for the misinformation. Is this not how Micaiah explained it? "The LORD has put a lying spirit in the mouth of all these prophets of yours; the LORD himself has decreed evil against you" (1 Kings 22:23). Because the four hundred spoke truly what God intended them to speak (a fatal deception for Ahab, a lie), God did not kill them. Rather, God used those prophets to punish Ahab for shaming the deity. Yes indeed, with the perverse God can be wily! This understanding continues into New Testament times: "Therefore God is sending them a deceiving power so that they may believe the lie, that all who have not believed the truth but have approved wrongdoing may be condemned" (2 Thess. 2:11-12).

God Is Not Fair?

Western readers find this kind of thinking difficult to accept. Western images of God (often based on selective reading of selected sections of the Bible) differ from this one. Is there a way to resolve these differences? There is one more consideration to add to our reflections. Secrecy, deception, and lying have always been acceptable cultural strategies in the Mediterranean world in the service of preserving one's honor. If humans have these strategies at hand, surely God must too, and God must be masterful at it. Our story of Ahab indicates that God indeed can be wily, devious, and deceptive when that is called for.

If that is the case, how can one trust God? When should one believe God? This was surely an abiding concern with all our ancestors in the faith from both covenants. This certainly was the question in the showdown between Jeremiah and Hananiah (Jer. 27–28) since the Hebrew Bible (and Hebrew people) did not have a word for "false prophet." Which of these conflicting messages should one believe in that "here and now"? This case is similar to the case of Ahab facing conflicting prophetic messages, except that the Deuteronomic historian laid the blame for the deceptive message to Ahab in God's hands.

Conclusion: The Pastor to the Rescue

The very-well-known verses penned by the Pastor (2 Tim. 3:16) provide an insight: "All scripture is inspired by God and profitable for teaching, for reproof, for correction and for training in righteousness. . . ." It is important to interpret this key verse in its total epistolary context, which is deception and lying. The statement is not about the inspired nature of Scripture so much as it is about the utility of Scripture for steering clear of deception and falsehood. In this community, Hymenaeus and Philetus have swerved from the truth and are upsetting the faith of some (2 Tim. 2:17-18). Foolish and ignorant debates are futile (2 Tim. 2:23). Who knows whether the opponents will repent and see the truth? In the last days there will flourish all manner of deception (2 Tim. 3:1-9). It is best to stick closely with what one learned from youth (2 Tim. 3:14-15), remembering the reliable people who taught it (2 Tim. 1:5; grandmother Lois and mother Eunice). "Toward the faithful you are faithful, toward the wholehearted you are wholehearted, toward the sincere you are sincere, but toward the crooked you are astute." Whoever remains faithful, wholehearted, and sincere before God has nothing to worry about. To such God will never lie.

4. The Middle Eastern Jesus

Early in 2003, the U.S. Army's 101st Airborne Division distributed *A Soldier's Guide to the Republic of Iraq*, a booklet intended to prepare troops for that culture. Among other tidbits of information, it observed that Arabs in general are very honorable, exceedingly polite, and frustratingly evasive. In general, this information about the culture is quite correct. Yet some critics found the information to be an odd omnium gatherum of stereotypes and gross generalizations. This is also correct, since there are always exceptions to general observations. Still, the booklet was intended to be a handy and "quick and dirty" resource. It would be impractical for a soldier to carry a comprehensive encyclopedia on Middle Eastern culture in personal gear along with other necessities. Since Jesus was born and lived in this same cultural world, what brief amount of cultural information would constitute a helpful guide to understanding and relating to him as a Middle Eastern male?

Like Us in All Things

Christians are fond of repeating that "Jesus was like us in all things except sin" (see Heb. 4:15). This is correct on a theological and a biological level. Human beings are God's creatures, and all human beings have the same biological constitution. But on an individual level, no human being — even an identical twin — is like another human being. Finally, on a cultural level, human beings are partly the same (by biology) and partly different (cultures interpret biology differently, as we know from the significance of gender differences in circum-Mediterranean and other world cultures). Thus from a biological point of view Jesus was no different from any other male, but from a cultural viewpoint he was definitely a typical Middle Eastern male very concerned about his honor, his reputation. His question to the disciples, "Who do men say that I am?" (Mark 8:27), was not a "theology quiz" but a serious interest in how the public viewed him (compare Mark 6:14-16). Like others in his culture and like 80 percent of the current world population, Jesus was a collectivistic personality. He drew his identity from his group and its opinions. That culture obliges one to live up to the reputation others attribute to him (or her). Clearly Jesus was recognized as a prophet and therefore should seek to measure up to that status.

Like other Middle Eastern males, Jesus was also masterful at being evasive. The parable, his favored form of teaching, is an evasive storytelling strategy. "To you [my disciples] has been given the secret of the kingdom of God, but for those outside everything is in parables . . ." (Mark 4:11). Realizing that his life was in jeopardy from his enemies, he was deceptive about his travel plans. "I am not going up to this feast. . . . But after his brothers had gone up, . . . he also went up, not publicly but in secret" (John 7:8-10).

On the other hand, it is not so evident that Jesus was "exceedingly polite." In fact, he doesn't come across as polite very often. He regularly resorted to insult, especially in response to hostile questions. In reply to the lawyer on a point of Torah, he asks: "How do you read?" (Luke 10:26). In Matthew, Jesus routinely addressed the Pharisees as "hypocrites" or "actors" who recite lines from Torah but do not live by its script (Matt. 23:3; see also vv. 13, 23, 25, 27, 29; etc.). And pity the poor, pleading woman whom he associated with dogs (Matt. 15:26)! Ever the master of language, one honorable trait in a Middle Eastern male, Jesus had an insult for everybody who threatened his honorable reputation.

Politically Oriented

Readers of the Bible who are unaware of Jesus' cultural character frequently miss his message. One of Jesus' clever insults is routinely misinterpreted: "Render therefore to Caesar the things that are Caesar's, and to God the things that are God's" (Matt. 22:21). Contemporary Western readers consider this to be an expression favoring the "separation of church and state." Apart from the fact that neither church nor state yet existed anywhere on the planet at that time, quite the opposite is true. If anything is certain about the preaching of Jesus, it is that he promoted theocracy, "the kingdom or reign of God." Theocracy is the union or identity of "church and state" (to use these anachronistic terms). Moreover, as Matthew makes quite explicit, Jesus was interested exclusively in "the lost sheep of the house of Israel" (Matt. 10:5). He had no use for non-Israelites (also known as "Gentiles"; Matt. 18:17). To spread the news of the establishment of theocracy and prepare Israelites for it, Jesus gathered around himself a group of like-minded followers who continued to await the kingdom after his death. This indeed was their agenda after Jesus' resurrection. Peter announced: "Let all the house of Israel therefore know assuredly that God has made him both Lord and Messiah, this Jesus whom you crucified" (Acts 2:36). After Jesus' expected imminent return, his apostles believed that God would initiate a theocracy in preparation for which Israelites ought to "repent, and be baptized . . . in the name of Jesus Christ for the forgiveness of sins" (Acts 2:38).

The Pharisee disciples who asked Jesus about the lawfulness of paying taxes to Caesar were attempting to entrap him as he walked in the temple. Recognizing their ploy, Jesus first insulted them ("hypocrites"), then tricked them into producing a coin (forbidden in the temple because it bore a graven image). The image on the coin is Caesar's, and rightfully belongs to him. But human beings bear God's image, and Pharisees took pride in claiming to know all the ways in which human beings might please God. Jesus' exhortation to "render to God what is God's" indicts the Pharisees for failing to do precisely what they claimed to specialize in. Politically, Jesus played this scene correctly and astutely.

Value Orientations

Jesus shared all the values of his contemporary, fellow Middle Easterners. Just like them, he was focused on the present, albeit a rather expansive present. "I tell you truly, there are some standing here," said Jesus to his audience, "who will not taste death before they see the kingdom of God" (Luke 9:27). Everyone in that audience has died, but the theocracy Jesus preached has still not been established. He was absolutely convinced that it was imminent. Indeed, no one but a prophet could know future events. If a prophet was aware of such, it was only because God informed him of it. "But of that day or that hour no one knows, not even the angels in heaven, nor the Son, but only the Father" (Mark 13:32).

Again, just like all peasants, Jesus lived with a conviction that everyone was subject to nature. No one could control it; they just had to suffer it. The fact that Jesus was able to walk on the sea, command the obedience of the wind and other spirits, or heal various human ailments did not so much indicate that he personally had power over these elements as that he was a "holy man." Indeed, this is the very first title ascribed to Jesus in the Synoptic tradition, and that by spirits! "I know who you are, the Holy One of God" (Mark 1:24; Luke 5:34; compare Matt 8:29). Holy men (and women) were characterized by rather ready entrée into the realm of the deity, with whose assistance they have socially beneficial abilities, most particularly the ability to heal. The reason for this is that they are believed to have direct and ready access to God, from whom they can broker these gifts to petitioners.

As for human nature, Jesus firmly believed what his tradition taught. Human nature is a mixture of good and evil because, when creating the first humanoid, God implanted in him an inclination or tendency toward good and toward evil. In Genesis 2:7, the first letter of the Hebrew word translated "formed" (*yāṣar*) is doubled. From this, interpreters concluded to God's implanting two tendencies (*yĕṣerîm*, a word with a different meaning than *yāṣar*) in the heart of humans. Subsequent tradition (Gen. 6:5; 8:21) observed that humans seemed to incline regularly toward evil rather than toward good. The first-century-c.e. book 2 Esdras notes, "For a grain of evil seed was sown in Adam's heart from the beginning [Gen. 2:7; see Sir. 15:14], and how much ungodliness it has produced until now, and will produce until the time of threshing comes!" (2 Esdr. 4:30). Jesus was aware of and enumerated the evils that come forth from the heart of a person (Mark 7:21-23) who follows the evil inclination or tendency.

Identity Theft

Contemporary Westerners are familiar with the concept of identity theft. Clever thieves steal personal information about their victims and benefit in many ways from the identity they have stolen. The thieves' benefits, of course, are injurious to the victim. In a certain sense, time has done that to the Middle Eastern person known as Jesus of Nazareth. Subsequent generations of believers reinterpreted the Middle Eastern Jesus in many ways, some of which ill fit his distinctive cultural heritage. Early on, the evangelists began to interpret Jesus, and as far as scholars can determine, these interpretations mesh well with Middle Eastern culture. Exegetes and theologians who continued the process through the centuries were not always so successful. In effect, some of these interpreters stole Jesus' identity by recreating it in an image more congruent with their own cultural situations. The challenge for any interpreter is "not to introduce imaginary additions at variance with the truth" (*Pontifical Biblical Commission Document on the Historical Truth of the Gospels,* no. XIII).

Conclusion

Midway through my course on the Middle Eastern cultural context of the Bible, a twenty-eight-year-old Kurdish student from northern Iraq, now a U.S. citizen, expressed gratitude for two things. The course was helping her to understand her native culture better but also helping her to articulate to others how her culture functions. Her absences from class usually meant that she was briefing State Department or CIA officials on how to deal with the cultural challenges they faced in Iraq.

Westerners who learn how to interpret Jesus in his Middle Eastern cultural context will inevitably have to learn to understand their own culture better so as to appreciate the alien culture better and with greater respect. At the same time, learning how the alien culture functions will help to understand and interpret Jesus as the evangelists did when they presumed their readers would supply the appropriate Middle Eastern details that they took for granted and omitted.

5. Spirits: Other-Than-Human Persons

Paul's use of the word "spirit" (Greek *pneuma,* 146 times [Hebrew *rûaḥ*]) manifests some inconsistency in his use of the term. Most often he uses the word in its prevalent Old Testament meaning: "breath" or "wind," that is, "air in motion." Yet when he uses the word in relation to Jesus, inconsistency takes on the dimensions of confusion. "Now the Lord is the Spirit, and where the Spirit of the Lord is, there is freedom" (2 Cor. 3:17) is one passage which puzzles contemporary interpreters as well as believers who are heirs of a highly developed theological understanding of spirits and the Spirit. The theological concept of the Trinity so familiar to modern believers frequently causes them to misunderstand and misinterpret the Bible's many references to spirit. Perhaps a brief review of the term may prove helpful.

Old Testament

Theologians point out that it is inappropriate to think that the Old Testament offers a trinitarian understanding of God or even a foreshadowing of that concept. As already noted, the basic meaning of the Hebrew word *(rûaḥ)* was "breath" or "wind." Palestinian peasants experienced strong and unpredictably violent winds in their climate. They especially feared the *ḥamsîn* (Italian: sirocco), the spring wind from the eastern desert which is both hot and dusty and can wilt vegetation in days. "A great and strong wind rent the mountains, and broke in pieces the rocks before the LORD" (1 Kings 19:11). They then transferred the experience of this powerful wind to Yahweh in typical anthropomorphic fashion. "But it is the breath *(rûaḥ)* in a man, the breath *(nĕšāmâ)* of the Almighty that makes him understand" (Job 32:8). Or again, "The spirit *(rûaḥ)* of God has made me, and the breath *(nĕšāmâ)* of the Almighty gives me life" (Job 33:4). This parallelism of the words "breath" and "spirit" *(rûaḥ)* reflects the eventual expansion of the word "breath" to include "spirit." God's breath, the divine vital power or "spirit," is as efficacious as Yahweh's "arm" (Isa. 51:5) or "hand" (Deut. 2:15). God's breath is a vivifying and creative power: "The LORD God . . . breathed into [the creature's] nostrils the breath of life; and man became a living being" (Gen. 2:7). Significantly, spirit, just like hand, points to activity, to doing. One knows the presence of the invisible wind by its effects on soil, plants, trees, animals, and humans. So, too, one knows the presence of spirits by their effects.

Moreover, in the Old Testament, God is never represented as a spirit or as an immaterial ("spiritual") being. After all, the wind is not immaterial. Yet the parallelism in Isaiah 31:3, "The Egyptians are men, not God; and their horses are flesh, and not spirit," indicates that the concepts of God and spirit are of the same order. More often the sacred writers report that God has a certain spirit, that he gives the spirit, and similar phrases. In the understanding of creation in the period, wind, fire, and water were considered to be liquids. Consequently, the spirit, even God's spirit, is perceived as a liquid-like substance that is "poured out" upon human beings to make an impact on their dealings with each other. "For I will pour water on the thirsty land, and streams on the dry ground; I will pour my Spirit upon your descendants, and my blessing on your offspring" (Isa. 44:3). The RSV translators' choice to capitalize "Spirit" in this quotation is an anachronistic reading of a trinitarian concept into an era when it did not yet exist. The ancient Israelites simply viewed "spirit" as a power that proceeds from

Yahweh and a power by which Yahweh acts upon all creatures. Spirit, like wind, signifies activity.

Later Judaism

Though contemporary Jewish scholars (and others) bristle at the term "later Judaism," it still serves technically to describe the period after Alexander the Great and closer to the turn of the millennia. At this time, the author of Wisdom (around 50 B.C.E.) personifies wisdom (as do Prov. 1:20-23; Job 28; etc.) yet not as a person distinct from God but rather as one function of Yahweh. As noted previously, wisdom was an effect of the spirit of God. After all, wisdom refers to the quality that directs proper interpersonal behavior, hence to activity. Thus in the book of Wisdom (Wis. 1:5-7; 7:22-23; 9:17), wisdom is identified with the spirit of the Lord as an internal principle of physical and moral life. A way appears to be opening to conceiving the spirit of God as a person, technically as an hypostasis (or a personified substance).

New Testament

While the New Testament continues to use the Greek word for spirit in the sense of breath (2 Thess. 2:8) and wind (John 3:8a), it is more often used in its derived meanings. Yet it always refers to wind-like or breath-like phenomena resulting in activity, doing, behavior. For instance, the spirit is a life principle (Matt. 27:50) that exists apart from the body (Luke 8:55). This same spirit abides in the sky (Heb. 12:23; compare Dan. 12:3) or in the netherworld (1 Pet. 3:19). Gradually the New Testament reveals that the spirit (or power) of God is a person even while most often it is "something" (a power) and not "someone."

Apart from the presumably trinitarian passage in Matthew (28:19), nowhere else in the Synoptic gospels is the holy spirit presented unequivocally as a person. Even in the Acts of the Apostles, with the exception of Acts 15:28, it is chiefly a power, not a person. Other apparent personifications (e.g., Acts 8:20; 10:19) can be viewed as rhetorical.

Paul, as noted above, most often follows the Old Testament usage and sometimes does not distinguish the spirit from Christ. For instance, in Romans 8:9-11 Paul uses the phrases "spirit of God," "spirit of Christ," and "the spirit of him who raised Jesus from the dead" to describe God dwelling in the individual believer. There are a handful of significant passages, however, which are clearly triadic (1 Cor. 2:7-16; 6:11; 12:4-6; 2 Cor. 1:21-22; 13:13; Rom. 5:1-5; 8:14-17; 15:10). In these passages, Paul aligns God or Father, Christ or Son, and the Spirit in a way that fit first-century Mediterranean understanding of how humans have an effect in interacting with others. In this way of understanding, humans relate in terms of eye-heart, mouth-ears, and hands-feet. Eyes-heart activity (know, love, understand, judge, etc.) relates to God as the Father of Jesus; mouth-ears activity (self-communication, self-revelation by speech) relates to Christ or the Son as the word of God and revelation of God; hand-feet activity (doing, power effects) relates to the Spirit, the hand of God (Luke 1:66), the finger of God (Luke 11:20), poured out like flames (tongues) of fire (Acts 2:3-4). This triple division served as the basis for the much later dogma of three distinct persons in the Trinity (Fourth Lateran Council, 1215, with roots already in Nicea, 325 C.E.). In Paul's letters, however, the relationship of the Spirit to the Son is quite unclear. John the evangelist seems to stand out in the New Testament tradition as one who thought of the spirit as a sort of person distinct from the Father and the Son (see John 14:16–19:26; 15:26; 16:7; 17:21; etc.).

Anthropological Insight

Not just theologians but no doubt every believer would agree that the Trinity is an absolute mystery and that the Spirit in this Trinity is very difficult to grasp and understand. Yet contemporary believers, among many others, routinely refer to the spirit (Spirit) as if it were something everyone understood and about whose identity and function everyone agreed. Denominational discussions tend to be very precise but often opaque. Anthropologists who study many diverse cultures offer some helpful insights.

To begin with, in their study of diverse cultures all over the globe, anthropologists observed that holy men and holy women (usually called shamans) are commonly characterized as capable of contacting and interacting with spirits and the realm of the spirits. Contemporary anthropologists, however, note that the word "spirit" mystifies matters and obscures more than it explains. In general, they understand spirit to mean nonvisible entities alleged in different cultures "to be responsible for the presence or absence of animals, health, sickness or enemies" (Harvey 2003: 9).

Similarly, the anthropologist A. Irving Hallowell, on the basis of his dialogue with the Ojibwa/Anishinaabeg of Berens River, Manitoba, substituted "other-than-human persons" for the word "spirit." "Spirits" were often contrasted with the "human persons" with whom they interacted or upon whom they had an impact. Considering that spirits entered into complex relations with human persons, Hallowell argued that the phrase "other-than-human persons . . . is more descriptively appropriate than labeling this class of person 'spiritual' or 'supernatural' beings, if we assume the viewpoint of the Ojibwa themselves. It is true that these entities have more power at their disposal than human beings, and this is why the humans need the help of other-than-human persons in achieving their goals. Nevertheless, other-than-human persons cannot be set off as categorically distinct" (Hallowell 1992).

Further, he argues that the term "spirit" suggests that all beings with whom holy men and women interact are of one kind, and that these beings are beyond sensual experience. Research, however, indicates that these beings ("spirits") are part of a larger community within the people under study. This community is sometimes called "nature," "environment," "life," "neighbors," and the like. In comparing indigenous with Western categories and language, Hallowell observed that similarities between human persons and "other than human" persons were more central than their differences. Beyond this, the relationships between various kinds of persons (human and other than human) are what constitute the essence of personhood.

Hallowell offers interesting illustrations from ethnography. He points out that "actual salmon, seals, caribou, tapirs, bears, jaguars, tigers, and so on are among the significant other than human persons with whom shamans communicate." Pilch reported how the Greek holy man Pythagoras communicated with an ox (Pilch 1999: 80). This helps understand the challenge hurled by the holy man Job against his (non-holy man?) discussion partner, Zophar the Naamathite: "Ask the beasts, and they will teach you; the birds of the air, and they will tell you; or the plants of the earth, and they will teach you; and the fish of the sea will declare to you" (Job 12:7-8). It is possible that Job was uttering more than a rhetorical response.

The Biblical World

Scholars note that the concept "supernatural" as contrasted with the "natural" is Western in origin and was not in use before Origen (3rd cent. c.e.; Saler 1977). In biblical understanding, the cosmos was one, and it was inhabited by human persons and other-than-human persons, namely, spirits. To separate the two into distinct realms does not reflect the understanding of our ancestors in the faith.

Conclusion

While it is inappropriate to change the terminology of trinitarian doctrine, it is also inappropriate to import that terminology and those concepts into the Bible, which lays only the barest foundation for them. Rather, it is helpful to incorporate the phrase "other-than-human" person(s) in contexts where "spirit" appears. Thus, biblical scholars propose that in practically all cases where the Hebrew term *ruach* can be translated as "disposition," it might also be designating an "other-than-human person." For instance, the "spirit of jealousy" which comes upon a husband and incites him to test his wife's virtue (Num. 5:14, 30) might be translated as an other-than-human person (a "true" spirit) rather than a disposition, as Western interpreters generally do. This is similar to Luke's notion that Peter's mother-in-law was afflicted by a spirit (an "other-than-human person") named "fever" (Luke 5:30, where Jesus "rebukes" the fever just as he rebukes spirits [Luke 5:41] and the wind [Luke 8:24]). It is preferable to be respectfully faithful to the concepts and imagination of the ancients rather than impose on them contemporary interpretations.

FURTHER READING: GOD AND THE SPIRIT WORLD

Hallowell, A. I. 1992. *The Ojibwa of Berens River, Manitoba: Ethnography into History.* Edited by J. S. J. Brown. New York: Harcourt Brace.

Harvey, Graham, ed. 2003. *Shamanism: A Reader.* London and New York: Routledge.

Kunkel, Mark A., Stephen Cook, David S. Meshel, Donald Daughtry, and Anita Hauenstein. 1999. "God Images: A Concept Map." *Journal for the Scientific Study of Religion.* 38: 193-202.

Malina, Bruce J., and Richard L. Rohrbaugh. 2003. *Social Science Commentary on the Synoptic Gospels.* Second Edition. Minneapolis: Fortress.

Murray, John Courtney, S.J. 1965. *The Problem of God.* New Haven: Yale University Press.

Neyrey, Jerome H., S.J. 2004. *Render to God: New Testament Understandings of the Divine.* Minneapolis, MN: Fortress.

Pilch, John J. 1999. *The Cultural Dictionary of the Bible.* Collegeville, MN: The Liturgical Press.

Saler, Benson. 1977. "Supernatural as a Western Category." *Ethos* 5: 21-33.

Part Eight

ENTERTAINMENT

Without electricity, and therefore without movies, TV, the Internet, and a host of other recreational devices to which the modern world has grown accustomed, how did our ancestors in the faith entertain themselves? Of course, they had games, amusements, and sports, after a fashion. But they also sang a good deal. So appealing was music to them that evidence indicates that they believed this would be the lot of those who had died. We conclude this part with a reflection on the "down to earth" language of some biblical authors (notably the prophets) and suggest some films that might help Bible readers get a better grasp on the very different cultural world of our ancestors in the faith.

1. The Sound of the "Flute"

When Jesus arrived at the home of a "leader of the synagogue" to attend to the recently deceased daughter (Matt. 9:23), he met with "flute players and the crowd making a commotion." Commentators offer various comments about the flute players. Most refer to the Mishnah (*Ketubbot* 4:4; early-3rd-cent.-C.E. compendium of opinions in the Israelite tradition): "Even the poorest in Israel must not furnish less than two flutes and one woman wailer (at the funeral of his wife)." As some interpreters often do, they explain the obvious: the "flute" is used in contexts of mourning. The context certainly makes that clear to even the most untutored of readers. But what exactly is the "flute" in the ancient world? What instrument are the people playing? Why are flute players playing their instruments at a wake? (Pilch 2011: 89-105).

Flute or Stringed Instrument?

Musicologists caution against thinking that instruments mentioned in the Hebrew and Greek texts and translated into modern terms (e.g., "flute") are the same instruments known by us today. The Hebrew words commonly translated "flute" are ʿûgāb and ḥālîl. Legend identifies Jubal, the brother of Jabal, as "the ancestor of all those who play the lyre and the pipe (= ʿugab; Gen. 4:21). The majority if not all modern translations render the Hebrew word ʿugab as pipe, that is, some sort of wind instrument. Lexicographers conjecture that since the word seems to derive from the Hebrew verb that means "to have inordinate affection for, to lust," the instrument produced a sensuous sound.

But the discovery of the Hebrew text of Psalm 151 at Qumran in 1956 sheds new light on this Hebrew word. Sanders' translation of verse 2, reported in the New Revised Standard Version, reads:

> "My hands have made an instrument *(ʿûgāb),*
> and my fingers a lyre *(kinnôr)."*

Identifying the parallelism of the two italicized words in this verse persuaded Sanders to translate ʿûgāb as a general word, "instrument." It would also be possible to identify it as a particular kind of stringed instrument which would also make a good parallel to "lyre." The Septuagint of Genesis 4:21 and Josephus agree with Sanders' translation. Clearly, then, Jubal was the ancestor of those who play stringed instruments and not the pipe. This stringed instrument could be used to express joy (Job 21:12; Ps. 150:4) as well as mourning (Job 30:31).

Flute or Reed Instrument?

Another Hebrew word customarily translated as flute, ḥālîl, derives from a verb that means "to bore, pierce, perforate," and the like. It actually describes a hollow tube into which holes have been pierced. The player blows into one end to make the sound, so it is more accurate to call this a pipe than a flute as we know it today. This ancient instrument is nothing at all like the contemporary transverse flute so familiar in marching bands or symphony orchestras. This modern flute descended from the German flute, which was revolutionized by Theobald Boehm in 1832.

In antiquity, the sound of a wind instrument was produced in one of two ways: one could blow into a pipe to make the sound like blowing into a reed instrument, or one could make the sound with one's lips and send it through the instrument as with a trumpet or bugle. The *ḥālîl* belongs in the first group; the *šôpār* belongs in the second group. Ancient monuments depict musicians playing the *ḥālîl* (pipe). Usually it is a "double-pipe" instrument, that is, it has two pipes or cones with a single mouthpiece. The player wrapped his mouth around the entire mouthpiece. His mouth became, as it were, the windbag of a bagpipe. He would inhale through his nose yet keep a steady flow of air through the pipe. Modern musicians, including singers, know this technique as circular breathing.

The mouthpiece contained a reed or reeds which produced the sound. In modern terms, we can imagine that the instrument might have sounded something like the clarinet (one reed) or oboe (two reeds). The player blows through these reeds to produce the sound. Of the two pipes descending from the mouthpiece, one had many holes while the other had just one. Thus the melody would be played on one pipe, while the other pipe served as a drone. Some commentators think that this is the instrument that was being played by the Canaanite band which led the band of prophets down from the shrine at Gibeath-elohim ("Hill of God"; 1 Sam. 10:5). What is noteworthy in this report is that the instruments — harp, tambourine, flute (better, pipe because the word is *ḥālîl*), and lyre — appear to induce and sustain an ecstatic state, an alternate state of consciousness. Saul, who was instructed by Samuel to meet these prophets and join their entourage, also entered into an ecstatic state.

A similar story is reported in the apocryphal *Acts of Thomas* (1.5ff.; 3rd cent. C.E.). The apostle Thomas was sent by the risen Lord to India to preach. After his arrival, he was swept up in a crowd going to attend the wedding of the king's only daughter. At the banquet, a "flute" girl was entertaining the guests but stayed a long time near Thomas. Her music threw him into an ecstatic state, and he began to sing. The crowd noticed that his appearance had changed. The crowd understood nothing since he sang in Hebrew. But the "flute" girl, a Hebrew also, understood, and loved him greatly.

Lest we be distracted by our familiarity with the modern flute and contemporary virtuoso flautists like James Galway, it is important to remember that both Saul and Thomas did not hear our modern flute. They heard instead a reed instrument which produced a shrill, strident tone. While we can imagine the instrument to be like a clarinet or oboe, it produced an almost ear-piercing sound. Contemporary research by members of the Felicitas D. Goodman Anthropological Institute with similar sounds made by Peruvian "whistles" helps to appreciate what our ancestors in the faith were hearing (Znamenski 2007: 254-55). These clay figurine whistles are wind instruments. They are shaped like a miniature person with a round belly and hands folded over the belly. The air is blown into the instrument through a mouthpiece and emerges through an opening behind the figure. The figurines produce a shrill sound depending on the force of air moving through the opening. This would seem to be the kind of sound reputed to have been heard from the ancient *ḥālîl*. It's not quite possible to play a melody on these whistles. One can only adjust the pitch of the sound (higher or lower). If too high, the sound will not induce a trance. It disturbs the neurophysiological harmonies that induce and sustain trances. True, these whistles do not contain reeds, but they come close to replicating the ancient instruments as musicologists have described them (Knochenklang 2000, Track 3).

The "Flute" and the Funeral

What, then, did Jesus hear at that wake? And what was its significance? Perhaps by now it is clear that modern Bible readers are at a loss to determine precisely what kind of instrument is being used at the funeral. It is certainly not anything like the modern flute. Moreover, its sound was very likely a shrill tone. Was it intended to send the mourners into a trance, an alternate state of consciousness? The answer may be "perhaps." The ancients were always eager to communicate with their dearly beloved departed, which explains why God forbids Israelites to be a medium or necromancer (Deut. 18:11).

But ancient sarcophagi give us some interesting clues. A stele in the museum at Fiesole, Italy, shows the deceased at a meal for the dead, and the lower panel shows a flutist and two dancing figures. The museum notes indicate that this is what the dead do in the afterlife: Music and dancing refresh them. More than that, it was believed that singing and instrumental music, playing and dancing were what the dead were consigned to in the afterlife. Lucian of Samosata (about 170 C.E.) writes about a sky journey to the Isle of the Blessed: "Now and then one could also hear very clearly different sounds — not noisy, but such as would come from a banquet when a few people are playing the flute or the cithara" (*Vera Historia* 2.5.108). This is one explanation of the depictions on sarcophagi of survivors giving musical instruments to their beloved departed.

Yet another interpretation indicates that music would render the deceased tractable to the survivors. With music the survivors could lead the spirit to the grave and the afterlife. The beliefs surrounding these practices are that the dead might want to return to life. Or that the dead needed to be protected from evil spirits who would interfere with their journey. A remnant of this idea remains in the Roman Catholic funeral liturgy. As the body is taken from the Church to the cemetery, the priest or the cantor sings: "May the angels lead you into paradise; may the martyrs receive you at your coming, and lead you into the holy city Jerusalem. May the choir of angels receive you, and with Lazarus, who once was poor, may you have everlasting rest."

Conclusion

Music in the ancient world is a fascinating if still puzzling topic. What were the flute players doing at the little girl's wake (Matt. 9:23)? Surely they were part of the mourning process. But perhaps they were leading the youngster to her eternal abode and her eternal occupation. Perhaps they were also keeping evil spirits at bay so that they would not interfere with the process of death and transition to the afterlife. Jesus' command that the flute players depart was, as the text indicates, a sign of his conviction that she was not really dead nor on her way to that realm.

2. Singing in One Voice

The November 2005 issue of *Clinical Geriatrics* reported an interesting case study of "musical hallucinations" (Zegarra et al. 2005). A 77-year-old, divorced Caucasian man hears well-formed musical hallucinations of songs including "Tiny Bubbles," "The Tennessee Waltz," and "The Star-Spangled Banner." They begin when he wakes and end when he falls asleep. These and other songs that he hears he had played in a marching band or remembers from church. At first he thought the music came from a neighbor's apartment, but then he realized that they were only in his head. He considers them a distracting annoyance but not frightening. No commands accompany them.

Among the seventeen risk factors for this symptom ("musical hallucinations") culled from the extant psychiatric literature, the researchers listed advanced age, hearing impairment, and female gender. Many standard medical treatments were reviewed, and for the man in this study repairing his hearing aid and initiating the use of relaxation techniques have helped to reduce the symptoms. Medication did not help. How then are we to understand biblical figures such as Isaiah, who heard the seraphim sing to one another in his vision: "Holy, holy, holy is the LORD of hosts . . ." (Isa. 6:3-4)?

Visions in the Bible

Whether one considers a vision such as Isaiah's to be a "factual report" or only a literary creation, the event must be culturally plausible for the audience to understand and appreciate it. Even if members of an audience have not had this personal experience, they will recognize it from the reports of others who have. Ethnographic evidence documents that some 90 percent of sample world cultures studied at the Human Relations Area Files at Yale University experience visions which also have sound tracks. Dreams are but one familiar example: they have visual content and a sound track which sometimes includes music. What appears to be distinctive in biblical visions is that the sound heard was in unison; the music was monophonic. There do not seem to be any biblical or extrabiblical reports, as in the psychiatric case study presented above.

Unison Singing

Though not specified as such, the singing in the book of Revelation must have been in unison since the visionary heard, understood, and recorded the texts he heard (e.g., Rev. 4:8, 11; 5:3, 12, 13, 14; etc.). In *The Martyrdom and Ascension of Isaiah* (5th-6th cent. c.e. but rooted in much earlier tradition), the author relates that during his journey through the heavens the prophet Isaiah saw choirs of angels, and they sang praises "with one voice" (*Ascension of Isaiah* 7:15). In the seventh heaven, Adam, Abel, Seth, and all the righteous "praised [God] with one voice," and Isaiah joined them (*Ascension of Isaiah* 9:28). In his letter to the Corinthians, Clement of Rome (about 96 c.e.), a successor to Peter, conflates citations from Daniel 7:10 and Isaiah 6:3 and then concludes: "In the same way ought we ourselves, gathered together in a conscious unity, to cry to Him as it were *with a sin-*

gle voice [emphasis mine] if we are to obtain a share of his glorious great promises . . ." (*1 Clement* 34:7).

Writing to the Ephesians during his journey to Rome, Ignatius of Antioch (about 107 c.e.) said: ". . . Jesus Christ is sung in your unity of mind and concordant love. And to a man you make up a chorus, so that joined together in harmony and having received the godly strain in unison, you might *sing in one voice* through Jesus Christ to the Father, that he might hear you and recognize you through your good deeds as members of his son. It is beneficial, then, for you to be in blameless unity so that you might always partake of God" (*Ephesians* 4.1-2).

The unison singing of antiquity (as of modern times) is actually singing at the octave. Since everyone sings together (men, women, and children), the differences in their respective renditions of unison are an octave. But experience also indicates that unison singing admits of wide variation. The measured and mellifluous chanting of monks and nuns stands in contrast to the voices of men in a contemporary synagogue service reading or chanting Hebrew prayers "in unison."

Monophony, Not Polyphony

One result of the Christian tradition's determination to imitate the unison singing of the angels was a prohibition of singing polyphony in primitive Christian liturgy (Quasten 1983). The reasoning behind this preference was clearly expressed by Paul: "May the God of steadfastness and encouragement grant you to live in such harmony with one another, in accord with Christ Jesus, that together you may *with one voice* glorify the God and Father of our Lord Jesus Christ" (Rom. 15:5-6). The singing, therefore, was to reflect the unity and harmony of the diverse believers in any congregation. Given that ancient Mediterranean culture is agonistic in nature, namely, that it is prone to conflict, one can appreciate the high value placed on unity and harmony in the biblical tradition. "Behold, how good and pleasant it is when brothers dwell in unity" (Ps. 133:1) expresses surprise and wonderment, for fraternal division is as common as unity in the biblical world. In the community at Corinth, disunity and disharmony were a major concern of Paul in the letters he wrote to them. Apart from their factions and divisive arguments, Paul also observed: "When you come together, each one has a psalm, has a teaching, has a revelation, has a tongue, has an interpretation" (1 Cor. 14:26-27). The psalm here is not one of the Old Testament psalms but rather a spontaneous creation produced by an individual inspired by the Spirit. Such a context hardly promotes unity and harmony and certainly no unison singing.

In the ancient world, polyphony and heterophany represented disharmony and duality. Such singing not only misrepresented the ideal unity expected of the community of believers, but it also threatened that unity, just as did the singing of creative psalms. In the history of the liturgy already from the earliest times, the prefaces invariably stated that human worshipers were joining their songs to those of the angelic choirs singing "Holy, holy, holy, LORD God of hosts." Often the phrase "with one voice" was explicitly mentioned. In his *Mystagogical Catecheses* (v. 6; 4th cent. C.E.), Cyril of Jerusalem wrote: "We call to mind the Seraphim also, whom Isaiah saw in the Holy Spirit, present in a circle about the throne of God . . . saying: 'Holy, holy, holy is the Lord of hosts' (Isa. 6:3). Therefore we recite this doxology transmitted to us by the Seraphim, in order to become participants in the hymnody of the super terrestrial hosts."

The Melody of Monophony

A papyrus dating from the end of the third century C.E. (*Papyrus Oxyrhyncus* 15.1786) contained a Greek text and musical notes on the opposite side of a grain invoice. Musicologists do not agree on the true significance of this song for the history of Christian music. Biblical scholars, however, observe that, in general, the papyri discovered at this archaeological site in Egypt (Oxyrhyncus) do reflect everyday Christian life at this time and place. Some musicologists claim that the melody was written down for private use and not for use at communal worship. Others think that it may have been a pagan melody to which a Christian text was later added. Be that as it may, the melody is of interest, for it suggests how unison singing might have sounded. The melody reflects a diatonic scale, that is, it contains five whole steps and two half steps. If sounded on the white keys of a piano, the melody would represent a scale extending from F below middle C to F above. One should hasten to add that scales are entirely arbitrary, and the number in use throughout the world (now and in antiquity) is incalculable.

Polyphony, Instrumental Music, Dancing

In the beginning, the Fathers of the Church in general were opposed to polyphony, to instrumental music, to hand clapping, and to dancing. Though a review of their writings uncovers many interesting arguments, the main objection seems to be that "they" do it. "We" are not "they." "They" are immoral, idolaters, given to great sensuality and the like. "We" are different. This is clearly rooted in the "in-group" and "out-group" distinctions that characterize group formation.

For example, the apocryphal *Acts of John* (of uncertain date and origin) relates the famous dance and hymn of Jesus in the Gnostic portion of this composite work. Before his arrest, Jesus gathered all together, and bade them to form a circle and hold each other's hands. He stood in the middle and said: "'Answer Amen to me.' Then he began to hymn and to say:

'Glory be to thee, Father,'
And we, forming a circle, responded 'Amen' to him.
'Glory be to thee, Word,
Glory be to thee, Grace.' 'Amen.'
'Glory be to thee, Holy One,
Glory be to thy Glory.' 'Amen.'
'I wish to play on the aulos;
Dance, all of you.' 'Amen.'
'I wish to mourn;
Beat your breasts, all of you.' 'Amen.'
'The one octad sings with us.' 'Amen.'
'The twelfth number dances above.' 'Amen.'
'To the universe belongs the danger.' 'Amen.'
'Who dances not, knows not what happens.' 'Amen.' . . .

After dancing thus with us, my beloved, the Lord went out, and we, confused and asleep, as it were, fled one way and the other" (*Acts of John* 94–97).

Gnostics had visions and claimed to receive messages from God which were at odds with what the faithful claimed to have learned about God from Jesus (Sloyan 1996). The conclusion of the quoted passage suggests that the author and/or the group who claimed to experience Jesus in this way had an experience in an alternate state of consciousness. Modern psychiatry might call it a "musical hallucination." Moreover, the "aulos" is an ancient Greek double-reed wind instrument used to accompany dithyrambs (intoxicated songs) in the orgiastic rites of Dionysus. The faithful would be scandalized by the idea of Jesus playing this instrument to induce a trance and direct his followers to an orgiastic trance dance. Anyone who had a vision like this would be considered insane by the faithful! Thus after a certain period of confusion, the community decided that no visions or messages other than those contained in the sacred books, the basic tradition, were valid and acceptable. "We" are and should continue to be different from "them."

The Power of Popular Piety

Try as they did to remain staunch defenders of the faith and to prohibit believers from doing what "they" did, the Fathers of the Church often realized that it was a losing battle. Historians of church music recognize that one or another of the Fathers often diverged from the opinion of other Fathers and permitted a "forbidden" practice. They thought that perhaps by allowing the practice, Christians could be gradually weaned from it. After all, like dependence on tobacco, it was an addiction that was difficult though not impossible to break. Another strategy was to attempt to "Christianize" the forbidden practice. If "they" sing songs, "we" will sing hymns and psalms. Still another strategy used especially by the Alexandrian interpreters was to allegorize texts that spoke explicitly of forbidden things (instrumental music, dancing, etc.). Thus Clement of Alexandria reads Psalm 150 and applies it entirely to the human body and its parts. It is not about instruments at all. The Antiochenes, on the other hand, like John Chrysostom, interpreted this psalm in its literal sense as a divine concession to human weakness in hopes that eventually the Israelites would be led away from such idolatrous practices. Popular piety, however, is a powerful force not easily harnessed or redirected. In many instances, it wins in the end.

Conclusion

The realities that some psychiatrists pathologize (e.g., "musical hallucinations") is recognized by many ordinary persons (nonpsychiatrists) as a normal part of life. Some people seek and enjoy such experiences. The number of biblical and extrabiblical authors who relate such accounts would belong to this rather large group (Pilch 2011a: 73-88). Others, like the man in the case study, find them a distracting annoyance. Whichever group one belongs to, it seems clear that music plays a central role in human life, especially life with God.

3. "After They Had Sung a Hymn"

According to the Passion accounts in Mark (14:26) and Matthew (26:30), Jesus and his disciples concluded their supper with a hymn and then proceeded to the Garden of Gethsemane, where Jesus prayed before his arrest. Though the Synoptics represent this meal as a Passover, scholars believe that the account of John the evangelist is more plausible. According to him, Jesus shared this meal with his disciples on the evening *before* Passover (John 13:1-2). By this calculation, Jesus died about the same time that the lambs were being slaughtered in the temple for the feast of Passover. While the symbolism is very appropriate and could be the evangelist's intention, scholars believe that John is right. Jesus' last meal with his disciples was not a Passover meal.

Our interest, however, is not to explore the historical plausibility of the date of the supper. Rather, we wonder how a contemporary Bible reader might *imagine* what the evangelists recount about the supper. Our challenge is similar to what Francis of Assisi attempted in the thirteenth century by designing a live tableau of Jesus' birth for his fellow citizens one Christmas eve. His was the first "Christmas Pageant." It is also similar to what Ignatius of Loyola proposed for the third week of his "Spiritual Exercises," which focuses on the Passion of Jesus. One might also say that this is what cinematographers like Pier Paolo Pasolini *(The Gospel according to Matthew)* or Mel Gibson *(The Passion of the Christ)* attempted to represent in film for contemporary audiences. Some critics have suggested that Gibson's film is a visual representation of responses to Ignatius's suggestions: "How do YOU imagine what you read in the Scripture?"

In this chapter we are specifically interested in the hymn sung by Jesus and his disciples, whether in fact or interpretation. How can we imagine it? What might the hymn have been? How might the melody have sounded? How well did these men sing it? Was music a special feature of this meal, or was it common at all meals?

The Meal

Perhaps it is best to begin with the meal. Everyone has to eat, of course. In the ancient Mediterranean world of the peasants, who constituted more than 90 percent of the population, food was relatively scarce. Banquets would be a rarity, perhaps only among the elite (not more than 2 percent of the population). Peasant families, however, were not nuclear as in the contemporary West: a father, mother, and children. They were nucleated, that is, the patriarch lived with all his sons, single and married, in the family compound. The girls always left their families to live with the husband's family. Thus, the activities of daily life were communal for these collectivistic personalities. There was a community well (Gen. 24:11; John 4:6-7), a community bath (Lev. 15), a community oven (Lev. 26:26, routinely misinterpreted by individualistic translators and commentators), and a community meal (Exod. 12). But since this world was rigidly divided along gender lines, so too were these places and events. Regarding the community meal, the men ate together and earlier (Esth. 1:3); women (including girls and boys younger than the age of puberty) ate together but after the men (Esth. 1:9). This was a typical "family" meal.

Thus while music and singing may or may not have been an element in the ordinary gender-divided family meal, the ancient evidence indicates that it definitely was an element in other communal meals (e.g., Sir. 32:3; 2 Sam. 19:35; Isa. 5:12; 24:7-9; Eccl. 2:8). It certainly was part of the Passover, at least in the first century C.E. (Mark 14:26; Matt. 26:30).

The Hymn

The New Testament does not specify which hymn the group sang. There does not seem to be a clear distinction between hymns and psalms in antiquity. A number of psalms are identified as hymns (8, 19, 29, etc., including 113, 114, and 117). Thus the group may well have sung one of the Egyptian Hallel Psalms (113–118), since traditionally these were associated with Passover and other occasions for singing God's praises. Psalms 113–114 were sung before the meal, and 115–118 after the meal. "Praise the LORD" (Hallelujah!) reverberates through these psalms (e.g., 113:1; 117:1). The first four verses of Psalm 118 repeat a refrain: "His steadfast love endures forever," suggesting responsorial singing. A leader (perhaps Jesus) would sing a verse with its response. "O give thanks to the LORD, for he is good; his steadfast love endures forever" (Ps. 118:1) Then as he sang subsequent verses ("Let Israel say"), the group would repeat the response ("for his steadfast love endures forever"). Hebrew poetry doesn't rhyme. Rather, the words and verses have weak and strong stresses. Such irregular meter gives a hint about how the music might have sounded.

The Melody

Musicologists agree that the melodies of ancient Israel will always remain a mystery. They are also agreed that sound tracks of biblical film epics definitely are not melodies of ancient Israel. The music of the contemporary synagogue (especially Conservative and Orthodox) is most often central European in origin and inspiration, and it is hardly two or three hundred years old. Even the cantillation symbols in the Hebrew Bible date from the end of the first millennium c.e. (Cantillation symbols are diacritical marks in the Hebrew Bible which aid in singing the text but also serve to indicate punctuation.)

Biblical scholars suspect that the "titles" of the psalms (the information placed just before the first verse of some psalms) contain important if mysterious musical information. (None of the Egyptian Hallel psalms has a title.) While many psalms are attributed to David, others are ascribed to different individuals or groups. The groups (e.g., the "sons of Korah") may have been hereditary guilds of musicians who possessed a distinctive traditional repertoire. Some contemporary *a cappella* groups are known for their distinctive arrangements and original songs, which applicants must memorize in order to belong to the group.

Thirteen psalms are identified as a "maskil" (three by the "sons of Korah"). The meaning of this Hebrew word especially relative to psalms is uncertain. But scholars think it might describe the manner in which the psalm should be sung (e.g., adagio, presto), or perhaps it indicates a category of song (e.g., Ps. 32, where maskil seems to be parallel to psalm, thus a sub-category of psalm).

"According to . . ."

Perhaps the most explicit but even more mysterious musical information provided in the "title" of some psalms is the instruction about how to sing it: "according to . . ." Everyone would agree that what follows is the name of a specific melodic formula familiar to those who were alive when these instructions were added to the psalm. These instructions, of course, were added a generation or two (or more) after the composer died, for who would remember the personal instructions of the composer beyond that time? At present, however, the melodic formulas and instructions are familiar to no one. Nevertheless, musicologists recognize that these melodic formulas are very likely similar to Indian *Rags (Ragas)* or Arabic *maqamat* (see Racy 2003).

The Indian *Raga* is not a tune, melody, scale, mode, or anything at all like that. In fact, there is no English word that can capture what this Sanskrit word means. A *Raga* is an acoustic method of coloring the mind of the listener with an emotion. (Etymologically, *raga* is related to the Sanskrit word for "color, or tone"; thus it is similar to "dye" in English.) As Indians know, a *Raga* is a combination of characteristics that can achieve that goal. The characteristics are many and varied. It is thus possible that some of the psalm titles gave a similar direction, a suggestion about how to color the mind of the listener with an emotion. In Israel, though they lack a title (musical directions), the Hallel Psalms were surely not recited monotonously, on a straight tone, without any feeling or emotion. The shout, "Praise the LORD!" (*Hallelujah!* in Hebrew), must have aroused strong feelings, especially when recalling the exodus (e.g., Ps. 114), or other timely interventions of God in the life of Israel (Ps. 115) or the life of an individual Israelite (Ps. 116). Since the Passover was a joyous feast, this must certainly have infected Jesus and the apostles even though the evangelists' reports suggest that Jesus' reflections at that meal may have cast a pall over their meal.

In Arabic music, a *maqam* (plural, *maqamat*) is a cluster of notes for which tradition has defined their mutual relationships, the habitual patterns of these notes, and their melodic development. Perhaps the nearest equivalent in Western classical music would be a mode, for example, major, minor, and the like. Modes are a way of ordering scales, and they are very familiar to Christians (even other than Catholics) from plain chant for more than 1,500 years (the time of Pope Gregory the Great — 590-604 C.E.). Actually this way of ordering scales goes back to Pythagoras (4th cent. B.C.E.). Essentially it gravitates around the "white keys" of the contemporary pianoforte or organ. But with the development of harmonized music (not favored in the ancient world and definitely prohibited in the early Christian world by many Fathers and Councils) the modal system disintegrated. What eventually remained were the "major" and "minor" scales, a poor reflection of the riches that existed prior to that time. The other modes did persist and are occasionally heard in the works of modern composers like Vaughan Williams (Australian), Bela Bartók (Hungarian), and Zoltán Kodály (Hungarian).

The Sound of the Melodies?

Since electronic recorders did not exist in the ancient world, and since we have not yet perfected a technology to capture melodies from antiquity which might still exist in the atmosphere, we moderns have no way of knowing what the ancient melodies sounded like. We can be certain that they did not sound like Bernstein's *Chichester Psalms,* which impressively set Hebrew Psalm texts to Bernstein's imaginary Hebraic tonalities. Neither did they sound like the melodies of Ernst Bloch's *Sacred Service* (the contemporary synagogue service), also set to Hebrew texts BUT with Ashkenazic pronunciation *(sic!).* Indeed, in that score only one small segment (a few measures) is cryptically and debatably identified as "ancient Hebraic melody" (with no documentation).

While we may not be able to track down and notate the melodies that Jesus and his disciples might have sung, they and their contemporaries surely were totally unaware of Ashkenazic (central European) pronunciation. As illiterate Galileans, Jesus and his disciples pronounced their words in a heavily guttural manner. People standing too close and face-to-face might have experienced an "eye wash." And everyone would recognize their geographic origins, as certainly as Americans can identify natives of the East Coast, for example, Boston, MA, or Brooklyn, NY, or the Midwest (especially after the movie "Fargo"), or the West Coast (whether California or Washington state).

Conclusion

Admittedly, this reflection on the hymn that Jesus and his disciples sang after their last supper is entirely speculative. We have no clue whether this event is veridical (really happened) or imaginal (created by the evangelists). Still, in trying to ascertain something about the hymn, we have drawn on a number of disciplines to fill in the blanks. History informs us of the place of music in different kinds of meals. Literary analysis of psalms (and hymns) helps us to understand instructions about how to sing them. Musicology enlightens us about the nature of music and songs in non-Western cultures (Arab, Indian). Knowledge of modern music cautions us that little if any of it has any relationship to Middle Eastern music of antiquity. We know for sure that the music we hear in church has no relationship to the music of our ancestors, even if the lyrics are the same. The chant extends back only to the sixth century c.e. While some Bible translations (e.g., the Jerusalem and New Jerusalem Bible) strive to reflect the metric patterns of Hebrew poetry in English, and some composers (e.g., Joseph Gelineau) attempt to capture those patterns and set them to music (e.g., the Gelineau Psalms), we can still only guess at what our ancestors in the faith experienced. However, some guesses are better than others, and the JB and NJB translations as well as Joseph Gelineau and others like him bring us closer to our ancestors than anyone else.

4. Solomon's, the Best of All Songs

One of the most popular books in the Bible is the Song of Songs (the Canticle of Canticles, the Song of Solomon). That title was added to the text much later by an editor who gave the audience a clue about the nature of the composition. The Hebrew word *šîr* can mean "poem" or "song." While recognizing this fact, scholars have tended to examine and interpret the composition primarily as a poem, that is, an oral/literary composition. They admit that it may have been sung or even dramatized or choreographed, perhaps at events such as a wedding, but few if any have attempted to analyze the composition seriously as a song. In other words, they concentrated on the lyrics without considering the melody.

While we have no evidence (no "recordings" or musical notation) for what the Song might have sounded like in the biblical period, insights from Middle Eastern ethnomusicology are helpful. They provide significant clues about the nature and purpose of Middle Eastern music (instrumental and sung) for contemporary Western Bible readers to imagine what the Song of Songs might have sounded like. This enterprise of constructing a "music scenario" for "imagining" ancient Middle Eastern song is similar to the familiar enterprise of constructing a "reading scenario" for understanding and interpreting ancient Middle Eastern texts and text segments (e.g., poems or "lyrics").

Ethnomusicology

The focus of ethnomusicology is the music, instruments, and dance, usually of an oral tradition in countries not linked with European art music. Many ethnomusicologists agree on the methodology of investigating "living oral traditions" as a sonic and technical resource for discovering old, indeed even ancient, melodies and practices (Shull 2006). This is especially true for conservative traditions that are believed to possess a certain longevity or at least a continuity with past traditions. The Lebanese-born and world-renowned ethnomusicologist and performer Ali Jihad Racy at UCLA has devoted his entire life and career to investigating Middle Eastern music (Racy 2003). He notes that there is a high level of historical continuity between the music and poetry of Moorish Spain, North Africa, Egypt, and the Eastern Mediterranean worlds. There has been very little change if any for over a millennium and more. It is worthwhile, then, to reflect on contemporary experience as it might inform the past record.

Middle Eastern Music

Many Westerners familiar with the music of biblical film epics think that this truly mirrors the past. Early films used strings and finger cymbals in "biblical" music. In 1948, MGM studios in Hollywood, CA, hired Hungarian-born Miklós Rózsa (1907-95) to score music for films, a position he filled from 1948 to 1962. During this period, three of his musical scores ("Quo Vadis." 1951; "Ben Hur," 1959; and "King of Kings," 1961) are recognized as having created the "vocabulary" of "biblical music." He composed in the European Romantic tradition and used huge orchestras with lush-sounding strings. The music was characterized by fifths (e.g., the opening words "Twinkle, twinkle [little star]") and minor thirds (the opening words of "Oh come, [oh come, Emmanuel]"). Sound tracks from these films can refresh the memory. When questioned about his sources, Rózsa admitted that it was solely his creative imagination. "No one knows what music in the biblical period sounded like!" (Pilch 2006).

Perhaps that is so, but we can be certain that music in the biblical period did *not* sound anything like what Rózsa composed. Western music in general relies on notation and harmony. Middle Eastern music, in contrast, places greater emphasis on improvisation, modal variety, and rhythmic flexibility. Western, and particularly European, music seeks to represent images and concepts. It is depictive, cerebral, and emotionally reserved ("The Moldau"; see below). Middle Eastern music strives to evoke intense emotions, powerful sensations, and direct interaction between performers and listeners, and even to induce alternate states of consciousness in both the performers and the listeners.

The basic theoretical system of Western music identifies equal tempered half-steps, whole steps, and the like, which are intervals derived from a theoretical scale of 24 equal quarter tones (one fourth of a tone) per octave. This system is highly detrimental to generating music that produces the ecstasy so essential to Middle Eastern music. Investigating medieval Arab treatises and attending to the pitch unit found in earlier Byzantine church modes, the Syrian theorist Tawfīq al-Ṣabbāgh divided the octave

269

into 53 "commas" (one-ninth of a tone)! The wealth of microtones (53!) in Middle Eastern music compared to the poverty (24!) of tones in Western music can and does induce trances in Middle Eastern listeners. However, these microtones are likely to strike Western ears as between the cracks, under pitch, off pitch, jarring, and unsettling. Not only would it not induce a trance for a Western listener, but it would likely leave that person on edge.

Middle Eastern Lyrics

In the Middle East, lyrics are a verbal genre possessing very distinctive stylistic features, aesthetic properties, and especially emotional efficacies. The most effective ecstatically oriented Middle Eastern texts are amorous. They belong to a major poetical genre known as secular love poetry *(ghazal)*. *Wasf's*, Arab poems that praise parts of the body, belong to this genre. Many biblical scholars have compared the Song to the *wasf*, but it is much more. While commentators have exhaustively analyzed its stylistic features, they have generally neglected to explore the Song's effective ecstatic potential rooted in the lyrics and enhanced by the melody. One reason for this deliberate neglect may be the historical critic's commitment to determining the literal meaning of biblical literature. What did the poet-lover intend in this Song? Obviously, to celebrate the beauty of the Beloved and vice versa by presenting detailed physical descriptions of the human body (male and female). But his singing of the poem was intended to produce other effects, too.

Contemporary Arab music, notably the *ṭarab* — which is a musically induced state of ecstasy — and especially its lyrics, manifests the mutual crossovers between the secular and mystical worlds in the Middle Eastern world. These texts represent a broadly shared Middle Eastern idiom just as reflected in the Song of Songs. Contemporary Arab music and love lyrics are rooted in medieval (13th cent.) Sufi poetry that reaches even further back into Arab history. In Sufi poetry, the poet speaks in the Lover's voice to the Beloved, who is a metaphor for God. Indeed the poet-lover seeks to experience God and ultimately to have union with God. Wine is a metaphor for mystic transformation. Such interpretation clashes with the historical-critical, literary perspective, but the Middle Easterner crosses over from one realm (secular love) to another (mystical union with God) with ease. The lyrics of Middle Eastern music make sense on a variety of levels and thus can serve different purposes. The ambivalent gender of the poet-Lover and Beloved (evident in some translations of the Song, but "smoothed out" to consistency in others, yet always evident in other Middle Eastern lyrics) contributes to multivalent interpretations of the lyrics.

Lyrics and Ecstasy

In the Middle Eastern musical tradition, especially that of the *ṭarab,* love lyrics are a primary agent of ecstatic evocation which can occur in three ways. First, emotionally loaded words and phrases directly evoke ecstasy. Notions of loneliness, togetherness, sadness, joy, pain, pleasure, love, and the like play a key role. This vocabulary flows from the universal and fundamental experience of unity/union followed by separation (e.g., Song 3:1-2; 5:6). It is a specialized vocabulary of emotions, hence it gains ecstatic effectiveness by being linguistically special. The singer-poet-Lover does not merely talk about these emotions. He rather "plays" them out and sings them as felt experiences.

Second, the lyrics of these songs have a "sonic-emotive" flavor and ethos that is intensely felt and experienced rather than merely conceived or visualized. The auditory-semantic impact of individual words and/or phrases mentioned above effects a transformation in the listener. Anyone who has heard the Qur'an chanted recognizes that though it is not love poetry, the chanted Sura can produce a similar somatic-emotive effect in the listener. The Qur'an has a very distinct auditory-conceptual dimension. Its verbal message makes an impact not only in terms of the notion conveyed but also in the sonic effect produced by the melody that encapsulates the words.

The most ecstatically effective love lyrics are those that follow a loose prosodic flow in contrast to lyrics that adhere to rigid metric or accentuated patterns. The majority of segments (cola) in the Song of Songs vary in length from five to ten (Hebrew) syllables, thus enhancing the ecstatic effectiveness of the lyrics. Contemporary Arab singers who are successful at triggering ecstasy in themselves and their listeners tend to highlight voweled syllables and elongated sound. This technique is confirmed by the French composer and Principal Guest Conductor of the Chicago Symphony Orchestra, Pierre Boulez, who observed regarding music in general that sometimes the highly compact "textual time" of the lyrics must yield to the more elongated "musical time" of the melody. "Musical time" in its turn can induce and contribute to "ecstatic time," which is in contrast to "nonecstatic or ordinary time." Because we have never heard the Song of Solomon sung in its ancient musical modality, this is difficult for us to comprehend. Contemporary Israeli settings of segments of the Song reflect contemporary, Western (or pseudo–Middle Eastern) melodies which have nothing in common with authentic traditional Middle Eastern music (e.g., *Songs from King Solomon's Song of Songs,* CBS LP S 63289).

In the music of the contemporary Middle Eastern world, song titles are selected for their appealing sonic-semantic effect. Racy reports some song titles such as *Bulbul Chayrān* (Bewildered Nightingale) or *ar-Rabī'* (Spring) that project into their song effects that are ecstatically inviting. The Hebrew title of the Song of Songs, admittedly appended later by an editor, seems to reflect this observation (*šîr haššîrîm 'ăšer lišlōmōh;* Song 1:1). The alliteration in this phrase, the repetition of the sibilant "sh" sound, is mellifluous, pleasing to the ear. Moreover, the sibilant is repeated in verses 2 and 3 in the "kiss" words. As J. Cheryl Exum observes, "Sense and sound work together to produce an aesthetic [and I would add, ecstatic] effect that cannot be captured in translation" (Exum 2005: 31). Try now to imagine that sound sung in Middle Eastern microtonal melodies.

Third, lyrics work their ecstatic effects through symbolic suggestion. Lyrics are of course heard and then imagined, visualized, and hopefully felt. The symbolic erotic references in the Song of Songs can easily be imagined and visualized (e.g., the mountain of myrrh, the hill of frankincense, 4:6; garden locked, fountain sealed, 4:12) and with the aid of ecstatic music even felt deeply and physically.

Conclusion

Early in my teaching career, it was my custom to conclude my course with a dramatic reading of the Song of Songs. A poet-Lover (male), the Beloved (female), and the Daughters of Jerusalem Chorus (females) would read the poem. As "background music" for the song, I would play Smetana's tone poem, "The Moldau," from *Má Vlast.* He wrote descriptive notes for this composition in which he wanted to portray the course of this river (Moldau, Vltava) from its source through Bohemia's valleys, past thick woods where a hunter's horn is heard ("catch us the little foxes"; Song 2:15), past the lowlands where a wedding feast is being celebrated with song and dance. At nightfall the nymphs revel in its waves as the river flows past castles. Then at St. John Rapids the stream rushes on toward Prague and the fortress, Vyšehrad, and then further on toward the sea. The imagery of the music could match the reading if the pace were right. The music could enhance the poetry.

This anachronistic and ethnocentric pairing of Smetana's music with an ancient Middle Eastern love poem was a very clumsy attempt at "actualization" or "contextualization," that is, making an ancient text relevant in a different time and a different culture. Today I search for music in the Middle Eastern repertoire to gain a better and more respectful appreciation of what our ancestors in the faith experienced when they sang or heard sung the Song of Solomon, *šîr haššîrîm 'ăšer lišlōmōh*. The desired result is a total human experience, emotional as well intellectual. The hope is to attain a transformative experience in an alternate state of consciousness, and perhaps even in transforming contact with God.

5. Games, Amusement, and Sports

In the third of seven oracles describing the restoration of Zion and Judah, Zechariah wrote: "Old men and old women will again sit in the open places of Jerusalem, each with a staff in his hand because of great age. The open places of the city will be filled with boys and girls playing in its open places" (Zech. 8:4-5). Jesus appears to describe one such game children played in the marketplace imitating elements of weddings and funerals: "We piped to you, and you did not dance; we wailed, and you did not mourn" (Matt. 11:16-17//Luke 7:31-32). How old were these children? How were they playing? What kinds of games did they play? While archaeologists have discovered game boards and other items relating to games, scholars caution that in the majority of cases we have no information about the rules of the games or how they were played. Recently replicated cross-cultural research on games offers new insights.

Games across Cultures

The standard definition of a game formulated in 1959 is "a recreational activity characterized by: (1) organized play, (2) competition, (3) two or more sides, (4) criteria for determining the winner, and (5) agreed-upon rules" (Chick 1998: 187). The researchers responsible for this definition subsequently removed the word "recreational" from the definition. Some activities like duels meet the criteria for games except for the word "recreational." Roman gladiators entertained the spectators, but they surely did not find the experience of death recreational. On the other hand, a colleague's husband writing a dissertation in 1988 on duels discovered that in modern, northern Europe one person always died in a duel, while in modern, southern (Mediterranean) Europe one person was wounded, though rarely mortally. The researcher believes that contrasting cultural values explain this variation.

Using the standard definition of games just cited, it is difficult to identify any games in the Bible. The information in Zechariah is too incomplete. Jesus' description of this children's game is similarly incomplete, although, on the basis of the text, the activity does not fit the definition of a game. Anthropologists classify such activities as "amusements." Modern examples would be non-competitive swimming, top spinning, and string-figure making.

Classifying Games

Analyzing information about games from a hundred societies in the Cross-Cultural Survey cited above, the researchers who were questioned suggested that the best way to classify games in their data was on the basis of the factor most critical for determining winners and losers. Thus, a general classification of games suggests three types: (1) games requiring physical skill; (2) games requiring strategy; and (3) games won by chance, pure luck.

From this perspective, was the riddle Samson wanted the Philistines to solve in Judges 14 a game or an amusement? Some biblical scholars have identified it as an example of a mental exercise. This would appear to be an ethnocentric suggestion. Driven as Middle Eastern cultures are by the core value of honor, a public claim to honor, and public acknowledgment of that claim, the audible eloquence and verbal dexterity of the competitors would determine the winner in antiintrospective Mediterranean culture. Moreover, the solution to the riddle did not occur by pure chance or physical skill. It required strategy first in having Samson's bride wheedle the clue out of Samson, but more importantly being able — as they were not — to cast the answer into properly impressive eloquence (Pilch 1999: 92-97). Researchers identify the riddle as a game of strategy.

Children Playing

In the Mediterranean world, young boys until the age of puberty were raised along with the girls nearly exclusively by all the women in the family. They would always be under the vigilant eye of the women. Since houses were generally dark inside, these boys and girls would play in the courtyard of the complex. If boys and girls were playing in the open places of the city or village, it is possible that the boys (perhaps the girls, too) might be older than the age of puberty. In this case, they would not be playing together. In any case, the vigilant women would be close by.

Many translations of Zechariah 8:5 say that the boys and girls are playing in the streets. This is inaccurate and inappropriate since the Hebrew word *(rēḥōb)* does not mean street. Anyone who has visited the old city of Jerusalem has a good basic image of "street" which can be retrojected centuries into antiquity. Since nothing like modern city-planning existed, houses were not organized in any orderly fashion. There would definitely not be anything comparable to "row houses." The spaces around these houses, therefore, were nothing like a modern "street." They were rather pathways for the use of people and animals. The pathways would form a challenging maze, as anyone who has ever gotten lost in the contemporary walled city of Jerusalem can testify. Moreover, the space around the house was often the convenient "garbage dump." Without sanitation or "pooper scooper" laws, animal droppings would contribute to the overall effect. It is difficult to imagine a game, strictly speaking, in this context and under these circumstances.

Wide open spaces would obviously be precious in the ancient walled city where space was at a premium. These were often located near the city gate (see Gen. 19:2; 2 Chron. 32:6). Here the residents would gather (Prov. 31:23, 31). Civic assemblies were held here (Neh. 8:1), as were commercial transactions (Neh. 3:1, 3). This was also where legal proceedings took place (Deut. 21:19; 22:24; Ruth 3:11; 4:1, 10, 11; Ps. 127:5). Given the busy nature of this relatively small area, boys and girls would find it difficult to play games as defined above. On the other hand, there would probably be much to mimic or imitate even for purposes of amusement.

Jesus' reference to children playing wedding and funeral "games" in the marketplace would make sense as a form of imitation. Since the dead had to be buried outside the walls, the funeral cortege would have to pass through this wide open space. Since the groom had to fetch his bride from her father's house, it is plausible that that procession, too, would have to pass through the wide open space. It might not be true that an actual wedding or funeral was taking place which children would be mimicking. But both events (wedding/funeral processions) would be a familiar sight in this place.

Of course, life for boys and girls in the Mediterranean world was different. Boys had ample opportunity to play. It was part of growing up under the care of the women. Girls, in contrast, were socialized as early as possible into the tasks they would be expected to perform for life, so there was little time for play. The only clue we have to pastimes among village boys is in the *Infancy Gospel of Thomas* (2) where Jesus played at damming up a stream and — together with other boys and perhaps girls — modeled animal figurines from wet clay. Some archaeologists conjecture that figurines excavated at various sites may have been dolls rather than cult figurines. They propose that the prohibition against graven images may not have applied to young girls. One reason for this conjecture is that some of these dolls appear to have been puppets or function like puppets for the youngsters. Cultural evidence to challenge this interpretation is that girls were intensely occupied with the real thing — babies! — from early on. The task of raising real-life children would likely leave little time for or interest in dolls.

Sports

Biblical scholars observe that there is little mention of sports in the Bible. References are brief and suggestive at most. The book of Judges refers to seven hundred men (selected from more than 26,000) who were left-handed and could sling a stone at a hair and not miss (20:12-17). Such skill suggests more than "basic training" to serve in the military. So, too, with archery. References to "shooting at a mark" (1 Sam. 20:20; Lam. 3:12) suggest that archery was at least a pastime if not a game. There is also a curious description of God's punishment for Shebna: "he will seize firm hold on you, and whirl you around, and throw you like a ball into a wide land; there you shall die . . ." (Isa. 22:17-18). Some scholars interpret this as a reference to a game like football, while others think that it may be a reference to wrestling. The story of Abner and Joab's men meeting at Gibeon, which both wanted to occupy, has been interpreted as a team wrestling match that turned violent and resulted in bloodshed (see 2 Sam. 2:12-18). Herod the Great encouraged Greek wrestling and chariot racing in the hippodrome outside the temple in Jerusalem.

While specific data on sports in ancient Israel is lacking, a general observation from anthropological research is worth remembering. All societies have games and sports, and these both reflect and reinforce cultural values. Indeed, the purpose of games and sport (apart from promoting physical fitness, which may not have been valid in antiquity with its minimal abilities to deal with mortal diseases) is to provide a form of buffered learning by which a young boy (and girl) is gradually enculturated into adult behavior. The violence that characterized ancient Israelite society was a learned value. The physical discipline proposed in Proverbs and Sirach for young boys was but one ingredient. Games that trained participants in skills useful for warfare would be another.

Board Games

Archaeologists have discovered a variety of gaming boards at different places in the ancient world: Ur, in the Tomb of Tutankhamen, and in Palestine (Debir, Tell al-'Ajul, Beth Shemesh, and Gezer). They are of various shapes. Inlaid with gold, shells, and ivory, they are also very elaborate. There are holes in some of them, presumably for pegs. Yet, we have no clue at all as to the nature or the rules of these games.

One "game" familiar to many is the one carved into stone pavement beneath the Convent of the Sisters of Sion in the walled city of Jerusalem. It was once thought to be the place (*lithostrōton; gabbatha;* see John 19:13) where Pilate judged Jesus. That most likely took place across the city, at the Citadel, the Palace of Herod (37 B.C.E.–4 B.C.E.), which the Roman Procurator used as his residence in Jerusalem when he was not in Caesarea. Nevertheless, the game on this stone has been identified as the King Game. This amusement derived from the Saturnalia, a feast originally celebrated in December but then extended to any period of unrestrained pleasure. The soldiers selected a mock king, endowed him with ridiculous honors, even allowed a measure of liberty to satisfy his pleasures, but put him to death at the end of the farce.

The King Game was played with dice (actually with astragali, or animal knucklebones, marked with letters or numbers) and was a favorite with soldiers, especially those off duty. On the flag-stones the rough outline of the circle is clear. In several places there is a "B" (for Basileus), and at the finish, a royal crown. The first to land on the crown was the winner. The mockery of Jesus (John 19:2-3) might have been related to this game, if it was available in the Citadel. Others have suggested that the mockery of Jesus reported by Luke (22:63-64) is a variation of blind man's buff in which young boys would learn how to practice the virtue of manliness, that is, suffering in silence (see Isa. 50:5-6; 53:7).

Greek Games

While Herod the Great promoted Greek games in Jerusalem, the prevailing attitude among Israelites would likely have been opposed to them (see 2 Macc. 4:7-17). Paul's letters, especially to the Corinthians, contain many more references. This should be no surprise given the frequency and popularity of games held at Corinth.

Paul speaks of boxing (1 Cor. 9:26; 1 Tim. 1:8; 2 Tim. 4:7) but especially of the footrace, perhaps the most popular of all athletic contests. He alludes to training (1 Cor. 9:15, 17), the racecourse (1 Cor. 9:24), and the starter's summons (1 Cor. 9:27, "I have called others to the contest"). Racers must strip naked (Heb. 12:1), concentrate on the task (1 Cor. 9:24; Phil. 3:13, 14; Heb. 12:2), and strive to endure (Heb. 12:1). Only then will the runner taste victory (Acts 20:24) and win the prize (1 Cor. 9:25).

Particularly motivating for circum-Mediterranean natives is the acquisition of honor, or public recognition (by spectators; Heb. 12:1; 1 Cor. 4:9). The judge would determine honor and dishonor (1 Tim 4:1; 1 Cor. 9:27) at the goal line, where he would award the prize (Heb. 12:2; Phil. 3:14).

Conclusion

Classical cultural research on games found no evidence for them among the ancient Hebrews. Anthropologists, even the primary researchers, are agreed that ethnographic error accounts for this lack of data in the cultural database. Astute Bible readers are in a good position to compensate for that deficiency with the aid of the precise definitions and distinctions offered by the social scientists.

6. The Bawdy Bible

Language that is tasteless and improper in one social system is often quite acceptable in another social system, and vice versa. Since kinship is the focal social institution of the Mediterranean world, it should not surprise readers that frank and frequent reference to procreation and procreative or other bodily functions are quite common and acceptable in the Bible.

During Elisha's journey from Jericho to Bethel, a gang of boys followed after him, yelling: "Go up, Baldy! Go up, Baldy!" In his turn, Elisha cursed them "in the name of the LORD"! Immediately two she-bears came out of the woods and tore forty-two of the boys. Elisha nonchalantly continued his journey (2 Kings 2:23-25). Even if this anecdote is fictional, it is appalling to most readers of the Bible. Why would the sacred author include such a tale in the story of Elisha? How could a holy man behave like this? After all, "baldy" is only a word. While not a flattering term, it does describe a physical attribute.

Symbolic Meanings

The American proverb declares, "Sticks and stone may break my bones, but names will never hurt me." Those Americans who believe this proverb would laugh at this biblical story. They might try to rationalize Elisha's response or conclude that the story is pure fiction. Other Americans would applaud Elisha. For their part, these Americans might retaliate against such taunts with violence.

What might have prompted Elisha's response? The key is likely in the significance of the word "bald/baldy." Herodotus said: "Egyptians shave their heads from childhood, and the bone thickens by exposure to the sun. This is also the reason why they do not grow bald; for nowhere can one see so few bald heads as in Egypt" (*Histories* 3.12.2-3). While Israelites did not normally shave their heads, the fact that they considered baldness a curse (Ezek. 7:18; Amos 8:10) suggests that it was not common in Israel either. Thus Israelites would have doubts about a bald man like Elisha, who presents himself as a holy man and successor to hirsute Elijah, an acknowledged holy man.

To this plausible literal meaning of the taunts, we can add a plausible symbolic meaning. Anthropologist Jeannette Mageo observed that head hairs are hairs, yet in some cultures they represent or symbolize sex organs and virility. Samson's strength (and sexual power?) was in his hair (Judg. 16:17). To call Elisha bald may amount to calling him sexually impotent. Even though at this point in the narrative Elisha has received a double share of Elijah's spirit (2 Kings 2:9-12), was able to part the Jordan just as Elijah did (vv. 13-14), and made the water of Jericho wholesome (vv. 19-22), this gang of boys publicly challenge his virility as well as his identity as man of God. Their taunts say that he is doubly cursed by God!

The only way for Elisha to preserve his manly honor is to summon God's help in leveling a curse at his accusers. God sends bears to maul a large number of the gang hurling insults, thus confirming that God is pleased with Elisha but not with them. Neither literal baldness nor suspected impotence reflects God's opinion about Elisha. He is indeed a holy man and successor to Elijah.

Eat There are other words in the Hebrew Bible that carry symbolic meanings. Scholars agree that in one or two places, the innocent word "eat" symbolizes the enjoyment of sexual intercourse. Thus the sense of the Sage's proverb is definitely: "This is how an adulteress behaves: she enjoys intercourse ["eats"], wipes away the traces ["wipes her mouth"], and says: 'I have done no wrong'" (Prov. 30:20). Using the same word, the foolish woman says: "Stolen intercourse ["water"; see Prov. 5:15] is sweet; and concealed intercourse ["bread eaten in secret] is pleasant." Finally, there is no mistaking the young woman's meaning when she sings: "Let my lover come to his garden and eat its choice fruits" (Song 4:16).

Thigh, Hand, Finger Other common words like thigh, hand, and finger also symbolize reproductive parts of the anatomy where the context makes this clear. When Abraham commands his servant: "Put your hand under my thigh, and swear to me by the LORD that you will do my bidding," the servant must swear while his hand touches Abraham's organ (see Gen. 24:2, 9). The deed is clear, but its significance is less clear. One interpretation is that the person is swearing by touching a sacred spot, namely, the location of the "covenant of circumcision." Another interpretation is that if the person does not fulfill his oath, he can expect punishment in this vital region of his body. He might not produce further progeny.

Philologists agree that a passage in *The Rule of the Community* at Qumran (1QS 7:15-16) demonstrates that "hand" is a euphemism for the genitals: "Whoever takes out his 'hand' from under his clothes . . . he shall be punished for thirty days." The word "hand" is used in Ugaritic in the same sense: "the hand of El grows long as the sea; and the hand of El like the ocean." Though others disagree, some scholars suggest that this is the symbolic meaning in the bride's statement in the Song of Songs (5:4-5): "My beloved put his 'hand' to the latch [literally in Hebrew, "from the hole"], and my innards thrilled about him; I rose to open to my beloved, and my 'hands' dripped with myrrh, my fingers with liquid myrrh. . . ."

Since hands and fingers frequently appear in parallelism (Ps. 144:1; Isa. 2:8; 17:8; 59:3; etc.), fingers might also be a euphemism for genitals, though a distinct meaning separate from the hand in Song of Songs is not clear. On the other hand, specialists in nonverbal communication note that in the circum-Mediterranean world extending far back to classical times, people used their fingers to send sexual messages or accusations. The *mano fica* (insertion of the thumb between the second and third fingers of a clenched fist) symbolized sexual intercourse. The *mano cornuta* (clenched fist with extended second and last fingers) was used to point to a cuckold. Both gestures are also considered effective protection against the evil eye because they distract the one giving the evil eye.

This perspective sharpens the contours of the worthless troublemaker described by the Sage (Prov. 6:12-14):

> A worthless person, a wicked man goes about with (A) crooked speech,
> (B) winks his eyes, (C) scrapes his feet, (C) points with his finger,
> (B) with perverted heart devises evil, (A) continually sowing discord.

This is a totally evil person in terms of speech (A — mouth-ears), thoughts (B — heart-eyes), and deeds (C — hands-feet). These are three zones of the human body interpreted symbolically in consistent fashion throughout the entire Bible (Malina 2001: 68-71). With regard to the zone of purposeful activity (C), this evil person who lies and has a perverse heart also makes deliberate, groundless sexual accusations. Though the finger gesture such as described above is common in this culture, such behavior is equivalent to playing with fire. His destruction will indeed be sudden and total (Prov. 6:15).

In all these passages, simple words and gestures not only have a plain and obvious meaning (bald, eat, pointing with the finger) but a symbolic one, too. Without an awareness of the symbolic meaning, a reader can miss the real point the sacred author is intending for the original audience. Does the Bible ever speak more explicitly, especially in matters related to human behavior or activity, especially if it relates to bodily function?

Explicit Meanings

If Ezekiel does not hold first place for speaking explicitly about the human body, it is difficult to imagine who else in the Bible does. Scholars properly identify Ezekiel 23 as an allegory. Ezekiel's subjects are Samaria and Jerusalem (23:4), but he discusses these cities under the figures of two sisters, prostitutes, Oholah (Samaria) and Oholibah (Jerusalem). (Cities in the ancient world were always considered to be females.) He speaks of their breasts and nipples (23:3, 8), their lust for Assyrian lovers and pleasure boys (23:5, 6). Leslie Allen translates the Hebrew of Ezekiel 23:20 literally:

"She [Oholibah, the worse of the two sisters] had love affairs with Egyptian paramours who rivaled asses in the size of their penises and horses in the amount of sperm they produced."

The entire passage is dominated by the Hebrew words for "to fornicate, be sexually loose," "lust, have an affair," "be or make unclean." Ezekiel does not have the delicate approach of the author of Song of Songs. He was obviously a spokesperson for God (a prophet) who did not shrink from using strong invective. His preached God's message in earthy language, yet he was not prurient.

This is a culture whose core value has always been honor (with its correlative, shame). Honor is replicated in gender and sexual behavior. Given the culture's expectation of sexual exclusivity from its females, the [female] cities' broken loyalty to God shames God. Though Ezekiel is speaking about a political situation, the language of sexuality suits his allegorical purposes perfectly.

Moreover, honorable men display their manliness not only by brute strength or the ability to absorb pain without crying but also by mastery of language. Samson is an excellent example of both abilities (Judg. 14–16). Ezekiel has the language of sexuality well in hand.

Relieving Oneself One bodily function is explicitly mentioned in the Hebrew Bible six times (1 Sam. 22:22; 25:34; 1 Kings 14:10; 16:11; 21:2; 2 Kings 9:8). Though most modern English translations render the phrase's meaning (appropriately and correctly) "male," or "man," the King James Version and the Douay-Rheims translate it literally: "[he/him/those] that pisseth against the wall." The Hebrew language has words for man and male. Obviously this Hebrew phrase was not offensive or one that reflects poor literary style, gutter talk. Modern readers have an opportunity to reflect upon their squeamishness with the literal rendition of Hebrew.

To Ravish, to Violate The Hebrew text of the Bible has a long and complex history. The text we possess at present contains in the margins various notes accumulated over centuries to help interpret the text. One such set of notes is known at the *kĕtîb* (written) and the *qērê* (read). Thus, the Hebrew word that means "to ravish or violate" (rape) a woman appears three or four times in the text (*šāgal:* Deut. 28:30; Isa. 13:16; Jer. 3:2; Zech. 14:2). This was what was written (*kĕtîb,* abbreviated "K"). It is very likely original. The people responsible for passing the text on to succeeding generations tried to maintain its integrity. They could not change words in the text or substitute others in their place. Yet, this particular Hebrew word was apparently considered obscene in its entire semantic range from "copulate" to "ravish."

Therefore, the Massoretes, medieval Jewish scholars who sought to preserve the text in its integrity, proposed in the margins that a different word should be spoken when this text was read in public: *šākab* (to lie down [with]; to have sexual relations with). Notice the different ways that English-language Bibles render those passages. The Massorete process would be similar in the English language to a reader seeing in a written text one of the seven words that normally gets censored (bleeped) on TV when someone says it (though not in movies) and substituting a euphemism instead. Still, the Massoretes were just as inconsistent in their substitutions (at least from our perspective) as Americans are concerning language that is permitted on TV and in movies.

Conclusion

Specialists are frequently baffled to explain why in some instances Hebrew authors used euphemisms and in other instances vocabulary and phrases that seem coarse to our ears. The philologist Edward Ullendorff (1979) describes some of the language of the Bible as bawdy. Synonyms for this word would be ribald, coarse, or loose. Bawdy language, however, is not lascivious, lewd, lustful, prurient, lecherous, erotic, or smutty. In the English language, these latter concepts belong to a related but very different semantic field.

He notes that a Hebrew vocabulary suspected of being lewd made it difficult for Song of Songs, Qoheleth, and Esther (dealing with human love, doubt, and patriotism) to be accepted by the rabbis into the canon. Gordon J. Bahr, my rabbinics teacher of happy memory, said the debate about accepting the Song of Songs into the canon was resolved when all agreed to include it in the canon but commanded that no one younger than the age of thirty-five should be allowed to read it (lest it cause a population explosion)! As the Latin proverb reminds us: *tempora mutantur et in illis mutamur.* Times change and we change with them.

7. Films That Illuminate the Bible

Only Matthew among the evangelists reports that the crowds Jesus fed were larger than 5,000 (14:21) and 4,000 (15:38) respectively. That number did not include the women and children! The Greek word for "men" in these passages is the exclusive Greek word *andres* (adult males). It does not include women as the word *anthrōpos* can. Two pieces of cultural information help understand this report. One, the women and children were not counted because in general they are not of primary concern in that culture. To this day, the answer a married man gives to the common question "How many children do you have?" is ordinarily, "Two sons." To learn whether that constitutes the entire family, the petitioner should ask: "Do you have any daughters?" Often the answer will be: "Oh yes, two daughters!"

Two, the groups into which these people clustered (see Mark 6:40) were very likely divided by gender. Men and boys older than the age of puberty would sit together. Women, young girls, and young boys up to the age of puberty would sit together, but apart from the men's group. While such gender-based separation is rather curious in our culture, it is rather common in other cultures of the world. A photograph of a Saudi Arabian family having a picnic at the Red Sea (published in *National Geographic,* October 1987) illustrates this custom.

Reading

In general authors are involved in a game with their readers. Every author assumes that the readers live in and understand the same world. The author then manipulates that common experience and understanding by building on it, rearranging it, or using some other literary strategy. Biblical authors wrote primarily for readers who lived in the same cultural world as they. No biblical author intended to write for all people of all times in all places. Because these authors and their readers shared this common understanding, it was never necessary to supply details. The story of Jesus' feeding the crowds omits many details which a modern reader in another culture needs to supply as appropriate. One way to learn these details is through pictures, such as those in the *National Geographic,* or through films.

"Educational" Films

Two kinds of films can assist Bible readers in creating appropriate scenarios for imagining what the biblical text envisions and often presupposes: educational and recreational. Educational films would include those based on anthropological research and fieldwork; recreational films are primarily fictional stories, though some intend to dramatize factual characters or events. Still, quality recreational films strive to present the historical and cultural circumstances of their subject with accuracy.

Family Matters: The Role of the Family in the Middle East is a very enlightening twenty-five-minute video in a series produced by Encyclopedia Britannica Education Corporation (see Further Reading). It explores the historical reasons behind the fact that very large patriarchal families form the basic social structure of the Middle Eastern family. Other topics include the role of family structure and kinship ties in hospitality, nepotism, and polygamy; the role of women in the patriarchal family and Islamic traditions; and the effects of Westernization, industrialization, and urbanization on modern Middle Eastern family values.

Though the film says practically nothing explicit about the Bible, many of its insights shed fresh light on familiar stories. The custom of the son marrying his father's brother's daughter (patrilateral cousin) is clear in the narratives about the patriarchs. Abraham sends a servant to Nahor, where he meets Rebekah, the daughter of Bethuel, son of Milcah, who was married to Abraham's brother, Nahor. Three times in the story, the narrator repeats the relationship for the reader, who can't fail to appreciate that this is indeed the right partner (Gen. 24:15, 24, 47). The proper partner for Jacob (father's brother's daughter) poses a problem. The brother of his father, Isaac, was Ishmael, who was removed from the family. Therefore Isaac sends Jacob to his mother Rebekah's brother, Laban, to find a suitable partner among his daughters (Leah and Rachel; Gen. 28:2, 5; 29).

The video also illustrates the importance of hospitality, which in the ancient Middle East is extended nearly exclusively by men exclusively to strangers. See how hospitality functions in the classic story about Lot and the strangers in Genesis 19. (What one offers relatives is not hospitality but rather steadfast lovingkindness, "ḥesed.") Jesus instructs evangelizers to rely on such hospitality, which would allow them to travel lightly and quickly preach more efficiently (Matt. 10:5-15). Those who fail to provide hospitality will pay a heavy price (Matt. 25:31-46).

Another helpful film is *Kypseli: Men and Women Apart — A Divided Reality* (see Further Reading). This forty-five-minute video is based on the fieldwork of Susanna M. Hoffman in Kypseli, a traditional peasant village on the Greek island of Thera (Santorini). It asks the question: "How do people structure daily life? How do people make sense out of life?"

The film illustrates how these peasants live in a rigidly gender-divided world which affects every aspect of their lives. Apart from the modern inventions (e.g., electricity), Abraham, Moses, Jesus, Paul, and other biblical personalities would feel quite at home in this world, with minor subcultural alterations. Greece, after all, is not Palestine. This film provides a very good scenario for reading and understanding the meeting between Jesus and the Samaritan woman at Jacob's well from a fresh perspective (John 4:4-42).

Almost all Westerners who view this video find it somewhat repulsive and incredible. Some of the discomfort comes from the narrative, which at times interprets rather than reports, and the interpretations are sometimes ethnocentric (Hoffman 1988). To avoid this problem, viewers might turn off the sound, watch the video, and attempt to interpret what they see. The experience would be similar to observing the behavior of people in a culture who speak a language the observer does not understand.

"Recreational" Films

Probably all readers recognize that the spectacular Hollywood biblical productions (e.g., *The Ten Commandments*) are faithful neither to the text nor to the cultural context. It is not even clear that they accomplish what other "creative" representations of historical events do, namely, inspire a viewer to seek the sources and read about the event from firsthand accounts. Some of the more helpful films are not explicitly related to the Bible at all.

Prizzi's Honor, based on a novel by Richard Condon, is an excellent contemporary story that illustrates the enduring Mediterranean values of honor and shame. The honor-and-shame vocabulary is explicit, and the story line dramatically demonstrates how these values govern the lives of people of Mediterranean ancestry. The Prizzi family (Don Corrado Prizzi, his sons Dominic and Eduardo, and Dominic's daughter, Mae Rose Prizzi) are friends with the Partanna family (Don Corrado is a friend of Angelo and godfather to his son, Charlie Partanna). Charlie's relationship with Mae Rose and her disappointment when Charlie marries an outsider to both families, Irene Walker (Walcewicz), lie at the heart of understanding the film's title, *Prizzi's Honor.* Of the many striking lines in the script, perhaps Don's are most poignant as he tries to persuade Charlie to regain the honor of the Prizzis: "She is your wife, but *we are your life!* . . . We are your blood!" At the very least, this film gives a viewer a new way of thinking about the commandment: "Honor thy father and thy mother," just one of 349 occurrences of the word "honor" in the Revised Standard Version.

In similar fashion, *The Godfather* and its various sequels not only illustrate the values of honor and shame but are based on the Mediterranean concept of patronage, a social institution that exists even to this day. A patron is a person with surplus who, according to the rules of the culture, is obliged to share his surplus with those in need. But he is free to select the beneficiaries whom he will treat as if they were family. The only reason for his choice is: "because I want to." This is a major element in Jesus' parable about the workers in the vineyard (Matt. 20:1-16). While some, like the first hired in the story, prefer to negotiate a contract with God, others, like the remaining characters, choose to trust God. In the long run, the story is about God, who, just like a Mediterranean patron, freely chooses to treat some people (the last hired) with favoritism, as if they were family.

The Greek term for favor is *charis,* in Latin *gratia* ("grace"). The theology of grace presupposes knowledge of patronage. Such grace or favoritism is underscored by a line like, "I loved Jacob, but hated Esau," says the Lord (Mal. 1:3; Rom. 9:13). No Mediterranean person has difficulty understanding this. Yet, just as the films indicate, potential clients will continue to knock at the patron's door, hoping to wear him down and obtain what they seek.

A truly exceptional film (also available on video) is *The Grandfather* (*El Abuelo,* Spanish with English subtitles). Here the intricacies of honor in Spain are portrayed in endlessly surprising twists of the basic story line. Attentive viewers with a good ear for music will get the point made brilliantly by the cinematographer, who uses a familiar theme from Elgar's "Enigma" variations toward the end of the film. Honor, the cultural value, as it is actually lived in the workaday Mediterranean world is an enigma indeed! The reversals in the film's story line help a Bible reader appreciate how Jesus, most notably in the beatitudes (Matt. 5:3-10), redefined the honor code of his culture. Those who followed his example were viewed by others in that culture as having "turned the world upside down" (Acts 17:6)!

Finally, an outstanding foreign feature film for Bible readers is *Wedding in Galilee* (Arabic/Hebrew, with English subtitles; 1987). It is not an explicit treatment of any biblical story, but it offers information, insight, and scenarios for understanding many aspects of families and family customs in the Bible. It is about a Palestinian father whose family lives in the occupied West Bank and who must seek permission from Israeli authorities to celebrate the wedding of his daughter. What he needs is the relaxation of some restrictions imposed by the occupiers to make the traditional wedding possible.

In the film one sees honor and shame in endless variations: in challenge and riposte (e.g., seeking permission from the authorities), in the behavior patterns of the village boys and girls, and the like. The behavior of the youngster who snoops in and out of male and female worlds and reports news to each quarter reminds one of Jesus scolding his disciples when they tried to keep such snoops away from him while he was teaching (Matt. 19:14). The old man whose constant babbling is ignored by everyone calls to mind the observation of Sirach (32:3-6). And, of course, all the preparations for, the celebration of, and the outcome of the wedding itself shed new light on Jesus' wedding parables as well as the dilemma Joseph faced when he learned that Mary was pregnant (Matt. 1:18-25). How did they satisfy the culturally required wedding customs (see Deut. 22:13-22) which this film graphically presents?

Conclusion

Many would wish that cameras had been invented ages ago so that we might have home videos and family photograph albums from the daily lives of our ancestors in the faith. Archaeological artifacts are of some help in imagining what their daily lives were like. But life in that part of the world has remained relatively unchanged over millennia until the discovery of oil. Even after that event, the cultural values have remained constant and can still be experienced in village life or tribal situations. The select films and videos mentioned in this article are those I use in the classroom and with adult audiences to great effect. At the very least, they help non-Mediterranean people to momentarily put aside their own cultural baggage in order to begin to appreciate another culture, on its own terms.

FURTHER READING: ENTERTAINMENT

Abu-Lughod, Lila. 1993. *Writing Women's World: Bedouin Stories.* Berkeley: University of California Press.

Alireza, Marianne. 1987. "Women of Saudi Arabia." *National Geographic* 172: 422-53.

Allen, Leslie C. 1990. *Ezekiel 20–48.* Word Biblical Commentary 29. Dallas: Word Books.

Altorki, Soraya, and Camillia Fawzi El-Solh, eds. 1998. *Arab Women in the Field: Studying Your Own Society.* Syracuse: Syracuse University Press.

Bailey, Kenneth E. 2007. *Finding the Lost: The Prodigal Son.* DVD (1 hour and 40 minutes; Arabic with English subtitles. www.cdbaby.com/DrKenBailey).

Chick, Gary. 1998. "Games in Culture Revision: A Replication and Extension of Roberts, Arth, and Bush (1959)." *Cross-Cultural Research* 32: 185-206.

Exum, J. Cheryl. 2005. *Song of Songs.* The Old Testament Library. Louisville: Westminster John Knox.

Family Matters: The Role of the Family in the Middle East. 1984. Encyclopedia Britannica Education Corporation. XO 4004, 25 minutes [XO = VHS].

Hoffman, Susanna M. 1988. "The Controversy about Kypseli." Pp. 161-69 in *Anthropological Film Making: Anthropological Perspectives on the Production of Film and Video for General Public Audiences.* Edited by Jack R. Rollwagen. Chur/London/Paris/New York/Melbourne: Harwood Academic Publishers.

Kypseli: Women and Men Apart — A Divided Reality. 1976. Produced by Paul Aratow, Richard Cowan, and Susanna M. Hoffman. 40 minutes. Berkeley: Berkeley Media LLC. 2600 Tenth Street, Suite 626, Berkeley, CA 94710.

Knochenklang–Paläolithisches Ensemble. 2000. *Knochenklang: Klänge aus der Steinzeit.* Wien: Verlag der Österreichischen Akademie der Wissenschaften. CD. Track 3.

Malina, Bruce J. 2001. *The New Testament World: Insights from Cultural Anthropology.* Third Edition Revised and Expanded. Louisville: Westminster John Knox.

Pilch, John J. 1999. *The Cultural Dictionary of the Bible.* Collegeville, MN: The Liturgical Press.

———. 2006. "Masters Corner: The Music of Our Ancestors." *GIA Quarterly* 18 (#1): 12-13; 40.

———. 2011a. "Music in Second (Slavonic) Enoch." Pp. 73-88 in *Flights of the Soul: Visions, Heavenly Journeys, and Peak Experiences in the Biblical World.* Grand Rapids and Cambridge: Eerdmans.

———. 2011b. "Flute Players, Death, and Music in the Afterlife (Matthew 9:18-19, 23-26)." Pp. 89-105 in *Flights of the Soul: Visions, Heavenly Journeys, and Peak Experiences in the Biblical World.* Grand Rapids and Cambridge: Eerdmans.

Quasten, Johannes. 1983. *Music and Worship in Pagan and Christian Antiquity.* Translated by Boniface Ramsey. Washington: National Association of Pastoral Musicians.

Racy, Ali Jihad. 2003. *Making Music in the Arab World: The Culture and Artistry of Ṭarab.* Cambridge: Cambridge University Press.

Shull, Jonathan. 2006. "Locating the Past in the Present: Living Traditions and the Performance of Early Music." *Ethnomusicology Forum* 15: 87-111.

Sloyan, Gerard S. 1996. "The Gnostic Adoption of John's Gospel and Its Canonization by the Catholic Church." *Biblical Theology Bulletin* 26: 125-32.

Ullendorff, Edward. 1979. "The Bawdy Bible." *Bulletin of the School of Oriental and African Studies* 42: 425-56.

Zegarra, Narcedallia M., M.D., Albert C. Cuetter, M.D., David F. Briones, M.D., and Frank L. Giordano, M.D. 2007. "Nonpsychotic Auditory Musical Hallucinations in Elderly Persons with Progressive Deafness." *Clinical Geriatrics* 15/11: 33-37.

Znamenski, Andrei A. 2007. *The Beauty of the Primitive: Shamanism and the Western Imagination.* Oxford: Oxford University Press.

Index of Authors

Index of Subjects

adultery, viii, xii, 105, 121-24, 126, 127, 129, 145, 149, 153, 155, 157
Ahab, 49, 238, 240-42
altered states of consciousness, 15, 36, 187, 189, 193, 194, 196, 197, 203, 210, 226
alternate reality, 2, 3, 13, 14, 17, 19, 20, 26, 37, 46, 57, 144, 188, 196-99, 206, 207, 209, 225
alternate states of consciousness, 13, 17, 20, 22, 25, 143, 183, 192, 193, 199, 200, 204, 205, 208, 212, 213, 269
Amarna period, 53
analogy, 1, 85, 126, 195, 209, 227, 229, 232, 238, 241
ancestors in the faith, 56, 78, 83, 121, 184, 189, 227, 242, 288
appearance, 19, 20, 23, 95, 134, 140, 151, 196, 199, 202, 255
ASC, 8, 13, 17, 19, 20, 22, 33, 34, 36, 80, 84, 88, 94, 100, 102, 108, 119, 123, 135, 175, 183, 187, 189, 191, 197-99, 202, 205-11, 232, 238, 246, 257, 258, 265, 267, 283

Baal, 16, 25, 45, 240, 241
bawdy, ix, 278, 283, 290
body guide, 174

citizen, viii, 28, 49, 59-64, 81, 130, 210, 247
client, 217-18
cognomen, 90
collectivist, 59, 78-83, 92-93, 96-97, 118-20, 143, 163, 170, 189, 222, 244, 264
commandments, 18, 25, 121, 147, 153-58, 166, 179, 213, 286
consensual reality, 12, 13, 14, 198, 206, 207
consensus reality, 184-85

cosmos, vii, 1, 11, 12, 14, 23, 25, 27, 41, 47, 50, 214, 251
culture, xi, xii, 2, 6, 13, 18, 20, 25, 27, 33, 37-39, 41, 46, 48, 50, 59, 65, 69, 72, 74, 78, 79, 81-88, 92, 105, 111, 114-16, 119-21, 123, 125, 127-29, 136, 141, 143, 144, 147, 151, 155, 158-60, 162, 163, 166-68, 171-74, 176, 180, 182, 184, 185, 189, 192, 196-99, 203, 211, 212, 227-32, 238, 239, 243, 244, 246, 247, 259, 273, 274, 281, 282, 284, 286-89
curses, 147, 159, 163-66, 221

dance, 261, 268, 272, 273
darkness, ix, 24, 41, 51, 219-24
daughter, 38, 48, 76, 85, 95, 97, 99, 102-3, 106, 110, 112, 124, 130-31, 162, 177, 240, 253, 255, 285-87
daydreaming, 183
death, viii, 3-5, 18, 34, 38, 39, 41, 45, 46, 51, 76, 80, 98, 105, 115, 125, 129, 130, 133-38, 141, 143, 144, 153, 163, 165, 167, 176, 177, 180, 182, 184, 188, 197, 203, 205-8, 220, 232, 240, 241, 245, 257, 273, 277, 289
deception, 49, 51, 125, 135, 136, 155, 166, 239, 240, 242, 243
dreams, ix, 143, 183-89, 205, 224, 258

ecstasy, 184, 270, 271
eisegesis, 114
emic, 46
endogamy, 112, 131
erotic, 272, 283
ethnomusicology, 268, 289
etic, 46,
evil eye, 180
exogamy, 112, 131, 132

Index of Scripture and Other Ancient Literature

Nehemiah

3:1	275
3:3	275
8:1	275
9:6	9
10	125
13:3	62
13:27	111-12

Esther

1:3	264
1:9	264
9:29	131

Job

1:2	49
1:7	24
4:13	200
6:16	55
7:21	4
9:8	196
9:16	12
12:7-8	251
14:13	2
17:13	4
21:12	254
26:10	12
26:11	7, 49
26:13	7, 49
28	249
28:17	54
30:31	254
32:6ff.	86, 248
33:4	248
37:10	55
37:18	7, 53
38:12-13	12
38:26	12, 29
38:29	55

Psalms

2	169
2:6	16
5	163
6:5	4, 163
7	163
8	264
9	169
10	163, 169
11:4	23
18	223
18:11	209
18:15	12
18:26-27	241
19:1	232, 264
21	169
22	82-83
27:8	101, 220
27:9	221
28:1	4
29:3	195
30	169
30:4	4, 169
31:17	4
32	169, 265
34	223
41	169
44	231
45	169
48:2-3	16
50	154
58:33-36	43
66:13-15	192
69	163
72:18-19	155
74:13-14	49
79	163
81	154
83	163
84:8	19
89:11	49
91:13	48
92	169-70
97:5	14
99:9	16
102:6	30
103	169
103:19	23
104:2	7
109:16	163
110	169
111:10	135
113-118	264
114	264, 266
115	266
116	169, 266
117:1	65, 264
118	169-70
123:1	23
127:3-5	113, 117, 275
133	154, 259
135:7	7
138	169-70
144:1	280
146:6	12
148:4	7
148:7	49
148:12	108
150:4	254

Proverbs

1:20-23	249
3:11-12	158, 229
5:15	280
6:12-14	281
6:15	280
6:19	154
6:29	173
8:29	12
11:26	165
12:17	154
12:23	44
13:24	118, 136, 140, 158, 229, 238
14:5	154
16:31	135
19:5	154
19:9	154
19:13	113
19:18	118, 136, 140, 158, 229
19:26	154
20:3	157
20:29	135
20:30	158
21:4	178
21:9	113
21:19	113
22:9	177
22:15	118, 136, 140, 158, 229
22:22	118
23:6	178
23:13-14	118, 136, 140, 158, 227, 229, 238
23:15	118, 136, 140, 158, 227, 229, 238
23:17	118, 136, 140, 158, 227, 229, 238
25:7c-10	157
25:18	154, 157
25:24	113
26:2	166
28:22	178
29:15	136, 140
29:17	136, 140
30:10	165
30:19	43
30:20	280

For an Index of References to the Roman Lectionary, see my web site:
http://mysite.verizon.net/vzewdxtw/drjohnjpilchwebpage/id67.html.